The Ismailis in the Middle Ages

The Ismailis in the Middle Ages

A History of Survival, A Search for Salvation

SHAFIQUE N. VIRANI

OXFORD
UNIVERSITY PRESS
2007

OXFORD
UNIVERSITY PRESS

Oxford University Press, Inc., publishes works that further
Oxford University's objective of excellence
in research, scholarship, and education.

Oxford New York
Auckland Cape Town Dar es Salaam Hong Kong Karachi
Kuala Lumpur Madrid Melbourne Mexico City Nairobi
New Delhi Shanghai Taipei Toronto

With offices in
Argentina Austria Brazil Chile Czech Republic France Greece
Guatemala Hungary Italy Japan Poland Portugal Singapore
South Korea Switzerland Thailand Turkey Ukraine Vietnam

Published by Oxford University Press, Inc.
198 Madison Avenue, New York, New York 10016

www.oup.com

Library of Congress Cataloging-in-Publication Data
Virani, Shafique N.
The Ismailis in the Middle Ages: a history of survival, a search for
salvation / Shafique N. Virani.
p. cm.
Includes bibliographical references and index.
ISBN 978-0-19-531173-0
1. Ismailites—History. I. Title.
BP195.I8V57 2007
297.8'2209—dc22 2006019105

1 3 5 7 9 8 6 4 2

Printed in the United States of America
on acid-free paper

Dedicated to the memories of

Muhammad b. Zayn al-ʿAbidin ‘Fida’i’
Khurasani ‘Hajji Akhund’

and

ʿAli Muhammad Jan Muhammad Chunara

الا ای طالب وحدت همی لافی که جویایم   کلام از من شنو زیرا کتاب الله گویایم

امام عبد السلام

Harken ye
Who quest for union
Who boasts
That he seeks

Heed my words
For I am
The Book of God
That speaks!

Imam ʿAbd al-Salam

Acknowledgments

O Our Lord!
Let thanks for your bounties
Be the litany of our tongues
And shelter us from the nethermost hell
Of ingratitude and thanklessness

From a seventeenth-century Ismaili prayer

Many people have given generously of their time, their resources and their wisdom to assist me in the writing of this book. In the initial stages, when the foundations were being laid, Roy Mottahedeh shared his wisdom about how to approach history, Robert Wisnovsky spoke at length with me about philosophical considerations, Wheeler Thackston motivated me with his learned opinions about literature, and Ahmad Mahdavi-Damghani assisted me with numerous intricacies in medieval texts. I must thank Ali Asani, in particular, for his constant support, his precious advice on the writing process, and for reading the initial drafts with such a keen eye.

During the course of my research, I spent a memorable year at the Institute of Ismaili Studies, London. I would like to thank Azim Nanji, the director, for facilitating my stay and making my residence so pleasant. I am indebted to the librarians at the Institute without whose help much of my research would have remained unfinished. Duncan Haldane was never too busy to help in locating obscure resources, Alnoor Merchant's wide knowledge of the Institute's collection was essential in procuring manuscript works, and whenever I was tired of poring over the manuscripts I would discover that a cup of hot tea and a plate of cookies had been prepared for me by Khadija Lalani, who always made the library a wonderful environment in which to work. The librarians at Harvard University in Cambridge, Mass., and at Zayed University in the UAE, particularly those working with interlibrary loans, were wonderful. I would like to thank Bonnie Burns of Harvard University, and Andrew Nicholson, Gerald Romme and

Magda Biesiada of the University of Toronto, who inducted me into the world of geographic information systems. Without their help, I would not have been able to design the maps included in this book.

This book has benefited from the sage advice and valuable information provided by many leading scholars in the field, including Aziz Esmail and Jalal Badakhchani. Farhad Daftary, Hermann Landolt, Wilferd Madelung, and Paul Walker took time from their busy schedules and read the penultimate draft of the book, providing me with the benefit of their immense erudition and incisive judgment. Through the years, I have always admired their superior scholarship, and am indebted to them for their guidance and observations. I must, in particular, single out Faquir M. Hunzai and Mrs. Rashida Hunzai who, from the very outset, bent over backward to assist me. Despite the demands of their own work, they were always eager to help with their characteristic selflessness. With his vast knowledge and expertise, Hunzai was able to decipher some of the most obscure and puzzling passages in the manuscripts I was dealing with and Mrs. Hunzai's vigilance saved me from many infelicities of expression. Both of them welcomed me with immense love and warmth, and I can never fully express my gratitude to them. In addition, my friends Hussein Rashid, Syed Akbar Hyder, and Sunil Sharma were sources of immense support and advice.

I am particularly indebted to my parents, my sister and my brother, who have always stood by me, unwavering in their encouragement and support. Never a day goes by when I don't remember how lucky I am to have them.

I'm grateful to the *Journal of the American Oriental Society,* which permitted me to use parts of my article "The Eagle Returns: Evidence of Continued Ismāʿīlī Activity at Alamūt and in the South Caspian Region following the Mongol Conquests," *JAOS* 123 (2003): 351–370, in chapter 2 of this book.

Lastly, I'd like to acknowledge the Government of Iran Ministry of Culture, the Iran Heritage Foundation, the Institute of Ismaili Studies, the Malcolm H. Kerr Dissertation Award of the Middle East Studies Association, the Foundation for Iranian Studies, the Harvard University Ilse Lichtenstadter Memorial Publication Prize, and the Whiting Foundation for their support, financial or otherwise, which made the publication of this book possible.

Contents

Note on the Text

Charles Lamb (d. 1834), the English author most famous for his collection *Essays of Elia*, writes in that anthology, "I can read anything which I call a book." However, he laments that there are many things that appear in the shape of books, but are no such thing, for they are quite unreadable. Among these he included scientific treatises, almanacs and the writings of Hume and Robertson. These he dubbed *biblia a-biblia*, "books that are not books." They were volumes "no gentleman's library should be without," yet tomes hardly anyone would actually wish to read.[1]

I wanted *The Ismailis in the Middle Ages* to be a book that people would enjoy reading as much as I enjoyed writing. At the same time, an academic book must maintain certain standards of scholarship that are absolutely sacrosanct. No such volume, particularly in a largely untouched field, can do without exhaustive documentation. Yet the general reader is unlikely ever to venture into the forbidding wilderness of documentary notes that authors of such books so painstakingly prepare. Specialist readers, however, cannot forgo consulting such apparatus, the very stock of their craft. Creative solutions in other areas, however, can greatly enhance the reading experience of the lay reader, without compromising scholarly fidelity.

NAMES AND TITLES

The title of Juwayni's famous work on the Mongol conquests, *Ta'rīkh-i Jahāngushāy*, while simple enough for the specialist, is nothing but an unpronounceable combination of letters for many casual readers. I have therefore opted to provide English designations for most works, in the case of Juwayni's opus, the one it was conferred by its able translator, John Andrew Boyle, who dubbed it *History of the World Conqueror*. Such titles will have greater relevance to the average reader. Meanwhile, for the benefit of specialists and curious generalists, the original titles are referenced in parentheses on their first (and occasionally subsequent) appearance. Along the same lines, I have also provided English equivalents for a number of technical terms. However, as many of these have no real equivalent in English, this has not always been possible. For the purposes of English grammar, occasionally the original word provided in parentheses will be in the plural, though it is singular in the source, or vice versa. The faint of heart turn pale when they have to read names such as Abū ʿAmr Minhāj al-Dīn ʿUthmān b. Sirāj al-Dīn Jūzjānī, and so I have spared them by trying to maintain the simplest form of such names wherever possible, hence Jūzjānī, while preserving the full forms in the index for those who are interested.

Computer software has made great strides in being able to accommodate languages in non-Roman scripts. Nevertheless, there are still many areas that need further development. The bibliographical software used for this book assumes that authors are identified by given name and surname. Traditional Eastern culture, however, knows no such convention, as authors may be identified according to any part of their name, not necessarily the last. The curious may therefore have to search a bit to find references to such sources in the bibliography, and may notice unconventional citations of figures in the notes, who may be better known by other names.

TRANSLITERATION

We are told in the Bible of humankind's arrogance in attempting to reach God by building the Tower of Babel. The Creator's punishment was swift and unequivocal. Henceforth, the peoples of the earth would speak a medley of mutually unintelligible tongues. This retribution falls particularly heavy on the shoulders of scholars of world religions, histories, and cultures, who bear the burden not only of making sense of the Babelian cacophony of their sources, but of trying to convey this intelligibly to their readers. Any work that draws upon sources written in languages and scripts as diverse as Arabic, Persian, Urdu, Gujarati, Hindi, Sindhi, Punjabi, Siraiki, and Khojki faces the perplexing question of what system of transliteration to adopt. No one solution can hope to satisfy everybody and it is difficult to decide whether to include a bewildering array of diacritics thereby sacrificing readability, or to oversimplify matters and thus sacrifice accuracy.

While the heaps of "dots and lines" (ahem, macrons) are a bugbear to many readers, these symbols of transliteration are actually of tremendous value, as they help us to know how a word is spelled and pronounced in its original language; otherwise, how would one distinguish between the names Nāṣir-i Khusraw (in which Nasir is pronounced with a long "a" and a short "i") and Nasīr al-Dīn Ṭūsī (in which Nasir is pronounced with a short "a" and a long "i")? Even with a fully transliterated text, though, many readers may remain blissfully unaware of such distinctions. The best compromise, I thought, was to correctly transliterate all foreign words, but to remove the macrons and subscript dots in the main text, while maintaining them in the notes, index, glossary, this note on the text, quotations and wherever such words or phrases would benefit from being fully transcribed, such as when incorporated within parentheses. In this manner, generalist readers are spared the confusion of muddling through symbols they may not fully understand, adventurous generalists (and I hope there are many such people) can learn the correct pronunciations of foreign words by referring to the glossary, and specialists can access the fully transliterated forms of non-English expressions quite easily. Other authors have opted for similar solutions, and in this I follow in their footsteps.

I have adopted a version of the Arabic transliteration system of the American Language Association (ALA) and Library of Congress (LC) for all Arabic script languages, with the usual additional characters for Persian, Urdu, etc., and the ALA-LC's Gujarati transliteration system for all South Asian languages not written in Arabic script, as these roughly fall into the paradigm of standard Devanagari. The following are the main modifications: For Arabic script languages, the *tā marbūṭa* (ة) is not represented by an h, the *alif maqṣūra* is represented by ā rather than á, iyy and uww are preferred to īy and ūw, and the prime symbol (") is never used. For Devanagari, च and छ (and their equivalents in related scripts) are transcribed as "cha" and "chha" respectively, rather than as "ca" and "cha," both श and ष (and their equivalents in related scripts) are transcribed as "sha," word final "a" is not retained unless the word ends in a conjunct syllable, and a distinction is not always made between short and long "i" and "u" sounds, particularly when transcribing from the Khojki script. Other minor modifications will be readily recognized by the specialist. The system adopted here does not solve all difficulties. For example, the Devanagari letter ट and the Arabic letter ط are both transcribed as "ṭ"even though their phonetic values are quite different. The Devanagari and Arabic characters (in order of appearance) are as follows: च छ श ष ट ط.

However, the context in which the letter appears should make it clear which sound is intended. A problem that is not easily resolved without resorting to an extremely convoluted system is that phonemes such as the Sindhi implosives (whether in Arabic script or Khojki) are not distinguished. Another unavoidable idiosyncrasy that results from transcribing several languages is that words and phrases that are precisely the same vary in pronunciation and spelling from one language to the next and are thus transcribed differently in English. For example, what would be *walī* and Ṣadr al-Dīn when transcribed from Arabic script (i.e., Arabic, Persian, Urdu or standard Sindhi) may become *valī* and Sadaradīn or even Sadharadhīn when transcribed from Gujarati, Hindi or Khojki script.

Foreign words that occur commonly in the text of the book, such as daʿwa and taqiyya, are not italicized. Moreover, the anglicized forms of foreign names and terms are preferred when these are well known: hence Tamerlane rather than Tīmūr-i Lang or, reproducing the elaborate vowel systems of Turkish and Mongolian, Temür. Similarly, the name of the city of western Afghanistan is spelled Herat rather than Harāt, but the name of a resident of that city remains, for example, Khayrkhwāh Harātī. Persian compound words, such as the name of the well-known opus *The Fire Temple* of the litterateur Ādhar, are written without a hyphen, hence Ātishkada rather than Ātish-kada. Along similar lines, Persianate compound names are written as one word, hence Islamshah rather than Islam Shah or Islam-shah. It is common for Arabic loanwords in Persian to have more than one accepted spelling; for example both ḥujja and ḥujjat are to be found. In such cases I have adopted what appeared more common and used that spelling in transliteration throughout, in this case ḥujjat. Occasionally, in transcribing from languages using Devanagari and related scripts, postpositions are written separately from the word that precedes them, though they are attached in the original text.

CALENDAR SYSTEMS

Not only are a plethora of languages represented in this book, but a number of calendar systems as well. Most common is the Islamic lunar calendar, commonly abbreviated with the Latin AH (= *Anno Hegirae*). This will generally be followed by the corresponding date in the Gregorian Christian calendar, now often abbreviated CE (= Christian or Common Era). In addition to both of these, in bibliographical references the reader will occasionally come across the Islamic solar calendar, adopted in modern Iran in 1925, abbreviated in this book as HS (= Hijrī solar or Hijrī Shamsī), and the Vikrama Samvat era, commonly used in South Asia and abbreviated here as VS. For conversion from lunar to solar dates the algorithms developed by John Walker and available at the following website were used: http://www.calendarhome.com/converter/. Approximations of other dates were calculated simply by subtracting 621 years from the Christian Era in the case of the Islamic solar calendar, and by adding either fifty-six or fifty-seven years in the case of the Vikrama Saṃvat era. Date conversions already provided in the sources are given as they were calculated by the composers of those sources. The abbreviations for the calendar will only be provided where ambiguity may arise. In most cases, the dates of only two calendar systems are shown, the first being the lunar Islamic and the second being the Gregorian. For simplicity's sake, where a date has only been provided for purposes of contextualization, it is given in the Gregorian system.

MAPS

This book is filled with the names of places, some famous, others not so familiar, and a few that have disappeared without a trace with the passage of time. Tremendous efforts have been made to determine most of the locations mentioned and to document their coordinates on the maps that have been included. To this end, the archives of the U.S. National Geospatial-Intelligence Agency, the Getty Thesaurus of Geographic Names Online, countless gazetteers and maps, and even reminiscences in travelogues have been sifted for information. On occasion, the data in different sources was contradictory. In such cases I have endeavored to select the most likely coordinates.

ABBREVIATIONS AND OTHER CONVENTIONS

Some of the common abbreviations that have been adopted include b. for *ibn* and *bint*, meaning "son of" and "daughter of" respectively, ca. for *circa*, meaning an approximate date, d. for died, fl. for flourished, r. for reigned, f. or ff. for folio(s), v. or vv. for verse(s), c. or cc. for canto(s), n or nn for note(s) vol., for volume, ed. for edition, edited by or editor, trans. for translation, translated by or translator, q.v. for *quod vide* (to cross-reference within the glossary), sv for *sub voce* or "see under," nd for no date, and np for no page number(s) available. The abbreviation # refers to the Ginan number in an anthology. Many of the Khojki Ginan books referred to are exceedingly rare and different editions do not generally maintain the same page numbers, while the Ginan numbers often (though not always) remain the same. This method has been adopted so as to assist scholars who may have different editions of the text. A list of abbreviations used in the notes and bibliography of works cited may be found at the beginning of that section.

It is common, in English, to capitalize pronouns referring to God. As Arabic, Persian and most of the other source languages for this book do not have a system of capital letters, this practice is foreign to them and is not consistently followed here, except in quotations of authors writing in Western languages who have used that system. At times, despite the fact that there is an existing translation of a particular text, I have furnished my own translation, often providing a reference to the earlier translation in the notes. In all cases, I am indebted to the earlier translators whose work has facilitated my task greatly.

During the course of writing this book, I have tried, wherever possible, to maintain consistency of the sources cited. However, frequent relocations in North America, Europe and the Middle East have meant that I have had to depend on the resources of a large number of libraries. Therefore the reader will occasionally find different editions of the same work being referred to. This will not even be noticed by the general reader, but can be a hindrance for specialists, who will, I hope, be understanding.

With regard to the manner of writing, I am inspired by the words of James Bissett Pratt, most famous for his work, *The Religious Consciousness*. He observed, "It would be possible to write a learned book on Buddhism which should recite the various facts with scholarly exactness, yet leave the reader at the end wondering how intelligent and spiritual men and women of our day could really be Buddhists." He contended that to give the true feelings of a religion, "One must catch its emotional undertone, enter sympathetically into its sentiment, feel one's way into its symbols, its cult, its art, and then seek to impart these not merely by scientific exposition but in all sorts of indirect ways."[2] In these pages, too, I have sought to bring to life the subject at hand, so that in the citations of religious poetry the readers can feel the palpitations of piety and earnestness, in the quotations from polemical sources, the vim and venom of the attackers, and in the personal reminiscences of academics, the trials, tribulations and adventures of the scholarly endeavor. In this manner, I hope that the volume in your hands will not remain, in the words of Lamb, a book that is not a book, a thing in book's clothing. *The Ismailis in the Middle Ages* is about a subject that held ever greater fascination for me the more I researched and wrote about it. I hope that in the pages that follow I will be able to convey something of this captivation to my readers.

Black Sea
GEORGIA
Caspian Sea
ARMENIA
ANATOLIA
AZERBAIJAN
Tabriz
R. Tigris
Alamut
Aleppo
R. Euphrates
Rayy
Qadmus
Masyaf
IRAQ
Qumm
Kahf
Salamiyya
Samarra
Anjudan
Mediterranean Sea
Hims
SYRIA
Baghdad
Maniqa
'Ullayqa
Karbala
Kufa
Jerusalem
Najaf
Cairo
Basra
Shiraz
Persian Gulf
EGYPT
ARABIA
Medina
Ghadir Khumm
R. Nile
Red Sea
Mecca
N
W
E
S
YEMEN
1:21,000,000

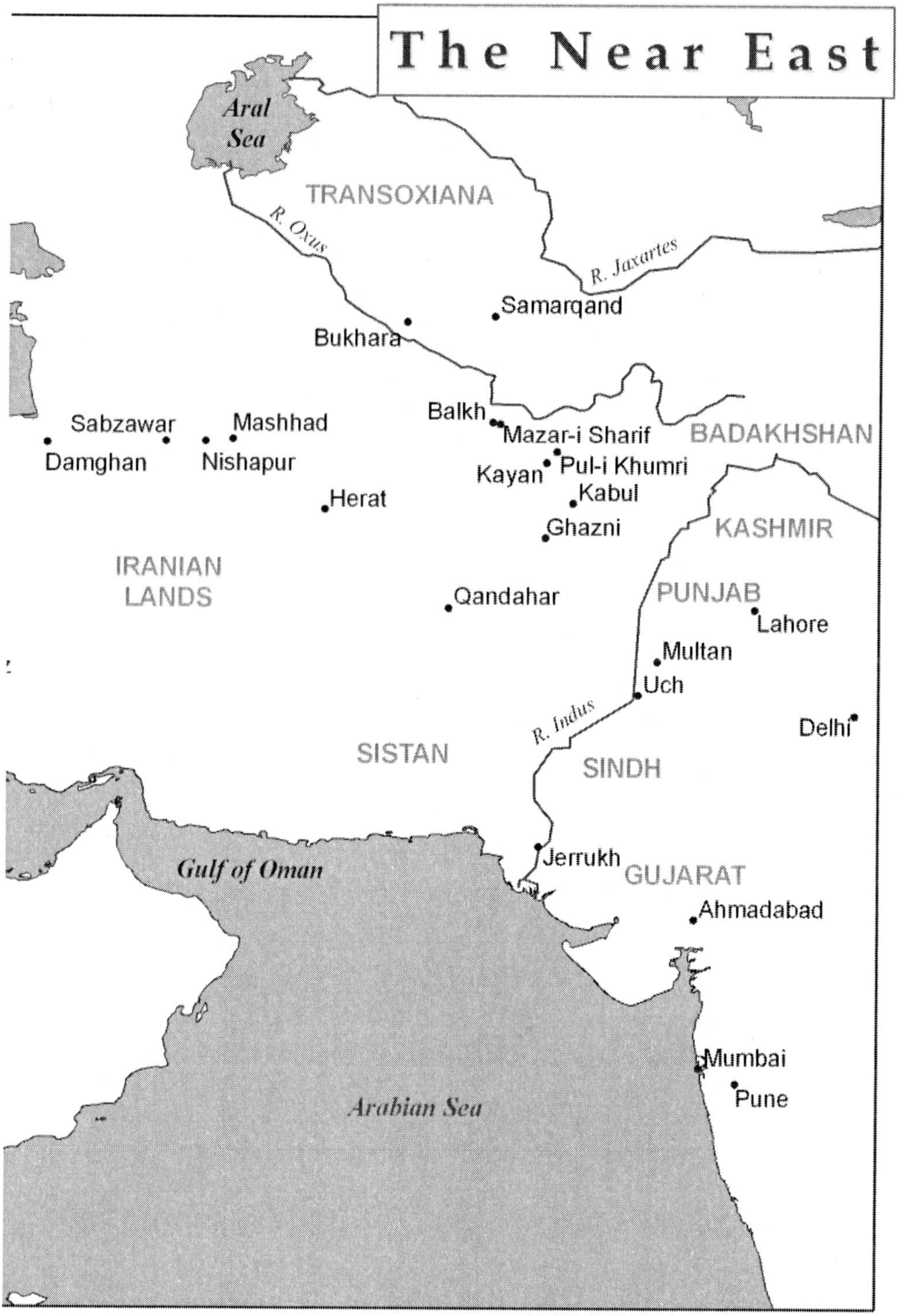
The Near East
Aral Sea
TRANSOXIANA
R. Oxus
R. Jaxartes
Samarqand
Bukhara
Balkh
Mazar-i Sharif
BADAKHSHAN
Sabzawar
Mashhad
Damghan
Nishapur
Kayan
Pul-i Khumri
Kabul
Herat
Ghazni
KASHMIR
IRANIAN LANDS
Qandahar
PUNJAB
Lahore
Multan
Uch
R. Indus
Delhi
SISTAN
SINDH
Jerrukh
GUJARAT
Gulf of Oman
Ahmadabad
Mumbai
Pune
Arabian Sea

AZERBAIJAN
Tabriz
Caspian Sea
Lahijan
Taliqan
Alamut
Rudbar
Lamasar
Nur
Sari
Kujur
Amol
GILAN
Qazwin
Sultaniyya
DAYLAM
MAZANDARAN
Kharaqan
Rayy
Sawa
Mushkabad
Hamadan
Kahak
Qumm
Arak
Anjudan
Kashan
Mahallat
Khistijan
'IRAQ-I 'AJAM
ISFAHAN
R. Tigris
Isfahan
Tushtar
Ahwaz
KHUZISTAN
R. Euphrates
Basra
Ramjird
Abiward
Shiraz
N
W
E
S
Persian Gulf
FARS
1:6,500,000

The Iranian Lands

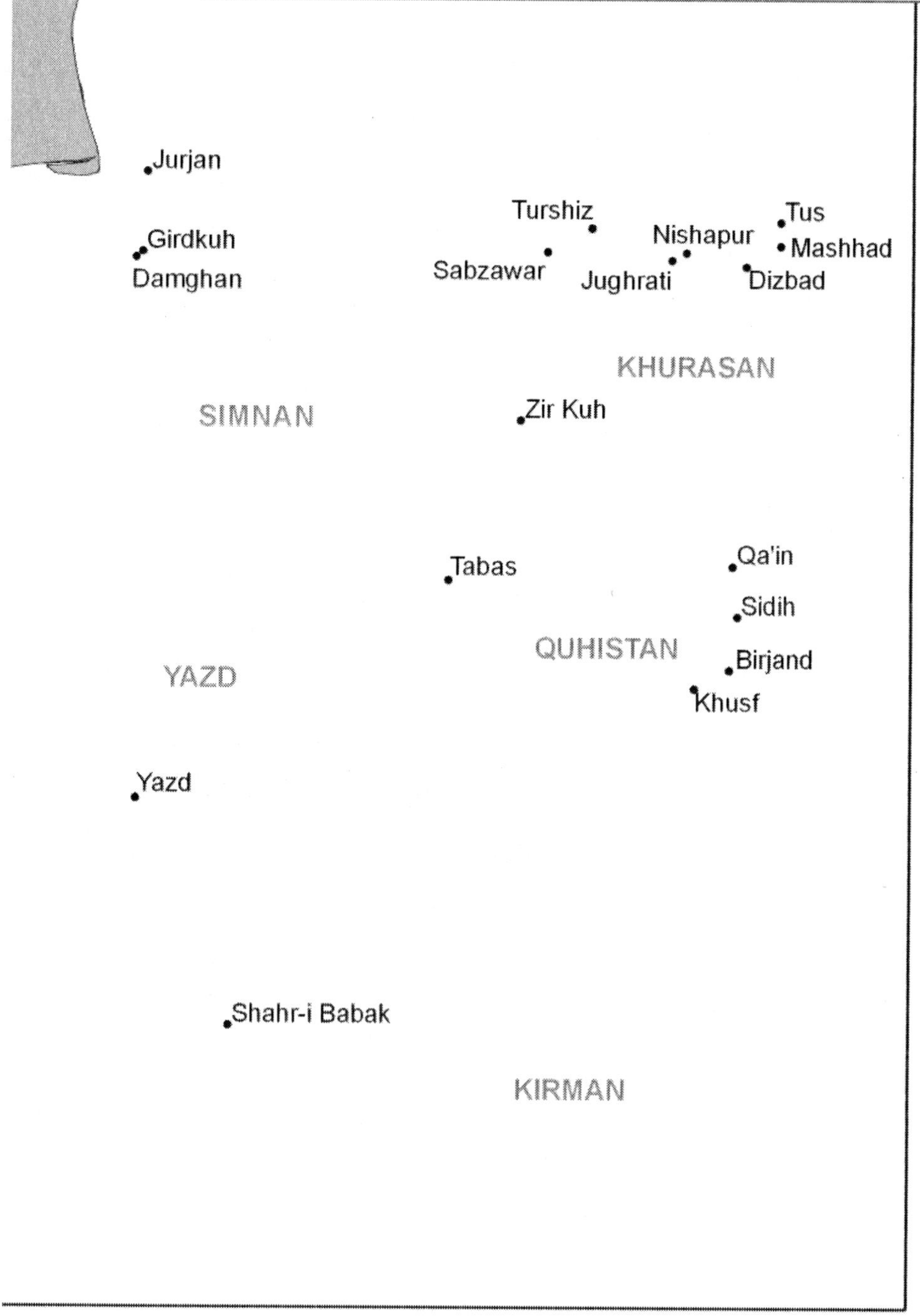

The Ismailis in the Middle Ages

Introduction

None of that people should be spared,
not even the babe in its cradle.

Edict of Genghis Khan as recorded in
History of the World Conqueror

The savagery of the Mongol invasions has perhaps no parallel in the history of humankind. Genghis Khan perpetrated more massacres, destroyed more states, reduced to rubble more monuments, razed more cities, and ruined more fields than any previous conqueror. The number of his victims ran into the millions. "My greatest joy," he is remembered for saying, "is to shed my enemies' blood, wring tears from their womenfolk, and take their daughters for bedding."[1] "I," he vaunted, "am the scourge of God!"[2]

E. G. Browne described the invasions as

> a catastrophe which, though probably quite unforeseen, even on the very eve of its incidence, changed the face of the world, set in motion forces which are still effective, and inflicted more suffering on the human race than any other event in the world's history of which records are preserved to us.... In its suddenness, its devastating destruction, its appalling ferocity, its passionless and purposeless cruelty, its irresistible though short-lived violence, this outburst of savage nomads hitherto hardly known by name even to their neighbours, resembles rather some brute cataclysm of the blind forces of nature than a phenomenon of human history. The details of massacre, outrage, spoliation, and destruction wrought by these hateful hordes of barbarians, who, in the space of a few years, swept the world from Japan to Germany, would, as

d'Ohsson observes, be incredible were they not confirmed from so many different quarters.[3]

The naked horror of the thirteenth-century Mongol irruption into the heart of the Muslim world caused devastation of disastrous proportions. Baghdad, the capital itself, was sacked, and its caliph was murdered. ʿAta-Malik Juwayni's eyewitness account, however, does not describe this as the pinnacle of Mongol conquest. Rather, for this Sunni historian, the Mongol invasions culminated in the remotest reaches of the Alburz mountains with the obliteration of the mini-state of the Shiʿi Ismailis, centered at the fortress of Alamut. In one of his imperial edicts, Genghis Khan had ordained that the Ismailis were to be annihilated: "None of that people should be spared," he decreed, "not even the babe in its cradle."[4] These chilling words heralded one of history's most lurid examples of mass extermination.[5] It is to this singular event that Juwayni dedicated the concluding one-third of his *History of the World Conqueror*.[6] The prominence given to this particular triumph reflects the enormous role played by the Ismailis in Muslim consciousness, belying their minority status. Contemporary Persian historians believed that the utter devastation of Alamut tolled their death knell. They celebrated the collapse of this center, home to a powerful voice of Shiʿi Islam, which had intellectually and politically challenged the reigning authorities.

The beginnings of Shiʿi Islam are connected with events surrounding the death of the Prophet Muhammad. The Prophet's family did not approve of Abu Bakr's assumption of the leadership of the Muslim community, and even withheld allegiance for a period of six months.[7] Many Muslims believed that the Prophet had, by divine decree, explicitly designated his cousin and son-in-law ʿAli b. Abi Talib as his successor. The group acknowledged ʿAli as its leader, or Imam, and thus became known as the *shiʿat ʿAli*, the party of ʿAli. It is widely narrated that at a place known as Ghadir Khumm the Prophet had declared, "ʿAli is the lord (*mawlā*) of those whose lord I am." Shiʿi authors have always been keen to point out the ubiquity of this narration not only in their own books, but in those of the Sunnis.[8] ʿAli's supporters thus tended to view the caliphs who were not members of the Prophet's immediate family (*ahl al-bayt*) as illegitimate usurpers.[9]

Quarrels came to a head in the reign of the third caliph, ʿUthman (d. 35/656), who distributed the governorships of all the major provinces as well as the important garrison towns to members of his own family, the powerful Banu Umayya.[10] Discontent with Umayyad hegemony gave rise to opposition movements in Kufa, Basra, and Egypt. It also instilled renewed vigor in the supporters of the Prophet's family. The malcontents soon broke out in open rebellion. ʿAli, despite his own reservations about the legitimacy of ʿUthman's leadership, had placed his sons al-Hasan and al-Husayn at the caliph's service to protect him against the mob.[11] However, the ensuing chaos culminated in ʿUthman's murder.

In the midst of these trying circumstances, ʿAli was acclaimed caliph in Medina, twenty-four years after the Prophet's death. His rule was almost immediately challenged by the Umayyads and their supporters, who wanted him to find the culprits and seek vengeance for ʿUthman's blood.[12] Within five years, ʿAli was murdered in the mosque of Kufa, and effective power passed into the hands of ʿUthman's kinsman, Muʿawiya. Henceforth, the Shiʿa and the Prophet's family were to be severely persecuted and to suffer a number of indignities, not least of which was the ritual cursing of ʿAli from the pulpits after the congregational prayers on Friday, a practice introduced during the rule of Muʿawiya.[13]

Over time, revolts by supporters of the Prophet's kinsfolk became ubiquitous, coloring the pages of early Islamic history. By 132/750, a Shiʿa-led revolution, with the support of a large cross-section of dissatisfied elements, managed to topple the Umayyad dynasty. They did not reveal who their leader was, naming him simply "the chosen one from Muhammad's family" (*al-riḍā min Āl Muḥammad*). With the defeat of the Umayyads in Iraq, Abu Salama al-Khallal, the "vizier of Muhammad's family" (*wazīr Āl Muḥammad*), was called upon to take power and disclose the name of the awaited "chosen one." He favored installing one of ʿAli's descendants, but his advances were rebuffed by both Jaʿfar al-Sadiq[14] (a descendant of ʿAli's son al-Husayn) and ʿAbd Allah al-Mahd (a descendant of ʿAli's son al-Hasan),[15] the two most prominent members of the family. After two months, the ʿAbbasids, descendants of the Prophet's paternal uncle al-ʿAbbas, managed to orchestrate a takeover of the rebellion, in which they had played a pivotal role, and succeeded in installing Abu al-ʿAbbas al-Saffah as the first ʿAbbasid caliph. Abu Salama was compelled to carry on as vizier for a time but was soon executed, almost certainly because of his ʿAlid sympathies.[16] The ʿAlid Shiʿi aspirations that had stirred the opposition to action were now crushed. Distancing themselves from those who had propelled them to power, the ʿAbbasids, particularly al-Mansur, the successor of Abu al-ʿAbbas, soon set out on a campaign of persecution against their ʿAlid cousins and supporters of the ʿAlid cause.

The aforementioned Jaʿfar al-Sadiq remained politically uninvolved.[17] While he had his own coterie of adherents who looked upon him as his father's successor and the sole legitimate source of religious authority, he also instructed a wider circle, which included, among other outstanding personalities, Abu Hanifa (d. 150/767) and Malik b. Anas (d. 179/796), the eponymous founders of two schools of law within what would later come to be known as Sunni Islam. Elaborating on the teachings of his father, Jaʿfar bequeathed to Imami Shiʿism a comprehensive enunciation of the doctrine of imamate.[18] This fundamental tenet was explained as the eternal need for a divinely appointed (*manṣūṣ*) and infallible (*maʿṣūm*) guide to instruct mankind by means of his sapiential knowledge (*ʿilm*).[19] Jaʿfar's quiescent policy and refusal to take up arms against the caliphate distressed a number of the Shiʿa. This activist branch soon joined in the ʿAlid revolts of personalities such as

Muhammad al-Nafs al-Zakiyya and his brother Ibrahim, sons of the aforementioned ʿAbd Allah al-Mahd.[20]

Following Jaʿfar al-Sadiq's death, amid confusion about his successor, the Imami Shiʿa split. Among other groups, one faction held to Jaʿfar's original designation (*naṣṣ*) in favor of his son Ismaʿil al-Mubarak, while another eventually came to recognize the imamate of a younger son, Musa al-Kazim.[21] In the course of time, the adherents of the elder line came to be designated as al-Ismaʿiliyya, while the younger line eventually became the Ithna ʿashariyya, or Twelver Shiʿa, after the disappearance of their twelfth Imam.[22]

The Ismaili Imams went into concealment (*satr*), away from the long arm of their enemies, the ʿAbbasids. Meanwhile, the Imams of the line of Musa were kept under the watchful eye of the government authorities and, according to Twelver tradition, were poisoned, one after the other, the eleventh Imam dying in 260/874. The Twelver Shiʿa affirm that this Imam had left behind a child, the twelfth and final Imam, whom they believe to have disappeared into a cave in Samarra, finally entering what later came to be known as the "greater occultation" in 329/940. Meanwhile, the Ismailis had prepared the ground for a revolution, which culminated when their Imam, ʿAbd Allah al-Mahdi, emerged in the Maghrib and established the Fatimid caliphate in 297/909, a direct challenge to the ʿAbbasids of Baghdad.[23] The Fatimid caliphate was the apogee of Ismaili political successes. At the height of power, the ʿAlid caliph eclipsed his ʿAbbasid and Umayyad rivals, claiming dominion over all of North Africa, Egypt, Sicily, the Red Sea coast of Africa, Yemen, Syria, Palestine, and the Hijaz with the holy cities of Mecca and Medina. Yet, despite their political power, the Ismailis always remained a minority, even within their own realms. There was no attempt at mass conversion. Significantly, however, the Fatimid Imams had supporters even within the territories of their rivals. In fact, it was one such adherent, the Turkish general al-Basasiri, who succeeded in capturing Baghdad itself, the very seat of the ʿAbbasid caliphs, albeit only for a short time in 450/1058.[24]

The political successes of the Fatimids alarmed their rivals, and the ʿAbbasids reacted fiercely, encouraging and commissioning numerous defamatory polemical works. The panic caused by the triumphs of the Shiʿi Ismailis can be gauged by the tone of some of the barbs directed against them. The Ashʿarite theologian, al-Baghdadi (d. 429/1037), excitedly charges:

> The damage caused by the Batiniyya [i.e., the Ismailis] to the Muslim sects is greater than the damage caused them by the Jews, Christians and Magians; nay, graver than the injury inflicted on them by the Materialists and other non-believing sects; nay, graver than the injury resulting to them from the Antichrist [*Dajjāl*] who will appear at the end of time. For those who, as a result of the missionary activities of the Batiniyya, have

> been led astray ever since the inception of the mission up to the present time are more numerous than those who will be led astray by the Antichrist when he appears, since the duration of the sedition of the Antichrist will not exceed forty days. But the vices of the Batiniyya are more numerous than the sand-grains or the raindrops.[25]

Following the death of the Caliph-Imam al-Mustansir in 487/1094, there was a succession struggle between two of his sons, Abu Mansur Nizar and Abu al-Qasim Ahmad, known as al-Mustaʿli bi'llah. Though Nizar was apparently captured and killed in the ensuing struggle, he was survived by a number of sons. The Ismailis were now divided into two factions, the Nizaris and the Mustaʿlians.

In 483/1090, shortly before this split, Hasan-i Sabbah, one of al-Mustansir's most senior dignitaries,[26] had successfully acquired the fortress of Alamut, which was to become the headquarters of the Nizaris. His remarkable organizational skills were indispensable in consolidating the Nizari community, and his writings, notably those on the concept of "spiritual edification" (*taʿlīm*), proved instrumental in attracting wide support. Under the able leadership of Hasan and his successors, Ismailism spread throughout the domains of its sworn enemies, the Turkish Saljuqs. The Saljuqs ruled in the name and with the blessings of the ʿAbbasid caliphs, who were now largely reduced to being the titular heads of Sunni Islam. Ismaili communities living within Saljuq territory were subjected to repeated massacres, but their dispersal across a number of fortresses made actions against them more difficult. Unable to confront the empire's massive military superiority head-on, they managed to defend themselves by identifying and assassinating those figures who led or encouraged the massacres against them. The Ismaili combination of both propagation and assassination yielded some astonishing results. According to Ibn al-Athir, whose work is considered the epitome of Muslim historical annals, so many of the Saljuq Sultan Barkiyaruq's (d. 498/1105) courtiers and soldiers had become Ismailis that some of his officers requested his permission to appear before him in armor lest they be attacked, even in his very presence.[27] Despite the adverse circumstances of the times, the literary output of the Nizaris of Alamut seems to have been considerable. As even their inveterate detractors have noted, the library of Alamut was famous for its holdings.[28] However, only a handful of Ismaili works have survived from this period.

Despite the ferocity of Saljuq actions against the Ismailis, an adversary of incomparably greater destructive abilities was on the horizon—the Mongols. We hear an ominous foreboding of the coming genocide from William of Rubruck, a Franciscan friar at the court of King Louis IX of France, who was sent on a diplomatic mission to the Great Khan Mongke. He tells that the Great Khan had sent his brother Hulagu to the lands of the Ismailis with an army, "and he ordered him to put them all to death."[29] The explicit targeting of the members of this minority group by the Great Khan betrays their influence in the region. When the fortress of Alamut was subjugated by the Mongols in 654/1256, ʿAta-Malik Juwayni, Hulagu's attendant and historian, requested permission to visit the celebrated library, "the fame of which had spread throughout the world."[30] There he found multitudes of books relating to the religion of the Ismailis, which he condemned to be burned, saving only copies of the Quran and a few other treatises.[31] Consigned to a fate similar to that of their religious books, the Ismailis themselves were hunted down and slaughtered indiscriminately. Henceforth, it would seem that they had simply ceased to exist, disappearing from the pages of history. Juwayni's account perhaps best describes what was believed to be the final destruction and ultimate annihilation of the community. It is so vivid that it is quoted here *in extenso*:

> And in that abode where monstrous innovations flourished, with the pen of violence the Artist of Eternity wrote upon the portico of each one's dwelling the verse: *These their houses are empty ruins* (27:53). And in the marketplace of the kingdom of those wretches the muezzin Destiny has announced, *Away then with the wicked people* (23:43)! Their luckless womenfolk, like their empty religion, have been utterly destroyed. The gold of those crazy, double-dealing counterfeiters, which appeared to be unalloyed, has proven to be base lead. Today, thanks to the glorious fortune of the World-Illuminating King, if an assassin still lingers in a corner he plies a woman's trade; wherever there is a daʿi there is an announcer of death; and every Ismaili comrade has become a thrall. The propagators of Ismailism have fallen victims to the swordsmen of Islam. Their Mawlana, to whom they addressed the words: "O God, our Protector,"—*dust in their mouths*!—(and yet *the infidels have no protector* (47:12)) has become the serf of bastards. Their wise Imam, nay their lord of this world, of whom they believed that *every day doth some new work employ him* (55:29), is fallen like game into the net of Predestination. Their governors have lost their power and their rulers their honor. The greatest among them have become as vile as dogs. Every commander of a fortress has been deemed fit for the gallows and every warden of a castle has forfeited his head and his mace. They have been degraded amongst mankind like the Jews, and like the highways, are level with the dust. God Almighty hath said: *Vileness and poverty were stamped upon them* (13:25). *These, a curse awaiteth them* (2:58). The kings of the Greeks and Franks, who turned pale for fear of these accursed ones, and paid them tribute, and were not ashamed of that ignominy, now enjoy sweet slumber. And all the inhabitants of the world, and in particular the Faithful, have been relieved of their evil machinations and unclean beliefs. Nay, the whole of

mankind, high and low, noble and base, share in this rejoicing. And compared with these histories that of Rustam, the son of Dastan, has become but an ancient fable. The perception of all ideas is through this manifest victory, and the light of the world-illuminating day is adorned thereby. *And the uttermost part of that impious people was cut off. All praise be to God, Lord of the Worlds* (6:45)![32]

EMERGING FROM OBSCURITY

The volume in your hands is not about the massacres that occurred. While there are numerous instances recorded in these pages of persecution and killings, particularly in the South Caspian region and Khurasan, this book instead seeks to identify and understand how the Ismailis managed to survive such circumstances, and how their religious doctrines and worldview helped them do this.

Juwayni had declared, "He [the Imam Rukn al-Din Khwurshah] and his followers were kicked to a pulp and then put to the sword; and of him and his stock no trace was left, and he and his kindred became but a tale on men's lips and a tradition in the world."[33] In the light of such unequivocal declarations, triumphantly announcing the complete and total annihilation of the Imam and his community, the extermination of the Ismailis in the face of the Mongol behemoth was accepted as fact in Western scholarship for centuries. This began to change about two hundred years ago.

One of the first people to draw attention in orientalist circles to the continued existence of the community as well as to their local traditions and literature was Jean Baptiste L. J. Rousseau (d. 1831), who was the French consul-general in Aleppo from 1809 to 1816 and a longtime resident of the Near East. He came across the Nizaris in Syria and highlighted their sorry plight after their 1809 massacre at the hands of the Nusayris, another sect of the region. When he participated in an official French mission at the court of the Persian monarch Fath ʿAlishah (d. 1834), he was taken aback to find that the community flourished in Iran as well. He wrote a letter about his findings to the famous Parisian scholar Sylvestre de Sacy, who quoted it at the end of his pivotal study "Mémoire sur la dynastie des Assassins, et sur l'étymologie de leur Nom." The letter was dated Tehran, June 1, 1808:

> I have collected some fairly exact notions about the Batinis or Ismaʿilis commonly called *Mélahédèhs*, a sect which still survives and is

widespread and tolerated, like many others, in the provinces of Persia and in the Sind. As I have very little free time, please excuse my putting off the task of going into a detailed discussion until some other time. Meanwhile, it may be useful to tell you that the *Mélahédèhs* even today have their imam or pontiff, descending, as they claim, from Jaʿfar Sadiq, the chief of their sect, and residing at Kehek, a village in the district of Qom. He is called Sheikh Khalil Allah and succeeded in the imamate to his uncle, Mirza Abu'l-Hasan, who played a great part under the reign of the Zends.[34] The Persian government does not bother him. On the contrary, he receives annual revenues from it. This person, whom his people grace with the pompous title of caliph, enjoys a great reputation and is considered to have the gift of performing miracles. They assure me that the Muslim Indians regularly come from the banks of the Indus to receive his blessings in exchange for the rich and pious offerings they bring him. He is more specifically known to the Persians by the name of *Seid Keheki.*[35]

Although this information was scarcely noted in orientalist circles at the time, shortly thereafter, the continued existence of the community was becoming apparent to the British government, which sought the help of the Imam, Aga Khan I, to secure the lines of communication in Sindh. General Sir Charles Napier, in his diary entry of February 29, 1843, wrote:

I have sent the Persian Prince Aga Khan to Jarrack, on the right bank of the Indus. His influence is great, and he will with his own followers secure our communication with Karachi. He is the lineal chief of the Ismailians, who still exist as a sect and are spread over all the interior of Asia. They have great influence, though no longer dreaded as in the days of yore. He will protect our line along which many of our people have been murdered by the Baloochis.[36]

By the early 1900s, there was a flurry of notices on the Ismailis of South Asia and greater Badakhshan, where the community was particularly prominent.[37] It was with the pioneering efforts of Wladimir Ivanow, though, that the Ismailis made substantial strides in their emergence from academic obscurity. This Russian scholar picturesquely describes his first encounter with them and the amazement his discovery elicited among his peers:

I came in touch with the Ismailis for the first time in Persia, in February 1912. The world was quite different then. No one imagined that the Great

> War, with all its misery and suffering, was just around the corner. Persia was still living in her ancestral mediaeval style, and her affairs were largely going on in their traditional ways, as they were going on for centuries.
>
> I was riding from Mashhad to Birjand, in Eastern Persia; travelling by day and taking shelter at night in the villages that were situated along the road. Icy winds blow in that part of the country in winter, raising clouds of dust and sand which make the journey a real torture. Tired and hungry, I arrived at the village of Sedeh, and was very glad to take shelter in the hut of a peasant. I sat warming myself by the side of a fire awaiting food which was being prepared for me. A man entered, conveying to me the invitation of the local landlord to shift to his house and accept his hospitality. It was, indeed, very kind of him, but, unfortunately, his invitation came a bit too late.... I therefore declined the invitation with thanks, promising that after a rest I would personally go to see the landlord and convey my thanks to him. This I did later on, and enjoyed a very interesting and instructive talk.
>
> Already in Mashhad I had often heard about these localities being populated by a "strange sect." My inquiries could not elicit any reliable information. Some people told me that the "strange sect" were the Ismailis, but I disbelieved it, having been brought up on the idea, universally accepted by Oriental scholars in Europe, that all traces of Ismailism in Persia were swept away by the brutal Mongols. And here, taking the opportunity of a conversation with the landlord on the spot, I tried to ascertain the truth. To my surprise, he confirmed what I had heard before, stating that the people really were Ismailis, and that the locality was not the only seat of the followers of the community but there were other places too in Persia in which they were found....
>
> My learned friends in Europe plainly disbelieved me when I wrote about the community to them. It appeared to them quite unbelievable that the most brutal persecution, wholesale slaughter, age-long hostility and suppression were unable to annihilate the community.[38]

It is thus only in recent times that the continued survival of the Ismailis has become apparent in Western scholarship. Today, they exist as a dynamic and thriving community established in over twenty-five countries.[39]

However, despite their newfound celebrity, the intervening centuries between what appeared to have been their total annihilation in 654/1256, and their modern, seemingly phoenix-like renaissance, remain shrouded in mystery. The destruction of the Ismaili mini-state centered at Alamut ushered in a period so dim and indistinct that the first half a millennium after the Mongol conquest has had to be classified by researchers under the amorphous title of "post-Alamut history."[40] In his monumental work, *The Ismaʿilis: Their History and Doctrines*, Farhad Daftary echoes the sentiments of over a century of previous scholarship in bemoaning this period as "the darkest phase" in the annals of the community.[41] He further writes, "Under the circumstances, modern scholars, including the specialists in Ismaʿili studies, have not so far produced major studies dealing with this phase of Nizari Ismaʿilism."[42]

The Ismailis in the Middle Ages is an inquiry into the most obscure portion of this period, beginning with the aftermath of the Mongol invasions and continuing until the eve of the Safawid revolution, that is, from the mid-thirteenth century to the end of the fifteenth century. While the historical investigation is largely circumscribed by these dates, the analysis of thought and doctrine spans a much wider compass, drawing on sources from over a millennium of Ismaili history to elucidate and shed light on the particular precepts and beliefs expressed in the works of this epoch. During the course of research, I discovered numerous previously unknown sources from many areas of Ismaili habitation, including documents in Arabic, Persian, Sindhi, Siraiki, Hindustani, Punjabi, Gujarati, and Latin, that help reconstruct Ismaili history and thought in this period. Most of these sources are still in manuscript form and uncatalogued. The significance of these newly recovered works is considerable and would more than double the number of entries for the Nizari Ismaili authors of this period recorded in the bibliographies of I. K. Poonawala and W. Ivanow, the most important scholarly references for primary sources on Ismailism.[43] These writings help us identify several hitherto unknown Ismaili authors, forcing us to reassess earlier judgments concerning the literature of this period. Many other works, some known only by name, others little-studied, have also been considered, often necessitating a revision of previously accepted theories or providing documentary support for ideas that have been conjectured by earlier scholars.

The book pieces together the existing fragments of information in order to reconstruct the history of how the community survived its political devastation. While it focuses chiefly on developments in the Iranian region, which was the primary home of the Nizari Imams throughout these two and a half centuries, it also touches on the existence of Ismaili enclaves in many other areas of the Near East. The book explains how three aspects of Ismaili thought were crucial to the community's survival: taqiyya (precautionary dissimulation), the Ismaili daʿwa, which literally means "summons" or, as it has sometimes been translated into English, "mission"; and the soteriological dimension of the imamate and, in particular, of the role of the Imam of one's time in leading the adept to salvation and a mystical recognition of God.

SIGNPOSTS FOR THE WAY

History is intimately connected with thought and doctrine. They are mutually entwined, each influencing the other. For this reason, in the pages that follow, analysis of the Ismaili belief system is often interwoven with historical narrative, as the history could not have unfolded as it did had its actors not conducted themselves according to a worldview inspired by their religious convictions. In some ways, the structure of the book mirrors the method of Ismaili pedagogy. The earlier chapters focus more on the exoteric, historical aspects of Ismailism. As the book progresses, however, greater emphasis is placed on the esoteric, on the system of thought that animated and gave life to the community. At the outset, the note on the text explained some of the nuts and bolts of the book, including the transliteration system, the calendars used, abbreviations and other conventions. The introduction that you are currently reading sets the stage by providing a background to Ismailism and an insight into the ravaging of the community by the Mongol hordes. The first chapter, "Recovering a Lost History," probes the meaning of history and the significance of historical information. It provides a bird's eye view of the sources used in this study. Chapter 2, "The Eagle Returns," explores the surprising tenacity of the Ismailis in the South Caspian regions of Gilan, Daylam and Mazandaran, including at the fort of Alamut itself, even after the Mongol devastation. The third chapter, "Veiling the Sun," is about the first Ismaili Imam of the post-invasion period, Shams al-Din Muhammad, as well as his disciple, the poet Nizari Quhistani, both of whose lives typify the practice of taqiyya and help introduce this fundamental concept. Chapter 4, "Summoning to the Truth," investigates the purport and structure of the Ismaili daʿwa, the biography of the successor of Shams al-Din Muhammad, known as Qasimshah, as well as his family, and the identity and writings of an Ismaili luminary by the name of Qasim Tushtari, who may have been a contemporary of the Imam Qasimshah. In addition to taqiyya and the Ismaili daʿwa, the concept of imamate was fundamental to the survival of the community. This concept is introduced in the fifth chapter, "Possessors of the Command," which examines the lives of the successors of the Imam Qasimshah, known as Islamshah and Muhammad b. Islamshah. It also assays the situation of the non-Iranian Ismaili communities in this period and contrasts the modes of taqiyya in Quhistan and Syria. Chapter 6, "Qibla of the World," considers the transference of the seat of imamate to Anjudan, the lives of the Imams Mustansir bi'llah, ʿAbd al-Salam and Gharib Mirza, and the vitae and writings of Ismaili luminaries contemporary with these three Imams. It further discusses the notion of the Imam as the spiritual *qibla*. The penultimate chapter, "The Way of the Seeker," continues by probing Ismaili thought in greater depth. It is about taqiyya and daʿwa, the latter viewed primarily through the eyes of Bu Ishaq

Quhistani, a contemporary of the Imam Mustansir bi'llah, who has left for posterity an invaluable account of his search for truth, his acceptance of Ismailism, and his progress in the Ismaili spiritual hierarchy. "Salvation and Imamate," the final chapter, delves into the central Ismaili belief in the eternal soteriological necessity for a present and living Imam to lead the adepts to gnosis and knowledge of God. This conviction was essential to the community's survival. The afterword is a reflection on some of the findings of this study.

It is a truism, but it bears repeating, that those who do not hold political power rarely write their own histories. Indeed, while we know of Ismaili chroniclers in the times when the community ruled Egypt and later administered a state from Alamut, no evidence exists that any Ismaili wrote a history of the Imams in the two and a half centuries following the Mongol invasion.[44] Not only was the community not in power, it was also a persecuted minority and therefore would have wished to avoid anything that could have drawn attention to its continued existence. However, there is also a more subtle reason for this lack of historical documentation that is connected with the spiritualized conception of imamate. To focus one's attention on the corporeal aspect of the Imam was to degrade him and to degrade one's own spirituality. The Imam's esoteric reality is consistently emphasized in Ismaili works of this and succeeding periods, with an equal emphasis on not focusing one's mind on his physical person. This is dramatically illustrated in a poem recording the journey of a certain Khwaja ʿAbd al-Maʿsum to deliver the religious dues of the Ismailis of Badakhshan to the Imam Dhu al-Faqar ʿAli (d. 1043/1634).[45] The Khwaja was granted an audience and received the beatific vision (*dīdār*) of the Imam. Excitedly, others gathered around him:

> Men and women, young and old, all fell at his feet, saying,
> "He has returned from the holy family (of the Prophet)!"
> Taking him aside they pleaded,"tell us what you beheld
> in that assembly!"He avidly began to relate to them his
> experience, "When the exalted lord mounted the throne,
> before him the rest of creation was of no account. . . ."

His narrative, however, was interrupted:

> A man, some fool, then asked him, "Is he old? A youth?
> Tell us!
> Perchance he's a babe in his cradle. Has he a wife and
> children at home?"

Distracted from his narrative and focusing on the physical aspect of his encounter, the traveler mused:

"His age must have been twenty years or so. . . ."

The composer of the poem then relates:

All the foolish men and women there were abustle,
saying oh and ah!
What do such people, material by nature, know of the
essence of the Imam?
There was a man in that assembly—a sage. When he heard this
babbling he reproached them, saying, "O worthless nightingale,
practice not your idolatry with the unique, the sublime!"

The wise sage then continued by quoting the Quran, drawing the questioners away from wondering about such mundane matters as the Imam's age and family and leading them to an understanding of his sublime nature and esoteric reality.

The poem is illustrative of the Ismaili attitude toward the Imam and gives a greater understanding of the reason histories that recounted facts about the earthly, and hence less important, aspects of the Imams' lives, would not have been valued nearly as much as treatises on matters of spirituality, which abound in the manuscripts containing works of this period. Hence, the annals of the community must be drawn from sources whose intention was not primarily historical but which, nevertheless, contain historical information. These include verses of poetry, epigraphs, and doctrinal works.

Without a state of their own in this period, the Ismailis did not have the luxury of grand libraries or professional scribes. Pious individuals, who may not always have been equal to the task, therefore took it upon themselves to copy religious works. Much of what we possess today of Persian Ismaili manuscripts originates from the region broadly termed Badakhshan, where Persian is not even a first language. Wladimir Ivanow frequently expressed his exasperation of working with these texts, passages of which had often been corrupted beyond recognition. He described working with the inferior copies as "a thankless task."[46]

Ivanow's annoyance became vividly apparent to me when I was poring over a Badakhshani manuscript at the Institute of Ismaili Studies, London, that had earlier been in the possession of the Ismaili Society, Mumbai. Portions of this manuscript had been used by Ivanow for his edition of *The Works of Khayrkhwah of Herat* (*Taṣnīfāt-i Khayrkhwāh Harātī*).[47] At the top of page 136, in the unmistakable hand of the learned orientalist, were the words, "Horrible! The copyist was an idiot."

After studying hundreds of manuscripts, some rendered incomprehensible at the hands of copyists, I can certainly sympathize with Ivanow's sentiments, amusing as they may be to modern-day readers. However, despite struggling over the often-impenetrable gobbledygook of errors arising from the haplography, dittography, homœoteleuton, and all the other malfeasances of the much-maligned scribes, I must admit that my reaction is completely different. Rather than the disgust that was felt by the Russian scholar, I feel a deep sense of admiration for the people, many of whom were not native speakers of Persian, who tried their best to preserve their religious heritage in the most adverse, and often hostile, circumstances. Were it not for these scribes, however humble, even the meager remnants of a literary tradition that today have found their way into the possession of both academic institutions and private holdings would have perished without a trace.

With regard to the dizzying number of variants in the manuscripts I have used, I find comfort in the words of Saint Jerome (d. 420), who faced much the same quandary with the texts from which he was translating to produce his Latin Vulgate. In reply to Pope Damasus, who had enquired as to their reliability, the most learned of Christian fathers was obliged to confess: *Pius labor, sed periculosa praesumptio. . . . Si enim Latinis exemplaribus fides est adhibenda, respondeant quibus: tot sunt paene quot codices*, "The labor is one of love, but at the same time both perilous and presumptuous. . . . For if we are to pin our faith on the Latin texts, it is for our opponents to tell us which; for there are almost as many variants in the texts as there are copies."[48]

A particularly poignant example of a scribe's acknowledgement of his limitations is that contained in manuscript RK 51 at the Institute of Ismaili Studies, entitled *A Bouquet of Poems by the Late Raqqami of Dizbad, Khurasan* (*Gulchīnī az ashʿār-i marḥūm Raqqāmī-yi Dīzbādī Khurāsānī*). Expressing his motivation for compiling the book, the scribe, a certain ʿAliquli b. Rajabʿali b. Imamquli, in tropes familiar to copyists, writes of his fear that the religious tradition preserved with such care by his forefathers would be snuffed out if it were not safeguarded. He thus took it upon himself, despite his own shortcomings, of which he was painfully aware, to recopy the work:

> Thanks be to our most exalted lord for giving such a helpless servant the strength and ability to complete this book. . . . This humble slave feared lest the lamp lit by our ancestors with such care be extinguished. . . . Thus, I withdrew my hand from the occupations of the world and with immense difficulty sat alone [to copy this book]. The entire book is cluttered, disorderly, in the language of the commoners and in the jumbled handwriting of this unworthy servant. . . . As this servant lacks elegant style and correct orthography, the writing of this book too lacks elegant style and correct orthography . . . transcribed by the most humble [of devotees], ʿAliquli b. Rajabʿali b. Imamquli.

One cannot help being moved by the apology of such a scribe to his future readers. Ivanow had described the task of using such inferior copies as "thankless." Granted, reading the exquisitely calligraphed and beautifully illuminated manuscripts of the royal courts, penned by richly rewarded and professional scribes, is a great pleasure. But there is a different type of pleasure to be gained from reading, often struggling over, the manuscripts penned by humble devotees who sought no reward from any earthly king for their labors. Far from "thankless," I have found the perusal of the texts used in this study to be, yes, difficult, extremely trying at times, but yet immensely edifying and truly inspirational.

ONE

Recovering a Lost History

Know that from [the time of the Imam] Rukn al-Din Muhammad onwards, the annals of this illustrious family do not appear in a single history that the eyes of this pauper have perused. This is because the family no longer possessed a worldly kingdom as in bygone times. . . . Hence it must be known that the Master of the House knows better than outsiders what goes on in his own household.

Fida'i Khurasani in *Guidance for the Seeking Believers*

In her historical mystery, *Daughter of Time*, Josephine Tey tells the tale of Inspector Alan Grant of Scotland Yard, who is bedridden in a London hospital with multiple injuries after a fall. A friend, knowing the sleuth's passion for faces, brings him a portfolio of historical portraits, hoping to make his convalescence less tedious. Scrutinizing the features of one particular character, he reads power and suffering in a face he associates with conscience and integrity. He is startled to discover that this is the likeness of one of history's most infamous villains, King Richard III. How could his astute intuition have so misjudged the face of such a monster? Most people remember Richard as Shakespeare had depicted him, a hideous hunchback who heartlessly murdered and plundered his way to the crown of England, whose most lamented victims were his own innocent nephews, "the little princes in the Tower." Grant begins to distrust the accusations against King

Richard, England's most vilified monarch, and is convinced by his keen instincts that the portrait could not be that of a killer. This suspicion leads the detective to turn historian, plunging with vigor into the archives and chronicles of the last half millennium. The more he learns, the more he begins to wonder: Could the history books be wrong? Could Richard have been innocent of the brutal double murder? The conclusions the author draws about the innocence or guilt of Richard are less important than her insightful discoveries along the way about the complexities of the past. History is written by the victors, she finds, and so alternative accounts must be found to balance it.

Following Grant as he investigates the facts surrounding the life of the maligned monarch, readers vicariously share the delight he feels as he finds Richard to be less a vicious tyrant than the victim of propaganda spread by the Tudors, the dynasty at whose hands Richard's Yorkist forces were defeated. Almost all the "authoritative" accounts, it turns out, were the products of Tudor patronage, which would hardly have been kind to the figure of the vanquished king. Virtually no testimony contemporary with Richard himself exists. Cross-examining these documents as he would cross-examine a witness in a criminal investigation, Grant finds many holes in the arguments. He discovers that once an accusation is made, it is often unquestioningly accepted, not to mention repeated. Historians following Sir Thomas More accepted his account as indisputable, though he could only have obtained his facts secondhand, almost certainly from John Morton, King Richard's bitterest enemy. In today's courtroom, such evidence would be inadmissible as hearsay.

There is great insight in the words of one of the characters in *Daughter of Time*:

> Give me research. After all, the truth of anything at all doesn't lie in someone's account of it. It lies in all the small facts of the time. An advertisement in a paper. The sale of a house. The price of a ring. . . . The real history is written in forms not meant as history. In Wardrobe accounts, in Privy Purse expenses, in personal letters, in estate books. If someone, say, insists that Lady Whoosit never had a child, and you find in the account book the entry: "For the son born to my lady on Michaelmas eve: five yards of blue ribbon, fourpence halfpenny" it's a reasonably fair deduction that my lady had a son on Michaelmas eve.[1]

These "small facts of the time" are precious—and often all we have to study communities like the Ismailis. Such discoveries force the historian investigating the case to question all that came before. In this particular instance, it is not enough simply to decide that Lady Whoosit had a son (as the entry in the account book apparently proves). One has to wonder why there was such insistence that she did not. It may or may not be possible to find out, but in searching for the answer, the investigator would have to uncover other casual documents, investigate the psychologies of those involved, and try to find more information about the good lady, her family, and their situation. A single clue, intriguing for its oddity, becomes the center of a web that spreads out in all directions.

Information on the Ismailis in the aftermath of the Mongol irruption is scattered. Not a single primary source containing a continuous historical narrative of the community in this period is known to exist. What survive are often nothing more than disparate references, laconic allusions, and suggestive passages in a sometimes bewildering array of sources. We have, as it were, snapshots, occasionally clips from a film, all strewn in sundry albums and spliced into a medley of reels. A single sentence in a fourteenth-century book by a Damascene geographer informing us that Ismailism survives in Egypt, a Siraiki poem heralding the Imam's advent in Multan, the travelogue of a Moorish voyager mentioning the Ismaili castles of Syria, the Latin tome of a Dominican traveler reporting on the holy land to the crusading King Philippe VI of France, a tract addressed to Tamerlane's son advising him to rid his lands of this community, the inscriptions on tombstones, a passage purporting to contain the words of an Ismaili Imam in a mislabeled Persian manuscript—these and sources like these constitute the bases of our inquiry. While the task is daunting, a careful sifting and assembling of the materials and a minute examination of the pictures they create allow us to see certain motifs appearing repeatedly, certain hues that are suggestive of themes, certain silhouettes that allow us to speak of continuity and change. While it is fruitless, with the resources available, to attempt a sustained historical account of these centuries, it is possible to bring together the remnants of what has been preserved of this period and to see the broadest outlines of a continuous, and fascinating, narrative.

What follows in this chapter is an exposition of some of the more prominent sources used in writing *The Ismailis in the Middle Ages*. It is, as it were, a roll call of the most important witnesses called to testify in the court of history. Some witnesses may be more credible than others on certain points, but less credible on others. Each has a point of view and particular strengths and weaknesses. In many instances, there may be but a single witness for a particular event—oftentimes one who lived centuries later, or whose testimony went through uncertain chains of transmission. Unfortunately, until such a time as a more credible witness comes to light, if one ever does, we are forced to rely cautiously on such testimony. For the academic specialist, this discussion of sources is essential information because it reveals in a summary form where the evidence for this book comes from. Further information on these and other materials used will, of course, also be found in the text of the chapters. For the more casual reader, the following analogy may be useful. If you are the type of person who watches a film and is then eager to read the credits to know who did what and how the film was put together, you'll want to give this chapter a close reading; but if you're already packing up your popcorn by that point, you may wish to skim through this chapter for the time being, pausing just long enough to read the final paragraph. You can always return to this later, if you so wish.

The non-Ismaili sources for this time period include both universal and local histories, geographical treatises, a travelogue, biographies of saints and poets (*tadhkira*), and polemical works. Ismaili sources include the works of the Imams, which tend to be philosophical, didactic, or mystical in nature; poetry, which figures very prominently in the texts of this period; works produced by members of the daʿwa, including some treatises on Ismaili thought; epigraphic evidence; and even the marginalia contained in some of the manuscripts. Attributions of authorship are generally provided as they appear in the received texts, since a detailed study of this question is not yet possible. The secondary literature is dominated by the textual editions, translations, and articles of Wladimir Ivanow. However, some more recent progress has also been made by scholars writing in both European as well as Eastern languages.

HISTORY IS WRITTEN BY THE VICTORS

The immediate aftermath of the fall of the Ismaili center at Alamut is first narrated by ʿAta-Malik Juwayni who was an eyewitness and, as an official for the Mongols, a key player in the events. His testimony in the *History of the World Conqueror* (*Taʾrīkh-i Jahāngushāy*) is therefore of particular importance.[2] The third volume of this work, completed in 658/1260, only four years after the destruction of Alamut, is primarily dedicated to the history of the Ismailis. As a Mongol officer, he was well placed to have access to accurate information; but by the same token, partisan interests color his work. Most important for our purposes is not only that he was present during those fateful last days before the Ismailis were massacred, but also that he had inspected the famous Ismaili library of Alamut, drawing selectively from the books there to write his own work before consigning his sources, and the rest of the library, to flames. William of Rubruck, a Franciscan friar at the court of King Louis IX of France, confirms for us Juwayni's testimony that a genocide was planned, for the Great Khan had sent his brother Hulagu to the Ismaili lands and "ordered him to put them all to death."[3] Another Latin work also has nuggets of information that are of use. In 1332, a treatise entitled *Directorium ad Passagium Faciendum*, most likely by Guillelmus Adae (William Adam), was submitted to King Philippe VI of Valois, providing advice on how to prepare for a crusade.[4] The book contains interesting information on the Ismailis.

Minhaj-i Siraj Juzjani, the foremost historian of the Delhi Sultanate, wrote his *Nasirid Generations* (*Ṭabaqāt-i Nāṣirī*) at the same time Juwayni was writing his *History of the World Conqueror*. However, in contrast to Juwayni, Juzjani was an old man by this time, one who had witnessed the horrors of Genghis Khan's invasion decades earlier. Writing in the safety of India, he was not compelled, as was his younger contemporary, to downplay the Mongol depredations. His testimony regarding the political activities of the Ismailis in India is particularly useful.[5]

Juwayni and Juzjani were followed by Rashid al-Din, perhaps the greatest historian of the period. He was one of the chief ministers of the Ilkhanids, the Mongol descendants of Hulagu Khan, and a talented polymath, skilled in fields ranging from medicine to theology. His *Universal History* (*Jāmiʿ al-Tawārīkh*) was commissioned by none other than Ghazan Khan, the great-grandson of Hulagu Khan.[6] Ghazan's brother and successor, Uljaytu, asked Rashid al-Din to expand his work by including the histories of peoples with whom the Mongols had come into contact, including the Ismailis. This expanded version was completed in 710/1310. While Rashid al-Din clearly follows Juwayni's basic narrative of the Alamut Ismailis (though omitting much of the opprobrium, despite his own patron's military activities against the community), he seems to have had direct access to other original sources, both Ismaili and non-Ismaili, and hence adds significant details missing in Juwayni, occasionally providing us with important and revealing divergent testimony.[7]

Immediately succeeding these historians we have Hamd Allah Mustawfi, who was a financial director in his native Qazwin and who dedicated his *Select History* (*Taʾrīkh-i Guzīda*), completed in 730/1330, to Rashid al-Din's son and successor, Ghiyath al-Din Muhammad.[8] This work follows the general accounts of the author's predecessors, while adding some unique material about the author's own times. Although earlier scholars have used this source to trace Nizari history, the same author's geographical treatise, *The Hearts' Bliss* (*Nuzhat al-Qulūb*), which contains references to the post-Alamut Nizaris, seems largely to have escaped notice.[9] The latter work was compiled in the year 740/1340 and hence provides valuable contemporary testimony. The author also produced a verse chronicle entitled *The Book of Triumph* (*Ẓafarnāma*), completed in 735/1335, which imitated the style of Firdawsi's immortal epic, *The Book of Kings* (*Shāhnāma*). This is an important source for the late Ilkhanid period and for some of Uljaytu Khan's activities in the Ismaili areas of Gilan. However, as it remained in manuscript form until recently, modern historians have largely neglected it.[10] Also useful for this region is the continuation of Rashid al-Din's *Universal History* written by Hafiz Abru (d. 833/1430)[11] and the *History of Uljaytu* (*Taʾrīkh-i Ūljaytū*) by Abu al-Qasim Kashani.[12] Slightly earlier than these is the *History of Herat* (*Taʾrīkhnāma-yi Harāt*) (probably written about 722/1322, exactly a century after Herat's complete destruction at the hands of the Mongols) by Sayf al-Harawi, a poet and historian of that city during the Mongol period.[13] This author has some incidental references to the Ismailis immediately after the fall of Alamut. Fasih al-Din al-Khwafi, a protégé of the Timurids of Herat in the first half of the 9th/15th century, also has some interesting details about the post-Alamut Nizaris in his well-known historical and biographical work, *Fasih's Compendium* (*Mujmal-i Faṣīḥī*).[14] With regards to areas in the immediate vicinity of Alamut, after the aforementioned sources, we find further information in a regional account, the *History of Gilan and Daylam* (*Ta'rīkh-i Gīlān wa-Daylamistān*) by Zahir al-Din Marʿashi (d. ca. 894/1489), a senior officer of the rulers of Lahijan who served in the Gilani army in a number of military operations in Mazandaran.[15] Though hostile to the sectarians, this author gives unique information about the remnants of the Ismailis in the mountainous region of Gilan. In fact, he had dedicated a section of his book to the history and doctrine of the Ismailis. As luck would have it, it is this very portion that is missing in the sole surviving manuscript of the work.[16] There is also the *History of Mazandaran* (*Ta'rīkh-i Māzandarān*) written in 1044/1634 by Mulla Shaykh ʿAli Gilani, who reports on Ismaili activities in that region.[17] One of the most important sources for the Ismailis of Quhistan is the *Counsels to Shahrukh* (*Naṣā'iḥ-i Shāhrukhī*). Written by Jalal-i Qa'ini of Herat, a fourteenth or fifteenth-century author and inveterate enemy of the community, the work is contained in a hitherto unpublished manuscript in the Imperial Library of Vienna.[18]

With regard to areas outside of Iran, there are some interesting notes on the Ismaili fortresses of Syria preserved in the *Book of Journeys* (*Riḥla*) by the famous Moorish traveler, Ibn Battuta, completed in 756/1357.[19] Shams al-Din al-Dimashqi (727/1327) has some surprising details about the remnants of the Ismailis in Egypt in his cosmography, *Selections of the Age on the Wonders of Land and Sea* (*Nukhbat al-Dahr fi ʿAjā'ib al-Barr wa-al-Baḥr*).[20] Similarly, Shaykh ʿAbd al-Haqq Dihlawi's (d. 1052/1642) account of the Muslim luminaries of India, *Reports of the Pious* (*Akhbār al-Akhyār*), includes information on the important Ismaili savant, Pir Hasan Kabir al-Din.[21] The lives of the Ismaili pirs of the Indian Subcontinent are further discussed in a later source, *Stations of the Poles and Gardens of the Lovers* (*Manāzil al-Aqṭāb wa-Basātīn al-Aḥbāb*) by Qadi Rahmat Allah b. Ghulam Mustafa of Ahmadabad, completed shortly after 1237/1822.[22] Lastly, a notice on his contemporary Nizari fellows turns up unexpectedly in the *Fountains of Histories* (*ʿUyūn al-Akhbār*) by the Tayyibi dignitary Idris ʿImad al-Din (d. 872/1468).[23]

Information about Tamerlane's attacks on the Ismailis in Mazandaran and Anjudan in the late 8th/14th century is recorded by four authors, Nizam al-Din Shami, Sharaf al-Din Yazdi, Mirkhwand, and Khwandamir. The first of these was one of the most important chroniclers of Tamerlane's conquests and a part of the royal entourage. He was appointed by the stalwart leader himself to record his victories. His *Book of Triumph* (*Ẓafarnāma*) was presented to Tamerlane in 806/1404.[24] Slightly later was another work of the same title by Sharaf al-Din ʿAli

Yazdi (d. 858/1454), a respected literary figure.[25] The third author, Muhammad b. Khwandshah b. Mahmud, well known as Mirkhwand (d. 903/1498), wrote a celebrated universal history entitled *The Garden of Purity* (*Rawḍat al-Ṣafā*ʾ).[26] His grandson, Khwandamir, continued to live in Iran for some time after the Safawid revolution before departing for India. He wrote the *Beloved of Biographies* (*Ḥabīb al-Siyar*).[27] Iskandar Beg Munshi (d. ca. 1042/1632) wrote one of the greatest works of Persian historiography, entitled *The World-Adorning ʿAbbasid History* (*Taʾrīkh-i ʿĀlamārā-yi ʿAbbāsī*).[28] When giving an account of the poets of Shah Tahmasp's reign, he mentions a certain Daʿi Anjudani and his brother Malik Tayfur, both of whom were apparently Ismaili poets.

Some Ismailis attracted the attention of the authors of poetic and other memorials (*tadhkira*), who were only rarely aware of the religious affiliation of their subjects. One such author, Dawlatshah, was closely associated with the Timurids, his father having been one of the most intimate courtiers of Tamerlane's son, Sultan Shahrukh. In 892/1487, shortly before Dawlatshah died, he completed his *Memorial of Poets* (*Tadhkirat al-Shuʿarā*ʾ).[29] Along the same lines was *Shem's Gift* (*Tuḥfa-yi Sāmī*), written by the third son of the Safawid Shah Ismaʿil I, Abu Nasr Sam Mirza (d. 974/1567).[30] It was finalized by 968/1561 and contains 714 short biographies of poets since the time the author's father came to power. The learned Shiʿi scholar Qadi Nur Allah Shushtari also wrote a book on the biographies of famous Shiʿis from the beginning of Islam to the rise of the Safawids, which he entitled *Gatherings of the Faithful* (*Majālis al-Muʾminīn*).[31] The account includes a few Ismailis. Finally, there was Lutf ʿAli Beg, who was known by the pen name Adhar. His claim to fame was the monumental *Fire Temple* (*Ātishkada*), completed shortly before his death in 1195/1781.[32]

ASKING THE PEOPLE OF THE HOUSE

A number of Nizari sources have also been used in reconstructing this period of Ismaili history and thought, many of them never before consulted by academics. These include texts by the Imams of the period, including what is most likely a 7th/13th century work, the *Pearl Scattering Words* (*Alfāẓ-i Guharbār*)[33]; an untitled quotation, perhaps attributable to the Imam Shams al-Din Muhammad (d. ca. 710/1310)[34]; the *Seven Aphorisms* (*Haft Nukta*) and the *Epistle of Sorrow* (*Risālat al-Ḥuzn*) of the Imam Islamshah, possibly the first of the three Imams with this name[35]; the *Five Discourses* (*Panj Sukhan*) of the Imam ʿAbd al-Salam, whom Ivanow identifies as the third Imam with this name[36]; an ordinance addressed to the Ismailis of Badakhshan and Kabul[37]; and an ode (*qaṣīda*),[38] both by the third Imam

ʿAbd al-Salam, a didactic work entitled *The Counsels of Chivalry* (*Pandiyāt-i Jawānmardī*) by the Imam Mustansir bi'llah, perhaps the second of the two Imams with this name who lived at Anjudan[39]; and a poem and an untitled treatise on the mystical significance of letters by the second Mustansir bi'llah of Anjudan, also known as Gharib Mirza.[40]

In addition to the works of the Imams, we have the various compositions of Persian Ismaili poets, most of whom were previously unknown. Besides Nizari Quhistani (d. ca. 720/1320),[41] these include ʿAbd Allah Ansari, Daʿi Anjudani, Ibn Husam Khusfi, Husayn, Zamani, and Darwish, all of whom flourished in the fifteenth century. There are also some anonymous poetic works that are historically significant, as well as an enlightening book entitled simply *Seven Chapters* (*Haft Bāb*) by an Ismaili proselyte, Bu Ishaq Quhistani.[42] The various prayers (*duʿā*) and poetic compositions known as Ginans—which are attributed to the great Ismaili preachers of South Asia, Pir Shams, Pir Sadr al-Din, Pir Hasan Kabir al-Din, Sayyid Imamshah, and Sayyid Nur Muhammadshah, among others—are equally important, as is the poem rhyming in the letter *Ta* (*Tāʾiyya*) of the Syrian Ismaili poet ʿAmir b. ʿAmir (d. after 700/1300)[43] and the poem *The Healing* (*al-Shāfiyya*),[44] which is of disputed authorship. The anonymous *Epistle of the Right Path* (*Risāla-yi Ṣirāt al-Mustaqīm*), tentatively dateable to the fourteenth or fifteenth century[45]; an opuscule on "Recognition of the Creator" by the poet Qasim Tushtari (or Turshizi)[46]; an anonymous fifteenth-century dialogue between an Ismaili ma'dhun and a mustajib entitled *The Epistle of the Discussion* (*Risāla-yi Munāẓara*)[47]; the *Gift (or Pages) for the Readers* (*Tuḥfat al-Nāẓirīn* or *Ṣaḥīfat al-Nāẓirīn*, also known as *Sī wa-shish ṣaḥīfa*, *Thirty-six Pages*), by the mid-fifteenth–century author Sayyid Suhrab Wali Badakhshani[48]; the anonymous *Epistle on the Explanation of the Ranks* (*Risāla-yi Sharḥ al-Marātib*), which is not dateable with certainty, but whose ideas mirror those of other works written in this period[49]; another anonymous treatise entitled *Guidance for Seekers* (*Irshād al-Ṭālibīn*), written before 915/1509; and *The Ladder of Ascent to the House of Eternity* (*Kitāb Sullam al-Ṣuʿūd ilā Dār al-Khulūd*) by Shihab al-Din Abu Firas[50] should also be mentioned. Some of the works of the sixteenth-century author Khayrkhwah Harati contain information on our period,[51] as do the anonymous *Opuscle on the Recognition of the Imam* (*Faṣl dar Bayān-i Shinākht-i Imām*)[52] and *The Sage's Discourse* (*Kalām-i Pīr*),[53] the latter a work traditionally ascribed to Nasir-i Khusraw but actually an amplification of Bu Ishaq's treatise mentioned above. Ivanow attributed both of these to the pen of Khayrkhwah, but this is not a definitive judgment. Works of authors writing in Fatimid and Alamut times, as well as those who wrote after the period under study, often shed tremendous light on questions of thought and doctrine. Therefore the writings of Abu Hatim Razi (d. 322/934), Jaʿfar b. Mansur al-Yaman (d. ca. 346/957), Abu Yaʿqub Sijistani (d. after 361/971), al-Qadi al-Nuʿman (d. 363/974), Hamid al-Din Kirmani (d. after

411/1020), Abu al-Qasim al-Maliji (fl. 5th/11th c.), Nasir-i Khusraw (d. after 462/1070), al-Mu'ayyad fi al-Din Shirazi (d. 470/1078), Nasir al-Din Tusi (d. 672/1274), and Salah al-Din Hasan-i Mahmud Katib (fl. 7th/13th c.), among others, have liberally been drawn upon to supplement, clarify, and elucidate many of the concepts contained in Ismaili works written from the time of Alamut's fall until the rise of the Safawids.

Wladimir Ivanow had made great efforts, though unsuccessful, to procure a copy of the *Pearl Scatterer* (*Gawhar Riz*), which he expected would be an apocryphal counterpart of Nasir-i Khusraw's *Book of Travels* (*Safarnāma*), describing his journeys to the East. In reality, it is a treatise in both prose and verse by a nineteenth-century Badakhshani author named Kuchak, which contains a great deal of interesting information, apparently culled from oral sources, about the activities of the Ismaili daʿwa in the author's time and earlier.[54] In addition to these, epigraphic evidence is invaluable in establishing dates for a number of the figures of this period.[55] There are several other late writings by Ismailis or those closely associated with the Ismaili community that are of value, particularly because their authors had access to written and oral traditions that are not otherwise available to us. These include *The Book of Supreme Admonitions* (*Khiṭābāt-i ʿĀliya*) by Pir Shihab al-Din Shah al-Husayni (d. 1302/1884),[56] *The Muhammadan Chronicles* (*Āthār-i Muḥammadī*) by Muhammad Taqi b. ʿAli Rida b. Zayn al-ʿAbidin Mahallati (d. ca. 1900),[57] and *Guidance for Seeking Believers* (*Hidāyat al-Mu'minīn al-Ṭālibīn*) by Muhammad b. Zayn al-ʿAbidin Fida'i Khurasani (d. 1342/1923), which, in its published version, has been updated by a certain Musa Khan b. Muhammad Khan Khurasani (d. 1937), all in Persian.[58] The last of these was also translated into Sindhi in the Khojki script by a certain Abhadharasul (i.e., ʿAbd al-Rasūl) Salemanani of Karachi.[59] The colophon is typical of those found in Khojki manuscripts and merits attention. The translator, who was also the scribe, writes:

> With folded hands, this particle of dust at the feet of the community (*jamāʿat*), this sinful wretch, Abhadharasul Salemanani, pleads in the presence of the lord that (the readers) may be merciful, correcting any mistakes as they read. May the community forgive my mistakes, may the Imam and pir forgive me. By the grace of the Imam and pir, by the bounty of the Imam of the time, I have completed copying this book, *Guidance for the Seekers*, on Sunday, the twenty-second day of the month of Shravan, 1960 (of the Vikrama Samvat era). O Mawlana! You are my support and I place my hope in you. I beg all who read this book to remember this sinful slave in their prayers.[60]

Another work of Fida'i Khurasani, *Wisdom for the People of Insight* (*Dānish-i Ahl-i Bīnish*), apparently contains some useful nuggets of historical information.[61]

Unfortunately, it is available only in manuscript and was not accessible to me. In Gujarati, of particular note are *Manifest Light* (*Nūram Mobīn*), in multiple editions and also translated into Urdu, by Alimamad Janmamad Chunara[62]; *Ismaili Mirror* (*Isamāilī Darpaṇ*) by Mastar Hasham Bogha[63]; *The Khoja Chronicles* (*Khojā Vṛttānt*) by Sachedina Nanjiani[64]; and *History of the Khojas* (*Khojā Kom no Itihās*) by Jafarbhai Rematula.[65] In Urdu, mention should be made of the *Garden of Shams* (*Gulzār-i Shams*).[66]

In perusing these sources, it soon becomes apparent that the task is, in many ways, similar to that of Inspector Alan Grant in Josephine Tey's *Daughter of Time*. The title of the novel derives from a famous proverb popularized by Francis Bacon but dating back at least to the second-century Latin author Aulus Gellius. In his only surviving work, *Attican Nights* (*Noctes Atticae*), which takes its name from the long winter's nights he spent in Attica, he recalls the lines of "an ancient poet whose name I cannot now remember" (*Alius quidam veterum poetarum, cuius nomen mihi nunc memoriae non est*). These were the immortal words *Veritas temporis filia*—"Truth is the Daughter of Time." But if this is indeed the case, it is proper to observe that time, by itself, can never give birth to such an offspring. In fact, the more time passes, the less likely the truth will ever be discovered. Records are lost, memories fade, sources disappear. As this happens, time itself becomes barren, or perhaps truth is stillborn. Time needs the tender care of the scholar to ensure a successful delivery. This, indeed, is the calling of researchers. The painstaking recovery and study of whatever remains of the past is absolutely essential. This is, in fact, the passion and joy of part of that venerable guild known as academe. As Johannes Kepler would say, voicing the feelings of many, *Temporis filia veritas; cui me obstetricari non pudet.* Truth is the daughter of time, and I feel no shame in being her midwife.

TWO

The Eagle Returns

It is generally believed that the fall of the castle of Alamut in A.H. 654 (AD 1256) marks the end of the Ismaili influence in Gilan. This is a great mistake.

H. L. Rabino in "Rulers of Gilan"

A charming legend set in the South Caspian province of Daylam records how the ruler Wahsudan was once on a hunting expedition. All of a sudden, he saw a soaring eagle alight on a rock. Noticing how strategically ideal the site was, he decided to build a castle there that was henceforth called *Aluh amu[kh]t*, which probably means "the eagle's teaching," (*taʿlīm al-ʿuqāb*). As noticed by a number of historians, in the traditional *abjad* system of alpha-numeric correspondence, the name is a chronogram for the year 483 AH (ا+ل+ه+ا+م+و+ت=1+30+5+1+40+6+400=483), corresponding to 1090 CE, the very year that Hasan-i Sabbah, the future champion of the Nizari Ismailis, came into possession of the castle. Alamut became the center of the community, the *taʿlimiyya* as it came to be known, reflecting their emphasis on the need for authoritative instruction (*taʿlīm*) and reminiscent of this delightful story about the *taʿlim al-ʿuqab*, the eagle's teaching.[1]

As their wave of devastation swept through the Near East, the Mongol hordes sought the complete destruction of Alamut. The Great Khan Mongke, grandson of Genghis Khan, perceived the Ismailis as a significant threat in his campaign. He therefore sent his brother Hulagu at the head of a mighty army with a dual purpose: to exterminate the entire Ismaili community and to destroy the Sunni caliph. Misled by the writings of Hulagu's courtier Juwayni, many of the Persian historians and later Western authors believed that the Ismailis had been annihilated in the face of the Mongol onslaught. While their continued survival has now become clear, this chapter is concerned with the hitherto largely underestimated, if not completely unnoticed, persistence of Ismaili activity in the South Caspian regions of Gilan, Daylam, and Mazandaran, including at the fort of Alamut itself, in the wake of the Mongol invasions.[2] Inconsistencies and exaggerations in Juwayni's testimony, a correction of his narrative based on other historians, including Rashid al-Din, and the statements of regional histories, geographical tomes, and inscriptions clearly point to a sustained Ismaili presence. This evidence is further supported by a Latin source on the Crusades, *The Counsels to Shahrukh* (*Naṣāʾiḥ-i Shāhrukhī*), and the testimony of South Asian Ismaili literature. From this, it becomes clear that the South Caspian region continued, perhaps sporadically, to be an important Ismaili center for over a century after the Mongol irruption. The eagle had, so to speak, returned.

A CORRECTIVE TO ʿATA-MALIK JUWAYNI'S NARRATIVE

The Mongol invasions were undoubtedly a singular event in Islamic history. The cataclysmic proportions of this catastrophe moved contemporary writers to predict the imminent end of the world.[3] Ibn al-Athir, who had witnessed with his own eyes the ravages of the marauding invaders, prefaced his account of the calamity as follows:

> I have been avoiding mentioning this event for many years because I consider it too horrible. I have been advancing with one foot and retreating with the other. Who could easily write the obituary of Islam and the Muslims? For whom could it be easy to mention it? Would that my mother had not given birth to me, would that I had died before it happened and had been a thing forgotten. However, a group of friends urged me to record it since I knew it first-hand. Then I saw that to refrain from it would profit nothing. Therefore, we say: this deed encompasses mention of the greatest event, the most awful catastrophe that has befallen time. It engulfed all beings, particularly the Muslims. Anyone would be right in saying that the world, from the time God created humans until now, has not been stricken by its like. Histories contain nothing that even approaches it.[4]

Indeed, by vicious conquests, the Mongols established the most extensive continuous land empire in the history of humankind, stretching at its height from

Korea to Hungary. As Morgan convincingly argues, it was no accident that Juwayni made the Mongol destruction of Alamut the culmination of his *History of the World Conqueror*. As a staunch Sunni Muslim, he could scarcely celebrate the devastation of his co-religionists by his own heathen patron whose service he had entered during his youth. He was therefore at pains "to discern some silver linings in the Mongol clouds."[5] What better way to do this than to celebrate his patron's victory over the "arch-heretics," something the Saljuqs had never been able to accomplish?[6] Though he was an eyewitness to the Mongol invasions, Juwayni selectively reports what suits his aim. Numerous authors from the time of d'Ohsson in the early 1800s to David Ayalon more recently have vigorously censured Juwayni for "extravagant flattery" of the Mongols, castigating him for being "servile"—even "nauseating."[7] E. G. Browne, the doyen of Persian literary studies in the Western world, is somewhat more forgiving, noting that his circumstances "compelled him to speak with civility of the barbarians whom it was his misfortune to serve."[8]

Juwayni's most glaring omission in his tome of the Mongol conquests speaks volumes. He neglects to mention that the invaders sacked Baghdad, the ʿAbbasid capital, and murdered the last Sunni caliph in 656/1258, unceremoniously rolling him up in a carpet and trampling him to death with elephants.[9] Meanwhile, the downfall of the tiny Nizari Ismaili state is given great prominence and is the pinnacle of his narrative. Juwayni himself composed the proclamation of victory (*fatḥnāma*) on this occasion.[10] While the desolation of such symbols of Sunni Islam are downplayed by the historian, he revels in the Mongol victories over the Shiʿi Ismailis, asserting that the "sons and daughters, brothers and sisters and all of [the] seed and family" of the last Ismaili Imam of Alamut, Rukn al-Din Khwurshah, were "laid on the fire of annihilation."[11] In concluding his history, he triumphantly declares, "He and his followers were kicked to a pulp and then put to the sword; and of him and his stock no trace was left, and he and his kindred became but a tale on men's lips and a tradition in the world."[12] While there can be little doubt that the community was devastated—we know independently from the *History of Tabaristan* (*Ta'rīkh-i Ṭabaristān*), for example, that Khurasan especially was flooded with captive Ismaili women and children, sold as slaves—this devastation was not as complete as Juwayni would have us believe.[13]

Our first clues of the author's embellishments are found in the contradictions within the *History of the World Conqueror* itself. Juwayni speaks of the writings of the Ismaili author Hasan b. Muhammad b. Buzurgumid as being "well-known to this very day amongst that people," writes in the present tense of the community's reluctance to visit the grave of Muhammad b. Buzurgumid, and curses the Ismailis, saying, "may what are left of them receive their deserts."[14] Clearly, the Mongols were not entirely successful in their efforts to exterminate their foes.

Writing not long after Juwayni, Rashid al-Din, who, like his predecessor, was in the employ of the Mongols, informs us that the Ismaili fortress of Girdkuh managed to hold out under extreme siege conditions for almost twenty years, falling only in 669/1270, over a decade after Alamut's capitulation.[15] In the same year, an attempt, ascribed to the Nizaris, was made on the life of ʿAta-Malik Juwayni himself, who had just written them out of existence. Contemporary witnesses clearly viewed the Ismailis as a force to be reckoned with and were not convinced of their extirpation by the Mongols.[16]

Soon after Girdkuh fell, rallying under a son of the Imam Rukn al-Din Khwurshah, a group of Ismailis managed to recapture Alamut itself in 674/1275.[17] The subjugation of the fortress by this son of the Imam Rukn al-Din, in league with a descendant of the Khwarazmshahs, led H. L. Rabino to assert, "It is generally believed that the fall of the castle of Alamut in A.H. 654 (AD 1256) marks the end of the Ismaili influence in Gilan. This is a great mistake. Either the destruction of Alamut cannot have been as complete as reported by the Persian writers, or the castle was rebuilt."[18] Regarding the destruction of the fortress Juwayni had gleefully asserted, "In that breeding-ground of heresy in the Rudbar of Alamut the home of the wicked adherents of Hasan-i-Sabbah and the evil followers of the practice of libertinism, there remains not one stone of the foundations upon another."[19] That this, too, is likely exaggerated is indicated by recent excavations. Hamideh Chubak, Iranian archaeologist and director of a team researching the remains of Alamut, describes how the digs of her team reveal another wave of destruction centuries later during the Safawid period, witnessed by two cast-iron catapult balls that were found near one of the towers in 2004, along with a huge pile of rubble dating from that time. Further evidence confirms an eighteenth-century Afghan military assault on Alamut as well, demonstrating that the fort itself probably survived Hulagu's assaults.[20]

A careful examination of the *History of the World Conqueror* reveals further inconsistencies and lapses in Juwayni's testimony, particularly with regards to a parenthetical remark that Rukn al-Din Khwurshah had but a single son—"he sent out his son, *his only one*, and another brother called Iranshah with a delegation of notables, officials and leaders of his people."[21] Prior to this pivotal assertion, the historian mentions a young son of the Imam Rukn al-Din who was sent together with a number of his chief officials to the service of the Mongol warlord. This, according to Juwayni, was a ruse, as a decoy of the same age had been dispatched in place of the real son.[22] Rashid al-Din, narrating the same incident, doesn't share Juwayni's doubts about the identity of the boy, who was about seven or eight years old.[23] His testimony regarding this event seems more plausible. Juwayni is convinced that even Khwurshah's ministers and advisers had been duped and were unaware that it was not the real son, which is scarcely a possibility.[24] If indeed this were a decoy, it would have been quite foolhardy to send a young child, who would easily have blurted out the truth of his identity under questioning.[25] Both Juwayni and Rashid al-Din mention that when the castle of Maymundiz was conquered in 654/1256,

Rukn al-Din Khwurshah sent another son to Hulagu together with the Imam's brother Iranshah and various notables and dignitaries.[26] This son was clearly not the same person as the child sent earlier, as Juwayni is confident of his identity.[27] Rashid al-Din provides the important additional detail that the name of this son was Tarkiya.[28] Thus, Khwurshah had at least two sons. This is further supported by Juwayni himself, who contradicts his own testimony about a single son by writing about Rukn al-Din Khwurshah's "sons and daughters, brothers and sisters."[29]

IN THE SHADOW OF THE ILKHANIDS

Hulagu Khan's military triumphs led him to found the Ilkhanid dynasty. His eldest son and successor to the throne, Abaqa Khan (d. 680/1282), managed to wrest Alamut once again from the Imam Rukn al-Din Khwurshah's son who had reconquered it.[30] The Mongols did not stay to rule though. Gilan was never completely subdued by them, and, until the time of Hulagu's great-grandson Uljaytu Khan (d. 716/1312), it was left relatively undisturbed due to its inaccessibility.[31] In fact, the area is scarcely mentioned in the earlier chronicles of the Mongol period.[32] Thus, the Nizaris were probably able to retain some sort of autonomy in Daylam, just as other groups ruled relatively independently in the surrounding areas. Indeed, Hulagu's other great-grandson, Ghazan Khan, the brother of Uljaytu, who succeeded to the Ilkhanate in 694/1295, refers to the continued presence of Ismailis in his time "who have been in these lands from long ago," noting that they had a practice of concealing their beliefs.[33] This state of relative independence continued until, hungry for the taxes of the Gilani chiefs and power over the silk of that region, Uljaytu brought in his army in 706/1307.[34] His foray into Daylam was marked by plunder and killing.[35] Though this Mongol incursion into Gilan was successful, it was, as J. A. Boyle correctly recognized, "at most a Pyrrhic victory."[36] Even if they managed to maintain some residual authority over the region after this expedition, it would have evaporated in 735/1335 with the death of Abu Saʿid, Uljaytu's successor and the last great Mongol Ilkhan. Henceforth, there was no central rule or strong government in the region, a circumstance that would have allowed any remaining Ismailis in the area a respite from the ravages of the previous decades.

The region's relative autonomy is confirmed in Mustawfi's geographical treatise, *The Hearts' Bliss* (*Nuzhat al-Qulūb*), written in 740/1340, which mentions that the districts in the area were under the control of independent governors, each of whom considered himself to be a sovereign king.[37] The work further goes on to state that many of these districts were populated by Ismailis.[38] It seems that during this period of respite, the community, still reeling from the slaughter of so many of its members, managed to regroup. By 770/1368, the whole of Daylam came under Ismaili rule once again and was governed by the Kushayji family, led by Kiya Sayf al-Din.[39]

THE TRIALS OF THE KUSHAYJI FAMILY

The lull in hostilities was short-lived though. Soon the Ismailis were to face the wrath of their neighbors, the Marʿashi dynasty and its allies, the Malatis.[40] Marʿashi power extended right to the frontier of Qazwin in the west, while the Malatis controlled much of Gilan.[41] Despite his clear hostility and stylized diatribes, it is to a member of the Marʿashi clan, Zahir al-Din (d. ca. 894/1489), that we owe much of our knowledge of the region's Ismailis in this period. In fact, he dedicated a whole section of his *History of Gilan and Daylam* (*Taʾrīkh-i Gīlān wa Daylamistān*) to the community, a section to which he repeatedly refers but which, regrettably is missing in the sole surviving manuscript of the work. In itself, the attention of this author is testimony to the Ismaili community's enduring presence and influence in the region two centuries after the Mongol destruction of Alamut.[42]

In Daylam, Kiya Sayf al-Din and the Kushayji family made a point of not broadcasting their Ismaili faith publicly. Despite this, the leader received a hostile letter from the neighboring Zaydi ruler, a Malati sayyid by the name of ʿAli Kiya b. Amir Kiya.[43] The letter caustically denounced the "Ismaili heretics" (*malāḥida-yi Ismāʿīlī*) and prevailed upon Kiya Sayf al-Din to rid his territories of the hated community. The Ismaili leader replied indignantly to the messenger, declaring his family's religion openly, "My ancestors followed the religion of Muhammad, upon whom be peace, and were followers and believers in the sayyids of the line of Ismaʿil b. Jaʿfar. Nobody has a right to dictate to us in this manner."[44] The stinging rejoinder moved ʿAli Kiya to prepare his forces for battle. When Kiya Sayf al-Din heard of these preparations, he immediately readied his own Daylami troops. The two parties clashed in 779/1377. In the battle, Kiya Sayf al-Din's troops were routed and the Ismaili leader was forced to flee. ʿAli Kiya quickly set about to "repulse and obliterate the path of impiety and depravity [of Ismailism] that the people of that realm had adopted for some years."[45] ʿAli Kiya's forces pursued Sayf al-Din, eventually capturing and beheading him. Uncowed by the loss, the members of the Kushayji family and their followers regrouped in Qazwin and managed to exact revenge on the lieutenant who had executed their leader. Numerous Ismailis then sought refuge in Qazwin, a city that, although itself largely

Sunni, was encompassed by Ismailis, who inhabited many of the three hundred villages in the district.[46] The Kushayjis made forays into Daylam from Qazwin, but in 781/1378, ʿAli Kiya's forces drove the Ismaili refugees out of that city. The Kushayji family then fled to Sultaniyya, originally a dependency of Qazwin, where they joined some of their co-religionists.[47] Nearby Taliqan, with a substantial Ismaili population, was ruled by the inimical Malik Bisutun, who was defeated by the Ismailis in 787/1385.[48] Shortly after this minor victory, however, Tamerlane's troops were to massacre the Ismailis in Mazandaran,[49] and shortly thereafter those in Anjudan as well.[50]

THE APPEARANCE OF KHUDAWAND MUHAMMAD

In his efforts to dominate the region, while still in conflict with the Kushayji family, on another front, ʿAli Kiya sought to enlist the support of a certain Khudawand Muhammad, who was evidently an Ismaili Imam. He therefore sent an emissary bearing a message proclaiming that "the Almighty God's gate of repentance and penitence was open" and that the way to it was for him "to forsake the corrupt beliefs" of his forebears and ancestors.[51] The message is further supposed to have proclaimed:

> Your folk have ruled over Daylam for a number of years, but due to abounding iniquity, the evil of impiety, and wicked beliefs, you have witnessed what you have witnessed.[52] If you turn away from the path reviled by the leaders of religion and companions of certainty and adorn and bedeck yourself in the garb of faith and certitude, accepting our generous counsel, we will show compassion and mercy to you and bestow the land of Daylam upon you.[53]

The highly stylized account then has Khudawand Muhammad hastily beating a path to Lahijan, ʿAli Kiya's Gilani capital. With Khudawand Muhammad's support, ʿAli Kiya hoped to overcome his rival, Kiya Malik. There followed, in the year 776/1374, a mighty battle in which the forces of Kiya Malik were routed by the combined efforts of Khudawand Muhammad and the forces of ʿAli Kiya. Kiya Malik fled and took refuge at Alamut.[54]

Rather than assigning Daylam to Khudawand Muhammad as had been promised, ʿAli Kiya double-crossed him and entrusted the area to his own brother, Mahdi Kiya.[55] Realizing he had been deceived, Khudawand Muhammad stole away by night to Alamut where he formed an alliance with the defeated Kiya Malik. In turn, Kiya Malik promised that Alamut would be entrusted to the Imam if he helped him to regain the city of Ashkawar. As Marʿashi narrates, upon seeing Khudawand Muhammad, the Ismailis of Alamut and Lamasar immediately rallied about him, joined the forces of Kiya Malik, and converged on Ashkawar. The combined forces inflicted heavy losses on the Gilani army of Mahdi Kiya, whose dead and wounded totaled close to two thousand, while many others were taken prisoner by the Ismailis.[56] Mahdi Kiya was himself taken captive and sent to the court of Sultan Uways (r. 757–776/1356–1374), the ruler of Azerbaijan, Iraq, and Kurdistan.[57] Mahdi Kiya remained incarcerated for a period of a year and six months, during which time, oddly enough, his brother made no attempt to have him released. It was only with the intercession of Taj al-Din Amuli, one of the Zaydi sayyids of Timjan, and the proffering of numerous gifts that he was freed.[58] When appealing to Sultan Uways, Taj al-Din explained that Kiya Malik was in cahoots with the Ismailis of Alamut (*malāḥida-yi alamūt*). Apparently the sultan required no further explanation. Even away in Tabriz, he seems to have been well aware of the continued existence of the Ismailis in Daylam and their survival of the Mongol depredations.

Soon after his brother was released, ʿAli Kiya once again set out to displace Kiya Malik from Ashkawar. Kiya Malik was bested in the ensuing struggle and fled to Alamut, where Khudawand Muhammad wanted nothing to do with him. He therefore took refuge with Tamerlane, the Turkic conqueror. Meanwhile, the army of ʿAli Kiya, which had pursued Kiya Malik right up to Alamut, decided to besiege the fort. Khudawand Muhammad refused to capitulate. However, dwindling resources forced him to surrender the castle. He was granted safe conduct and also made his way to Tamerlane's camp.[59]

ʿAli Kiya wrote a letter to Tamerlane about the collusion of Kiya Malik and the Ismaili Imam, prevailing upon him to take the appropriate measures. Upon receipt of this letter, the ruler sent Kiya Malik to Sawa, while Khudawand Muhammad was sent to confinement in Sultaniyya. Marʿashi writes that the Imam's descendants continued to reside there until his own days, that is to say, until the late fifteenth century.[60]

ʿAli Kiya's death in 791/1389 allowed Kiya Malik to return to Daylam from Sawa. There he received help from the locals to regain Alamut and Lamasar.[61] He was, however, murdered by his own grandson, Kiya Jalal al-Din, who then succeeded him but was hated by the Daylamis. Amidst this confusion, Khudawand Muhammad reappeared in the area, and the Ismailis of the region, who apparently resided at Alamut, gave the fortress to him. However, it was soon lost once again, this time to Malik Kayumarth (d. 857/1453), a ruler of Rustamdar.[62]

Later, the fortress was taken over by ʿAli Kiya's son, Radi Kiya (d. 829/1426). This ruler perpetrated such massacres in Daylam that in the year 819/1416, in the words of Marʿashi, "the waters of the White River (*Safidrūd*) turned red with the blood of those killed."[63] Among those done away with were many Ismaili leaders, including some descendants of the Ismaili Imam Khudawand ʿAla' al-Din Muhammad (d. 653/1255).

CONTINUED ISMAILI ACTIVITY

However, even this terrible massacre did not completely end Ismaili activities in the region. While it would appear that the Ismaili Imams had now abandoned the area, perhaps in favor of Shahr-i Babak or Anjudan, there is epigraphic evidence of a continued Ismaili presence in Gilan. The tombstone of the Malati ruler, Muhammad Kar Kiya b. Sayyid Nasr Kiya, located in Lahijan and dated 883/1478, boasts that for forty years he battled against the innovations of the Ismailis (*bidʿa mulḥidiyya*).[64]

Meanwhile, in his *History of Mazandaran* (*Ta'rīkh-i Māzandarān*), written in 1044/1634, Mulla Shaykh ʿAli Gilani reports Ismaili activities in that region as late as the end of the sixteenth century, that is to say, even into Safawid times. When the aforementioned Malik Kayumarth died in 857/1453, his territories were divided between his two sons, Kawus and Iskandar, the former ruling from Nur and the latter from Kujur. In 975/1567, Sultan Muhammad b. Jahangir, a Nizari Ismaili, succeeded his father to the leadership of the Iskandari line. Gilani expresses his distaste for this ruler, but reports that he was tremendously popular among his subjects. With the help of his adoring citizenry, he spread his creed throughout Rustamdar and established his suzerainty over Nur and other areas of Mazandaran, even as far as Sari. When his eldest son Jahangir succeeded him in 998/1589, he continued his father's religious policies. The South Caspian region could not remain free from Safawid hegemony for long, however, and after Shah ʿAbbas I subjugated much of the area in 1000/1591, Jahangir hastened to his court. Shortly after returning to Rustamdar, he was captured by a force under the command of the shah's local lieutenant, sent to Qazwin, and executed there in 1006/1597.[65] This is the last we hear of Ismaili political activities in the area. Some faint whisperings of the possibility of the community's continued habitation in this region, however, are found in a verse of the Ismaili poet Khaki Khurasani, who flourished in the first half of the seventeenth century, which refers to Mazandaran.[66] The traveler Macdonnell Kinneir's "Topographical History of Persia" has also been cited as observing in about the year 1813 that "the castles in the district of Rudbar, in the mountains of Kuhistan, particularly in the vicinity of Alamut, are still inhabited to this day by Ismailites who . . . go by the general name of Hosseinis."[67] This single allusion may represent the last vestige of Ismailism in the South Caspian.

After Alamut's capitulation to the Mongols, while the Ismailis had continued their activities in the area for an extended period, and tenuously and sporadically tried to reassert control over the fort,[68] repeated reversals of fortune weakened them considerably. Command over all the fortresses formerly under Ismaili suzerainty eventually passed into the hands of the Malati rulers who used them as prisons until the Safawid conquest.[69]

An interesting question arises here about the identity of Khudawand Muhammad, who played such a central role in rallying the Ismailis of the area. As mentioned above, Marʿashi records that people in Daylam, Rudbar, Padiz, Kushayjan, and some of the regions of Ashkawar owed their allegiance to this figure, a descendant of the Imam ʿAlaʾ al-Din Muhammad. This lineage, Marʿashi's description, and the title "Khudawand" all indicate that he was considered the Imam by his followers. The confusion arises because of the existence of evidence, first brought to light in a seminal article by Wladimir Ivanow published in 1938, indicating the possibility that the Nizari Ismailis split into two sects in the fourteenth century: the followers of Qasimshah and the followers of Muhammadshah.[70] Further evidence from Muhammadshahi sources was later provided by the Syrian scholar ʿArif Tamir in his article "Branches of the Ismaili Tree" (*Furūʿ al-shajara al-Ismāʿīliyya*)[71] and his book *Imamate in Islam* (*al-Imāma fī al-Islām*).[72] A reconstruction of the family tree and its branches can be found in chapter 4.

While a detailed discussion of the split is beyond the scope of this study, it should be mentioned that scholars have cautiously identified Khudawand Muhammad with Muhammadshah b. Muʾminshah (d. 807/1404) of the Muhammadshahi line on the basis that there was no contemporary Imam of the Qasimshahi line with the name Muhammad.[73] However, new evidence in a work entitled *Seven Aphorisms* (*Haft Nukta*), associated with Islamshah, a Qasimshahi Imam, may suggest a different identification.[74] While the Muhammadshahi line is never explicitly mentioned in this work, there is an allusion to rivalry in the family. This source specifies that the author's adversary had influence in four areas: Badakhshan, the fort of Zafar (likely in Badakhshan as well), Egypt, and Narjawan. Daylam is not mentioned at all, and we may therefore assume that it remained loyal to the Imams of the Qasimshahi line. This would significantly reduce the possibility of the earlier identification of Khudawand Muhammad. Given that the first of the Qasimshahi Imams named Islamshah was also known as Ahmad,[75] and that the names Ahmad and Muhammad are often interchangeable (as in the case of the Prophet himself), it is possible to cautiously suggest that Khudawand Muhammad may be identified with Islamshah b. Qasimshah. In view of the fact that the Nizari tradition of the Indian Subcontinent, which is discussed below, connects the residence of Islamshah with Alamut, this is conceivable. At the same time, ʿArif Tamir, a Muhammadshahi author, asserts that Muhammad b. Muʾminshah died in 807/1404 and was buried in Sultaniyya, the same place where Khudawand

Muhammad had been sent to confinement.[76] No authority is given for this information however, and Tamir himself associates the recapture of Alamut with the Qasimshahi Imams.[77] In the absence of further information, the question of Khudawand Muhammad's identity must remain open.[78]

The material outlined above clearly indicates that the Ismailis continued their activities in the South Caspian region, perhaps sporadically, through the fourteenth and fifteenth centuries. This hypothesis finds further support in materials foreign to the region.

TESTIMONY FROM LATIN, KHURASANI, AND SOUTH ASIAN SOURCES

Immediately upon his accession to the throne of France in 1328, King Philippe VI of Valois already had aspirations of embarking on a crusade to the Holy Land. In 1332, a Latin treatise entitled *Directorium ad Passagium Faciendum* was submitted to him, providing advice on how to prepare for his campaign.[79] While the text has sometimes been attributed to a certain Brocardus or the French Dominican Raymond Étienne, it most likely comes from the pen of Guillelmus Adae (William Adam), who is known to have voyaged for twenty-four years in the Near East, through Constantinople, Persia, and Armenia, the same number of years mentioned in the prologue to this work.[80] In book nine of his tome, "On People Against Whom the King Must Be on His Guard," he includes Greeks, Armenians, and the Assassins, i.e., the Ismailis. Information on this community is scanty, and it is unlikely that the author actually met any Ismailis. However, his lengthy residence in the region, and particularly the two years he spent in Sultaniyya, so close to the former centers of Ismaili power, would certainly have exposed him to local traditions about their continued survival. Their inclusion among those of whom the king must be wary indicates some degree of political clout as well. So worried was Adae about the continued strength of the community that he advised the French sovereign to take precautions by requiring sufficient security clearance for all the staff of his royal household, even in far-off Paris!

While it is possible that Adae's advice to the King of France was based on rumor and gossip, Jalal-i Qa'ini's advice to his Timurid ruler, entitled *Counsels to Shahrukh* (*Naṣāʾiḥ-i Shāhrukhī*), for all its venom and malice against the Ismailis, was based on his own family's attempts at eradicating the community. We will return to this very interesting source further on, but most noteworthy at this juncture is that the author, who completed his work in 820/1417, writes that it had been hoped that the Mongols would decimate the Ismailis once and for all.

However, such was not the case. Some of them returned to Alamut after the death of Rukn al-Din Khwurshah and renewed their preaching activities, even dispatching envoys to Quhistan. Yet more significant is his testimony that the Ismailis of Quhistan continued to send their religious dues (*wājibāt*) to Alamut, following an age-old practice that had existed since the time of Hasan-i Sabbah.[81] There can be no reason for this *modus operandi* other than the continued existence of the daʿwa structure, if not the Imam's own residence, in that region. Qaʾini's testimony is based on a thorough investigation. In the space of eleven months he traveled the length and breadth of Quhistan on his mission.[82]

Further evidence of continued Ismaili activity in the region of Alamut comes to us in the form of what are sometimes called "unintentional" historical sources—that is, sources that were not composed with the express intention of recording history, but which, nevertheless, may serve a historical purpose, particularly where writings with an expressly historical intent are wanting. With the destruction of the Ismaili state at Alamut and the devastation of Iranian lands by the Mongols, literary activity among the Ismailis was stymied. As would be expected under the circumstances, no chronicles of Ismaili activities written by members of the community are known to have been composed in this volatile period, although there was a tradition of historical writing in Fatimid and Alamut times.[83]

While the Mongol onslaught laid waste to the Iranian regions, South Asia was largely spared these assaults. Accordingly, we find testimony in the Ismaili literature of the Subcontinent to the continuation of activities in the South Caspian area and, most notably, to continued connections with Alamut.[84] Hitherto, however, there has been no thorough study of the textual transmission of this literature, which goes by the name Ginan, derived from a Sanskrit word meaning "gnosis."[85] As the name suggests, the subject matter of this corpus is often esoteric, with a predominance of didactic, mythic, and allegorical motifs. Historical references, while they certainly exist, may sometimes be understood symbolically. Furthermore, the texts have suffered from a long period of transmission, both oral and written, occasionally resulting in anachronisms in a composition. While we can be certain that at least a few manuscripts dating back to the sixteenth century survived until recent times,[86] the oldest manuscript currently preserved in an institutional collection dates to 1736.[87] Bearing these factors in mind, however, as it has survived, the Ismaili literature of South Asia potentially preserves memories of this most obscure period of history.

The ancient mausoleum of the Ismaili savant, Pir Shams of Multan, which likely dates to the thirteenth century, witnesses the community's presence in the region at the time of the Mongol invasions.[88] Traditional accounts, preserved both in the Ginans as well as in later, non-Ismaili sources, maintain that the son and grandson of Pir Shams, known as Pir Nasir al-Din and Pir Shihab al-Din (or Sahib al-Din, as his name often appears) respectively, assumed the leadership of the Ismailis in South Asia from the late thirteenth to the mid-fourteenth century.[89] The Ginans confirm that religious dues continued to be submitted to the Imam in this period and that propagation activities were conducted in secret.[90] Procedural details provided in these accounts give us greater reason for confidence in the testimony. Of the sum collected, 20 percent was for local use, while the remaining 80 percent was dispatched to the Imam who, we are informed in the Ginanic account, resided in a fortress by the name of "Mor." Juzjani reports that prior to the Mongol invasions, the Ismailis were in possession of seventy forts in Quhistan and thirty-five in the Alamut region.[91] In fact, an Ismaili citadel from Alamut times, known as Mahr Nigar or Mahrin, still exists in the South Caspian, not far from Damghan. The similarity of names is striking, as the Persian word *mahr* is often rendered as *mor* in South Asian languages. Peter Willey, who made researching Ismaili castles his life work, comments on the "exceptionally well built" stone walls of the Ismaili forts in the area of Mahr Nigar, demonstrating the builders' "architectural expertise."[92] Whether this particular fort is the same as the one in the Ginanic narrative is difficult to ascertain. Regardless, according to this Ginanic testimony, emissaries (*rāhī*)[93] traveled from Uch to Mor to convey the funds to the Imam, who was in concealment (*alop*). Such a system of delivering religious dues is presumed in the *Counsels of Chivalry* (*Pandiyāt-i Jawānmardī*) of the fifteenth-century Imam Mustansir bi'llah.[94] Similarly, the sixteenth-century Ismaili author Muhammad Rida b. Sultan Husayn, known as Khayrkhwah Harati, also refers to the comings and goings of Ismaili dignitaries from various places, including India, to see the Imam as well as to submit religious dues.[95]

A striking feature of the literature attributed to the Indian Ismaili leadership in this period is the candor with which it speaks of the Imam's continued residence in Daylam, or even the fort of Alamut itself. A work attributed to Pir Shihab al-Din that alternates between addressing the disciples and the Imam trumpets:

> Come hither! O assembly of vassals, that the king may fulfill your desires. We are sinful, paupers, slaves—O king! Succor us. In serving your court, no other comes to sight. The four aeons have run their course. O chivalrous ones, perform deeds of virtue. Brother, build a raft of truth, believer, steady your heart, for in the land of Daylam the great king, my lord has descended. O king, the earth's nine continents are your vassalry. You are our lord, the Mahdi. O lord Islamshah, the granter of boons! Be pleased, O great Mahdi. O king, bestow on the faithful salvation, deliverance and your beatific vision. How blessed is the region of Alamut where you have established your physical residence![96]

Most remarkably, Alamut or Daylam are mentioned in no less than twelve of the compositions attributed to Shihab al-Din's son and successor, Pir Sadr al-Din.[97] Under the able leadership of this fourteenth-century luminary, perhaps the most prolific of the South Asian Ismaili authors at this time,[98] the community in the Subcontinent experienced something of a renaissance. Pir Sadr al-Din often mentioned the name of the reigning Imam Islamshah in his compositions.[99]

While the need for a proper study of the textual transmission of the Ginanic corpus has been alluded to, along with the attendant necessity for prudence in deriving historical data from it until such a study is completed, there is remarkable consistency in the testimony of the Ginans in this particular instance. There are repeated references in the Ginans of Pir Sadr al-Din to Daylam as the residence of the Imam Islamshah, references that completely disappear in the compositions attributed to the successors of this pir. There is not a single Ginanic composition ascribed to any figure that lived after Pir Sadr al-Din that mentions Alamut or Daylam as the current residence of the Ismaili Imam in any of the over six hundred works consulted.[100]

While this concentration of references to the residence of the Imam at Alamut or Daylam in the works attributed to Pir Sadr al-Din to the exclusion of works credited to later authors is, in itself, compelling evidence to argue for the authenticity of the traditional attribution of authorship, the argument does not rely on this ascription. There is a consensus among scholars that in the event that particular compositions are incorrectly ascribed to their purported authors, the provenance of these compositions must, in all events, be later than that attributed to them, and hence after the Mongol offensive. This is fairly compelling evidence that at some time after the Mongol invasions, an Ismaili Imam, almost certainly one of those named Islamshah, again took up residence in Daylam.

The fact that no author after Pir Sadr al-Din mentions the Imam dwelling at Alamut strongly suggests that the Imams must have moved their base at some point during his lifetime. That the Imam's residence was in the Alamut region at the time when the Imam Islamshah succeeded his father, Qasimshah, is implicit in the Sindhi Ginan "Serve the lord single-heartedly" (*shāhāke hek man āṃhī sirevo*), in which the audience is assured that Islamshah, the light (*nūr*) of ʿAli, is none other than Qasimshah himself, established at the fort of Alamut.[101] This kind of statement, celebrating Islamshah's succession to his predecessor, would most likely have been made at the outset of the new Imam's reign.

One of the most striking details that emerges from a reading of Pir Sadr al-Din's compositions is that he himself made a pilgrimage to the Imam's residence. This is suggested in the following emotive verses:

> Blessed, blessed is this day, for we have attained the supreme lord. Effaced are the sins and misdeeds of the four cosmic ages. Gather in the assembly of love with the true guide; gather in the assembly of hearts with

> Pir Sadr al-Din, the savior of the twelve crore souls.[102] Forsake this deceitful world. Cross the vast ocean of the deceptive world with the name of the Imam. Work deeds of righteousness in the world. The Imam has descended in human garb[103] at the fort of Alamut, the capital of the land of Daylam. I scaled towering mountains and negotiated treacherous passes; now I await the light of the true guide. How pitiful are lofty trees without leaves; how the human soul wanders lost without gnosis of the guide![104]

The reference to scaling the difficult mountain passes of Daylam, while evocative of a spiritual pilgrimage, is also redolent of the arduous journey that would have confronted believers making the trek to see the Imam from far-off places. That it was Islamshah whom Pir Sadr al-Din met is expressed elsewhere: "We received the lord Islamshah who bestowed on us the mysteries of faith. We recognized him in a form beyond description and he fulfilled all our desires."[105] Yet another composition mentions the author's departure from Alamut: "Brothers, Pir Sadr al-Din, the true guide, departed from the fort of Alamut, the capital of the land of Daylam."[106] Extremely noteworthy is an exultant Sindhi composition that suggests that proselytization was once again set afoot from Alamut:

> The Imam's herald travels throughout the world. Blessings be upon the Imam, the pir and the community, for the Imam has appeared in the fortress of Alamut. Brother, we are perpetually blissful. By God, he has arrived; the community enjoys its fortune. Hail the advent of the lord ʿAli in the west. Recognize the supreme man, lord of light. Friends, know the pir to be he who has led you to the recognition of the lord of twelve splendors.[107] Serve none other than that very lord, my brother. Friend, never doubt in this. Hail the advent of the lord, as glorious as the risen sun![108]

CONCLUSION

Upon examination of the evidence, it becomes immediately apparent that even after the Mongol onslaught, Ismaili activity continued in the South Caspian region. Juwayni had definite political motives for omitting any reference to the destruction of Baghdad and the murder of the Sunni caliph, and for making the subjugation of the Shiʿi Ismailis of Alamut the climax of his narrative of the Mongol conquests. The historian wished to celebrate the great service his pagan patron had rendered to the Islamic world by destroying this "community of infidels." He could scarcely dwell on the depredations visited upon the rest of the Muslim world by the Mongols, and certainly not the destruction of the Sunni caliphate. He thus had to overstate the iniquities and the political significance of this minority group, emphasizing how the Saljuqs and others had failed to subdue them. He also had to exaggerate the extent of their defeat and stress their absolute and complete extermination. Anything less than a total annihilation would have been seen as failure on the part of his patron. As virtually all future Persian historians drew on Juwayni's testimony for their narratives of the Ismaili community, they accepted his conclusions.

Nevertheless, we know that after their initial subjugation in 654/1256, the Ismailis attempted several times to recapture the fortress of Alamut and were often successful. Within five years of the fall of Girdkuh, a son of the Imam Rukn al-Din Khwurshah had already managed to rally the Ismailis of the area and retake the fort. However, the blows they had sustained at the hands of the Mongols had seriously undermined their strength, and it was soon lost once again. The Mongols did not maintain a strong presence in the area though, and it is likely that the Ismailis resided there unmolested until Uljaytu Khan entered Gilan with his army in 706/1307. Once again, this attack was short lived. After the departure of these forces, Daylam and the surrounding areas likely reverted to their semi-independent status. Certainly, after the death of the last great Mongol Ilkhan, Abu Saʿid, in 735/1335, there was no strong central rule or government in the region. This gave the remaining Ismailis a respite from the ravages of the previous decades. At this time, the great mountainous districts between Persian Iraq and Gilan were controlled by independent governors. Contemporary accounts inform us that much of the region remained dedicated to Ismailism in this period. By 770/1369, the whole of Daylam seems once again to have come under the Ismaili rule of the Khushayji family, led by Kiya Sayf al-Din. However, he did not openly proclaim his identity until provoked by a Zaydi rival, ʿAli Kiya.

ʿAli Kiya extended his control over the region, ousting this Ismaili leader. Nevertheless, much of the population in Daylam, Rudbar, Padiz, Kushayjan, and Ashkawar remained Ismaili and was dedicated to an Imam by the name of Khudawand Muhammad. Khudawand Muhammad was intricately involved with the political struggles of the area and managed to reoccupy Alamut for a spell. At this time, the matter-of-fact communication of a certain Taj al-Din Amuli with Sultan Uways (r. 757–776/1356–1374) regarding the Ismailis of Alamut (*malāḥida-yi Alamūt*) demonstrates that the continued presence of the community in its ancestral center was well known, even at the court of Tabriz. That Alamut, or at least the region of Daylam, remained an important center of the Ismaili community in this period is testified to by Khurasani and South Asian sources. These make it clear that after Hulagu conquered the region, the Ismailis returned and religious dues continued to be delivered to the area. There is even testimony, albeit from sources whose history of transmission has yet to be fully studied, that the Imam Islamshah lived at the fort of Alamut itself.

Though the Ismailis continued to inhabit Alamut and the South Caspian for much of this period, their former political power had been shattered. Henceforth, at least politically, the Ismailis were of minor, regional significance. Soon enough, in 819/1416, they were subject to yet another massacre in which "the waters of the White River (*Safīdrūd*) turned red with the blood of those killed."[109] Among those executed were many Ismaili leaders, including some descendants of the Ismaili Imam Khudawand ʿAla' al-Din Muhammad. It must have been around this time, about one and a half centuries after Alamut first capitulated to the Mongols, that the Ismailis gave up all hopes of regaining the fortress as their center. While Ismaili activity continued in this region, the Imams appear to have already moved away to safer, more politically quiescent surroundings.

THREE

Veiling the Sun

The earth is never devoid of someone who stands as the proof of God, either manifest and well known or wary and hidden.

Imam ʿAli to Kumayl b. Ziyad
in *The Path of Eloquence*

In a passage of his book *Commencement of the Mission* (*Iftitāḥ al-daʿwa*), the tenth-century Ismaili jurist, al-Qadi al-Nuʿman, narrates the encounter between the preacher Abu ʿAbd Allah al-Shiʿi and the Kutama tribe of Berbers, who would prove critical in bringing the Ismaili Imam to power in North Africa. Meeting a group of Shiʿi Kutama pilgrims in Mecca in 280/893, Abu ʿAbd Allah persuaded them to join the Ismaili cause and accompanied their caravan to their native country. Reaching a locale called Ikjan in Kutama territory, he inquired about a place known as the Valley of the Pious (*fajj al-akhyār*). They were astonished by his knowledge of this name and told him that they were in that very region. When they asked how he knew about it, he replied, "By God, this place is named in your honor!" and quoted the following tradition of the Prophet Muhammad: "The Mahdi shall emigrate far from his home at a time full of trials and tribulations. The pious (*al-akhyār*) of that age shall support him, a people whose name is derived from *kitmān* (secrecy)." He continued, "You, Kutama, are those people. Because you come from this valley, it is called the Valley of the Pious."[1]

The maintenance of secrecy, *kitman*, was thus intimately associated with the virtue of piety. This should not surprise us, as taqiyya, the more common synonym for *kitman*, is derived from an Arabic root meaning godliness, devotion, and piety.

Taqiyya, precautionary dissimulation, has been a significant feature of Islam, and particularly of Shiʿi Islam, since its earliest days.[2] Muslims of virtually all persuasions acknowledge the legitimacy of its use in certain circumstances.[3] The Quran (3:28) advises that the company of believers should not be forsaken for that of doubters, unless this be as a precaution, out of fear.[4] Verse 16:106, which refers to the blamelessness of those who feign disbelief under compulsion, is explained by both Sunni and Shiʿi commentators as referring to the case of the companion ʿAmmar b. Yasir, who was compelled under torture to renounce his faith.[5]

Over the course of time, the majority Sunni Muslims, who had gained political supremacy, only rarely found it necessary to resort to precautionary dissimulation. The Sunni scholars who took recourse in taqiyya during the inquisition (*miḥna*) at the time of the caliph al-Maʾmun may be cited as an example, as they affirmed that the Quran was created, though they believed otherwise.[6] By contrast, the precarious existence of the minority Shiʿa forced them to develop taqiyya as an almost innate and instinctive method of self-preservation and protection.[7] The Shiʿa even have a specific legal term for regions in which taqiyya is obligatory, *dar al-taqiyya*, the realm of precautionary dissimulation.[8] For the Shiʿa, taqiyya has two aspects: hiding their association with the cause of the Imams when its open declaration would expose them to danger and, equally important, keeping the esoteric teachings of the Imams hidden from those who are unprepared to receive them.[9] The Shiʿi Imam Jaʿfar al-Sadiq is reputed to have said, "Our teaching is the truth, the truth of the truth; it is the exoteric and the esoteric, and the esoteric of the esoteric; it is the secret and the secret of a secret, a protected secret, hidden by a secret."[10]

For the Ismaili Shiʿa, a minority within a minority, whose creed emphasized the paramount importance of the *batin*, or esoteric dimension of the revelation, this need was even more pronounced.[11] The destruction of Alamut ushered in a period in which, more than ever, taqiyya was required for survival. The hazards constantly facing the stateless community in the aftermath of the Mongol invasions forced it to make taqiyya not just an expedient to be used on occasion, but a way of life. While this held the advantage of deflecting unwanted attention, it also harbored its own risks. Dissimulation through generations was liable to obscure the identity of sections of the community, which would gradually forget their ancestral heritage. Over time, these segments would drift, eventually adopting the identity that had once been nothing more than a cover. Nevertheless, there was probably little choice in the matter. In the wake of the wholesale slaughter perpetuated by the Mongols, it was not possible to betray an Ismaili identity to the outside world. Where taqiyya failed, the community attracted unwanted attention and was attacked. It is thus ironic that in many of the regions in which we know of Ismaili political activity from outside sources, it is because the existence and identity of the community had been detected and it was thus crushed. Hence, in these areas, the Ismailis were eradicated, while those in areas that attracted scant attention managed to survive until present times. Ismaili tradition maintains that the son of the Imam Rukn al-Din Khwurshah, Shams al-Din Muhammad, was smuggled away to safety. This chapter is about the life of the Imam Shams al-Din and that of one of his disciples, the poet Nizari Quhistani, whose life and writings shed light on the practice of taqiyya.

IMAMATE OF SHAMS AL-DIN MUHAMMAD

The sons (or son, if they are the same individual) of Rukn al-Din Khwurshah who find a place in the Persian histories, Tarkiya and Abu Dawlat, were alluded to in chapter 2. The son who succeeded him, however, was known as Muhammad and had the title of Shams al-Din, the Sun of the Faith.[12] Without any further information, it is not possible to ascertain whether he can be identified as Tarkiya or Abu Dawlat, or was yet another individual. A very late source, the *Muhammadan Chronicles* (*Āthār-i Muḥammadī*), completed in the city of Mahallat in 1310/1893 by a certain Muhammad Taqi b. ʿAli Rida b. Zayn al-ʿAbidin, contains some interesting information about Shams al-Din Muhammad. The family of this author, whom Wladimir Ivanow opined was not an Ismaili,[13] had been in the service of the Ismaili Imams for many generations. In his account, he mentions a small booklet (*kitābcha*) to which he had once had access, passed from hand to hand by the successors of the Imam Rukn al-Din, which contained autobiographical information in the handwriting of Shams al-Din Muhammad himself, as well as in the hand of the following Imams. According to this source, Shams al-Din Muhammad had been sent away to Tabriz, accompanied by his paternal uncle Shahanshah.[14] The *Muhammadan Chronicles* tells us that the Imam maintained complete anonymity, living unassumingly in this city as an embroiderer, whence his epithet *zarduz*. The booklet on which this information appears to have been based, if it was authentic, would have been of tremendous value. It was, unfortunately, destroyed when the Ismailis and their Imam, Aga Hasan Alishah (Aga Khan I) were attacked and their possessions plundered by Baluchi tribesmen in Jerrukh on March 23, 1843.[15] Writing in about 1015/1606, Muhammad Qasim "Firishta," the well-known historian of South India who was apparently in contact with descendants of the Imam Shams al-Din Muhammad, affirmed that the son of Rukn al-Din Khwurshah was known as Muhammad Zarduz, with the title of Shams al-Din.[16]

Fortunately, contemporary evidence also specifies the main center of activity of the Imam Shams al-Din Muhammad as Azerbaijan, likely in Tabriz or its vicinity. It was in Tabriz that the Ismaili poet Nizari Quhistani evidently met him when he journeyed there in 678–679/1280–1281, recording the encounter in his versified *Travelogue* (*Safarnāma*). This locale is also alluded to in his poetic *Omnibus* (*Dīwān*).[17] Two treatises, the anonymous *Epistle of the Right Path* (*Risāla-yi Ṣirāṭ al-Mustaqīm*)[18] and a later interpolation in the Arabic ode, *The Healing* (*al-Shāfiyya*), which mentions that the Imam Shams al-Din Muhammad was living in the town of Qusur, in the vicinity of Tabriz, lend support to this testimony.[19]

The Suns of Tabriz

The residence of Shams al-Din Muhammad in Tabriz seems to have caused a number of authors to conflate the biography of the Ismaili Imam with that of his near contemporary and townsman Shams-i Tabrizi, the spiritual preceptor of the famous Muslim mystic, Jalal al-Din Rumi, who shared the Imam's name. The confusion is first apparent in the *Memorial of Poets* (*Tadhkirat al-shuʿarāʾ*) of Dawlatshah, completed in 892/1487.[20] This was later taken up by prominent figures such as Nur Allah Shushtari (d. 1019/1610), who also makes Shams-i Tabrizi, Rumi's preceptor, a descendant of the Ismaili Imams.[21] Early orientalist scholarship adopted this view. The venerable E. G. Brown, for example, considered Shams-i Tabrizi to have been a descendant of the Ismaili Imam Jalal al-Din Muhammad.[22] The problem is further compounded by the additional identification of the Ismaili luminary (*pīr*) of South Asia, Shams al-Din, with Rumi's Shams.[23]

With regard to the former identification, the first evidence of an Ismaili source combining the two personalities (though, even here, not explicitly) is in Khayrkhwah's *Epistle* (*Risāla*), written in about 960/1553, in which he makes "Muhaqqiq-i Rumi" the Imam's hujjat, a dignitary in the Ismaili hierarchy.[24] The verses he quotes in this connection, written under the pen name "Shams-i Tabrizi," are indeed from a popular poem found in Jalal al-Din Rumi's currently accepted oeuvre.[25] The *Epistle of the Right Path*, which is likely even earlier, similarly preserves a poetic quotation from "Pir-i Rumi," but the particular verse is not found in Jalal al-Din Rumi's known works.[26] The *Epistle* suggests that this Pir-i Rumi was the Imam's hujjat. A more explicit identification of the Imam Shams al-Din Muhammad and Rumi's Shams occurs in Fidaʾi Khurasani's (d. 1342/1923) *Guidance for the Seeking Believers* (*Hidāyat al-Muʾminīn al-Ṭālibīn*).[27] Other Ismaili sources, however, vigorously deny the association. Pir Shihab al-Din Shah (d. 1302/1884),[28] for example, writes:

> O Partisans of Truth! Know that, as I have mentioned, after the death of Rukn al-Din Khwurshah, our ancestor Shams al-Din Muhammad arrived and stayed in Tabriz. In order that information about his situation not reach the enemies, he went to the shop of an embroiderer and occupied himself in that craft. Because of the extreme handsomeness, beauty and

> excellence of his face, which was like the sun, it was not long before he came to be known as Shams-i Tabriz, the Sun of Tabriz. But it should not be imagined that Shams-i Tabrizi, whose disciple was the Mullah of Rum, was the same person. Rather, that (particular) Shams-i Tabrizi was originally from Tabriz. They used to call him Shams-i Tabrizi (Shams, the Tabrizite) in the same manner in which it may be said, Sulayman-i Badakhshani (Sulayman, the Badakhshanite) or Ismaʿil-i Hunakiri (Ismaʿil, the Hunakirite).[29]

That the two figures could not have been the same is suggested by the fact that Aflaki's *Eulogies of the Gnostics* (*Manāqib al-ʿārifīn*) gives the name of Shams-i Tabrizi's father as ʿAli, and that of his paternal grandfather as Malikdad.[30] Unfortunately, Aflaki's reliability has often been called into question.[31] Rumi's own son, Sultan Walad, who, unlike Aflaki, had actually met Shams, was himself unsure of the saint's origins or lineage.[32] Likely drawing on Shams's own *Conversations* (*Maqālāt*), Aflaki dates the saint's arrival in Konya to Saturday morning, the twenty-sixth of the month of Jumada II, 642/November 29, 1244,[33] when the Imam Rukn al-Din Khwurshah would have been about fifteen years old,[34] scarcely old enough to have a son traipsing off to Turkey.[35] In his *Conversations*, most of which appear to date from his sojourn in Konya, Shams already speaks of himself as an old man, which accords well with the tradition of the Mevlevi dervishes that he was over sixty when he arrived in that city.[36] This casts further doubt on the possibility of the two figures being the same. Of course, while this would seem to preclude the possibility of Shams the mystic being the same as Shams the Imam, it still leaves the question of his descent from the Imams of Alamut open, not to mention his identification with the Ismaili pir of Multan, whose ancient shrine in that city is still frequented by Muslims of all persuasions as the burial place of Rumi's preceptor.[37] Both of these questions, however interesting they may be, are beyond the scope of this book.

What is noteworthy is that Dawlatshah, among other biographical writers,[38] has applied the epithet of the Ismaili Imam, *zarduz*, "the embroiderer," to Rumi's mentor. The *Conversations of Shams-i Tabrizi* (*Maqālāt-i Shams-i Tabrīzī*), a record of the "table talk" of Rumi's preceptor, do not mention this as his occupation. Hence, elements of the Imam's biography must somehow have become known to the biographers of Rumi's preceptor, who then incorporated these into their memoirs, but the exact mode of this transfer remains unknown. Scattered throughout the Persianate Islamic world, there is also poetry of a remarkably Shiʿi tenor containing the pen name Shams-i Tabriz. Scholars have generally dismissed these as incorrect attributions. Gabrielle van den Berg, for example, in her study of minstrel poetry from the Pamir mountains, notes that Shams-i Tabriz is first and foremost among the poets whose *ghazals* are sung in this heavily Ismaili populated region. She assumes this to be the pen name of Jalal al-Din Rumi but is mystified by the fact that while the *ghazal*-singers' renditions of Hafiz and Hilali, for example, can be found in the edited *Omnibuses* of their poetry, the overwhelming majority of those attributed to Shams cannot be found in Rumi's traditionally accepted oeuvre.[39] The prevalence of these poems in other regions as well is remarkable. The Ahl-i Haqq of Kurdistan, for example, join the Badakhshanis in singing the highly popular verses of "Shams-i Tabriz":[40]

تا صورت پیوند جهان بود علی بود   تا نقش زمین بود زمان بود علی بود

ʿAli has existed since the dawn of the world's creation
ʿAli has existed since the appearance of time and terre

Likewise, the Ismailis of Afghanistan are joined by the Sindhi Sufis in singing another well-known composition attributed to Shams, made even more popular by the lively rendition of Pakistan's favorite female *qawwali* singer, ʿAbida Parwin:[41]

ساقی با وفا منم دم همه دم علی علی

A faithful cupbearer am I, with every breath I cry ʿAli! ʿAli!

In considering the Ismaili minstrel tradition of Badakhshan, van den Berg laments, "In case of poems by Shams-i Tabrezi the search for printed versions of sung texts was unsuccessful, since the text of the majority of the poems attributed to Shams-i Tabrezi cannot be found in the current editions of the diwan.... These poems are either unknown or considered apocryphal."[42] Despite the fact that approximately 94 percent of the poems attributed to Shams-i Tabriz by the Ismailis of Badakhshan were not available to van den Berg in the well-known printed editions of Rumi's *Omnibus* (*Dīwān*),[43] these versions have indeed been published. The first poem cited above, for example, is quoted from page 220 of one such edition in the *Rose Garden of Shams* (*Gulzār-i Shams*) by Mulukshah, a descendant of the Ismaili Pir Shams.[44] It is also recorded in the *Assemblies of the Faithful* (*Majālis al-Muʾminīn*) by the prominent Twelver Shiʿi jurist, Nur Allah Shushtari.[45] It would be interesting to examine the question of whether these writings, popular in South and Central Asia as well as in Iran and Kurdistan, do indeed belong to Shams-i Tabriz—not Shams the preceptor of Rumi, but Shams the Imam of the Ismailis, or perhaps to the Ismaili sage (*pīr*) of the same name, whose writing in a Shiʿi voice would not be at all surprising.[46]

The Travels of Shams

Further light may be shed on the life of this Imam by a nineteenth-century manuscript, formerly in the possession of the Ismaili Society Bombay, which is now to be found at the Institute of Ismaili Studies, London. The document, number 814 in the collection, is incorrectly labeled as containing only two works, *Forty Worlds* (*Chihil Dunya*) and *Epistle on Horizons and Souls* (*Risāla dar Āfāq wa-Anfus*), hence it seems to have escaped the notice of scholars that, among other works, it contains a section, perhaps apocryphal, that purports to contain the words of an Ismaili Imam. While the name of the Imam is not mentioned, there are certain elements in the passage that suggest an association with the Imam Shams al-Din Muhammad. The short address is translated here in full:

> May it not remain hidden from all the servants that as Mawlana ʿAli and Mawlana Husayn (on whose mentions be peace) have said, "We will have to pass through Jabalistan (i.e., Gilan) and Daylam, which will be the final Karbala. The palace of Caesar and the fortress of Alamut [will be reduced to such straits] that were they given to even a poor old woman, she would not accept them."[47] All of this came to pass and was seen by the people of the world. Aught of what I said was belied. Now I have left the land of Iran for Turan and traveled through its cities to see them. I passed through Samarqand, Bukhara, Cathay, Scythia, Balkh, China and the land beyond China (*Chīn wa-Māchīn*), Tibet and Kashmir. I also passed through the land of the Franks. In short, I actually beheld the world from one end to the other. I clearly manifested myself in the cities of Uch and Multan and fulfilled the promise that I had made to the loving devotees. [After experiencing] the kindness of the loving devotees and friends of Hindustan, I returned to Iran. In all these lands through which I traveled, in every place I practiced taqiyya for *taqiyya is my religion and the religion of my ancestors*.[48] That is to say, "dissimulation is my religion and the religion of my ancestors." In every place we portrayed ourselves in a manner and form that we deemed prudent for the task of the people. However, my disciples know best what is prudent for our (own) task! If someone knows better the task and what is advisable, let him come forward. Nobody in the world can claim this. If someone doubts this it is because of depravity and the whisperings of the devil. May God keep all the servants in his protection![49]

The reasons that the words appear to be connected with the Imam Shams al-Din Muhammad are several. The citing of a prediction auguring the destruction of

Alamut and comparing it to the devastation that occurred when the Imam al-Husayn and his companions were massacred at Karbala suggest that the Mongol triumph was still fresh in mind. This is also implied by the mention of the fall of Caesar's castle, which may be an allusion to the ʿAbbasid caliphate in Baghdad, viewed as a dynasty of worldly rulers.[50] References to the extensive travels of the Imam Shams al-Din Muhammad are strongly supported by Nizari tradition as recorded in both Shihab al-Din Shah's *Book of Supreme Admonitions* (*Kitāb-i Khiṭābāt-i ʿĀliya*) and Fida'i's *Guidance for the Seeking Believers* (*Hidāyat al-Muʾminīn al-Ṭālibīn*).[51] The latter work, for example, speaks of the Imam's itinerary as follows: he departed Tabriz for Gilan, remaining there for a spell. He then went to Kashan and Waramin, where he tarried for a bit before heading for Qazwin, and then to Damghan and Rudbar, where he received the religious dues of his followers. After this he traveled to Khurasan, including Herat. From Herat he went to Bukhara and then back to Herat and the surrounding regions, including Kabul and Badakhshan, until he arrived in Punjab, including the city of Multan, and parts of Sindh. He then went back to Multan where he took up residence before finally returning to Tabriz. From Tabriz he went to Daylam and thence to the Maghrib, Egypt, Syria, and Anatolia, spending some time there before coming back to Tabriz. He then returned to Multan in the Punjab where he lived out the rest of his days.[52] This source is, of course, very late, but it does indicate the existence of a tradition affirming the wide travels of Shams al-Din Muhammad. Interestingly, a number of Ginans also speak of the journeys of Shams (presumed to be the pir, but perhaps in the light of this evidence, a reference to the Imam) through twenty-four countries.[53] Aflaki, possibly transposing an account of the Ismaili Imam into his biography of Rumi's Shams, mentions that because of his extensive travels, Shams was known as "the flier" (*parinda*) while in Tabriz.[54] Such an attribute would certainly have been befitting of the Imam, if indeed it refers to him rather than to the other Shams.

Especially remarkable in the Persian source quoted above is the Imam's reference to his voyage to Uch and Multan in India in fulfillment of a promise made to his devotees in that land. This allusion finds striking corroboration in the Ginans attributed to Pir Shams (fl. ca. 13th–14th c.), the Ismaili savant who spent time in these areas and whose ancient mausoleum in Multan remains a major center of Muslim pilgrimage. Compositions ascribed to him record not only the making of such a promise, but also its fulfillment.

In one Ginan, whose striking Siraiki features have piqued the interest of local literary historians in Pakistan,[55] the Imam's imminent arrival in Multan is forecast:

> O fortunate one! Traveling from way-station to way-station
> the Imam will cross Sindh, arriving in Multan.
> O fortunate one! Through the four corners and four crossroads
> [he will arrive] at the main square of Multan[56]

Another composition records the Imam's establishment in the city:

> The Imam was born in the land of Daylam and
> took up residence in Multan[57]

However, most impressive are those verses in which a promise of arrival is explicitly mentioned, such as in the following:

> Rouse yourselves in the Imam's service, for he
> has arrived in fulfillment of his promise[58]

Of course, these verses are more suggestive than conclusive. None of them specifically mentions that it was the Imam Shams al-Din Muhammad who arrived in India. However, given the period sometimes attributed to Pir Shams, this is a possibility.[59] The fact that Shams al-Din Muhammad's son, Mu'minshah, was married to a woman named Dawlat Sati (see below), a very Indian-sounding name, further suggests the possibility of his having spent time in the Punjab.[60] Indeed, if these verses are truly references to a promise of coming to India that was fulfilled by the Imam Shams al-Din Muhammad, they are remarkable for their consonance with the statements in the Persian manuscript.

Wary and Hidden

The Imam's declaration, "In all these lands through which I traveled, in every place I practiced taqiyya for *taqiyya is my religion and the religion of my ancestors*," is revealing and resonates deeply with the Imam ʿAli's statement to his disciple Kumayl, "The earth is never devoid of someone who stands as the proof of God, either manifest and well known or wary and hidden."[61] In the dangerous times in which this Imam and his immediate successors lived, it has often been assumed that they concealed their identities. The document quoted above, whether it is a reflection of the actual words of the Imam or of later community sentiment, is the earliest witness to come to light from an Ismaili source that authenticates this obvious hypothesis. Clearly, one of the reasons that we know so little of the Imams of this period is precisely because they didn't want their existence to be commonly known. Attracting unwanted attention in such a hostile environment would have been exceedingly dangerous, even fatal, and success in concealing the identity of the Imams contributed to the survival of the lineage. Faithful members of the community in areas in which the threat was most acutely felt would have been loath to reveal the names and whereabouts of their Imams, or indeed their own identity. This is confirmed in the geographical part of Mustawfi's *The Hearts' Bliss*

(*Nuzhat al-Qulūb*), in which he writes with regard to the city of Taliqan, to the east of Qazwin, that the citizens "declare themselves to be Sunnis in religion, but have leanings towards the Ismaili doctrines."[62] As noted in chapter 2, Hulagu's great-grandson, Ghazan Khan, also referred to the continued presence of Ismaʿilis in his time and their practice of concealing their beliefs.[63]

The aforementioned *Epistle of the Right Path* (*Risāla-yi Ṣirāṭ al-Mustaqīm*) sheds light on this fact and its circumstances. Speaking of the Imams after Hasan ʿala dhikrihi al-salam (d. 561/1166), the anonymous author writes:

> Since then, the Imams have been in concealment (*satr*) until our day. However, this concealment is for the exotericists (*ahl-i ẓāhir*), not for the esotericists (*ahl-i bāṭin*, i.e. the Ismailis). Even when there is concealment for the esotericists, it is not for all of them, for it is stated that the epiphany of the Universal Intellect (*ʿaql-i kull*), who is the proof (*ḥujjat*) of the Imam, always has access to the Imam of the Age and Time in the world of the esoteric.
>
> *There is a path from the heart of the hujjat to the Imam*
> *He is aware by the divine support* (taʾyīd) *of his heart . . .*
>
> Because of this, the noble hujjat is the lord of divine support (*taʾyīd*). However, it is possible for there to be concealment for the other ranks of the faith (*ḥudūd-i dīn*) because of the disobedience of the servants, as it happened during the time of Mawlana Shams al-Din Muhammad Tabrizi.[64]

It should be noted that in Alamut times, the concept of *satr*, concealment of the Imam, had an additional dimension. It was not necessarily a time when the Imams were hidden from view. They could be fully apparent to people, as were the Imams who ruled Alamut after Hasan. However, it was particularly characterized by the Imam's command to observe precautionary dissimulation, or taqiyya.[65] Nasir al-Din Tusi comments that the period during which he wrote *The Paradise of Submission* (*Rawḍa-yi Taslīm*) was one of *satr*, "The time during which these deliberations (*tasawwurat*) are being recorded is an epoch of concealment (*satr*) and prudence (*taqiyya*), and it is his eminence [i.e., the Imam]—exalted be his power—who ordains *taqiyya*."[66] The word *satr* mentioned above may also be understood in this sense.

The author of the *Epistle* informs us that in times of concealment, the Imam is accessible only to members of his community, not to outsiders. Apparently, in periods of extreme danger, only those who were enrolled in the highest levels of the daʿwa, such as the hujjats, were in direct contact with the Imam. They would convey his guidance to the believers. This, the author informs us, is what happened at the time of the Imam Shams al-Din Muhammad.

A hitherto unpublished text encountered in several Ismaili manuscripts records *Pearl Scattering Words* (*Alfāẓ-i Guharbār*) of an Ismaili Imam, Khudawand Muhammad, who is identified specifically in some manuscripts as Shams al-Din Muhammad b. Rukn al-Din Khwurshah.[67] The document warns the believers to beware the ephemeral nature of the physical world and exhorts them to take up the spiritual life, certainly poignant guidance in the wake of the general massacre of the Ismailis by the Mongol hordes. But what concerns us here is that in the message, the Imam addresses himself to the faithful scattered throughout "Khurasan, Hindustan, Badakhshan, Turkistan, Daylam, Quhistan, Rudbar, Azerbaijan, Qaznin (sic),[68] Qaniyat (sic) and so on, and the inhabitants of the land of Syria, Zanzibar, Qasran, the people of Egypt, Ashkawar, Punjab and elsewhere."[69]

This remarkable dissemination of the Ismailis in about the thirteenth century, notably in areas where even the long arm of the invading Mongols could not reach, assured the continued survival of the community, albeit largely under the cloak of taqiyya. If the earlier quoted passage is indeed to be attributed to the Imam Shams al-Din Muhammad, it seems highly likely that he was traveling throughout the regions in which his followers lived in order to reinforce their allegiance in the aftermath of the Mongol invasion and the evaporation of Ismaili political power. In his *Book of Supreme Admonitions*, Pir Shihab al-Din Shah poignantly points out that at this time, many of the Persian Ismailis abandoned their faith for fear of their lives.[70] Certainly, trying to reconnect with these scattered communities would have been a high priority for the Ismaili leadership.

The Setting Sun

In his well-known historical and biographical compendium written in the sixteenth century, Fasih-i Khwafi mentions the grave in Khuy of Shams al-Din al-Tabrizi, who died in 672/1273.[71] While he presumes this Shams to have been Rumi's teacher,[72] Franklin Lewis, one of Rumi's foremost biographers, considers the date provided to be "surely wrong."[73] Could this, then, possibly be the burial place of the Ismaili Imam? An eighteenth-century family tree (*shajaro*), later published by Suleman Gulamhushen Haji of Karachi, states that this Imam passed away in Azerbaijan.[74] About seven years after this date, the Ismaili poet Nizari Quhistani was to pass through Khuy, near Tabriz, a city in which there had been an Ismaili population,[75] in the retinue of Shams al-Din Juwayni, the Ilkhanid vizier and brother of ʿAta-Malik Juwayni.[76] However, he provides us with no indication that he had a specific motive in visiting the place. Muhammad ʿAli Muwahhid, the editor of the *Conversations* (*Maqālāt*) of Shams-i Tabrizi[77] and biographer of this personality, points out that at least since the turn of the fifteenth century there has been a grave with a minaret outside of Khuy known as the minaret of Shams-i Tabriz.[78] In his *History of Khuy* (*Ta'rīkh-i Khūy*), Amin-Riyahi recalls the sojourn of the Ottoman Sultan and grand vizier in that city in 1535, when they visited the tomb.[79] It would be possible to imagine that the sultan and his vizier inadvertently payed their respects to an Ismaili Imam rather than to the teacher of Rumi. However, the death date proposed by Fasih-i Khwafi for the figure buried there seems far too early to be that of the Imam Shams al-Din Muhammad. If it is assumed that Rukn al-Din Khwurshah's (b. 627/1230) successor was born when the Imam was aged a youthful twenty years, Shams al-Din Muhammad would have been a mere twenty-five years old in 672/1273.[80] The question therefore remains open.

Wilferd Madelung, Farhad Daftary, and others accept a date of 710/1310 for the death of Shams al-Din Muhammad, which is chronologically more acceptable.[81] However, the ultimate source of this date was apparently unknown to them, as only very late secondary materials have been cited as references for the assertion.[82] Daftary's immediate source seems to have been ʿArif Tamir's Arabic work *Imamate in Islam* (*al-Imāma fī al-Islām*).[83] Tamir, in turn, likely obtained his information from the Urdu translation of Alimamed Janmamed Chunara's well-known Gujarati history of the Ismaili Imams, *Manifest Light* (*Nūram Mobīn*).[84] The first appearance of these dates in modern times, though, was in the published version of a Ginan entitled *The Offspring of the Tales of Truth* (*Satveṇī nī Vel*), attributed to an Ismaili savant by the name of Nur Muhammadshah (d. 940/1534), which appeared in 1962 of the Samvat era, i.e., 1905.[85] While Ivanow was aware of the source of this date and mentioned it in one of his articles,[86] it seems he was not cognizant of the fact that the date is a later addition to the composition.

The Offspring of the Tales of Truth is, in part, a versified history of the Ismaili Imams. The late manuscript version that has come down to us is clearly a composite work, with many interpolations.[87] While internal evidence suggests that the core of the composition probably does date back to the time of Nur Muhammadshah,[88] it is obvious that later scribes have incorporated into it writings of their own. For example, the narrative about the Imams of Alamut occurs in cantos 71–78, but another version of the narrative, with different dates, is given in cantos 95–101. The twentieth-century editor(s) of the text were clearly aware of these interpolations. The published version therefore eliminates large portions of the original and recomposes sections to maintain a continuous narrative. Most significantly, the dates of the Imams are not the same as those found in the original manuscripts. Even the original dates were chronologically of highly questionable value. In canto 94 of the revised publication, the date given for the accession of the Imam Qasimshah is 1366 of the Vikrama Samvat calendar, which works out to 1310 CE, the date popularly adopted by modern-day historians.[89]

The question arises of how this and other dates in the published version of *The Offspring of the Tales of Truth* were determined. Writing in the same year as the appearance of this publication, the learned Ismaili, Jafarbhai Rematula (d. 1912), a British-educated barrister-at-law, made no mention of the dates of the Imams who were the immediate successors of Rukn al-Din Khwurshah in his *History of the Khojas* (*Khojā Kom no Itihās*).[90] These dates were therefore not common knowledge in the community. It is possible that they were provided by an Ismaili named Hasham Bogha (d. 1912) who, because of his teaching activities, was known as "Master."[91] Familiar with Arabic, Persian, Sindhi, and English in addition to his native Gujarati, he was a prolific author. One of his first publications was *Ismaili Mirror* (*Isamāilī Darpaṇ*), which appeared in 1323/1906, a year after the publication of the aforementioned Ginan. He informs us that "we have copied the . . . blessed names of the Ismaili Imams from the book of worship of the Ismaili faith (*isamāīlī dharma nī bandagī nī kitāb*),"[92] i.e., presumably from the daily prayer manual known as *duʿa*, which contained such a list. In the register itself, then, there was nothing particularly original. However, Hasham Bogha also provided the dates of the imamate of these Imams, which corresponded closely to those published a year earlier in *The Offspring of the Tales of Truth*. He explains that he had taken "these dates from the Christian and *hijra* calendars from a number of documents (*sanad*) found in the books of Ismaili religious literature (*isamāīlī dharmashāstra nī kitābo*), the writings of English historians, a number of manuscripts and several reliable materials."[93] He also attached the following caveat to his work:

> Nevertheless, if any of our gentle readers may possess a more authoritative date, and if such learned readers should kindly assist us by bringing it to our attention, and if that date is supported by greater authority than those provided by the documents in our possession, we will know that in the second edition of this book, or in our future publications on the subject of Ismailism, we must incorporate the correction.[94]

Either Hasham Bogha had taken his dates from the Ginan that had just been published or, more likely, had himself been involved in the earlier publication and had furnished materials for the recomposed portions. He was closely associated with the publisher, Mukhi Lalajibhai Devaraj (d. 1930), with whom he had established a school in Mumbai in 1901.[95] Some Ismaili authors, writing soon after Hasham Bogha, occasionally proposed different dates.[96] Others, including the prominent non-Ismaili polemicist, Edalji Dhanji Kaba, adopted the information provided in the newly published materials.[97] Chunara, too, accepted these dates, found in both the published version of the Ginan and the books of his predecessors, incorporating them into his own popular work, *Manifest Light* (*Nūram Mobīn*), which was widely quoted (often without acknowledgment) by later historians. Henceforth, scholars writing in European languages, who had very little knowledge of these sources in Khojki and Gujarati, and usually accessed these dates through later Ismaili writings in Arabic, presumed them to be those "traditionally" accepted by the community. This they were not. Unfortunately, we do not know exactly which documents and manuscripts Hasham Bogha had in his possession and are therefore dependent upon his findings without knowledge of their ultimate source.

NIZARI QUHISTANI (D. 720/1320)

Illumination of the Moon

During times of *satr* when the Imam was concealed, Ismaili tradition maintained that he continued to be accessible through the hierarchy of the daʿwa, particularly through its highest ranking official, the Imam's supreme hujjat. The *Paradise of Submission* explains the role of this hujjat as follows:

> His supreme hujjat is the manifestation of the First Intellect, that is to say, the visibility and power of the illumination of the First Intellect is made manifest through him. His position has been likened to that of the Moon. For just as the body of the Moon is in itself dark but illuminated by the Sun, taking the Sun's place in its absence (*khalīfat-i ū bāshad*), and lighting up the Earth in proportion to the amount of light that it has been capable of obtaining from the Sun, so the soul of the supreme hujjat, which by itself knows nothing and is nothing, is illumined by the effulgent radiation of the divine assistance (*ta'yīd*) from the Imam. In the absence of the Imam, he acts as his vicegerent. By virtue of his capacity to receive the grace of the lights of knowledge (*fayḍ-i anwār-i ʿilm*) and according to the measure of his aptitude, he enlightens people about the Imam, showing the way to him—may salutations ensue upon mention of him.[98]

There is a very revealing passage in one of the poems of the contemporary Ismaili literary figure Nizari Quhistani that further substantiates the statements regarding the situation of the hujjat in the time of the Imam Shams al-Din Muhammad, as expressed in the *Epistle of the Right Path*. Every couplet of the poem ends with the phrase "I found" (*yāftam*):

Salvation is in the Imam of the Time
But before that, in the command of his Regent faith itself I found!

I forsook all save *descendants, one after the other*[99]
When the permanent (*mustaqarr*) imamate in the essence of
The Man (*insān*) I found!

I know none save the living, eternal, exemplary Imam
In whose command the sanctuary of both worlds I found!

Turn your back on the wasteland of times astray
For the way to ʿAli's gate by the light of Salman I found![100]

In Ismaili thought, Salman al-Farisi is often considered the archetypal gate (*bāb*) and supreme hujjat.[101] A fifteenth-century Ismaili author of Badakhshan, writing on this topic, quotes the Prophet's declaration, "Indeed, paradise longs more for Salman than Salman for paradise!"[102] Nizari's allusion to the fact that his contact with ʿAli was through Salman is therefore significant. In the tenth missive of the *Epistle of the Right Path*, it is explained that the highest ranks of the daʿwa, i.e., the hujjat and the bab (called the supreme hujjat in the passage above), who are the epiphanies of the Universal Soul and Universal Intellect respectively, must always be in contact with the Imam. Speaking of the periods of concealment, the anonymous author asserts, "Mawlana ʿAli must have a slave like Salman, as has been mentioned in the Blessed Epistles (*fuṣūl-i mubārak*). Thus, it is never possible for there to be a (period of) concealment such that nobody has access to him, may he be exalted and hallowed."[103]

Nizari's allusion to Salman must therefore be understood in this manner. Clearly, the Imam Shams al-Din Muhammad communicated with the community only through this dignitary, who acted as a veil who would conceal his whereabouts, a moon who would reflect the light of the sun. It further demonstrates that even Nizari, whom some have considered to have been a dignitary in the daʿwa, did not always have direct access to the Imam. It was the Imam's hujjat with whom he dealt and through whom he must have eventually met the Imam during his journey to Azerbaijan. Nizari's reference to the *mustaqarr* or "permanent" imamate is also significant in relation to the period of concealment (*satr*). This concept will be discussed in the next chapter.

A Poet of His Time

The poet's testimony in this regard, as well as with regard to all matters concerning the period immediately following Alamut's initial capitulation to the Mongols, is valuable, as he is the only major Persian Ismaili author of the Imam

Shams al-Din Muhammad's time whose works have been preserved. Within twenty years of the poet's death, the fact that he hailed from Birjand bestowed on that provincial town a claim to fame.[104] In his *Literary History of Persia*, the redoubtable orientalist, Edward G. Browne, displays palpable excitement at chancing upon a rare manuscript of some of Nizari's poetry that had been acquired by the British Museum. An Indian copyist by the name of Mawlawi Isma'il 'Ali transcribed the volume for him in the autumn of 1913. Browne writes:

> This transcript I desired because of the strong probability that Nizari belonged to the sect of the Ismailis, Malahida, or Assassins, and I hoped that his poems might afford proof of this fact, and perhaps reveal a genius comparable to that of the one great Ismaili poet hitherto known, Nasir-i Khusraw."[105]

Indeed, it was Nizari's poetic virtuosity that secured his place in Persian history. Writing in 1002/1594, the prominent biographer Amin Ahmad Razi commented that Nizari's adherence to Ismailism was inconsequential to his place in history. He was, after all, one of the best exemplars of Persian verse.[106]

Born nine years before the fall of Alamut and a young adult when Girdkuh finally capitulated, he would have been painfully aware of the trauma his people, as well as all people engulfed by the Mongol calamity, had suffered. His poetry testifies to the hardship and penury endured by residents of his province and chastises the landlords for hoarding food while others hungered:

> When will the price of wheat be equal again to that of clay and soap, so that the tears of grief can be removed from the purchase of a wheat-bag? My heart is wounded at the thought of no bread, at that wheat which leaves me destitute. . . . In such times when wheat is hoarded in storage, (I say) that they are oppressors. The problem is that without gold, gems and silver, they will not sell wheat to the poor. Even if wheat were to rain from the clouds they would not allow a single seed to go to the needy. . . . Even if Nizari were on his deathbed a hundred times, those who are to blame would not offer him any wheat.[107]

During this period, Quhistan was generally held to be a dependency, or part, of its northern neighbor, Khurasan, though it was still governed by independent rulers.[108] As one of the most important centers of Ismaili population, the community was particularly hard hit by Mongol policies in the area. As Lewisohn notes, "The naked horror and utter terror of the Mongol conquests brought with them genocide and a scorched earth policy."[109] This destruction devastated the capacity for agricultural production in the area, hence Nizari's plaint. Despite being born into a family of landed aristocracy, the poet had fallen on hard times.[110] We can presume the same or worse for other Ismailis in the area who, along with their compatriots, inherited the ruined fields and farms. Hamd Allah Mustawfi, as an Ilkhanid financial officer, was well placed to judge the economic carnage inflicted on Iran by the invasions. Noting the plunge of revenues in the country (and here he excludes Khurasan, which had been hit even harder), he writes:

> The state of fertility of the land (in past times) may be compared with its ruin (in the present day) as a result of the irruption of the Mongols and the general massacre of the people that took place in their days. Further, there can be no doubt that even if for a thousand years to come no evil befalls the country, yet it will be impossible to repair the damage completely, and to bring the land back to its former state. Least of all can this be in our times, by reason of the numerous unhappy events that so constantly befall. Thus the following couplet has become the continual utterance of the people:
>
> *Every day that passes makes cares of yesterday appear light:*
> *Each new year that comes makes the losses of last year seem trivial*[111]

Nizari's talents, however, helped him to brave the tumultuous times. After completing his early education in Birjand and Qa'in, he became versed in Arabic and Persian literature, along with philosophy. He would serve at the Herat court of the founder of the Kart dynasty, Malik Shams al-Din Muhammad (d. 684/1285), and later at that of his heirs.[112] Shams al-Din Kart had interacted with the Ismailis on occasion and was probably ill-disposed toward them. He had been Hulagu Khan's envoy to Nasir al-Din, the last Ismaili chief of Quhistan. Then residing at the fortress of Sartakht, this elderly Ismaili leader was persuaded by Shams al-Din Kart's overtures to present himself before Hulagu, though he refused to bring down the garrison, stating that it would obey the Imam alone.[113]

At about this time, in 649/1251, Shams al-Din Kart was confirmed by the Great Khan Mongke as the governor of Herat, Balkh, and the territory between those two provinces and the Indian frontier. Sayf b. Muhammad, a local historian, records that he had ordered an Afghan chief by the name of Malik Taj al-Din to be imprisoned. However, in the year 659/1262, one of Shams al-Din's intimates, whom he considered fondly as his own brother, paid one thousand dinars to have Taj al-Din released from his prison in Tiginabad. The historian tells us that this intimate was an Ismaili by the name of ʿAla' al-Din Harir.[114] The snub would scarcely have been appreciated by the Kart ruler.

The same historian also relates an incident that occurred in the year 666/1268. One day, as Shams al-Din was crossing a bridge, he saw two Ismailis. When asked who they were, they replied that they were from Abiward. The ruler realized they were lying and ordered Malik ʿIzz al-Din to interrogate them. They were tortured until they finally confessed that they had been dispatched to Quhistan to assassinate Shams al-Din. They also conceded that they had ten companions in Jughrati. All twelve were then executed.[115] It was, thus, an invidious position for any Ismaili, much less the outspoken, headstrong, and often overly vocal Nizari Quhistani, to be in the service of this ruler. It is little wonder then that he had to exercise extreme caution in dealing with his patron.

In his official capacity, Nizari traveled extensively throughout Quhistan, Sistan, Rayy, and Khurasan. His most important journey, however, was one he undertook in 678/1280 at the age of thirty and about which he has bequeathed to us a poetic *Travelogue* (*Safarnāma*). This valuable historical source has recently been edited and studied by Nadia E. Jamal.[116] Speaking in allegories, Nizari describes his journey and meetings with people who, in Jamal's opinion, were Ismaili dignitaries in Armenia, Georgia, Arran, and Azerbaijan. He evidently met with the successor of the Imam Rukn al-Din Khwurshah during this journey, an Imam whom he names Shah Shams, who was then apparently residing in Tabriz.[117] This versified travelogue testifies to the wide distribution of the community. Indeed, there is an enigmatic poem in Nizari's poetic *Omnibus* (*Dīwan*) that begins, "How fortunate are the lands under the command of the friends (*awliyāʾ*, presumably a reference to the Imams or perhaps the leaders of the daʿwa)." He then proceeds to name numerous regions, presumably those in which the daʿwa had been preserved.[118]

Nizari also wrote a number of other poetic works, including a short *mathnawi* entitled *The Debate of Night and Day* (*Munāẓara-yi Shab wa-Rūz*), said to be a metaphorical dispute between exoteric Islam, represented by the darkness of night, and esoteric Islam, represented by the light of day. Perhaps his most overt defense of Ismailism is an epic poem with the title *Resplendent and Luminous* (*Azhar wa-Mazhar*). Baiburdi, a Russian authority on Nizari, describes it as "the embodiment of the high ideals of the Ismaili Nizari. Mazhar, the hero, is a representative of Ismailism and esotericism and he is fighting the tyranny of Halil, who represents Sunnism and the *ẓāhir* [the exoteric]."[119]

The poet's religious training likely reflects that of his co-religionists in his native Quhistan. His spiritual upbringing was at the hands of his father, to whom he pays tribute in very tender verses ending with the word *pidaram*, "my father":

> O God! May he live long in security—my father
> For he has been abundantly generous to me—my father
>
> What obligation is greater than following the Prophet's Family?
> Of the proof of the imamate he gave me certainty—my father

Though I may have been a dastardly and unworthy son
He fulfilled all the conditions of paternity—my father[120]

Clearly, in this hostile age, with no secure Ismaili state as in earlier times, no Ismaili institutions of learning that we know of, where the community lived as a minority wherever it was established, the Ismaili tradition must have passed from generation to generation, from parents to their children as a cautiously guarded oral heritage. This teaching would have been supplemented by the dignitaries of the Ismaili hierarchy, the daʿwa, who, we are constantly reminded in Ismaili works, operated in every *jazira*, or "island" of Ismaili activity. While the practice of *taqiyya* in Iran had the advantage of allowing the community to live largely unnoticed, a great danger was also inherent in it. After a few generations of nominal adherence to Sunnism, there can be little doubt that over time many Ismaili families really did become Sunni, not only in appearance, but also in fact, especially in homes in which devotion to the Imam was not discussed, unlike in Nizari's home. This is confirmed by an observation of Hamd Allah Mustawfi. Considering the Ismailis to be heretics, he notes that in his days, though Rudbar was Ismaili, its people "profess to be Muslims [i.e., non-Ismaili Muslims], and at the present day some part walk in the way of the faith."[121] In other words, they were no longer simply practicing taqiyya, but had really become absorbed into the general community. Nizari's poem gives us remarkable insight into this process. He notes that he had been brought up in the tradition of loyalty to the Prophet's family at home, but when he went for higher education, he was surrounded by people hostile to the doctrines of his ancestors. While Nizari came from a highly educated and devout Ismaili family, there would have been many other children whose faith had not been so inculcated by their parents, leaving them open to the beliefs of their peer group and environment. Over time, this undoubtedly must have led the community to atrophy in size.

Nizari's training at home in his native Birjand was in stark contrast with that he was to receive when he attended a college (*madrasa*) for his higher education. In poetry addressed to his father, he bemoaned the sorry plight at the school:

> I wasted my time with a bunch of complete idiots, never finding in them an iota of manliness, of humanity. They are enemies of the Prophet's descendants—all of them are, and yet they claim to be Muslims! I bite my hand in grief and weep, "Alas, what a disgrace!"[122]

Nizari had to be very careful about his outspokenness. We know from his writings that he had been accused of heterodoxy. Indeed, in his poetry, he rails against those who would call him a heretic: "If I am a heretic, then where is this 'Muslim?' Who is he?!"[123] And again:

> Why do you say "heretic" to one who has established his faith with a hundred proofs from the Qur'an and the hadith? When you understand he who attains the perfect *maʿrifa* [gnosis], then by knowing him, you will confess your own ignorance.[124]

It has been suggested that Nizari chose verse and Sufi forms of expressions for camouflaging his Ismaili ideas.[125] Indeed, we do find repeated references in his works to such figures as Rabiʿa, Bayazid, and especially Hallaj, as well as to literary tropes that were used by contemporary Sufi poets.[126] However, whether this was a conscious "choice" is open to interpretation. With their emphasis on the esoteric dimension of Islam (the *bāṭin*), both Sufism and Ismailism, even Shiʿism as a whole, shared a common intellectual heritage. Writing toward the end of the fourteenth century, a figure of Ibn Khaldun's stature was to assert in his *Prolegomena*, "It is obvious that the Sufis in the Iraq derived their comparison between the manifest [exoteric] and the inner (world) [esoteric] from the Ismaʿiliyya Shiʿah."[127] This shared heritage, combined with the fact that Persian poetry had become, *par excellence*, a vehicle for conveying esoteric wisdom by Nizari's time, strongly suggests that no conscious decision to use this medium had to be made. As Wheeler Thackston has noted:

> Fairly early in the game the mystics found that they could "express the ineffable" in poetry much better than in prose. Usurping the whole of the poetic vocabulary that had been built up by that time, they imbued every word with mystical signification. What had begun as liquid wine with alcoholic content became the "wine of union with the godhead" on which the mystic is "eternally drunk." . . . After the mystics had wrought their influence on the tradition, every word of the vocabulary had acquired such "clouds" of associated meaning from lyricism and mysticism that the two strains merged into one. Of course, some poets wrote poetry that is overtly and unmistakably mystical and "Sufi." It is much more difficult to identify poetry that is not mystical. It is useless to ask, for instance, whether Hafiz's poetry is "Sufi poetry" or not. *The fact is that in the fourteenth century it was impossible to write a ghazal that did not reverberate with mystical overtones forced on it by the poetic vocabulary itself.*[128]

The case of Hafiz is replicated in that of Nizari in the previous generation. The poetic idiom of the time dictated certain norms, norms that were felicitous for writing on the esoteric beliefs of the Ismailis, as well as for "camouflaging" those very beliefs. There is no doubt that regardless of the medium of his expression, Nizari had to be cautious. Any Ismailis left alive after the Mongol massacres would have had to tread softly, avoiding drawing attention to themselves. That Nizari was sympathetic to Sufism is mentioned in his own verses.[129] That he considered it an incomplete form of spirituality in the absence of the Imam is equally clear. He writes:

> The Sufis say, "O you who anxiously wait, be a child of the time!" Well, I'm not one of those who remain in waiting. Were the Sufis on our path, how wonderful it would be; but we believe in the divine designation of the Imam, they in the dictates of their own choice. O friend, I won't divulge any more of this secret to you. How fortunate are those who understand this reproof. Heed Nizari's counsel that you may remain safe. Fearlessly, seek authoritative instruction and submit to it.[130]

The passage is charged with meaning. Those who anxiously wait (*muntaẓir*) are the Ithna ʿashari Shiʿa, who pray that their twelfth Imam hasten his return. The Sufis chide the Twelvers for believing in a guide who has disappeared from the face of the earth and hence is of no benefit. They admonish these Shiʿa, in the words of the popular maxim, based on a Prophetic tradition, to be children of the time (*abnāʾ al-waqt*). This criticism seems to have been commonplace, even among those with express Shiʿi sympathies. The prominent messianic leader of the following century, Muhammad Nurbakhsh, while connecting himself to the Twelver Imams by his concept of "projection" (*burūz*), contends in his Arabic treatise, *Epistle of Guidance* (*Risālat al-hudā*), that the belief in no more than twelve Imams was misleading. He claims that this numerical limitation was a myth propagated by the ʿAbbasids to demean the ʿAlids and deprive them of capable leaders.[131]

Nizari agrees with the Sufis on this point but begs to differ on a matter of crucial importance. The Imam of the time (*imām-i waqt*) cannot be chosen at whim, like the shaykhs and pirs of the Sufis. He must be designated by divine authority (*manṣūṣ*). For those who understand Nizari's intent, this allusion is sufficient. He refuses to elaborate and says, "I won't divulge any more of this secret to you."

Within a century of Nizari's death, Ibn Khaldun was to observe that the Sufis had appropriated this central concept of the Ismailis and, in particular, had been influenced by the Nizaris:

> The early (Sufis) had had contact with the Neo-Ismaʿiliyah Shiʿah extremists. . . . In Sufi discussion, there appeared the theory of the "pole" (*quṭb*), meaning the chief Gnostic. The Sufis assumed that no one can reach his station in gnosis, until God takes him unto Himself and then gives his station to another Gnostic who will be his heir. Avicenna referred to this in the sections on Sufism in the *Kitāb al-Ishārāt*. . . . The theory of (successive "poles") . . . is identical with the theory of the extremist Shiʿah about the succession of the imams through inheritance.

> Clearly, mysticism has plagiarized this idea from the extremist Shiʿah and come to believe in it. . . . The (Ismaʿiliyyah Shiʿah) considered the leadership of mankind and its guidance toward the religious law a duty of the imam. Therefore, they assumed that there could be no more than one imam if the possibility of a split were to be avoided, as is established in the religious law.[132]

The Sufis against whom Nizari argues clearly had not adopted this doctrine. He is thus able to turn their argument against them, claiming that he is the true "child of the time." He follows a guide who is present among mankind, unlike the Twelvers, but who is chosen by God, not man, unlike the Sufis.

Nizari's following counsel is poignant. "Seek authoritative instruction (*taʿlīm*) and submit to it (*taslīm*)," he advises. Both terms reverberate with their Ismaili connotations, for *taʿlim* is the teaching dispensed by the Imam through his daʿwa hierarchy, while to submit to this *taʿlim*, *taslim*, is to be truly Muslim, that is, to submit to God's will. It seems that on the pattern of Ismaili antecedents, the Sufis even adopted the concept of the daʿwa hierarchy that would dispense *taʿlim*. Ibn Khaldun notes:

> The (Sufis), furthermore, speak about the order of existence of the "saints" [*abdāl*] who come after the "pole," exactly as the Shiʿah speak about their "chiefs" [*nuqabāʾ*]. . . . [The Sufis] then regarded as a duty of the "pole," who is the chief gnostic, the instruction (of mankind) in the gnosis of God. Therefore, they assumed that there could be only one, on analogy from the imam in the manifest (world), and that he was the counterpart of the imam. They called him "pole," because the gnosis revolved around him, and they equated the "saints" with the ʿAlid "chiefs," in their exaggerated desire to identify (their concepts with those of the Shiʿah).[133]

As the doctrine of the *taʿlimiyya*, i.e., the Ismailis, insisted, the intellect is essential in the quest to recognize God. It is, however, insufficient. Since God is beyond the intellect, how can the intellect comprehend him? At the zenith of its search, the intellect must submit (*taslīm*) to the instruction (*taʿlīm*) of those who have recognized God, whom God himself appointed to lead mankind to knowledge of him. Nizari elaborates:

> The way of the lovers is not to be traversed on the feet of the ordinary intellect, for the intellectuals are like birds and the path of love, a snare. Reflect on all the sciences, then come hither, that I may lead you to God's Proof, the perfector of the imperfect. You stand behind anyone who

winds a turban around his head and steps before you, thinking, "this is the Imam." Not for an instant is the world bereft of the Imam of the time! Does what I say bother you? Well, what can I do about it if the Quran says so? As the Imam was and always will be, what would you respond to me if I were to ask, "Who is your Imam?"[134] If you do not know the Imam of your time with certitude, then know certainly that your wealth, wife, even the head upon your shoulders, all are forbidden to you.[135] I'll barter your type of Imam for the sweets at the tavern. After all, that turban on his head would be a good pawn for wine and a goblet. And if you have two Imams, what would you reply if I asked which one was your real Imam? Let all the world's clerics gather and issue an edict that the drunken Nizari is the dregs of humanity! I fear not being killed, nor am vexed at the thought of my flesh burning. I care not a wit for their flowing beards, for their long whiskers are naught but infantile![136]

In this, one of Nizari's most outspoken *ghazals*, he castigates his adversaries with unusual daring. The poem begins with a keystone of Ismaili thought, that a study of all the sciences, of all knowledge, will lead the truly realized intellect to seek a preceptor, a guide who can lead it along a path that is beyond its grasp. Nizari calls this the path of the lovers, a path on which those who try to tread with the intellect alone will be trapped like birds in a snare. A truly realized intellect is one that comes to terms with the fact that it is imperfect and must seek out the one who would perfect it, Nizari's "Proof of God."[137] But who is this guide, this Imam, to whom one must turn? Is it the fellow who leads the prayers with an imposing turban wrapped around his head? Certainly not, Nizari scoffs. How could such a person be the one referred to in the Prophetic hadith that Nizari alludes to, لو خلت الأرض من إمام ساعةً لمادتْ باهلها "Were the world to be bereft of the Imam for but an instant, it would be convulsed with all its inhabitants."[138] This is followed by a reference to the Qur'an, likely to 17:71, "On the day we shall call all men with their Imam," after which he questions his opponent pointedly whether he would be able to answer if asked to identify his Imam. If it happens to be the fellow with the turban, Nizari seemingly mocks, a turban does not an Imam make! This turban may as well be bartered at the local tavern.

Realizing how audacious he has been, Nizari concludes that he doesn't care if all the religious clerics join in condemning him. He doesn't consider their opinion worthy of worrying about, nor their power to have him killed particularly frightening. Despite their flowing beards, in Nizari's eyes, they are little more than infants.

The copy of Nizari's poetic *Omnibus* (*Dīwān*) available at the Kitabkhana-yi Milli-yi Malik in Iran is very revealing. It consists of four parts, the first of which visibly differs from the others. It is written in a different hand and, unlike the second and third volumes, is not arranged according to rhyme. Most important, it appears to have been entirely expunged of Ismaili elements. It would be very difficult, on the basis of this volume, to conclude anything of Nizari's Ismaili affiliation. The second and third parts, however, are very outspoken about Nizari's religious convictions. The beliefs of his religious opponents are roundly condemned. Based on the marginalia of these volumes, it can be concluded that it was written in the early seventeenth century and, shortly thereafter, was received as an inheritance by an Ismaili dignitary (ma'dhūn-i akbar) named Darwish Qutb al-Din Muhammad of the village of Yahn in Quhistan. Unfortunately, between the second and third volumes there appears to be a huge lacuna as the first contains poems rhyming in the letters *alif* to *dal*, while the third contains those rhyming in *nun* to *ya'*. Hence, more than half the letters are missing. The fourth volume contains poetry of some other poets.[139] The question arises as to who expunged the more openly Ismaili verses of Nizari's *Omnibus*, the poet himself, the later Ismailis, or non-Ismailis who found such verses distasteful? The last of these would not have been unusually uncommon. Michael Sells notes the possibility of the Quran commentary of the Shiʿi Imam Jaʿfar al-Sadiq being adopted into Sufi circles and stripped of its Shiʿi elements.[140] Similarly, the non-Ismaili scribe of Nasir-i Khusraw's *Unfettering and Liberation* (*Gushāyish wa-Rahāyish*) deliberately suppressed and censored explicitly Ismaili portions of the work.[141] It is also possible that the Ismailis themselves censored their own works or the works of their co-religionists to ensure that they wouldn't give offense to the majoritarian community. Perhaps there were other Ismailis of this time whose religious convictions are unknown to us because their works no longer contain explicit indications of their allegiance.

Doubtless, Nizari's open espousal of his convictions caused him much grief. Even maintaining the pen name "Nizari," if it refers to one of the Imams, was audacious. It was perhaps his outspokenness in matters of religion, Jamal muses, that allowed his detractors to poison the Shah's ear against him.[142] When a friend of his was put to death, the poet criticized his patron. His insolence was not to be tolerated, and he was dismissed from his position at court. He passed his last days in relative obscurity, dying in 720/1320, just a decade after the date ascribed to the death of the Imam Shams al-Din Muhammad in 710/1310.[143] He bequeathed to posterity gems of Persian poetry, strewn among which were pearls hinting at the faith and conviction that he nurtured in his heart, unable to divulge them openly in the realm and time of taqiyya. In this manner, he attempted to veil the Sun of Faith, Shams al-Din, his Imam. However, to those able to understand his allusions, the rays of that light hinted at their source. As he writes:

It is well that one should follow the Imamate
For the light of God is in his pure heart
That light will set you free from darkness
Follow that light and may peace be with you[144]

FOUR

Summoning to the Truth

The Imam Maʿadd [al-Muʿizz] summons to the absolute oneness of God, the Eternal.

Inscription on a Fatimid coin

In the last chapter, we met with the daʿi Abu ʿAbd Allah al-Shiʿi, whose activities among the Kutama Berbers set the stage for the advent of the Fatimid Imam in the Maghrib. As town after town fell under the daʿi's sway, the Aghlabid leader, Ziyadat Allah III, despaired, abandoned his capital, and fled in 296/909. In that very year, the daʿi minted the first Fatimid coins in Qayrawan. The inscription on the coins, exemplars of which are still in existence, is illuminating. In the center they read, *There is no deity but God, the Unique, without partner.* Encircling this declaration are the Quranic words *Muhammad is the messenger of God, who sent him with the Guidance and the Faith of Truth that it may be manifested above all other faiths* (9:33, 61:9). With the conquest of Egypt in the time of the Imam Maʿadd, known as al-Muʿizz, the legend on the obverse of the first coinage bore the same Quranic verses, while the reverse included the words: *The Imam Maʿadd summons to the absolute oneness of God, the Eternal. Al-Muʿizz li-Din Allah is the Commander of the Faithful.*[1]

The numismatic evidence reveals a central tenet of Ismailism. At the center is the absolute, uncompromising unity of God. The very fact that God had sent his messengers, including Muhammad, indicates that he seeks to communicate with humankind. In the words of the Quran, the message is one of guidance and a revelation of the Faith of Truth. In fact, the Ismailis did not call their religion "Ismailism." This was a name given to them by the early heresiographers, notably al-Nawbakhti and al-Qummi.[2] They referred to themselves simply as the Faith of Truth (*dīn al-ḥaqq*) or the Summons to the Truth (*daʿwat al-ḥaqq*). The fifteenth-century Ismaili author, Bu Ishaq Quhistani, states quite plainly that "the people of the Truth are the people of the Summons."[3] Such designations remained common even when the community spread to South Asia, where it came to be known as the Path of Truth (*satpanth*). The declaration, *The Imam Maʿadd summons to the absolute oneness of God, the Eternal*, is one of the most remarkable features of the coin. As the successor to the prophet, the Imam is responsible for calling all of humankind to the Faith of Truth; to a recognition of the absolute divinity and oneness of God. The Imam's call was conducted through an organization known as the daʿwa, simply "the summons."[4] Like the practice of taqiyya, the daʿwa was one of the central features of Ismailism that allowed it to survive the Mongol depredations. This chapter investigates the concept of daʿwa and its structure, analyzes the existing data on the immediate progeny of the Imam Shams al-Din Muhammad, including the Imam Qasimshah, and probes the identity and writings of Qasim Tushtari, an Ismaili author who was perhaps a contemporary of the Imam Qasimshah.

THE DAʿWA

The term daʿwa and other words derived from the same Arabic root are found numerous times in the Quran. It is, for example, used to refer to the occasion when God summons the dead from their graves to eternal life: "Among his signs is this: the heavens and the earth stand by his Command. Then, when he summons you by a daʿwa, lo! You will emerge from the earth" (30:25). It is also understood as God's summons to believe in him and the true religion: "And warn mankind of a day when they will be punished. Those who did wrong will say, 'O our lord! Grant us a short reprieve. We will respond to your daʿwa and follow the prophets" (14:44). While Muslim groups including the ʿAbbasids and even the Shiʿi opposition to Saddam Husayn's rule in Iraq used this term extensively, it has most particularly been associated with the Ismailis, who also referred to their community as "the summons that guides aright" (*al-daʿwat al-hādiyya*). The wide appeal and extensive reach of the Ismaili daʿwa, even in the heart of the ʿAbbasid empire, alarmed both the caliph and other rulers. The tremendous attraction of the daʿwa provoked the young ʿAbbasid caliph al-Mustazhir (d. 512/1118) to commission the most outstanding Sunni scholar of the age, Abu Hamid Muhammad al-Ghazali (d. 505/1111), to attempt a refutation of the Shiʿi Ismaili doctrines, a task that he undertook in his *Infamies of the Batinis and Virtues of the Mustazhiris* (*Faḍāʾiḥ al-Bāṭiniyya wa Faḍāʾil al-Mustaẓhiriyya*).[5] The Saljuq Turks were particularly nervous about the independent existence of the Ismaili daʿwa within their territories. Nizam al-Mulk, the all-powerful Saljuq vizier, dedicated a long section of his *Books of Politics* (*Siyāsatnāma*) to repudiating the Ismailis.[6] Some scholars have interpreted his efforts at establishing theological schools of an Ashʿari-Shafiʿi ilk across the empire—the famous Nizamiyya madrasas—as an attempt to counteract the immense intellectual influence that Ismaili thought and doctrine were exercising even beyond the borders of Ismaili dominion.[7]

The Ismaili daʿwa was characterized by a system of gradations, known as the ranks of faith (*ḥudūd-i dīn*).[8] Each rank received knowledge from its superior rank and conveyed it to the rank immediately below, reflecting the Quranic dictum, "We raise by grades whom we will. And over every possessor of knowledge there is one more knowing" (12:76). Through this process of edification, or instruction (*taʿlīm*), the faithful drew ever closer to their ultimate goal, the recognition of God. Each rank was to submit to its superior, based on the injunction, "He who transgresses the ranks (*ḥudūd*) of God, he certainly wrongs his own soul" (65:1).

The names of the ranks described differed slightly among various authors. The system elaborated hereunder is drawn primarily from the *Epistle on the Explanation of the Ranks* (*Risāla-yi Sharḥ al-Marātib*), which is based on the number seven and seems to have been one of the most popular and widely circulated texts of the post-Mongol period, though it cannot be dated with any degree of certainty.[9] The text begins with a verse of the Quran, "It is God who has created the seven heavens and of the earth the like thereof. The Command descends through them so that you may learn that God is powerful over all things and that God encompasses all things with knowledge" (65:12). In the esoteric exegesis that follows, each of these seven ascending heavens is understood to be a rank of the faithful.

The lowest heaven, occupying the seventh rank, is the respondent to the summons (mustajīb). The respondents are revived from the death of ignorance in accordance with the above quoted Quranic verse, emerging from the earth in response to the daʿwa of God (30:25). The name "mustajib" is likely based on the verse, "Only those who listen can respond (*yastajību*). And God will raise the dead, then they will return to him" (6:36). Those who do not seek recognition of God are as though dead, but by responding to God's daʿwa, they are brought to life and begin their return to him. The mustajibs cannot convey the daʿwa, only receive it from the upper heavens. Immediately above the respondents are the junior and senior licentiates (ma'dhūn-i aṣghar and ma'dhūn-i akbar). They are authorized by the daʿi to conduct the daʿwa and to establish its claims by both intellectual and scriptural proofs. If the respondents ask the junior licentiates any questions that they cannot explain, they must not disregard the matter, thus closing the gate of bounty. Rather, they are required to inquire and find the answer from those who are of a higher rank, and hence who are more knowledgeable than they are. The senior licentiates must convey the commands of the daʿi to every region. Some members of this rank were also referred to as muʿallim, teacher, a term that may have first acquired this technical meaning with the writings of Hasan-i Sabbah.[10] The daʿi is referred to as the "candle of guidance and light of gnosis" and is referred to in the Quranic verse, "O our people! Respond to God's daʿi and believe in him" (46:31). The rank of daʿi specified in the *Explanation of the Ranks* is likely a reference to the limited daʿi (*dāʿī-yi maḥdūd*), while the next rank, the junior proof (*ḥujjat-i aṣghar*), is a reference to the absolute daʿi (*dāʿī-yi muṭlaq*). The junior proofs, or absolute daʿis, were considered the epiphany of the Universal Soul (*nafs-i kull*). Hence, they do not receive their knowledge by instruction (*taʿlīm*), as do the lower ranks. Rather, their knowledge is by a type of inspiration from on high, a support (*taʾyīd*) that the text explains to be the power of the divine light (*quwwat-i nūr-i ilāhī*). A couplet found in this text as well as in many other Ismaili treatises, but of unknown authorship, explains this inspiration as follows:

> A path exists from the hujjat to the Imam
> He becomes aware by the divine support (*taʾyīd*) of his heart[11]

One of the proofs is considered the greatest proof (ḥujjat-i akbar) or the most hallowed gate (bāb-i aqdas). Just as a city must be accessed by its gate, the Imam must be accessed through the greatest proof, who is the epiphany of the Universal Intellect (*ʿaql-i kull*). Meanwhile, the Imam himself is the epiphany of the creative fiat *kun*, "be," a reference to the Quranic verse, "His command when he desires a thing, is to say to it 'Be!' and it is" (36:82). He is thus the personification of God's command and will and is the one through whom recognition of God is attained. Our text thus refers to him as the vicar of God on earth, the true supreme name, the Kaʿba and qibla toward truth, and many other epithets. He is the most exalted of the seven heavens. The arrangement of the ranks in this text can be seen in figure 4.1.

A Syrian text by Shihab al-Din Abu Firas entitled *The Ladder of Ascent to the House of Eternity* (*Kitāb Sullam al-Ṣuʿūd ilā Dār al-Khulūd*) gives unique insights into the concept of the ranks of faith (*ḥudūd al-dīn*).[12] It also evinces the mutual influence of Ismailism and other esoteric interpretations of Islam, including Sufism. There appear to have been two authors named Abu Firas. The better known of them was born in 872/1468, lived in the Ismaili fortress of Maniqa, and died in either 937/1531 or 947/1540.[13] In the mid-nineteenth century, Joseph Catafago, a dragoman at the Prussian consulate in Syria, discovered a manuscript containing a hagiographic account of the life of Rashid al-Din Sinan, a celebrated Syrian daʿi.[14] The text is commonly attributed to Abu Firas, but the manuscript dates to 724/1324, and so could not have been by the sixteenth-century figure. It may

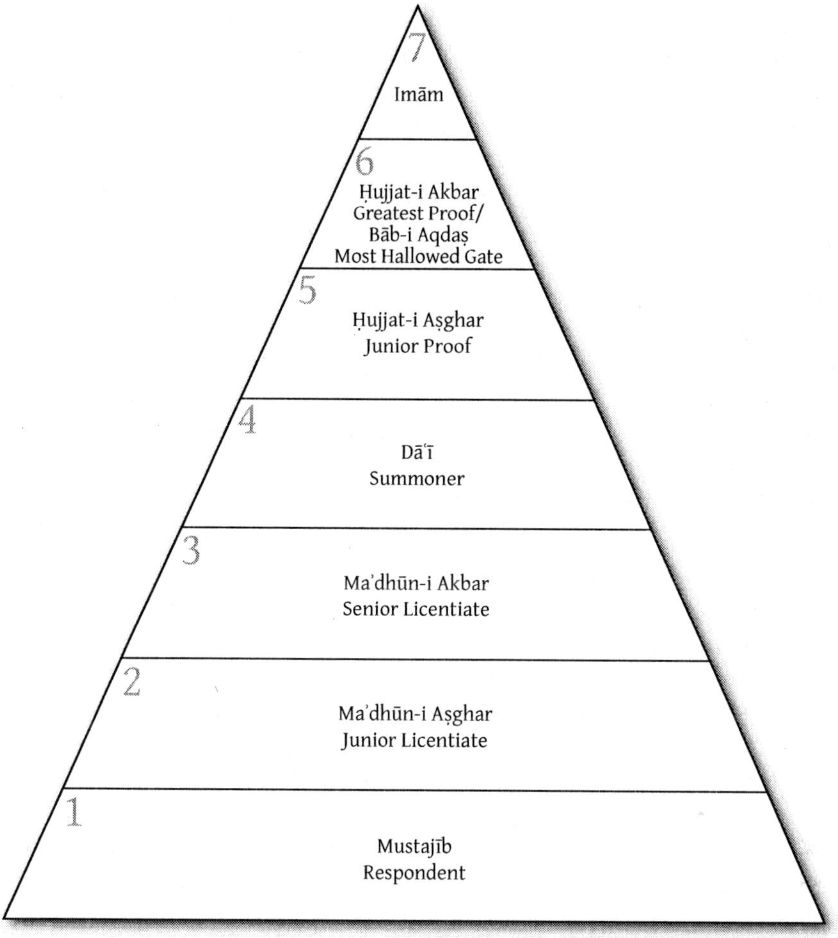

FIGURE 4.1 The Seven Heavens of the *Ḥudūd-i Dīn*

It is God who has created the seven heavens and of the earth the like thereof. The Command descends through them so that you may learn that God is powerful over all things and that God encompasses all things with knowledge (65:12)

perhaps be by a fourteenth-century author of the same name. It is thus difficult to determine in which of these two periods *The Ladder of Ascent* was composed. In any case, it comprises three volumes, each containing numerous chapters. Each volume details the progressive stages through which a believer must pass in order to attain spiritual beatitude. Commencing with *The Book of Souls* (*Kitāb al-Nufūs*),

The Ladder of Ascent describes the nature of the soul and its struggle to free itself from the physical world as it seeks to draw nearer to the divine light. This theme continues in *The Book of Lights* (*Kitāb al-Anwār*), the largest of the three volumes. Here, the author speaks of the heavenly lights and explains that the light of the celestial spheres and other higher lights are only temporal. They always seek the primordial source of light, the origin of all existence. The heavenly ranks (*ḥudūd ʿulwiyya*) correspond to the ranks of the religious hierarchy on earth (*ḥudūd ʿālam al-dīn*), who symbolize the universal divine order. By scaling the ranks of the daʿwa, the believers mount the ladder of ascent to the house of eternity. In the final volume, *The Book of Knowledge of the Divine Presence* (*Kitāb ʿIlm al-Ḥuḍūr*), the author explains the necessary qualities of the seeking soul. The soul's passage from darkness to light is possible through recognition of the Imam of the time. Through such knowledge it comes into the presence of the divine light, at which stage there is eternal happiness.

Earlier authors have suggested that in the confusion following the Mongol invasions, this daʿwa hierarchy collapsed, perhaps surviving in name alone.[15] Daftary notes that the blow of the death of Rukn al-Din Khwurshah, the leader in whose reign Alamut capitulated to the Mongols, deprived the "confused and displaced Nizaris" of access to their Imam or his local representatives.[16] While there can be little doubt that the singular catastrophe stunned the whole community, many parts of the Ismaili world, such as Syria, South Asia, and Badakhshan, were largely spared from the Mongol debacle, and the disruption in these areas would have been considerably less. Moreover, we have clear evidence in the newly found manuscripts that even in areas destroyed by the invaders, the daʿwa continued not only to provide religious instruction to the believers, but also to deliver the religious dues to the Imams who succeeded Rukn al-Din Khwurshah. The assumption of the daʿwa activities being curtailed in the absence of a centralized Ismaili state is actually contrary to the theoretical vision of how it should function. A post-Mongol Ismaili author explains that it is in fact when the Imam is apparent, "like the sun," that the dignitaries of the daʿwa cease to be seen. However, in periods of concealment (*satr*) and dissimulation (*taqiyya*), which are like night, the believers must be guided by the moon and stars, which are like the hujjat and the daʿis. When the sun reappears, the moon and stars are no longer visible.[17] Ibn Khaldun (d. 784/1382) noted this aspect of the Ismaili daʿwa: "According to the Ismailis, an imam who has no power goes into hiding. His missionaries remain in the open, in order to establish proof (of the hidden imam's existence) among mankind. When the imam has actual power, he comes out into the open and makes his propaganda openly."[18] Hence, the daʿwa hierarchy is most active precisely at times when the Imam lacks political authority or is hidden from the eyes of his enemies and the lower ranks of the daʿwa.

IMAM QASIMSHAH

Upon the demise of the Imam Shams al-Din Muhammad, there may have been a succession dispute. In a seminal article entitled "A Forgotten Branch of the Ismailis" that appeared in 1938, Wladimir Ivanow revealed his findings about the possibility that a second branch of the Nizaris had come into existence at this time.[19] Ivanow's work was based primarily on his discovery of a manuscript of a work entitled *Guidance for Seekers* (*Irshād al-Ṭālibīn*). He had obtained a copy of Nasir-i Khusraw's *Face of Religion* (*Wajh-i Dīn*) from Badakhshan, which was transcribed in 929/1523. In addition to this work, the volume included a few short Ismaili treatises, among them *Guidance for Seekers*, copied by the same scribe, Muhibb ʿAli Qunduzi, who, in Ivanow's estimation, was a well-educated man with a sound knowledge of Arabic.[20] He thus cautiously postulates that the scribe may have written this treatise himself. In his later work, *Ismaili Literature*, he lists Muhibb ʿAli Qunduzi as the author but qualifies the supposition with a question mark.[21] I. K. Poonawala in his *Biobibliography of Ismāʿīlī Literature* lists this scribe as the definitive author,[22] and this opinion has been adopted by subsequent scholarship.[23]

We can be fairly certain, however, that the true author of the treatise was not Muhibb ʿAli Qunduzi. In listing the Imams of the Muhammadshahi line, the author ends with the Imam of his own time, Radi al-Din b. ʿIzz al-Din Tahirshah. Ivanow based his hypothesis concerning the authorship on the assumption that this figure was still alive in 929/1523 when the manuscript was transcribed. It has since been determined, however, that Radi al-Din died in 915/1509.[24] Had Muhibb ʿAli been the true author, it would have been highly unusual for him not to have included in his list Radi al-Din's successor, Shah Tahir Dakkani, the most famous son of this line. It is thus unlikely that Qunduzi wrote this treatise, and therefore the author of the *Guidance for Seekers* remains anonymous. Nevertheless, as Ivanow claimed, the work provides strong evidence that a split did indeed take place and that a group of Ismailis followed the descendants of an Imam named Qasimshah, while another group followed the descendants of an Imam named Muhammadshah, as already alluded to in chapter 2. Later scholars have all accepted Ivanow's conclusions. In this book it is the line of Qasimshah that concerns us; therefore, here it is sufficient to discuss the details of the family of the Imam Shams al-Din Muhammad that are recorded in *Guidance for Seekers*. The anonymous author gathered the information from the oral tradition he had heard and explicitly affirms this, introducing his narrative by stating, "It is thus related" (*chunīn riwāyat mī kunand*). It should therefore be treated with some degree of caution. The repetition of both male and female names in different generations of the lineage may indicate a lacuna in the memory of the oral tradition narrated by the author of the text. However, this is not necessarily so. It seems that repetition of names in the family was common at this time. Hence we have Islamshah b. Islamshah (or Salamshah b. Salamshah) in one branch of the family tree, and a plethora of Muhammads, Tahirs, and Radis in the other branch. As this work is the only extant source that deals extensively with the offspring of Shams al-Din Muhammad, its testimony has been relied on here to draw tentative conclusions and to sketch the outline of the family presented below.

The family relationships described in the text are rather intricate, and an attempt has been made to represent them in as simple a form as possible while remaining faithful to the source. While expressions such as "the first" (*awwal*), "the second" (*thānī*), etc., do not appear in the manuscript, the majuscules *A, B* and *C;* the *ibn* and *bint* or "son of" and "daughter of" construction (abbreviated as b.); and other devices will be used here to help distinguish between people of the same name.

Shams al-Din Muhammad had two sons, ʿAlaʾ al-Din Muʾminshah and Salamshah A. Muʾminshah had two wives, one named Bibi Sharaf Khatun, by whom he had a son named Muhammadshah (the ancestor of Shah Tahir Dakkani), and the other named Bibi Dawlat Sati A, by whom he had a son named Qasimshah A. When Muʾminshah passed away, his two wives were taken into the household of his brother, Salamshah A, who married the widows.

Salamshah A had a daughter by Sharaf Khatun and two sons by Dawlat Sati A, Nizarshah (who was also known as Qasimshah B) and Qadirshah. Qasimshah A had no sons, but he had three daughters, Muhammadumshah,[25] Dilshad, and Dawlat Sati B. Dawlat Sati B was given in marriage to Nizarshah (Qasimshah B). The couple had three sons, Qasimshah C, Salamshah B, and Zayn al-ʿAbidin.[26] This is most easily seen in figures 4.2 and 4.3.

The anonymous author's argument seems to be that the Qasimshahi line claimed that Qasimshah C b. Nizarshah (Qasimshah B) was the son of Qasimshah A, whom the author had previously referred to as *Mawlana* Qasimshah. The use of the term "mawlana" is a strong indication that he believed that Qasimshah A was an Imam, having received the *nass* or designation for the imamate from his father, Muʾminshah. However, as Qasimshah A had no sons, our author prefers the Imam to be Muʾminshah's other son, Muhammadshah. Meanwhile, it would seem that his opponents claimed that the true Imam was Nizarshah (Qasimshah B) b. Salamshah. Throughout this whole debate, *Guidance for Seekers* affirms that all the people mentioned as Imams by both groups are the descendants of the Imam Shams al-Din Muhammad and, ultimately, of ʿAli b. Abi Talib. What is at issue is which line is the rightful one.

A late alternative tradition is preserved by some of the Muhammadshahis of Syria. According to this oral narrative, the eldest and youngest sons of Shams al-Din Muhammad, ʿAlaʾ al-Din Muʾminshah and Qasimshah, had a dispute about the succession. A middle son, Kiyashah, was not involved in the conflict. Since no

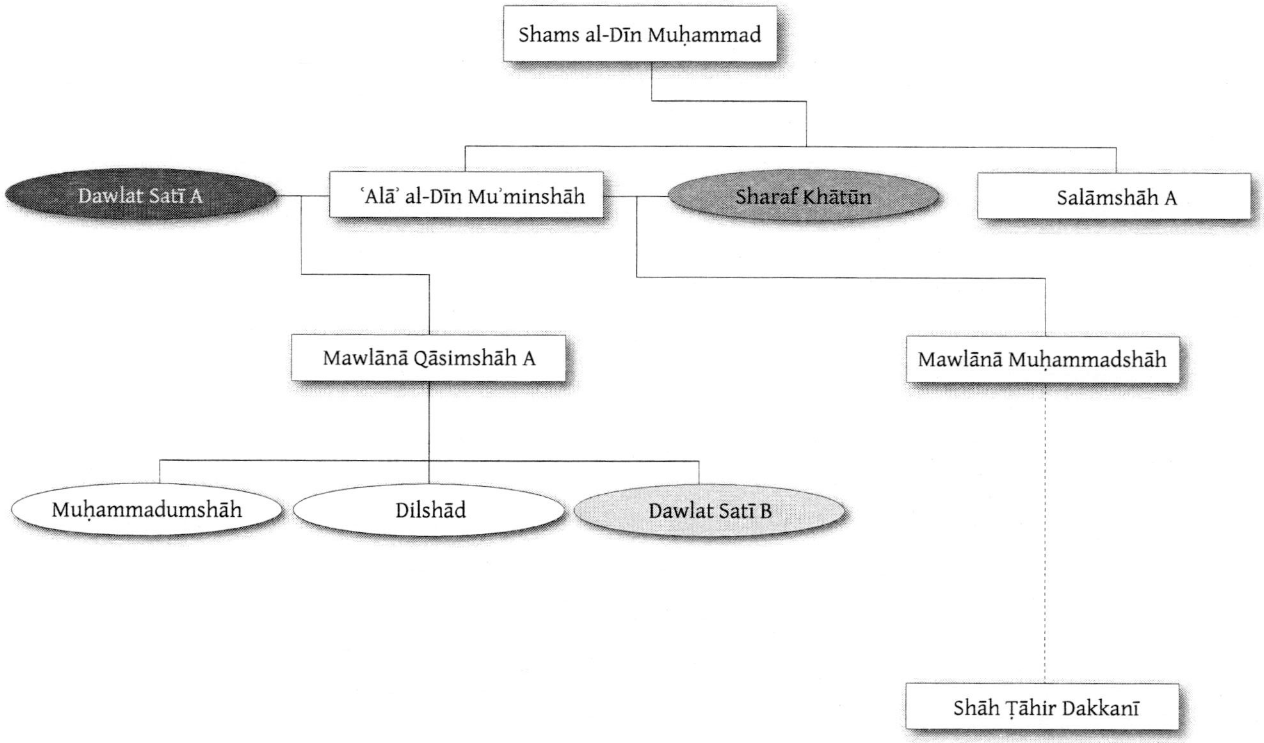

FIGURE 4.2 The Family of the Imam Shams al-Dīn Muḥammad

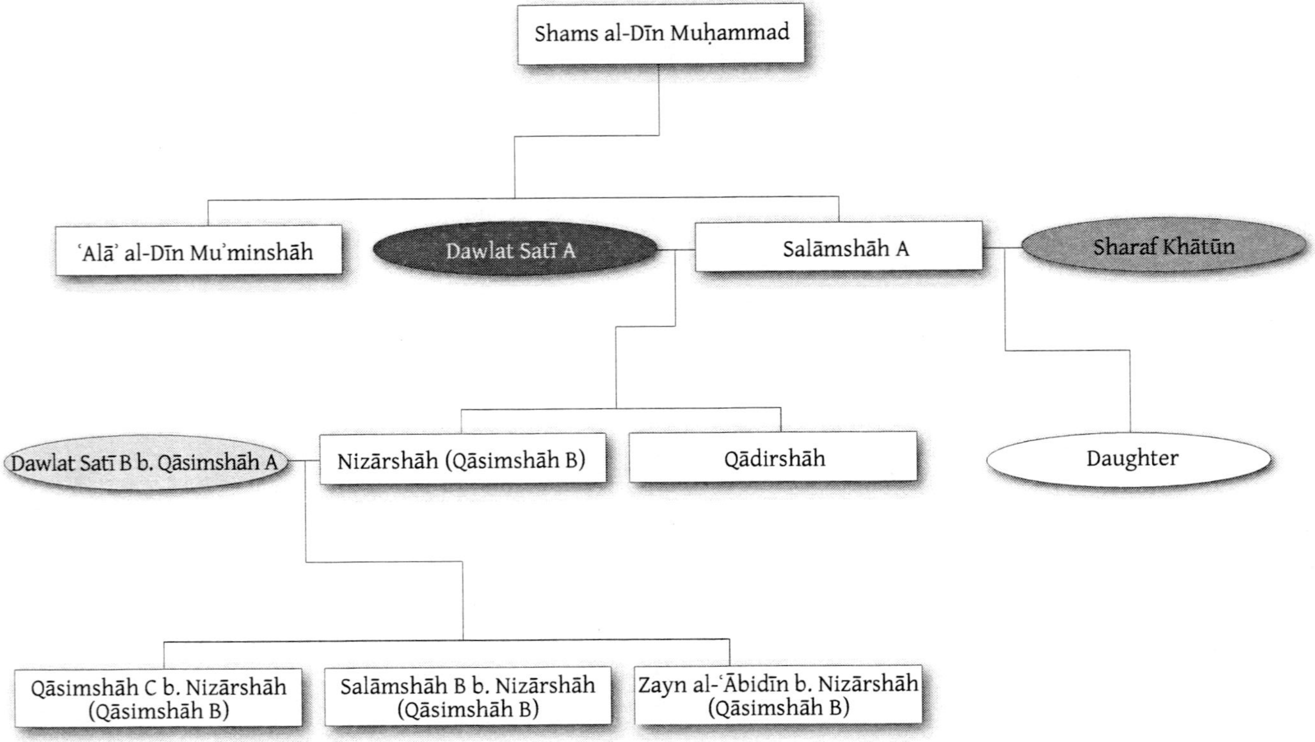

FIGURE 4.3 The Family of the Imam Shams al-Dīn Muḥammad

supporting evidence of any significant antiquity has been adduced to support this version, we may presume the scenario provided by the much earlier *Guidance for Seekers* to be the correct one.[27] Furthermore, the earliest Qasimshahi sources, adduced below, all include Mu'minshah in their register of Imams, so the split must have occurred after his death. Remarkably, an Indian Ismaili writing in 1892 mentions that Mu'minshah was born and lived in Anjudan and that his tomb (*turbat*) was located there.[28] Ibrahim Dihgan (d. 1984), a native of the region, mentions the same tradition, providing further substantiation by noting that a castle exists in Anjudan called Sharfa, which he assumes to be named after Mu'minshah's wife Sharaf Khatun.[29] He observes, however, that the region's oral tradition is against his speculation, as it associates the castle with Sharaf Nisa Begam, the wife of the Imam Khalil Allah (who was also known as Dhu al-Faqar ʿAli, d. 1043/1634) and sister of Shah ʿAbbas I (d. 1038/1629).[30] This greatest of Safawid sovereigns—whom the French traveler Chardin immortalized in his oft-quoted declaration, "When this great prince ceased to live, Persia ceased to prosper"[31]—did indeed have some interaction with the Ismailis of the area, as testified to by a royal edict addressed to the Imam and issued in 1036/1627 in which the shah exempted the Shiʿis of Anjudan from paying certain taxes.[32]

The oldest extant lists of Qasimshahi Imams, provided by three fifteenth-century Ismaili authors, Bu Ishaq Quhistani (fl. 9th/15th c.), Daʿi Anjudani (fl. 9th/15th c.), and an anonymous author of a *mathnawi*, provide unanimous testimony about the order of succession. The latter two works are not mentioned in Ivanow's or Poonawala's bibliographies. Both Bu Ishaq and Daʿi will be discussed in greater detail elsewhere in this book. The *mathnawi* is preserved in an old manuscript, dated 986/1560.[33] It is an account of all the Imams from the time of Adam to ʿAli, and then from ʿAli until the author's time. It will be noted that the names in the *Ode* (*qaṣīda*) of Daʿi Anjudani and the *Mathnawi* use constructions such as Qasimshah II (*Qāsimshāh-i Dīgar*) to distinguish between personalities of the same name. In transcribing the family trees derived from *Guidance for Seekers*, this form was deliberately avoided in favor of the majuscules *A*, *B*, and *C* in order to prevent confusion between the different sources. The three lists are to be found in Table 4.1.

It was common in this period for respected persons to be addressed with titles meaning such and such "of the faith" (*al-Dīn*) or such and such "of the truth" (*al-Ḥaqq*), a practice also apparent in these lists. Franklin Lewis notes the propensity for such designations in encomia or in the addresses of letters, and hence we find Shams-i Tabrizi referred to as "The Sun of the Truth and the Faith" (*Shams al-Ḥaqq wa-al-Dīn*).[34] Similarly, here we find names such as "Qasimshah, the Exalted One of the Truth and the Faith" (*ʿAlāʾ al-Ḥaqq wa-al-Dīn Qāsimshāh*).

In the Ismaili Ginans of South Asia, we find corroboration for one of the Imams being known as both Nizarshah and Qasimshah (hence Qasimshah B in our genealogical tree). In the cycle of *Garbis* attributed to Pir Shams, the Imam of the

TABLE 4.1 The Oldest Lists of Qāsimshāhī Imams

Fifteenth-century *Mathnawī*[1]	*Ode* of Dāʿī Anjudānī[2]	*Seven Chapters* of Bū Isḥāq[3]
Shams al-Dīn Muḥammad	Shams al-Dīn Muḥammad	Shams al-Dīn Muḥammad
Mu'minshāh	Mu'minshāh	ʿAlā' al-Dīn Mu'minshāh
Qāsimshāh	ʿAlā' al-Ḥaqq [wa-al-]Dīn Qāsimshāh	ʿAlā' al-Dīn Qāsimshāh
Qāsimshāh-i Dīgar	Qāsimshāh Thānī	ʿAlā' al-Ḥaqq wa-al-Dīn Qāsimshāh b. Qāsimshāh
ʿImād al-Dīn Salām	ʿImad al-Ḥaqq [wa-al-] Dīn Shāh al-Salām	ʿImād al-Ḥaqq wa-al-Dīn Salāmshāh
Shāh Salām	Shāh al-Salām-i Duwwum	ʿImād al-Dīn Salāmshāh b. Salāmshāh
Shāh Mustanṣir	Shāh Mustanṣir bi'llāh	Jalāl al-Ḥaqq wa-al-Dīn Mustanṣir bi'llāh
		ʿImād al-Ḥaqq wa-al-Dīn Salāmshāh
		Mustanṣir

[1]Anonymous manuscript dated 986/1560 in the possession of G. Mihrābī of Khushg, in the vicinity of Bīrjand, Iran.

[2]Dāʿī Anjudānī, "[Qaṣīda-yi dhurriyya]," in *Institute of Ismaili Studies Library*, Persian ms. 15030 (London).

[3]Quhistānī, *Haft Bāb*, ed. Ivanow, trans. Ivanow, *Haft Bab or "Seven Chapters"* (Mumbai, 1959), ed. 24, trans. 24.

time is frequently referred to as Qasimshah.[35] However, in one instance, the composition states: "The name of the last of the Prophets, Muhammad, is divine light. Meditate upon it, and obey the lord ʿAli. Shall I reveal to you the name of his present manifestation? It is Shah Nizar!"[36]

The pen name of the Ismaili poet "Nizari" Quhistani, who was introduced in the last chapter, has been the cause for some speculation. Dawlatshah, in his well-known *Memorial of Poets* (*Tadhkirat al-Shuʿarā'*), reports two theories concerning the nom de plume, the first being that he was slender and thin (*nizār*) and the second that he was a partisan of the Imam Nizar.[37] He adopts the latter view, as did the historians Mirkhwand and Khwandamir.[38] E. G. Browne likewise found derivations from the Persian adjective meaning thin to be "quite untenable."[39] But did this poet choose the name Nizari as a sign of allegiance to the Imam Nizar

b. al-Mustansir bi'llah, or to the Imam Nizar, the successor of Shams al-Din Muhammad, who was also known as Qasimshah? The possibility of his having taken his nom de plume based on the successor to Shams al-Din Muhammad is problematic because he would have adopted the name when Shams al-Din Muhammad, to the best of our knowledge, was still alive.[40] At the same time, in the Persian-speaking regions, we know of no Mustaᶜlians. All Ismailis of the region had, it seems, unanimously rallied around Nizar's descendants, and so it strikes a somewhat odd note that the poet would have identified himself with a particular branch of his faith when the other branch would scarcely have been known in his region. Furthermore, in the wake of the Mongol invasions, why would he have wanted to draw attention to his religious inclinations through his choice of pen name? This is a vexed question, and one for which no answer is readily forthcoming.[41]

The Imam Mu'minshah and one of the Imams named Qasimshah (most likely Qasimshah b. Mu'minshah, designated as Qasimshah A in the genealogical tree) are omitted from later Qasimshahi registers of the Imams. This is most easily explained by the Ismaili conception of permanently established (*mustaqarr*) and trustee (*mustawdaᶜ*) Imams.

Mustaqarr and Mustawdaᶜ Imams

The succession of brothers to the imamate evoked differing responses among the Shiᶜa. The first case of this was, of course, the Imam al-Husayn's succession to his brother, al-Hasan. A similar situation arose after the death of the Imam Jaᶜfar al-Sadiq. Most of his followers took his son ᶜAbd Allah al-Aftah as his successor. ᶜAbd Allah, however, died within months of his father. The partisans of ᶜAbd Allah, who were known as Aftahiyya or Fathiyya, then joined the party of Musa al-Kazim, acknowledging both of the brothers as Imams. Others sought to exclude ᶜAbd Allah from the line of the Imams and declared Musa as the direct successor of his father. Numerous similar situations arose, most noticeably with the death of Hasan al-ᶜAskari. As this Imam apparently died without a successor, many of his partisans then affirmed the imamate of his brother, Jaᶜfar. With the evolution of what later came to be known as Twelver Shiᶜism, however, the opinion that prevailed asserted that Hasan al-ᶜAskari did indeed have a son, but that this son had disappeared to return sometime in the future. The imamate of Jaᶜfar was therefore considered invalid. Such situations gave added importance to the well-known doctrine that "After the two Hasans, two brothers will never hold the imamate," انّ الامامة لا تكون في اخوين بعد الحسنين[42] i.e., with the single exception of al-Hasan and al-Husayn, the imamate must always pass in a single lineage.[43] This dictum was also upheld by some of the early partisans of the Imam Ismaᶜil al-Mubarak. Known as the Mubarakiyya, they contended that since Jaᶜfar had explicitly designated his son Ismaʿil as the next Imam, the imamate could not pass to his brothers, but only to his offspring.[44] Meanwhile, other Ismaili thinkers spoke of different types of imamate, namely, *mustaqarr*, or permanently established, and *mustawdaʿ*, or trustee, based on the following verse of the Quran: "And it is he who has produced you from a single soul, and then given you a permanent residence (*mustaqarr*) and a temporary abode (*mustawdaʿ*). We have detailed our signs for a community that understands" (6:98).[45]

According to the *Epistle on the Recognition of the Imam*, which draws inspiration from the words of the Imam Hasan ʿala dhikrihi al-salam:

> It must be known that the offspring of the Imam are of four kinds. One is his physical offspring, like Mustaʿli; one is his spiritual offspring, like Salman; one is his offspring both physically and spiritually, like Imam Hasan, who is called the trustee Imam (*imām-i mustawdaʿ*); and one is his offspring physically, spiritually and in reality, all three, like Mawlana Husayn, who is called the permanently established Imam (*imām-i mustaqarr*).[46]

The difference between the latter two is expounded upon by the author of *The Sage's Discourse* (*Kalām-i Pīr*):

> Now we have to explain the difference between the real hereditary Imam, *mustaqarr*, and the trustee Imam, *mustawdaʿ*. The difference between them exists only in so far as the question of inheritance is concerned, as in the case of Imam Hasan and Imam Husayn. The trustee Imam, *mustawdaʿ*, is a son of the Imam . . .[47] who also knows all the mysteries of imamate, and so long as he discharges his duty he is the greatest of all people of his time. But he is not endowed with the privilege of transmitting his imamate to his descendants, who can never become Imams, only Sayyids. The hereditary Imam, *mustaqarr*, is endowed with all the privileges of imamate, and transmits them to his successors.[48]

Thus, the *mustawdaʿ* Imams, in Ismaili thought, are considered to be descendants of the previous Imams both physically and spiritually, while the *mustaqarr* Imams are descendants physically, spiritually, and "in reality." Al-Hasan b. ʿAli was therefore a *mustawdaʿ* Imam in that while he was an Imam "in the full sense," his descendants could not inherit the permanent, *mustaqarr*, imamate from him.[49] Meanwhile, al-Husayn b. ʿAli was a *mustaqarr* Imam in that he was physically and spiritually his father's successor and was also able to transmit the *mustaqarr* imamate to his progeny. Thus, while acknowledging the imamate of al-Hasan b. ʿAli, Nizari Ismailis do not generally include him in the list of Imams, which is understood to include only those who were *mustaqarr*.[50] It seems to be that for the same reason the second Imam in table 4.1, Mu'minshah b. Shams al-Din Muhammad, and either the third or the fourth, both named Qasimshah, were omitted in later Ismaili lists. They were likely *mustawdaʿ* Imams who, as Bu Ishaq Quhistani informs us, only held the imamate "in trust" (*amānat*).[51] It is likely that the first Qasimshah referred to in the table is Qasimshah A b. Mu'minshah of figure 4.2, and the second is Nizarshah (a.k.a. Qasimshah) of figure 4.3. Since Qasimshah A had three daughters, the *mustaqarr* imamate seems to have been transferred through another line, almost certainly that of Nizarshah, the grandson of Shams al-Din Muhammad, who appears in the genealogical chart as Qasimshah B.[52] The succession to the imamate by a grandson of the previous Imam, rather than by a son, was repeated in recent times, when Karim al-Husayni succeeded Sultan Muhammadshah to become the forty-ninth Ismaili Imam. Qasimshah B would then have been succeeded by his son, Salamshah.

The Paradise of Submission explains that trustees were appointed when the Imams felt that the precarious situation demanded it. The Imams sought that "an interval and a trial (of faith) take place, deeming that concealment and strict protective dissimulation (*tasattur wa-taqiyya*) were necessary."[53] Hence, their permanent, or *mustaqarr*, successor is hidden by a trustee (*mustawdaʿ*) Imam, who conceals his master, generally his own brother.[54] The status of the *mustaqarr* Imams would have been a highly guarded secret during their own lifetimes. That an Imam was acting as a regent for the true (*mustaqarr*) Imam would be a matter known only to the highest dignitaries of the daʿwa. In this context, Tusi quotes the words of an Imam, saying, "Our affair is one hardship after another, one mystery after another, one ordeal after another. No one can bear it except an angel close (to God), a Prophet sent as a messenger, or a believer whose heart God has tested with faith."[55] This is the reason common believers would not have been privy to information that could have put the community at risk. In fact, *The Paradise of Submission* lambasts those followers who "were foolishly indiscreet, and began to point out, identify and venerate the real (*mustaqarr*) Imam, without his consent and permission."[56] Such actions would have been extremely dangerous to the *mustaqarr* Imam. As the text notes, it would have been a heinous crime for them to reveal the true Imam's identity or in any way jeopardize his safety. The anonymous *mathnawi* cited earlier states that the four Imams succeeding ʿAla' al-Din Muhammad, i.e., Rukn al-Din Khwurshah, Shams al-Din Muhammad, Mu'minshah, and Qasimshah I, were all in concealment (*satr*), thus alluding to the precarious situation.

In the case of the Imam Mu'minshah, it would appear that it was Pir Shihab al-Din Shah (d. 1302/1884), who predeceased his father, the Imam Agha ʿAlishah, by a few months, who first omitted his name from the register of the Imams in his *Book of Supreme Admonitions* (*Kitāb-i Khiṭābāt-i ʿĀliya*). Khojki manuscript number 22 in the Harvard University collection contains a register of the Imams transcribed during the imamate of Khalil Allah b. Abi al-Hasan ʿAli (r. 1792–1817), which includes Mu'minshah's name between Shams al-Din Muhammad and Qasimshah;[57] whereas manuscript number 19 of the same collection, which contains a register that apparently dates to immediately after the death of the Imam Agha ʿAlishah, omits the name.[58]

Murder Most Foul

That the Imams in this period were in real danger is confirmed in an ode (*qaṣīda*) of a certain Daʿi Anjudani, who informs us that the Imam Qasimshah (and here his reference is to the first Qasimshah) was murdered. It appears from these verses that there were numerous attempts to have him poisoned, one of which finally succeeded. Unfortunately, this poet provides us no further details regarding the perpetrators of the crime, nor any information about their identities, referring to them simply as "his enviers, worthy of hellfire" and "the accursed."[59] One late manuscript of the poem does furnish us with the date of the tragedy, 770/1368.[60] This line, however, is not present in the sixteenth-century manuscript of the *qasida* available to me. Moreover, it is metrically deficient. Both of these details strongly suggest that the verse is spurious. Nevertheless, the fact that the line may be inauthentic does not necessarily mean that the date is incorrect. Actually, it is very close to the date provided in a different calendar system in the published version of *The Offspring of the Tales of Truth* and the *Ismaili Mirror*, 1426 VS/771 AH/1370 CE.[61]

The murder of Qasimshah is also alluded to in the work *Seven Aphorisms* (*Haft Nukta*), which is associated with one of the Imams by the name Islamshah, perhaps the first. While not explicit, this work is highly suggestive that the murderer was from the Muhammadshahi line, which, however, is never mentioned. Nevertheless, it is very clear that a family member was involved:

> There is a physical and spiritual pharaoh in the cycle of every Imam. By means of the power and influence of his defiled soul he leads astray the simple-minded servants who are not yet firm-footed on the way of the bearer of truth, diverting them from the path of the most sublime paradise and supreme heaven to the nethermost hell, which is the land of the hypocrites (*munāfiqān*). This is what happened in the time of the lord of the age and caliph of the Merciful, ʿAla' al-Haqq wa-al-Dunya wa-al-Din, Khudawand Qasimshah the first,[62] on whose mention be prostration, peace and glorification. A group of the accursed[63] who, on the face of things, were among his family members, led several servants in every region, who were soldiers, on the path to hell. Previously, the people of Badakhshan, the fortress of Zafar, the realm of Egypt and Narjawan and

> other places followed the true summons, but at the instigation of that faction they have been drowned in the ocean of iniquity. Now, the foremost duty for the muʿallims (teachers) of the present time is to make every possible human effort to guide them according to the decree.
>
> One of the lords of decree has proclaimed a mystery regarding this matter. "If, for example, a community were to live in a mouse hole, it behooves the daʿis and teachers to seek it out and summon its people to the right path." Those who previously followed the true summons must already know that the words of the community of the wicked, which is opposed to the path of God, have veiled their guide. Clearly, the proofs of recognition of the truth must be made known quickly, and there is no demonstration more evident and manifest than their own meaningless claim. What beauty or intellect could consider reasonable the imamate of someone who was so immersed and seduced by status in this world that from the height of envy and jealousy, by deadly poison he made sweet life bitter on the palate of his brother and gave his paternal cousin[64] a drink of diamond, cutting off his hope for life? In short, the teachers of Badakhshan and in the other aforementioned places must make great efforts, especially in areas where the dervishes are virtuous.[65]

This passage, while itself not entirely transparent, is the clearest statement available from an accessible Qasimshahi source that seems to allude to a second claimant to the imamate in the time of one of the Imams named Qasimshah, presumably the first Qasimshah.[66] This rival apparently poisoned two individuals, his brother and his paternal cousin. The evidence suggests that the culprit may have been Muhammadshah b. ʿAlaʾ al-Din Muʾminshah, whose brother, Qasimshah, and paternal cousin, Nizarshah, who was also known as Qasimshah, may have been the two victims. This would further substantiate the theory expressed above that these are the two of the three known persons named Qasimshah in the family who were considered Imams, the first being a *mustawdaʿ* Imam and the second being a *mustaqarr* Imam. The eighteenth-century family tree mentioned earlier indicates that an Imam by the name of Qasimshah lived and was buried in Azerbaijan.[67]

QASIM TUSHTARI (OR TURSHIZI)

An Ismaili luminary and poet by the name of Qasim Tushtari (or Turshizi) may have flourished at about this time. In his *Ismaili Literature*, Ivanow tentatively makes him a contemporary of Raʾis Hasan, placing him in the first half of the

7th/13th century. He notes that "very short quotations of his poetry appear in early Nizari works" which, unfortunately, he does not identify.[68] Ivanow's periodization is not far from the mark. A newly discovered prose work of this figure, untitled but on the subject "Recognition of the Creator," suggests that he may have lived in the generation immediately succeeding Nizari.[69] In one of the manuscripts he is identified as Khwaja Qasim Turshizi rather than as Tushtari, Turshiz being a town in Khurasan.[70] That we are dealing with the same individual is clear from the appearance of the same work in a second manuscript, this time attributed to Qasim Tushtari.[71] The Nizaris had a number of castles in the Turshiz district, most notably the fortresses of Barda Rud, Mikal, Mujahidabad, and Atishgah.[72] It is therefore likely that remnants of the community had survived in the area. While Turshiz itself had been devastated, Hamd Allah Mustawfi notes that in this period the nearby villages had "lands producing excellent crops. Corn is in plenty, good fruit is abundant—such as grapes, figs and pomegranates—and silk is also produced. Thus they have crops of all kinds. . . . The city of Turshiz is itself now in ruin, but the lands round are extremely well cultivated."[73]

Meanwhile, Tushtar (also known as Shushtar and Shustar, among other variants) was, along with Ahwaz, one of the two main towns of Khuzistan. It is possible that there were Ismailis in Khuzistan at this time, as we are aware of their prior residence in this region.[74] In the present state of our knowledge it is difficult to determine whether this Qasim hailed from Turshiz or Tushtar, or perhaps that his ancestral home was one and his place of residence the other.

Several figures are mentioned in the tract, a few of whom are identifiable, thus helping us suggest a date for the author. These include the poet Sana'i (d. ca. 535/1140),[75] a certain poet by the name of Fakhr al-Din Muhammad, Hakim Nizari (d. ca. 1320), and a certain Sharaf al-Din Muhammad.

Our dating is based on the quotation of a couplet by Hakim Nizari Quhistani in the text. Unfortunately, this couplet ends with the letter *ha'*, while the only volume of Nizari's edited poetry available to me breaks at the letter *lam*.[76] It is thus not easy to confirm that the verse appears in Nizari's known oeuvre. Moreover, in one manuscript[77] the name of the poet appears as Hakim Nizari, while in another[78] it appears simply as Hakim, further complicating the issue. If the verse is not Nizari Quhistani's, Qasim Tushtari may have lived earlier than we have placed him.

The poet by the name of Fakhr al-Din Muhammad is difficult to identify with any degree of certainty. However, while in Tabriz, the city of Imam Shams al-Din Muhammad, Nizari Quhistani had met an individual whom he identifies as Khwaja Fakhr al-Din.[79] Jamal suggests that this may have been a high-ranking Ismaili da'i. While it is possible that this Khwaja Fakhr al-Din of Tabriz is the same as the poet Fakhr al-Din Muhammad mentioned by Qasim Tushtari, nothing conclusive can be said on the issue.

The case of the last individual mentioned, Sharaf al-Din Muhammad, is very intriguing. Qasim Tushtari has the greatest respect for this figure, whom he identifies as a high-ranking member of the daʿwa, the upright teacher (*muʿallim-i ṣādiq*) "by whom I mean the glory of the verifiers of truth (*muḥaqqiq*), leader of the people of certainty, guide on the path of certainty, who was chosen by the lord of the worlds."[80] Had it not been for the reference to the later figure of Nizari, it would have been tempting to identify this individual as the learned son of Ra'is Muzaffar, who succeeded him at the fort of Girdkuh and who was named Sharaf al-Din Muhammad. Ra'is Muzaffar was well connected with the Saljuq officers of Isfahan and had secretly accepted Ismailism at the hand of the famous daʿi ʿAbd al-Malik b. ʿAttash himself.[81] However, it is clear from Qasim Tushtari's description that Sharaf al-Din Muhammad was alive at the time of his writing and so could not have been this 5th–6th/11th–12th century figure. If our dating of Tushtari is correct, his remarks about Sharaf al-Din's involvement in the daʿwa as well as his own writings are strong testimony for the continuation of a formal network of Ismaili dignitaries at this time. The primary purpose of this network, spread throughout the Ismaili world, was to lead the believers on the path of knowledge. At the same time, it was this very system that kept the cells of the community, scattered in often hostile surroundings, connected with one another and ultimately with the Imam.

The work itself, untitled but on recognition of the Creator, addresses the believers in the following words:

> May the congregation of mustajibs (respondents to the Ismaili daʿwa), seekers on the path of certainty and friends of the noble and pure family [of the Prophet]—*may God improve their conditions*—know that in the opinion of the possessors of insight and the companions of belief, it is as clear as the sun that the decrees of the speakers (*nāṭiqān*) of the divine laws and the proofs (*ḥujjatān*) of the divine realities—upon whom be peace—in every age and epoch were and will be this: The purpose of the creation of the 18 000 worlds is the composition of man's existence. The goal of human existence is to attain recognition of the Exalted God so that the spiritual meaning of, "We have favored the children of Adam" (17:70) may pass in human beings from potentiality to actuality.[82]

The motif here echoes that evoked by the inscriptions on the Fatimid coins that were discussed at the beginning of this chapter. The entire purpose of creation is the existence of humankind, but such existence is meaningless unless human beings attain recognition of the exalted God. Of all creatures, it is only the lot of human beings to be able to seek gnosis of the Creator. This is the reason the Quran states, "We have favored the children of Adam" (17:70). But so long as they do not seek

God, they are no different from other animals; as the text states, quoting the Quran: "They are like cattle—nay! Even more astray" (7:179). This was one of the favorite Quranic verses quoted by Ismaili authors. In his *Gift for the Readers* (*Tuḥfat al-Nāẓirīn*), also known as *Thirty-six Epistles* (*Sī wa-Shish Ṣaḥīfa*), the fifteenth-century writer of Badakhshan, Sayyid Suhrab Wali, for example, quotes this verse in alluding to "those who have fallen from the rank of humanity, remaining with but the apparent meaning (*ẓāhir*) of the words of their prophets and daʿis and, in the manner of livestock, are satisfied with straw and grass, never reaching the seeds of grain."[83] Hence, there must always be a people summoning humankind to the truth, led by God's caliph from among the descendants of the Prophet. It is for this reason, Tushtari continues, that when questioned about the recognition of God, the Imam Zayn al-ʿAbidin replied that this was only possible through a recognition of the Imam of the time. After fashioning the heavens and the earth, hadn't God announced to the angels the perfection of his creation with the words "Indeed, I am placing a caliph on the earth" (2:30)? Tushtari advises us that knowledge of God's caliph, the Imam of the time, is gained through the upright teachers, who are the members of the daʿwa hierarchy. "That which reaches the hujjat from the light of the Imam of the time is conveyed to the daʿi. By the command of the hujjat the daʿi conveys this to the licentiates of every 'island' (*jazīra*) or region of Ismaili activity according to their level." This Ismaili network held the community together and kept isolated cells in communication with one another. Its purpose, however, was conceived in more lofty terms. By means of the daʿwa, Tushtari informs us, those who seek recognition of God are raised by degrees and are brought from potentiality to actuality. The existence of this summons to the truth, and ultimately of its head, the Imam of the time, was to lead people on the path of God's recognition, "that they may become gnostics (*ʿārifīn*)."[84]

FIVE

Possessors of the Command

The meaning of the Book of God
is not the text, it is the man who guides.
He is the Book of God, he is its verses,
he is scripture.

Shams-i Tabrizi in *Conversations*

THE COMMAND AND THE COMMANDER

In his *Book of Assemblies and Travels* (*Kitāb al-Majālis wa-al-Musāyarāt*), the tenth-century jurist, al-Qadi al-Nuʿman, recounts an illuminating episode from the life of the Fatimid Imam-Caliph al-Muʿizz. One day, al-Muʿizz was searching for a book in the palace library. In its time, this was possibly the largest trove of literature anywhere on earth. The Twelver Shiʿi chronicler Ibn Abi Tayyiʾ had described it as a "wonder of the world."[1] When the librarian came back empty-handed, al-Muʿizz decided to take a look for himself, though it was already past nightfall. He set himself in front of one of the cabinets, where he thought the book may be, and pulled a volume off the shelf. As he leafed through it, he became fascinated by certain passages and began to read more closely. Before he knew it, he was reaching for another volume, and then another, and another. In the Imam's own words, "I completely forgot why I was there and didn't even think of sitting down. It wasn't until I felt a shooting pain in my legs from standing so long that I even realized where I was!"[2]

Book enthusiasts will immediately identify with the Fatimid sovereign's absorption in his reading till the wee hours of the morning. The enchantment of the written word transcends boundaries of space and time. The Fatimids and their successors at Alamut were great lovers and patrons of books, and their vast libraries attracted scholars of every creed from far and wide. The Imam al-Hakim even provided ink, pens, paper, and inkstands free of charge for all who sought learning in the "House of Knowledge" (*dār al-ʿilm*).[3]

We can only imagine the horror the Ismailis would have felt when they witnessed the destruction of the literary legacy they had so painstakingly fostered. al-Maqrizi (d. 845/1442) describes how great hills of ashes were formed when the slaves and maids of the Luwata Berber tribe burned the Fatimid books. As an act of further desecration, they used the precious bindings of the volumes to make sandals for their feet.[4] Similarly, Juwayni exults at torching the Ismaili library of Alamut, "the fame of which," he adds, "had spread throughout the world."[5] It ranks among history's great ironies that one of the world's oldest manuscripts of Juwayni's own *History of the World Conqueror* is today carefully preserved at the library of the Institute of Ismaili Studies, an organization established by the Ismaili Imam in 1977.

The destruction of the Alamut library was not the first time books had been the victims of a conqueror, nor would it be the last. In 1562, as Spanish troops entered Mexico, a Franciscan friar decreed that thousands of volumes containing Mayan hieroglyphics should be burned. The obliteration of this store of local spiritual beliefs was to pave the way for the spread of Christianity. In a single afternoon, the recorded memory of an entire civilization was turned to ashes; it is believed that only four codices ever survived. The Belgian city of Louvain was the site of another such travesty. When the German army invaded in 1914, in a senseless act of wanton destruction with no military significance whatsoever, the city's splendid library, containing 300,000 volumes, including close to a thousand irreplaceable illuminated manuscripts, was set ablaze.[6] Invaders throughout history have not been content with massacring their foes, but have often sought to destroy every possible trace of a people's recorded memory. Such was the fate of the vast Ismaili libraries. George Orwell, with his penetrating insight, identified well the motivation of conquerors in his celebrated novel *Nineteen Eighty-four*. Describing the situation of his main character, Winston Smith, who worked for the Ministry of Truth, the government agency responsible for putting forth the version of history approved by those in power, Orwell writes:

> The Party said that Oceania had never been in alliance with Eurasia. He, Winston Smith, knew that Oceania had been in alliance with Eurasia as short a time as four years ago. But where did that knowledge exist? Only in his own consciousness, which in any case must soon be annihilated. And if all others accepted the lie which the Party imposed—if all

records told the same tale—then the lie passed into history and became truth. "Who controls the past," ran the Party slogan, "controls the future: who controls the present controls the past."[7]

Seeing the accumulated knowledge of generations go up in flames would have been heartrending for the Ismaili community, passionate as it was about its books. But *The Voyage* (*Sayr wa-Sulūk*), a spiritual autobiography of Nasir al-Din Tusi, one of Islam's greatest luminaries, in which he recounts how he became an Ismaili, sheds light on why the literary devastation, in itself, could not have crushed the community's spirit. One of only a handful of Ismaili texts to survive Juwayni's torch, this work informs us that Ismailism, for all its love of books, gave primacy not to the recorded word, but to the living Word. It is not simply to the command (*farmān*) that the hearts of the believers should be attached, but to the one who issues the command (*farmān-dih*).[8] The Commander is the Prophet in his age and the Imam in his own time. Hence, Muslims are divided into two groups—those who hold solely to the command, and those who hold fast to the Commander. "By this distinction the hypocrites are distinguished from the faithful, the people of external forms from those of inner meaning, the partisans of the law from those of the resurrection, and the adherents of multiplicity from those of divine unity."[9] Echoing this identical sentiment, Shams-i Tabrizi, the master of the great mystic Jalal al-Din Rumi, asserted that it is a person, and not a bound volume, that liberates the believer: "The meaning of the Book of God is not the text, it is the man who guides. He is the Book of God, he is its verses, he is scripture."[10]

The Shiʿa had always laid particular emphasis on the Quranic injunction to "obey God and obey the Messenger and the Possessors of the Command" (4:59). An old command may be superseded by a new command, and at that point to hold to the old command is to stray into error. However, those who held fast to the Commander could never be led astray, for he is the ever-present, ever-living Word of God.[11] The Possessors of the Command succeed one another in a never-ending chain, until the Day of Judgment.[12] It was therefore imperative that the Imam Rukn al-Din Khwurshah shield his offspring from the Mongols, and so, Ismaili tradition informs us, his son Shams al-Din Muhammad, the next "Possessor of the Command," was taken to safety in Azerbaijan. It was not without reason that the coin described in the last chapter identified the Imam as the Commander of the Faithful (*amīr al-muʾminīn*). This, in itself, was a declaration that the descendants of the Prophet were the rightful Possessors of the Command (*amr*). This chapter is a study of the lives of two of the Possessors of the Command, the successors of the Imam Qasimshah, known as Islamshah and Muhammad b. Islamshah. It also includes an examination of the situation of the non-Iranian Ismaili communities in this period and a comparison of the modes of taqiyya in Quhistan and Syria.

THE IMAMS ISLAMSHAH B. QASIMSHAH AND MUHAMMAD B. ISLAMSHAH

The sources record that the two Imams following Qasimshah were both named Islamshah (or Salamshah or ʿAbd al-Salamshah), the first being identified as Ahmad, and the second as Muhammad or Malik al-Salam.[13] The variations on the name Islamshah were common. In sixteenth-century South Asia, for example, the son and successor of Sultan Shershah Suri was known as both Islamshah and Salimshah.[14] An uncorroborated reference in Chunara's *Manifest Light* suggests that the mother of the first Islamshah was named Khalifa Bibi.[15] It is difficult to distinguish the biographies of these two Imams from each other because of the repetition of their name, a difficulty compounded by the fact that another Imam, within two generations, also had a similar name. The two are therefore considered together here.

At the beginning of the imamate of Islamshah b. Qasimshah, the whole of Daylam had already come under the Ismaili rule of Kiya Sayf al-Din Kushayji, who did not proclaim his religious identity openly until provoked. The details of his struggles against his Zaydi rivals, along with those of Khudawand Muhammad, who may perhaps have been the same individual as Islamshah, were addressed in chapter 2.

The anonymous *Epistle of the Right Path* (*Risāla-yi Ṣirāṭ al-Mustaqīm*) credits the Imam ʿAbd al-Salam with a work entitled *The Epistle of Sorrow* (*Risālat al-Ḥuzn*).[16] If the dating of the *Epistle of the Right Path* to the 8th or 9th/14th or 15th century is correct, the text is presumably by one of the two Imams succeeding Qasimshah. I have been unable to discover any manuscript containing this work in its entirety, and it is possible that it has been lost. However, the *Epistle of the Right Path* does preserve a short quotation from it:

> The first thing that the Exalted God brought forth was the Command. As a result of the Command, the Universal Intellect was produced. The Universal Soul was produced as a result of the Universal Intellect and the hyle, the heavens, the four natures, minerals, plants and animals were produced as a result of the Universal Soul. In reality, the purpose of creating these substances is humankind's existence. Then, the issuance of the existents from the Exalted God, who is the first origin, is through the mediation of something which, in the parlance of this community, is called his Command or his Word, may he be exalted. Thus, the first cause is the Command and the first effect is the Universal Intellect, for the Exalted God is pure from being a cause or an effect.[17]

We thus see a reaffirmation in this period of the Ismaili belief in the utter and complete transcendence of God, creation itself being predicated from his Command, the *amr*, rather than from God *qua* God, for Ismaili belief asserts that God is beyond all causation. As in the treatise of Qasim Tushtari, here the existence of humankind is again portrayed as the very purpose of the entire creation, which exists solely so that human beings may come to recognize the Creator.

One of the texts attributed to an Imam by the name of Islamshah is *Seven Aphorisms* (*Haft Nukta*), quoted earlier with reference to the murder of the Imam Qasimshah. While the text itself contains no explicit indication of authorship, the compiler of the volume in which it appears, Haji Qudrat Allah Beg, attributes it to "Mawlana Islamshah."[18] Its ascription to an Imam is also suggested by an introduction to the work that appears in Persian manuscript 43 at the Institute of Ismaili Studies. This preamble refers to the work as "the noble words" (*kalām-i sharīf*), an epithet that one would scarcely expect to be used of an author of little consequence.[19] It further prevails upon the believers to carry the spiritual message of the aphorisms in their hearts and not to divulge their contents to the uninitiated. We can therefore provisionally accept the attribution to the Imam Islamshah. The vividness of the description of the Imam Qasimshah's murder allows us to cautiously posit that the event had occurred recently. This suggests that the author was the first of the three Imams named Islamshah.

Seven Aphorisms is largely didactic in tone, exhorting the believers to submit every aspect of their existence to the service of the Imam and constantly to strive to be virtuous. The daʿis and muʿallims (teachers) are instructed to provide guidance to the initiates, never withholding their knowledge from those who sincerely seek it. Their duty is to save the disciples "from the waves of the ocean of error and ignorance by the ark of gnosis of the Imam of the time." The believers must also faithfully submit their religious dues and be prepared to obey the Imam in all circumstances. While the way of the people of the religious law (*sharīʿa*) is deemed to be simple and straightforward, the way of the people of truth (*ḥaqīqa*) is intricate and subtle, like the web of a spider. In order to negotiate the spider's web, one must become delicate and meek like a spider.

A Call for Unity

In guidance that must have been essential for the survival of the small community, the author of *Seven Aphorisms* admonishes the Ismailis to live in harmony with one another, and not to be at one another's throats like the followers of other communities who fight over the world's worthless trappings:

> If the people of this community sow or harbor the seeds of envy, rancor and enmity for the sake of the world, just as others do, they are not worthy of being the disciples of Mawlana. They will despair of the hope of salvation in the next world, as in the dictum *humiliation in the world and punishment in the hereafter,*[20] and will not be among the companions of the bench of purity.[21] . . . A community that is and will be on a single path must be united in blood and veins, body and spirit. If such is not the case, their names shall not be inscribed in the volume of the lord of the resurrection. The disputes of worldly people are because of the greed for the world, wealth and fame. It is of paramount importance that the members of this community not show greed for the world nor sacrifice their noble spirits and precious lives for a much fought over corpse:
>
>> This world is like a corpse. Circling it are thousands upon thousands of vultures. One scratches the other with his talons, the other pecks the first with his beak. At the end of the matter all of them will die. Naught will remain save this corpse[22]

Indeed, Ismaili works depicted those who did not follow the Prophets and Imams as the people of discord (*ahl-i taḍādd*), for they were constantly bickering among themselves, not only about the material world, but especially on the subject of the Creator. In the Chapter of the Angels, also known as the Chapter of the Creator, the Quran speaks of three categories of humankind: "And among them are those who wrong their own souls, and among them are those who strive, and among them are those who lead the way in goodness" (35:32).[23] Sayyid Suhrab Wali Badakhshani states that this refers first to the people of discord, who wrong their own souls, then to the people of ranks (*ahl-i tarattub*), who have entered the daʿwa and seek to mount the ever-ascending degrees of gnosis—"For them are grand chambers above which are grand chambers" (39:20)—and finally to the people of unity (*ahl-i waḥdat*), "who lead the way in goodness," as they are those who have lost their own individuality through cognizance of the divine unity.[24] Bu Ishaq Quhistani laments the plight of the people of discord, for they see themselves at the center of existence, and not God. They must seek to follow the Prophets and the Imams, thus entering among the people of ranks, the members of the daʿwa. However, even the members of the lower ranks of the daʿwa see both themselves and God, which is like polytheism (*shirk*). They too must endeavor to traverse the ranks of spiritual understanding so that they may enter among the people of unity

> who see naught but God in everything. They have so immersed themselves and their knowledge of self in the divinity of God that they see nothing but God, know nothing but God and know that they are nothing

without God. This is the realm of unity and truth, and the world of God and divinity.[25]

Echoing the sentiment in *Seven Aphorisms*, Bu Ishaq informs us of how the believers must conduct themselves with one another:

> Each one should care more for his companion than himself and endeavor with might and main for the sake of his comrade, keeping nothing from him. In every matter, he must consider expenditure for him like expenditure for his very self—this is the law (*sharīʿa*) of this community—for the reality is that the (followers of this community) see nothing save our lord (*Mawlānā*), may his mention be exalted, and consider everything—self, friend, all that exists—to be for the sake of our lord.[26]

Such sentiments are found repeatedly in Ismaili works purporting to date from this period. In a Ginan of Pir Sadr al-Din, we read: "With humility and forbearance, gather together O chivalrous ones. Laughing and smiling, forsake both anger and ire."[27]

The Ismailis of Arab Lands

One of the most startling revelations in *Seven Aphorisms* is the mention of Nizari Ismailis living in Egypt. It had hitherto been assumed that this branch of the Ismailis had eventually died out in that land after the takeover of the Mustaʿlians. The continued survival of the Egyptian Nizaris is also testified to in *Pearl Scattering Words* (*Alfāẓ-i Guharbār*) cited earlier. The Damascene geographer, Shams al-Din Abu ʿAbd Allah Muhammad, writing in about 723/1324, records the precious detail that Ismailism survived in the village of Usfun in Egypt, though he gives no information about which division of the community this was.[28] Al-Maqrizi (d. 845/1442), the famous Egyptian historian, also mentions the presence of a Persian (and hence almost certainly Nizari) Ismaili doing business with the upper classes in Cairo during his own lifetime.[29]

Some Syrian Ismaili authors contemporary with the Imam Islamshah also draw our attention. The first, a certain Nur al-Din Ahmad (or Nur al-Din b. Ahmad) (d. 849/1445), wrote several books.[30] Among these, his *Missives and Reports* (*Fuṣūl wa-Akhbār*), a massive work of almost nine hundred pages, is of particular interest, as it is said to deal with the history of the Syrian Ismailis. Unfortunately, no critical edition exists, nor are there any manuscript copies of it in accessible institutional collections. Three Syrian scholars, however, apparently had copies available to them.[31] The second author, named Muhammad b. Saʿd (or Ahmad)

b. Da'ud al-Rafna, was born in 789/1387 in Rafaniyya, a town in the district of Hims. He visited the Imam Islamshah in Iran and died in Masyaf in the year 859/1455. One of his works, *The Sufficient Epistle* (*Risālat al-Kāfiyya*), has been edited,[32] but two of his other known works, both of which hold promise of containing historical information, are not readily available.[33] We know precious little about two other authors who flourished sometime in the 9th/15th century, the first named Muhammad Abu al-Makarim who wrote *Lanterns of Guidance* (*Maṣābīḥ al-Hidāya*) and a book (which occupies some three hundred pages in manuscript) entitled *The Law* (*al-Qānūn*), and a second author named Abu al-Maʿali Hatim b. ʿImran who wrote *Decrees and Intervals* (*al-Aḥkām wa-al-Fatarāt*) and *The Origin and the Return* (*al-Mabdaʾ wa-al-Maʿād*).[34]

Expansion of the Daʿwa

A reference to the Nizari Imams of this time unexpectedly turns up in a contemporary account of Idris ʿImad al-Din (r. 832–872/1428–1468), the chief daʿi (*al-dāʿī al-muṭlaq*) of the Tayyibi community, a branch of the Mustaʿlians that had parted ways with the Nizaris after the death of the Fatimid caliph al-Mustansir bi'llah in 487/1094. In the seventh volume of his monumental history, *The Fountains of Histories* (*ʿUyūn al-Akhbār*), Idris records that he was writing in the fortress of Shibam in 839/1435 when he was approached by a man from Samarqand in Persian Iraq. This individual met the senior-most leaders of the community in Yemen and invited them to the rightful Imam whom he named and whose ancestry he recited going back to Nizar b. al-Mustansir bi'llah. He further mentioned that this Imam and his followers were resident in Samarqand and that the disciples continued to submit their religious dues to him.[35] The more famous Central Asian Samarqand, which had been devastated by the forces of Genghis Khan in the thirteenth century, was given new life when Tamerlane chose it as his capital in the late fourteenth century. It later fell under the sway of Tamerlane's son, Shahrukh (d. 850/1447). Shahrukh's son, Ulugh Beg (d. 853/1449), governed from that city.[36]

The brief but important notice in *The Fountains of Histories* is noteworthy in that it suggests (assuming we have an accurate date for Islamshah's death) that during the time of Muhammad b. Islamshah, despite strict dissimulation, the Nizaris were actually proselytizing among their sister communities. Unfortunately, it is impossible to know from this information whether the anonymous emissary represented the Qasimshahi or the Muhammadshahi line, if indeed there were two lines claiming the imamate. The existence of a dynamic Qasimshahi daʿwa at this time is supported by the remarkable daʿwa activities in the Indian subcontinent contemporary with these events. In chapters 2 and 3, the endeavors of Pir Nasir al-Din, Pir Shihab al-Din, and Pir Sadr al-Din in South Asia were alluded to, the latter two being contemporaries of the Imam Islamshah. Both of them mention his residence as Alamut. The family of pirs claimed descent from Ismaʿil b. Jaʿfar, but through a line different from that of the Imams, and provided the most gifted and dedicated exponents of Ismailism in South Asia. The leaders of the community seem to have continuously been appointed from their ranks. Their activities are alluded to in a contemporary Iranian source, the anonymous treatise entitled *Epistle of the Right Path.* Describing how the Imams from ʿAli through Ismaʿil were manifest (*ẓāhir*) while those from Ismaʿil through Mahdi were concealed (*mastūr*), it continues:

> Mawlana Ismaʿil manifested in the cities of Uch and Multan, leaving indications among the people of India and displaying marvels. A community from among that Imam's descendants still remains in that realm, and by means of those indications those people will never entertain doubts.[37]

This startling passage suggests that the Imam Ismaʿil had traveled to the Indian subcontinent. The testimony is supplemented by some unexpected sources. Juwayni himself remarks that Muhammad b. Ismaʿil fled to Sindh with his sons,[38] and Rashid al-Din tells us that Muhammad b. Ismaʿil's sons, who were in concealment, spread out into Sindh.[39] Clearly, in the time of Juwayni and Rashid al-Din, it was believed that very early on, the Ismaili Imams had made inroads into South Asia. This is further substantiated by *The Canon of the Astrologers* (*Dustūr al-Munajjimīn*), which mentions that Muhammad b. Ismaʿil found refuge in India.[40] The sole surviving manuscript of this work, anonymous but apparently from the pen of a Nizari Ismaili daʿi writing at the end of the eleventh century, is now preserved at the Bibliothèque Nationale in Paris. Both P. Casanova and M. Qazwini were of the opinion that this manuscript was once actually part of the collection of the famous library of Alamut.[41] The genealogy and various family trees (*shajara*) of the leaders of the Ismaili community in South Asia, traced to Ismaʿil b. Jaʿfar, are readily found in Indic Ismaili manuscripts as well as in manuscripts in the possession of the keepers of the shrines of these saints.[42]

Immediately upon establishing a base in Yemen in 270/883, the Ismaili daʿi Ibn Hawshab dispatched his nephew, al-Haytham, to spread Ismailism in Sindh.[43] Active Fatimid propagation activities in South Asia are confirmed by the earliest known work that identifies the twelve "islands" (*jazāʾir*) in which the daʿwa operated. Among them are included both Hind and Sindh.[44] In 346/957, al-Qadi al-Nuʿman wrote that the daʿwa was doing well in Sindh.[45] He further tells us in his *Book of Assemblies and Travels* about an anonymous daʿi in Sindh who operated in the middle of the tenth century and converted a large group of unbelievers as well as a Muslim prince in the region, thus establishing an Ismaili vassal state.

However, the daʿi's unconventional beliefs provoked controversy at the Fatimid headquarters.[46] In 345/965, this daʿi died in a riding accident and was replaced by Halam b. Shayban,[47] who conquered Multan in the name of the Imam.[48] Visiting Sindh in 375/985, al-Maqdisi noted that the city was Shiʿi and wrote, "In Multan the Friday sermon (*khuṭba*) is in the name of the Fatimid and all decisions are taken according to his commands. Their envoys and presents go regularly to Egypt. He (the ruler of Sind) is a powerful and just ruler."[49]

This state of affairs did not last long. Attacks by the Ghaznawids left the Ismailis of Multan vulnerable on their western flank. In 396/1005, the famous Mahmud of Ghazna invaded Multan, returning again a few years later to finish the job, and massacring the Ismaili inhabitants.[50] Hamdani suggests that after this disastrous setback, the Ismailis took refuge in Mansura, where the Habbarid Arab ruler, perhaps named Khafif, may have accepted the Fatimid daʿwa.[51] In any case, in 416/1025, Mansura also fell to the Ghaznawids. However, the persistence of the daʿwa is remarkable. Only two years after the Multan massacre, the Fatimid Imam-Caliph al-Hakim sent an envoy to Mahmud of Ghazna in an attempt to gain his allegiance.[52] Stern asserts that Mahmud's purges eliminated Ismailism from the area and hence "the later phases of the history of Ismailism in Sind and in India stand in no direct connection with this first successful attempt to establish territorial rule in Sind."[53] It is clear that Stern was mistaken. We see continued evidence of Ismaili activity in the period immediately following these setbacks. The Ghaznawids, apprehensive about the resurgence of Ismailism in Sindh and other eastern territories under their dominion, tried and executed Mahmud's vizier Hasanak in 423/1032 because he had accepted a cloak from the Fatimid Imam-Caliph al-Zahir and was suspected of adhering to the Ismaili doctrine. His was no ordinary execution. He was strangled, his head was mockingly given to his adversary, the finance minister Sawsani, and his corpse was tied to a pillory for seven years.[54] In 425/1034, the famous Druze leader, al-Muqtanaʿ, attempted to win Shaykh Sumar Rajibal, the chief Fatimid daʿi in India, to the Druze cause.[55] In 443/1051, less than three decades after Mahmud's purges, this same Sumar Rajibal appears to have repossessed the entire region of lower Sindh from the Ghaznawids.[56] Letters dating from 476/1083 and 481/1088 indicate that the Fatimid Ismaili daʿwa continued to operate efficiently in India as the Imam-Caliph al-Mustansir designated new daʿis to the area to replace those who had died.[57]

By the time the Ismaili Imams established themselves at Alamut, the Nizari daʿwa was asserting itself strongly in Multan and other areas. Juzjani notes in his *Nasirid Generations* (*Ṭabaqāt-i Nāṣirī*) that the Ghurid Sultan ʿAlaʾ al-Din (d. 556/1161) welcomed some envoys from Alamut and treated them "with great reverence; and in every place in Ghur they sought, secretly, to make proselytes."[58] This area of proselytization presumably included Sindh, which had been annexed to the Ghurid territories. However, Muhammad Ghiyath al-Din (d. 599/1202), ʿAlaʾ al-Din's successor, reacted violently to the Ismaili presence. Juzjani records:

> In every place wherein the odour of their impure usages was perceived, throughout the territory of Ghur, slaughter of all heretics [Ismailis] was commanded. . . . The area of the country of Ghur, which was a mine of religion and orthodoxy, was purified from the infernal impurity of the Qarmatians [i.e., the Ismailis].[59]

It was at about this time that the Ismailis again lost their power in Multan, for in 570/1175, Sultan Muʿizz al-Din Ghuri "delivered Multan from the hands of the Qarmatians."[60] After these setbacks, the daʿwa in South Asia appears to have gained new life during the imamate of Islamshah. That the Imam laid emphasis on daʿwa activities is testified to by the remarkable statement in the *Seven Aphorisms* quoted earlier: "If, for example, a community were to live in a mouse hole, it behooves the daʿis and muʿallims (teachers) to seek it out and summon its people to the right path." The sixteenth century author Khayrkhwah Harati's quotation of this maxim in his *Epistle* (*Risāla*) also indicates its currency.[61] The earlier activities of the Ismailis in South Asia would have paved the way for the strong assertion of the Indian daʿwa in the time of this Imam. It was already mentioned in chapter 3 that Pir Nasir al-Din and Pir Shihab al-Din conducted their propagation activities in secret and continued to dispatch the religious dues to the Imam in Iran.[62] Immediately after Pir Shihab al-Din, the daʿwa experienced its heyday under the able leadership of the fourteenth-century Pir Sadr al-Din, perhaps the most prolific of the Ismaili authors in the Subcontinent at this time. As Nanji has mentioned, the Ginans are clear that he was in the service of the Imam Islamshah (or Salamshah).[63] It is doubtful that this refers to the thirty-third Imam ʿAbd al-Salamshah who died in about 899/1494[64] as has been suggested by some authors.[65] In all likeliness it refers to the thirtieth Imam, Islamshah b. Qasimshah, who probably lived in the 7th/13th and 8th/14th centuries, and whose period thus overlaps with that ascribed to Pir Sadr al-Din.

The Persian accounts of the life of the Imam Islamshah recorded by Pir Shihab al-Din Shah and Muhammad Taqi b. ʿAli Rida b. Zayn al-ʿAbidin are dominated by narratives of the activities of the charismatic figure of Pir Sadr al-Din, to whom much of the modern Ismaili community in South Asia attributes its existence. He is credited with bestowing on his followers the title of *Khwaja*, as it is pronounced in Sindh, or *Khoja*, as in Gujarat, derived from the Persian honorific used for people of stature or sages of high achievement. In his *Book of Supreme Admonitions*, Pir Shihab al-Din Shah writes:

> O partisans of truth! Know that this path and true religion of ours have been organized and have appeared in splendor in all corners of the world. . . . Among [our notables] was Sayyid Sadr al-Din whose lineage extends to al-Wasi Muhammad, the son of Imam Ismaʿil. . . . Sayyid Sadr

> al-Din lived in Sabzawar among the ranks of the learned. His pure nature inclined him to serve Islamshah so he entered the service of that holy personage. It is from this that the very clay of the being of the *Khwaja* communities became kneaded in the love of his excellency Mawla [ʿAli]. Islamshah appointed him to the summons (daʿwa) and gave him the blessed command (*farmān-i mubārak*) to accomplish the summons.[66]

The Ginans of Pir Sadr al-Din frequently refer to Islamshah as the Imam of the time, though without providing extensive biographical details.[67] Evocative verses such as the following abound:

> Our lord's arrived! ʿAli Salamshah
> Our lord's arrived! Resplendent Salamshah
> Venerate the lord of the age, the resplendent Salamshah
> Venerate the man of the age, ʿAli Salamshah
> The faithful are those who entertain no doubts[68]

The Ginans record that Pir Sadr al-Din was successful in establishing *jamaʿat khanas*, or Ismaili religious centers, in three areas, Sindh, Punjab, and Kashmir.[69] Annemarie Schimmel suggests that since the Ithna ʿasharis did not play a major role in the area, the attacks on the Shiʿa (*rawāfiḍ*) by Firuzshah Tughluq (r. 752–790/1351–1388) in this period were probably directed against the Ismailis.[70] The time of the persecutions certainly follows this upsurge of Ismaili activity.

Taqiyya in Quhistan and Syria

"They must be slain," "attack them and snatch the wealth from their hands," "their property and children are to be distributed as booty," "may Almighty God abase them and curse them!"[71] Jalal-i Qaʾini, writing at the beginning of the fifteenth century, opens his discourse on the Ismailis in this manner, spewing fire and brimstone. His *Counsels to Shahrukh* (*Naṣāʾiḥ-i Shāhrukhī*), one of the most important sources for the Ismailis of Quhistan after the Mongol invasions, is contained in a hitherto unpublished manuscript in the Imperial Library of Vienna.[72] Qaʾini is less concerned with the question of whether the Ismailis should be massacred than with the legal nicety of whether this should be done because they are apostates (*ahl-i riddat*), rebellious (*ahl-i baghy*), or non-Muslims against whom war was required (*ahl-i ḥarb*). An adherent of the Hanafi school of Sunni Islam, he was charged by Sultan Shahrukh with the task of suppressing "heretics" (*bad-madhhabān*), who presumably included not only the Shiʿa, but perhaps even non-Hanafi Sunnis.[73]

He quotes approvingly from the most famous work of the jurist al-Qadi al-ʿAdud al-Iji (d. 756/1355), *The Way-Stations* (*al-Mawāqif*), which accuses the Ismailis of everything from wearing red clothes and considering what is prohibited as lawful, to being Magians (*majūs*) in disguise. Even this, Qa'ini fulminates, "is but a whiff of what has been written about the depravity of that community, may God curse them!"[74] One of the most frightening aspects of his tirade is its vilification of those in his own religious community who wished to live in peace with the Ismailis. He threatens the lives of these moderates with the same dire fate as those whom he deemed heretics. In this respect, history very much repeats itself. Hodgson remarks that during Alamut times most of the Sunnis lived on relatively good terms with the Shiʿi Ismailis among them, until "a mob or a ruler would set the goal of destroying all Ismailis at once."[75] When Muhammad Tapar (d. 511/1118), the great Saljuq Sultan, personally led a campaign against the Ismaili community of Shahdiz at Isfahan, the Ismailis argued that they differed little from their Sunni neighbors except in the matter of the imamate. The sultan therefore had no cause to attack them so long as they accepted him as their political leader, which they were willing to do. Apparently the Ismailis had many Sunni friends in the Saljuq army who argued their cause and delayed engagement of the battle, but certain elements among the religious authorities urged it on. Even among the clerics there were differences of opinion but the extremists finally managed to silence the moderates, the Ismailis were assaulted, and the community suffered terrible losses. Their leader Ahmad b. ʿAttash was ignominiously paraded through the streets of Isfahan before being skinned alive.[76] Centuries later, Qa'ini tells us that the last of the great Ilkhanids, Abu Saʿid Bahadur Khan (d. 735/1335), was greatly concerned that much of Quhistan remained dedicated to the tenets of Ismailism. This is certainly a possibility. Just decades earlier, recalling the ubiquity of the Ismailis in the area, Juzjani opprobriously dubbed the province "Heretic-istan" (*Mulḥidistān*).[77] At the instigation of Shah ʿAli Sijistani, the lieutenant of Quhistan, the Ilkhanid ruler sent a mission to the area to effect a mass conversion to Sunnism in 718/1324. At the head of the mission was Qa'ini's grandfather, a certain Shaykh ʿImad al-Din Bukhari, a distinguished jurist and old friend of Sijistani, who had fled to Quhistan from Bukhara when the latter city was destroyed. ʿImad al-Din was accompanied by his two sons, Husam al-Din and Najm al-Din Muhammad. The details of this expedition were related to the author by his father, Najm al-Din, whose presence on the mission makes this testimony very valuable. The efforts of the group were directed primarily at Qa'in, which, even until that time, was in the control of the Ismailis. In fact, Najm al-Din narrated to his son that most of Quhistan was still under Ismaili influence. Apparently, the group was successful in its purges. Tamerlane's son and successor, Sultan Shahrukh (r. 807–850/1405–1447), who cultivated an image of strict Sunni piety, sent Jalal-i Qa'ini many decades later in 818/1415 "to exterminate, suppress . . . kill, banish and expel the [Ismaili] community from Quhistan."[78] Shahrukh was intolerant of certain religious movements, such as the Nurbakhshis. In 830/1427, a member of the Hurufi sect tried to assassinate him. In retaliation, he commanded a number of executions and exiled the poet Qasim-i Anwar (d. 837/1433), whom some later Ismailis seem to have considered a co-religionist.[79] When Qa'ini arrived, he found that Sunnism had already made inroads. The clerics (*ʿulamāʾ*) were zealous Sunnis who were accused of Shiʿism and Ismailism (*rafḍ* and *ilḥād*) if they showed any weakness. While the sayyids of Junabad appeared to be genuine Sunnis, many of the other sayyids of Quhistan were charged with Ismailism. If these figures were indeed Ismailis, they must have been practicing taqiyya in order to avoid the purges. Indeed, as Qa'ini worries, "Only Almighty God knows if the rest of the Mutasayyids of Quhistan are cured of the disease of Shiʿism or not."[80] The princes of Tabas and Zir Kuh (except for a handful) were Sunnis, though Qa'ini is uncertain about whether the remaining princes of Quhistan had leanings toward Shiʿism and Ismailism. Pleased, he writes that Farʿan, Tijarar, Makhzafa, and Sa'ir were free of the taint of Ismailism. In what may be paranoia rather than reality, Qa'ini notes that Ismailis occupied important positions in the political administration (*dīwān*), thereby seeking to avert the persecution of their co-religionists and to harm others. In a remarkable aside, Qa'ini observed that a group of people in Quhistan appeared as Sufis but were really Ismailis.[81] While earlier scholars have frequently supposed the Ismailis of this period practiced taqiyya under cover of Sufism, this is the first positive evidence we have of the fact. Certainly, no Ismailis living in such hostile circumstances could openly practice their faith. Taqiyya was the only way to survive. Qa'ini's investigation was thorough. In the space of eleven months, he traveled the length and breadth of Quhistan and concluded, "In appearance (*ẓāhir*), the community has ceased to exist, but secretly (*bāṭin*), only God knows."[82]

The situation of the Syrian Ismailis was in marked contrast to that of their Quhistani co-religionists. They do not seem to have practiced taqiyya with the same vigilance, and even casual observers, such as the fourteenth-century Ibn Battuta, one of the world's most distinguished travelers, were readily able to identify them as Ismailis. There are several possible reasons for this disparity. In contrast to their Persian co-religionists, the Syrian Ismailis managed to escape the immediate devastation wrought by the Mongols, perhaps saved by Hulagu's withdrawal in 658/1260 upon hearing of the death of the Great Khan Mongke. Sultan Baybars then extended Mamluk authority throughout the region, thwarting the Mongol advances. The Nizaris had ambivalent relations with the sultan, but in 671/1273, they lost their last independent fortress to the Mamluks, just three years after their co-religionists lost Girdkuh to the Mongols.[83] It is very likely that the internal disunity of the Syrian Ismailis expedited their antagonists' victory. When Rashid al-Din Sinan, their most famous leader, took over the helm of the community a century earlier, he brought with him a letter from the Imam urging the Syrians to set aside their differences and unite behind him:

> May God preserve you all, brethren, from conflicts of opinion and from following your passions, for that is the temptation of the first generation and the doom of the last, and in this is a lesson for those who heed. Whoever renounces the foes of God, his friend [the Imam], and his faith, must rally to the friends of God [the Imams]. . . . Be united in following the teaching of a person appointed by the designation of God and his friend [the Imam], and [unify] your passions in obeying him. Accept willingly whatever commands and prohibitions he vouchsafes to you. No, by the lord of the worlds, you do not believe until you make him judge in your tangles, and do not afterwards find difficulty in his decisions but assent [to them] heartily.[84] And this uniting is the unity which is the sign of truth that saves from destruction and leads to everlasting felicity, since disagreement is the sign of falsehood, which leads to shameful perdition.[85]

The call to unity is remarkably similar to that of the Imam Islamshah centuries later. While the Syrian community rallied behind this talented leader, after his death in about 589/1193, the earlier discord seems to have set in once again; and their leader Shams al-Din tried in vain to organize his co-religionists against Sultan Baybars.[86] This internal disharmony was capitalized on by Baybars in his subjugation of the Syrian Ismailis.

Unlike the Mongols, however, the Mamluks did not attempt to exterminate the community. Rather, they made use of the services of the *fidaʾis* for their own ends against their enemies. An interesting account of this is found in the narrative of the aforementioned Ibn Battuta. While passing through Syria for the first time on his journey in 726/1326, the Moorish voyager noted that the fortresses of Maniqa, ʿUllayqa, Qadmus, Kahf, and Masyaf were in Ismaili possession. He further recounts, in some detail, the compacts that existed between the *fidaʾis* and the reigning Mamluk Sultan, al-Nasir Nasir al-Din Muhammad.[87]

The community did not provoke nearly the same hostile reaction in Syria as it had in Persia. Thus, while Persian historians are ever ready to revile the Ismailis, never remiss in heaping their opprobrium on them, the Arabic historians are remarkably mild, sometimes even positive about the Syrian community. In an article on the appellations of the Ismailis in Arabic historiography, Shakib Saleh writes that Ibn Kathir (d. 774/1373) "was probably the only Arab historian at his time to curse the Nizaris, though this was done only once when he reported the murder of the Abbasid Caliph al-Mustarshid."[88] In contrast, the earlier Ibn al-Qalanisi (d. 555/1160) acknowledges the Ismailis' assistance to the Sunni community. In describing the part taken by the Nizaris in the defense of Damascus when it was attacked by the Franks, he hails them as "heroes, men of honour and pride."[89]

The positive imprint left in popular memory as well as in Arabic literature by the Syrian Ismailis of Mamluk times is remarkable. In *The Epic of al-Zahir Baybars* (*Sīrat al-Ẓāhir Baybars*), they are among the most dashing of figures—chivalrous cavaliers, invincible warriors, adventurous mountain people strongly holding to their independence and averse to the grips of outside interference and authority.[90] This romantic depiction is mirrored in the folklore of the Ismaili community itself.[91] Not surprising, in the Mamluk context all their gallantry is stripped of its explicitly religious connections. They appear not as despised heretics, but rather as the Banu Ismaʿil, a family descended from the valiant figure of ʿAli, inheritors of his legendary courage and strength, unimpeachable sense of justice, and intrepid aplomb. This halo of valor extends even to the female members of the Banu Ismaʿil, including the daring Shamsa, who takes on the identity of a Byzantine count and thus renders valuable services to a secret agent sent by Sultan Baybars to the Emperor Michael. The Banu Ismaʿil is often assigned special missions, such as saving the Muslim captives of Yanisa or even delivering Baybars himself when he is captured by Genoese pirates. The sense of astonishment expressed by Western authors writing about the self-sacrificing mission of the Ismaili *fida'is* who were willing to risk their lives to protect their community was combined with a sense of wonder and approbation. Thus, the Provençal poets would liken their own romantic devotion to their sweethearts to the loyalty of the *fida'is* to their leader.[92] Similarly, popular Muslim sentiment expressed a sort of grudging admiration for the lofty sense of mission harbored by the minority group in the face of overwhelming odds.

It was this comparatively positive attitude that allowed the Syrian Ismaili community to dispense with the strictest forms of taqiyya adopted by their co-religionists in Iran. However, as with the writings of some of their Persian Ismaili fellows, the general idiom of esoteric Islamic currents, including Sufism, is readily apparent in the Syrian Ismaili writings of this period. Not long before Ibn Battuta traveled to the region, an Ismaili dignitary of Basra by the name of ʿAmir b. ʿAmir composed a long didactic poem in Arabic, rhyming in the letter *ta*ʾ. This mystical treatise is analogous to the *Taʾiyya* of the celebrated Sufi poet Ibn al-Farid, who had lived a century earlier. The first editor of this poem, ʿAbd al-Qadir Maghribi, seems to have been unaware of the Ismaili faith of its author.[93] Within four years of this edition, in 1952, the same poem was edited by ʿArif Tamir of Syria. Tamir had access to over fifteen manuscripts of the work, most likely all of Syrian Ismaili provenance.[94] However, he was apparently unaware of Maghribi's edition, which was based on a very early and reliable copy of the text. The poem was finally edited critically, translated into French, and commented on by Yves Marquet in 1985. It is a remarkable attestation to the continuity of literary activity among the Syrian Ismailis and to the profound influence of Sufism in this area.[95]

To return to the Imam Islamshah, Fidaʾi Khurasani relates a very late tradition about his peregrinations. Toward the end of his life, he left Azerbaijan for the

Iranian lands, first visiting Shahr-i Babak in Kirman, then proceeding onward, by way of Yazd and Kashan, to Qazwin, where he remained. Here, he was visited by his followers from Isfahan, Kashan, Shiraz, Kirman, Damghan, Rudbar, Jurjan, Khurasan, Qainat, Herat, Kabul, Badakhshan, and Hindustan (South Asia). "They would take with them," says Fida'i, "healing water (*āb-i shifā*) from that sage for every ailing person."[96]

Both the manuscript and printed versions of *The Offspring of the Tales of Truth*, along with the register provided by Hasham Bogha, suggest 1480 VS/827 AH/1424 CE as the date of death of the first Islamshah.[97] The manuscript offers no date for the second Islamshah, but both the printed version and Bogha give 1520 VS/868 AH/1464 CE.[98] The eighteenth-century family tree from South Asia states that both of these Imams were buried in Shahr-i Babak.[99] The information of this late source should be treated with a degree of caution. Its assertion that Mustansir bi'llah, the successor of Muhammad b. Islamshah, was buried in Shahr-i Babak has proven incorrect, as his mausoleum is still in existence in Anjudan. However, in the case of Islamshah and Muhammad b. Islamshah, material evidence adds weight to the family tree's assertion. While traveling to Shahr-i Babak in 1370 HS/1991, the Iranian scholar Maryam Muʿizzi came across two large marble gravestones that were in a dilapidated state, but notably different from the surrounding grave markers, in the graveyard of Ramjird, a small village just outside of the city. After cleaning them she found that they bore a remarkable resemblance to the gravestones of the Ismaili Imams in Kahak, with inscriptions also resembling some of those of the Imams in Anjudan. Local Ismaili tradition in Shahr-i Babak also maintains that this is the burial place of the Imams Islamshah and Muhammad b. Islamshah, and till today the locale is known as that of Imamzada Muhammad, i.e., "Muhammad, the offspring of the Imam." Unfortunately, the inscriptions on the two gravestones had become worn to the extent that Muʿizzi was unable to decipher any historical information, other than poetry on one of the stones that suggests the person interred there had died at a young age.[100]

Fida'i Khurasani's allusion to the distribution of healing water by the Imam Islamshah is significant, as the practice of drinking water blessed by the Imam is frequently attested in the Ginans and continues to form part of the Ismaili tradition to this day.[101] The use of such consecrated water is widely practiced in several religious traditions. Many Twelver Shiʿa, for example, dissolve the dust of Karbala (*khāk-i shifā*), where the Imam Husayn is buried, or that of Najaf, the resting place of the Imam ʿAli, and drink the resulting healing water (*āb-i shifā*) as a cure for illness, both spiritual and physical. The Ismaili emphasis on the spiritual aspect of this healing is clear from the names used to designate the water, which include light (*nūr*) and ambrosia (*amṛt, amī, amīras, amījal*). Their use of the blessed water is also distinctive in another regard. It is taken in the name of the Imam of the time, who is physically present on earth.[102] In the old prayer associated with this ritual, preserved in many of the manuscripts, the water is sanctified with the following formula when poured into the vessel:

> Pure is the water, pure is the wind
> Pure is the earth, pure is the sky
> Pure is the moon, pure is the sun
> Pure is the lord's vessel, pure is the lord's name
> By the name of the lord, pure becomes the lord's congregation[103]

In the remainder of this long prayer, the primordial existence of a manifest divine authority is repeatedly evoked. The lineage of this authority is traced through the cosmic ages and is ultimately affirmed to be vested in the living Imam of the age. The sections of the prayer end with a declaration that the Imam is alive and eternally present. At this point the reciter of the prayer would announce the word *farman*, to which those in attendance would reply *shah-pir*—a reaffirmation of their allegiance to the command (*farmān*) of the reigning Imam (*shāh*) and his representative (*pīr*). The current practice is similar, but the expression *shah-pir* has been replaced by Ya ʿAli-Ya Muhammad. In this manner, the community members voiced their allegiance, in the words of Nasir al-Din Tusi, not solely to the command, but to the Commander (*farmān-dih*) of their time, the Possessor of the Command.

SIX

Qibla of the World

Hidden in every nook of the plains of Persian Iraq, at the foot of the mountains, are treasures of the life-secrets of those who have passed on. In every cranny a trove is deposited in trust. The plains of its deserts, teeming with hills and subterranean valleys since before the dawn of history, the hearts of its mountains, filled with tales of yore, encompassing ancient settlements and fabled cities, all look toward us with expectant eyes, hoping that we will unveil their mysteries. . . . The great fort of Anjudan was once the seat of the Ismailis. From far and wide the adherents of the community made the dust of that place the collyrium of their eyes and illuminated the land of Mushkabad by lighting the candles of devotion. . . .

Ibrahim Dihgan in *Memoirs* (*Kārnāma*)

In his *Rashidian History* (*Taʾrīkh-i Rashīdī*), Mirza Haydar Dughlat, a sixteenth-century cousin of the Mughal Emperor Babur and scion of a tribe that had served Genghis Khan, wrote about what moved him to undertake the chronicling of the Mongol successor dynasty:

> Most nations, indeed all the people of the world, practice this science [of writing history] and tell stories and tales of their forebears. . . . It is for this reason that I, Muhammad-Haydar, son of Muhammad-Husayn Kuragan, who am known familiarly as Mirza Haydar, am forced by circumstances, despite my lack of talent and ability, to undertake the grave task of this history. Since for a long time now the Moghul khaqans have ceased conquering territory and have contented themselves with the civilized world, no one among them has ever written a history, and they remember their ancestors merely by oral accounts. As of this date, which is the year 951 (AD 1544–1545), there is not a soul left of this group who remembers these stories, and my audacity in this important task is based on necessity, for if I were not so bold, the history of the Moghul khaqans would disappear entirely from the pages of time.[1]

If Mirza Haydar's words demonstrate to us the fragility of the historical memory of a mighty empire, what can be said of a people living in the shadow of fear, geographically scattered, the revelation of whose identity would lead to renewed persecutions? Despite having had an earlier tradition of historical writing in Fatimid Egypt and then at Alamut, no systematic history of the Ismailis dating from this period is known to have existed. Indeed, even if such a history were ever recorded, the chances of its survival are dismal. In the last chapter we learned of the ravaging of the Ismaili libraries in Egypt and at Alamut. These were not, unfortunately, the last instances of such destruction. The literature of the Syrian Ismailis, which was potentially one of the richest sources of Arabic Ismaili literature, has been the victim of predatory assaults on the community, primarily by the more numerous Nusayris, even in recent memory. When Wladimir Ivanow toured Syria for two months in 1937 in search of Ismaili literature, he had to "hear the story, over and over again repeated on every occasion, of the books gone with the loot."[2] Similarly, much of the Ismaili literature of Afghanistan, along with that of many other Persian speakers, whether Shiʿi or Sunni, was systematically destroyed during the Taliban reign of terror that devastated that country.

In 1987, the collaborative efforts of several civil society and academic institutions, leading scholars, and members of the Ismaili community led to the establishment of the Nasir-i Khusraw Foundation in Kabul.[3] The premises included video and book publishing facilities, a museum, and a library. Numerous Ismailis and members of other Muslim communities had donated their personal collections of books and manuscripts to the library, and a delegation was also sent to Iran for the acquisition of further items. The facilities were open to all students and researchers, with pencils and copybooks provided free of charge to those who could not afford them. Artistic wonders of the school of Herat were carefully preserved, including miniatures, illuminated manuscripts, and calligraphic masterpieces of Timurid times. Among the fifty-five thousand books could be found the great classics of Western literature, including writings of Flaubert, Kafka, Dostoievski, Pasternak, and Hemingway. Visitors to the library could read Kant, Hegel, Sartre, Max Weber, Alain Touraine, and Noam Chomsky. While the library housed items in Arabic, English, and Pashto, its greatest strength was in its magnificent Persian collection, which included among its most precious items an extremely rare twelfth-century manuscript of Firdawsi's epic masterpiece, *The Book of Kings* (*Shāhnāma*). The Ismaili collection featured a number of exceptional articles, including letters from Hasan-i Sabbah to his co-religionists in Isfahan, the writings of Nasir-i Khusraw, and seals of the first Aga Khan.

The Soviet withdrawal from Afghanistan in the late 1980s left the country in a state of even greater chaos than before, when it had been a pawn of Cold War politics. With the capital Kabul now vulnerable, many fled. The Foundation itself was relocated to Pul-i Khumri, an industrial town of some 200 000 inhabitants, which swelled to about a million as refugees attempted to escape the onward march of the Taliban. Kabul fell in 1996, but the library was safe in its new home, idyllically situated among groves of green trees. This state of affairs was not to last long, however. By 1997, the Taliban forces had already entered Mazar-i Sharif and were closing in on Pul-i Khumri. The inhabitants were forewarned and were prepared. The library collection was swiftly spirited off to the valley of Kayan for safekeeping. Attempts by the Taliban to take Pul-i Khumri were unsuccessful, as their forces were driven out by a local insurrection. The library was damaged slightly in the fighting, but was soon repaired, and the books returned to the shelves. The following year, however, a Taliban offensive against the North succeeded in recapturing Mazar-i Sharif, where terrible atrocities were committed. Thousands of Hazaras, a predominantly Shiʿa people who speak a dialect of Persian, were executed. Pul-i Khumri was taken completely unawares on August 11, 1998, as thousands of armed soldiers entered the city at 4:00 PM. Latif Pedram, the director of the library, fled for the nearby hills and later took refuge in the house of a friend, just opposite the Foundation. He later learned that his was one of the first houses to be searched by the Taliban, and had he been discovered, he would have been executed. From his hideout, on August 12, 1998, a day he describes as one of the blackest of his life, he witnessed a horrifying scene as he furtively peaked out from behind a curtained window. Taliban fighters were arriving in four-by-four vehicles armed with rocket launchers. After ransacking the press, the museum, and the video facilities, amidst a terrible pandemonium, they launched rockets at the locked doors of the library. Over the course of the next several hours the books were massacred. A fire broke out as flames and smoke billowed through the windows. As though the carnage was not proceeding quickly enough, more books were thrown into the river bordering the library. By evening all was finished. Every book had been set ablaze or destroyed in the flowing water. Even the library's thousand-year-old Quran had not been spared. Pedram described his feelings of shock and horror at the atmosphere of madness that prevailed. This had not been a random act, but a calculated attempt to destroy. In Herat, the Taliban had ravaged the arts center and personal library of the former minister for culture, which included thousands of ancient volumes. In Kabul, they devastated the university library. All private book owners and booksellers were hunted down. Streets whose designations had a Persian connotation were renamed. Even tombstones with Persian epigraphs were profaned. "It is the book," mused Pedram, "which preserved history, politics, philosophy, grammar, logic, esotericism, mathematics and the visual arts. Our pride is the book. We have survived thanks to books. They are the memory of Afghanistan. The Taliban knew well that to annihilate all resistance of a people, they had to efface their memory."

While the Taliban were not, in the end, triumphant, they were successful in destroying large portions of the cultural and literary heritage of many of Afghanistan's minority groups. One can only hope that those who were the victims of such atrocities somehow managed to safeguard some remnants of their past. The contents of this chapter depend heavily on such remnants. It is about the Imams Mustansir bi'llah, ʿAbd al-Salam and Gharib Mirza, all of whom lived in Anjudan, and about the Ismaili luminaries who were their contemporaries. It also explores the notion of the Imam as the spiritual *qibla*.

Till today, a few of the elderly Afghan Ismailis preserve in their litany of prayers a remarkable invocation, calling out *Ya Shah-i Kashan*, "O lord of Kashan."[4] One can speculate that this practice must hark back to the time when the Ismaili Imam lived in that very region. About a hundred years before the Safawid revolution transformed Iran, virtually overnight, into a Shiʿi state in 907/1501, steps were being taken to transfer the headquarters of the Ismaili imamate to Anjudan, a village near Qumm and Kashan, age-old Shiʿi strongholds and centers of learning. On the eve of the Safawid revolution, an Ismaili poet with the pen name "Husayn" wrote, "We make Anjudan our Kaʿba of reality."[5] In this period, Anjudan became firmly established as the heart of the Ismaili world.

TRANSFERENCE OF THE SEAT OF IMAMATE TO ANJUDAN

With the exception of the reign of Tamerlane and his son Shahrukh, Persia had remained largely fragmented after the death of the Ilkhanid ruler, Abu Saʿid (d. 735/1335). This ruler's demise shattered the ideal of a single, if merely symbolic, sovereign governing the area. It is not coincidental that a number of often chiliastic religious movements arose in such a vacuum. The absence of a strong central authority must have afforded favorable circumstances to the numerous religious communities, many tinged with Shiʿi sentiment, that surfaced in this period. These included the Sarbadar movement, the Hurufiyya, the Nuqtawiyya, the Mushaʿshaʿ and numerous Sufi fraternities. The most politically successful of these messianic movements was the Safawid Qizilbash organization that propelled Shah Ismaʿil I to power in 907/1501. The dramatic upheaval and declaration of Shiʿism as the official state religion led many of the Sufi orders openly to proclaim their Shiʿism or, in the case of some, to quickly adopt a Shiʿi stance. It is particularly noteworthy that the founder of one of the most prominent of these Sufi orders, Nur al-Din Niʿmat Allah (d. 834/1431), while apparently a Sunni, traced his genealogy to the seventh Ismaili Imam, Muhammad b. Ismaʿil. He vaunts this lineage in an unpublished epistle as well as in one of his poetic compositions.[6] Soon after the establishment of Safawid power, the Niʿmat Allahi order declared itself to be Shiʿi.[7] As will be seen, the Iranian Ismailis too, who had hitherto largely practiced taqiyya as Sunnis, now began to adopt the cover of Twelver Shiʿism.

The reason for the transference of the Ismaili headquarters to Anjudan cannot be ascertained with any degree of certainty but may have been the result of a number of factors. As mentioned earlier, attempts to consolidate their position at Alamut had repeatedly proved futile. In the South Caspian region, their failure to conceal their identity provoked the hostile reaction of their more powerful neighbors. Meanwhile, Anjudan, situated not far from Arak (formerly Sultanabad) had the advantage of being far from the two centers of Sunni power: the seat of the Aq Qoyunlu in Tabriz and that of the later Timurids in Herat. It was also in the environs of the traditional centers of Shiʿism in Persia. Other Shiʿi-influenced movements of this period had also initiated their activities in relatively remote regions. We could cite, for example, the Shaykhis in Sabzawar, who were associated with the Sarbadar state in Khurasan (ca. 1336–1381), the movement of Muhammad b. Falah Mushaʿshaʿ (d. 886/1461) in southern Iraq, and that of Fadl Allah's (d. 796/1394) Hurufis in Astarabad (Jurjan).[8]

The first we hear of an Ismaili presence in Anjudan is at the very end of the fourteenth century when Tamerlane himself led a foray in Rajab 795/May 1393 against the Nizaris of the area.[9] The mighty conqueror's exploits were to become legendary. By 1587, they were the subject of one of the greatest plays of Elizabethan theater, "Tamburlaine the Great" by Richard Marlowe, also author of the equally popular "Doctor Faustus" and a contemporary of William Shakespeare. The prologue to the play read:

> From jigging veins of rhyming mother-wits,
> And such conceits as clownage keeps in pay,
> We'll lead you to the stately tent of war,

Where you shall hear the Scythian Tamburlaine
Threatening the world with high astounding terms,
And scourging kingdoms with his conquering sword.
View but his picture in this tragic glass,
And then applaud his fortunes as you please.[10]

In typical Elizabethan fashion, the playwright described Tamerlane, "Who, from a Scythian Shephearde by his rare and woonderfull Conquests, became a most puissant and mightye Monarque."[11] At the time of his incursions against the Ismailis, Tamerlane was engaged in his Persian campaigns and was traveling from Isfahan to Hamadan and Baghdad. While he was well known for his pro-ʿAlid (and, as many have suggested, pro-Shiʿi) sympathies, there appears to have been no love lost between Tamerlane and the community. David Morgan writes,

> "Temür's own religious persuasion is difficult to discern: he professed a reverence for ʿAli and the Shiʿi imams, and on occasion attacked Sunnis on what were represented as religious grounds. But at other times he attacked Shiʿis on Sunni grounds. All in all he remains one of the most complex, puzzling and unattractive figures in the history of Persia and Central Asia."[12]

Tamerlane is portrayed as the eighth in a line of religious restorers who appeared in every century to promote Islam and reinstate its original purity. In this regard, he lauds the fifth champion of the line, Sultan Sanjar b. Malikshah, for waging war against the Ismailis of Alamut.[13] One is led to wonder whether Tamerlane viewed his own sortie against the Ismailis of Anjudan, carried out just a year after he had attacked their co-religionists in Mazandaran, in the same light, or indeed what it was about the activities of the community in this small village that had attracted his attention at all. From the accounts preserved by the Persian historians, it seems as if Anjudan had been fortified against attack. Mirkhwand informs us that they had a fortress in the village.[14] Moreover, they had built special underground tunnels and burrows for protection and took refuge there at the time of Tamerlane's assault. However, this device proved futile when the assailants cut a channel from above, allowing the invading troops to pour water into the hollows, drowning the Ismailis. After destroying the unfortunate denizens of the village, Tamerlane tarried in the area, which seems to have been well known for the chase, and set up camp to hunt wild asses and gazelles.

Khwandamir, in his *Beloved of Biographies* (*Ḥabīb al-Siyar*), provides us with an interesting detail not found in any of the other historical sources for this event. He writes that the Ismaili community was on the increase at this time and had organized itself in Persian Iraq, extending its authority in the region. Some of the locals were not pleased with these developments and provoked the attack by reporting the matter to Tamerlane. Thus, it may be that even at this early stage the rudiments of a new center were being established, perhaps in consideration of the extremely tumultuous situation at Alamut. While the exact occasion for the assault is ambiguous, it seems to have been the result of spreading Ismaili influence and political authority in the region. Clearly it was the attenuation, perhaps the abeyance, of taqiyya that drew the attention, and the wrath, of the famous conqueror. It is ironic but true that whenever we hear of the community in non-Ismaili sources, this seems to be a result of a political failure, and is almost always indicative that taqiyya had lapsed. Thus we find prudence and caution being emphasized in the works of the period, such as in the verses of Husayn advising the believers to "expound the secrets of faith to the lovers" but to "conceal the path of the summons from the enemies of the faith." The Imams were well aware of the dangers inherent in the lapse of dissimulation. Thus we find very strict instructions of the Imam in *The Counsels of Chivalry* not to reveal his identity to outsiders.

Mirkhwand notes in his account that the people of Anjudan were still Ismaili at the time of his writing, that is, in the late fifteenth century. The first evidence we have of an Ismaili Imam actually inhabiting the village, however, is with Mustansir bi'llah (d. 885/1480), whose mausoleum is found in Anjudan and who may have been the first of the Ismaili Imams to have been interred there.

The late Russian scholar Wladimir Ivanow is often given credit for the "discovery" of the mausoleum of Mustansir bi'llah as well as of the other Ismaili antiquities at Anjudan.[15] While this astute researcher certainly played an indispensable role in bringing these important historical monuments to the attention of the scholarly world, he cannot be dubbed their discoverer.

Ivanow's first major contact with Ismaili literature occurred when he was associated with the Asiatic Museum of the Russian Academy of Sciences in St. Petersburg. In 1916, he examined the collection donated to the museum by the well-known Russian specialist of Tajik dialects, I. I. Zarubin, that, despite its small size, contained the largest collection of genuine Ismaili literature in a Western library at that time. This piqued Ivanow's interest, and through the following decades, his indefatigable efforts made him the undisputed father of modern Ismaili studies. It was in 1937, the same year he paid his second visit to Alamut, that Ivanow stumbled upon the tombs of several Nizari Ismaili Imams in the villages of Anjudan and Kahak, about which he published an invaluable study.[16] While not detracting from the significance of this achievement, it should be mentioned that the family of the later Ismaili Imams was well aware of the existence of the antiquities of Anjudan long before Ivanow's find. The Iranian scholar Ibrahim Dihgan recalls that

> the first Aga Khan [d. 1298/1881] and his son, ʿAlishah, who was known as Aga Khan II [d. 1302/1885], did not neglect their original cradle, Anjudan. They used to send aid to the needy people and impoverished

sayyids of the area and maintained their ancestral monuments (*āthār*), preserving the memory of their grandsires by the restoration of the buildings of Anjudan.[17]

IMAMATE OF MUSTANSIR BI'LLAH (D. 885/1480)

While there is clear evidence of organized Ismaili activity in Anjudan from at least the late fourteenth century, the first definitive confirmation we have of an Imam's residence in this area is the aforementioned mausoleum of Mustansir bi'llah, who died shortly before 885/1480, this date being recorded in the edifice.[18] The date is close to that provided by the printed edition of *Offspring of the Tales of Truth* and Hasham Bogha, 880/1476.[19] *The Muhammadan Chronicles*, *The Garden of Shams*, and the eighteenth-century family tree from South Asia all indicate that his full name was Mustansir bi'llah ʿAlishah.[20]

This Imam has been credited with a work entitled *The Counsels of Chivalry* (*Pandiyāt-i Jawānmardī*).[21] That the book pertains to the Imam Mustansir is certain; however, both this Imam and his grandson bore the same title. While it is indeed possible that the text belongs to this Imam, and this is what has been assumed by all scholars to date, there seems to be a preponderance of evidence suggesting that it belongs to the second of the two Mustansirs. The *Counsels* will therefore be discussed in connection with that Imam, who was also known as Gharib Mirza.

The tomb of Mustansir bi'llah, known locally as Shah Qalandar, contains an exquisitely carved casket-like box (*ṣandūq*). On the borders of the three sides is engraved a Quranic passage, well known even in English as "The Throne Verse" (*āyat al-kursī*, 2:255), in *naskhi*-style calligraphy, the remaining side bearing the Quranic lines,

> The messenger believes in what has descended unto him from his lord as do the believers. All believe in God, his angels, his scriptures and his messengers—we make no distinction between any of his messengers—and they say, "We hear and we obey. (Grant us) your forgiveness, our lord. Unto you is the journey." (2:285)

The edges have elaborately carved floral designs in the *islimi* style.[22] Most important, the following information is recorded on the inscription at the top of the casket, "This is the purified, hallowed and luminous grave of the noble Shah Mustansir bi'llah, [erected] by the command and direction of the noble Shah ʿAbd al-Salam."[23] A further inscription near the bottom of one of the shorter sides gives the name of the scribe as ʿAbd al-Jalil [Nay?]saburi, and the date of the inscription as 885/1480. The Imam must therefore have died shortly before this date, his mausoleum having been commissioned by his son and successor, ʿAbd al-Salam.

Daʿi Anjudani

Contemporary with the Imam Mustansir bi'llah was a poet who had the pen name "Daʿi."[24] It is likely that this high title, a rank in the Ismaili hierarchy, had been bestowed on him by the Imam; it may otherwise have been presumptuous for him to adopt it as his pen name (*takhalluṣ*). In a similar fashion, centuries earlier, Nasir-i Khusraw had adopted "Hujjat" as his nom de plume. We can be fairly confident that this Daʿi is the same as the poet Mawlana Daʿi Anjudani named by Iskandar Beg Munshi the Turcoman in his register of poets of the time of Shah Tahmasp I (r. 930–984/1524–1576) as recorded in *The World-Adorning ʿAbbasid History* (*Taʾrīkh-i ʿĀlamārā-yi ʿAbbāsī*).[25] The fact that this poet was from Anjudan is particularly suggestive. While this account is not clear about the exact period of Mawlana Daʿi, it is chronologically possible that he lived toward the end of the imamate of Mustansir bi'llah and died within the first decades of the reign of the Safawid Shah ʿAbbas.[26] Iskandar Beg Munshi considers him together with his brother Mawlana Malik Tayfur Anjudani, who was also a poet. He writes:

> Mawlana Malik Tayfur Anjudani and his brother Mawlana Daʿi were both among the literati and were among the people of excellence and perfection. In the time of the late Shah, Malik Tayfur used to be at the school (*madrasa*) and pulpits of Qazwin. He was an accomplished world-traveler, explorer and lover (of God), a righteous and pious man among the fair-faced youths, possessing good fortune and happiness. His temperament was dominated by a sense of whimsy. In the time of his exalted majesty, he left Qazwin for Kashan. He had such an independent nature that despite his poverty and destitution, he was content with barley bread. He never arrayed himself in the garb of the greedy. . . . At that time he would sometimes go with his brother Mawlana Daʿi to Kashan and meet with the poets and other people there. Mawlana Daʿi was an abstemious person as well, like a dervish. He wrote many limpid verses, including powerful odes (*qaṣāʾid*) and beautiful love lyrics (*ghazaliyyāt*).[27]

Daʿi and his brother appear to have attracted some attention for their poetic virtuosity. Both are also mentioned in the celebrated anthology of poets, *The Fire Temple* (*Ātishkada*) by Lutf ʿAli Beg, whose pen name was "Adhar."[28] A notice in *Compendium of Eloquence* (*Majmaʿ al-Fuṣaḥāʾ*), a later source by Rida Qulikhan

Hidayat, also mentions a certain Daʿi Anjudani, giving his proper name as Mir Muhammad Mu'min.[29] However, it makes him a contemporary of the eighteenth-century poets Hatif (d. 1198/1783) and Adhar (1195/1781), which is impossible. It is likely that Hidayat is in error, or perhaps that he refers to a completely different individual.

Ibn Husam Khusfi

Ibn Husam, whose poetry is found scattered in the manuscripts of the Iranian Ismaili community, was another Ismaili poet who flourished at this time. This is almost certainly the poet Muhammad b. Husam b. Shams al-Din Muhammad Khusfi. While considered one of the literati, he preferred to live far from others and earned his living by farming.[30] He was born in either 782 or 783/1380 or 1381[31] and, according to Dawlatshah Samarqandi and Nur Allah Shushtari, died at an advanced age in 875/1470 or, according to Khwandamir, even later in 893/1487.[32] Much of his oeuvre is dedicated to praising the Prophet and ʿAli, and he became well known for this genre of poetry, known as *manqaba*. A number of the poems in Ismaili collections match those in his published *Omnibus* (*dīwān*).[33] However, at least one of the poems that is explicitly Ismaili in tone is not to be found in the manuscripts that were used by the editor for establishing the critical text, these all having apparently been gathered from non-Ismaili milieus. The Ismaili author of *Words of the Sage* (*Kalām-i Pīr*), however, definitely had access to this poem, a verse of which he quotes on no less than three occasions:[34]

> If you don't recognize the Imam of the time in truth
> You will head for hellfire, despite your hundred thousand devotions

The poet's association with Khusf in Khurasan is suggestive, as this was a village known for its Ismaili affiliations. Nizari Quhistani had earlier set out from Khusf on his trek to see the Imam Shams al-Din Muhammad. Ibn Husam's mausoleum continues to exist in that locale.[35] Furthermore, as we know from his poetry, he was accused of being a heretic and infidel (*mulḥid* and *kāfir*) in his lifetime, accusations that were commonly leveled against the Ismailis by extremists. He responded hotly to these allegations:

> That dastardly foe accuses me of infidelity
> God forbid! What infidelity? What is faith and what is infidelity?[36]

He also penned an elegy in memory of Qasim-i Anwar (d. 837/1433), another poet whom Ismaili writers, very early on, claimed as one of their own, though explicit evidence of his affiliation with the community is merely suggestive rather than conclusive.[37]

Sayyid Suhrab Wali Badakhshani

Another author who likely lived in the time of this Imam was Sayyid Suhrab Wali Badakhshani, who was active in the mid-fifteenth century, the date 856/1452 being found in one of his works.[38] His *Gift to the Readers* (*Tuḥfat al-Nāẓirīn*) incorporates the thought of Nasir-i Khusraw as well as Nasir al-Din Tusi and Hasan-i Mahmud, direct quotations from whose *Paradise of Submission* (*Rawḍa-yi Taslīm*) are apparent in his work. In fact, an apocryphal and anachronistic tradition believes him to have been Khusraw's student.[39] In this book, he also alludes to another composition of his, *The Paradise of Apprentices* (*Rawḍat al-Mutaʿallimīn*), which may still be extant.[40] It is clear that his work was influential, as the anonymous author of *The Sage's Discourse* (*Kalām-i Pīr*) clearly had access to it and quoted large sections from it. This fact is interesting in and of itself. While the Badakhshani origin of Suhrab Wali suggests that he may have been attached to the Muhammadshahi line of Imams, the fact that he is liberally quoted in what is clearly a Qasimshahi work either precludes this possibility, indicates that the Ismailis of Badakhshan were never unanimous in their devotion to the Muhammadshahi line, or else suggests that by the time *The Sage's Discourse* was written, Badakhshan had returned to the Qasimshahi fold. Unfortunately, the contents of Suhrab Wali's work give us no indication of his own affiliation. Suhrab Wali's progeny continued to be active in the Badakhshani Ismaili community; and the *Pearl-Scatterer* (*Gawhar-Rīz*), a work of one of his descendants named Kuchak, is a source for the history of this period.[41] The adherence of the author of this later composition is itself interesting. While it is clearly written by a devotee of the Qasimshahi Imams, it freely invokes the line of Muhammadshah as well.

IMAMATE OF ʿABD AL-SALAM (D. CA. 899/1493)

When the Imam ʿAbd al-Salam succeeded to the imamate, the occasion appears to have been commemorated by the composition of an ode by a poet with the pen name Salik or Saliki. While not explicitly naming the Imam, the poet alludes to him as Mustansir's successor:

> He's arrived! With healing breath like Christ, son of the saved Mary. Greetings unto him. Whence came he? From the Kaʿba of Mustansir bi'llah, the Imam. All who heard these glad tidings were revived. All who distance themselves from him, well, God knows best their lot. Salutations, salutations, for this wonderful news, which arrives without doubt from the heavenly orb of the world of religion. Every breath there is a message in the soul. Doubtless those who disregard this command, their place in the afterlife will be the inferno. . . . Saliki! If a few verses have brashly been strung together, perchance they may be arrayed on the thread of correction.[42]

The *Muhammadan Chronicles* describe an incident in which this Imam, named Mahmud, had mentioned to his father that contentment was more important than conquest. Mustansir bi'llah, pleased with his son's wisdom, gave him the title ʿAbd al-Salam, "the servant of peace."[43] A. J. Chunara notes that an epistle (*risāla*) of the poet Khaki Khurasani states that ʿAbd al-Salam was also known as Salam Allah.[44] This epistle is not recorded in the bibliographies of Ivanow and Poonawala.

The Imam ʿAbd al-Salam is best known for an ode he authored, addressed to the "seekers of union," portions of which are analyzed in greater detail in chapter 8.[45] There are also three other writings attributed to him. The first, in the copy available to me, is entitled *Five Discourses Uttered by Shah Islam* (*Panj Sukhan kih Ḥaḍrat-i Shāh Islām farmūda and*).[46] In his *Ismaili Literature*, Ivanow describes the work as

> an instructive opuscule of 30 small pages, dealing with the virtues appropriate to good believers. References to *fuṣūl-i mubārak*, to (Hasan) ʿalā dhikri-hi's-salām, Bābā Sayyid-nā, *"Faṣl-i Fārsiyān"*, poets Qāsim Tushtarī, Thanāʾī, and a certain Fakhru'l-muḥaqqiqīn Sharafu'd-Dīn Muḥammad.[47]

This is incorrect. It is possible that Ivanow was misled by the frequent appearance in manuscripts, immediately after *Five Discourses*, of the treatise on the subject "Recognition of the Creator" by Qasim Tushtari (or Turshizi) that was described earlier. This sequence likely existed in an early manuscript tradition and later proliferated.

Ivanow's attribution should also be taken as tentative. In the copy of the work available to me, consisting of approximately a page of text, while the name of the author is certain, there is nothing that would indicate which of the three Imams of the same name this opuscule pertains to. It is, in essence, an ethical passage, urging the faithful to be generous and honest and to keep the society of their fellow believers. It affirms that those who remain ignorant of the Imam (*mawlānā*) and his friends (*dūstān*, apparently in reference to the officials of the Ismaili hierarchy) will incur his wrath. It further describes the path of the religious law (*sharīʿa*) to be formal prayers and fasting. Meanwhile, the way of the truth (*ḥaqīqa*) is "prostrating one's forehead on the earth so as never to remain heedless of the lord for even a single breath and to endeavor in good works in order to earn God Almighty's pleasure in this world and the next."

The next work, titled simply *Decree of the Imam ʿAbd al-Salām* (*Farmān-i Shāh ʿAbd al-Salām*) by Ivanow, is found in a chrestomathy (*majmūʿa*) in Kirman and bears the signature of Shah ʿAbd al-Salam. It is, however, a copy of the original. In this case, we can be certain that it pertains to the third of the three Imams of this name as it contains the date 895/1490. The subject matter is extremely interesting. Ivanow describes it as "an epistle addressed to the Ismailis of Badakhshan and Kabul who followed the Imams of the Muḥammad-Shāhī line, inviting the erring people to reconsider the grounds for their allegiance and return to the fold of the right line of the Imams, that is to say, the Qāsim-Shāhī."[48]

If Ivanow's assessment is correct, this would be the only known Qasimshahi source explicitly testifying to a rivalry between the two lines. Unfortunately, this work apparently remains in a personal collection, and Ivanow has not furnished any further information concerning its whereabouts.

The last work, not mentioned in the writings of Ivanow, is noticed in Poonawala's *Biobibliography of Ismāʿili Literature*, in which it is titled *A Poem of Shah ʿAbd al-Salam b. Shah Mustansir bi'llah* (*Bandī az Shāh ʿAbd al-Salām [b.] Shāh Mustanṣir bi'llāh*).[49] It is contained in a manuscript—a copy or microfilm of which appears to be at the Tehran-Markazi library—that may have been written in the lifetime of this Imam himself, whom it styles the Imam of the time (*imām-i zamān*).[50] It is possible, though, that the work is the same as the ode mentioned above. Hasham Bogha and both the manuscript and printed versions of *Offspring of the Tales of Truth* place the death of the Imam ʿAbd al-Salam b. Mustansir bi'llah in 1550 VS/899 AH/1494 CE.[51] This seems to be roughly correct, as we know he succeeded his father as Imam shortly before 885/1480, that he wrote the aforementioned letter to the Ismailis of Badakhshan and Kabul in 895/1490, and that his own successor, known as ʿAbbas Shah, Mustansir bi'llah, and, most commonly, Gharib Mirza, died shortly afterward, in about 904/1498.

IMAMATE OF GHARIB MIRZA (D. 904/1498)

Pir Shihab al-Din Shah al-Husayni relates a tradition that the Imam ʿAbbas Shah,[52] "due to the opposition of some enemies, was forced into exile (*ghurba*) from his ordinary residence for a time. He thus had the title of Gharib Mirza, the

Exiled Prince."[53] The Imam apparently had a younger brother by the name of Nur al-Din, after whom one of the most prominent fortresses near Anjudan was named Nurabad.[54] Despite his short period of imamate, he is named as the reigning Imam by at least four contemporary Ismaili writers and authored both poetry and prose.

A hitherto unknown work is found in a Persian manuscript copied in Poona, India, in the early years of the last century, entitled simply *From the Discourses of Shah Gharib Mirza* (*Min Kalām-i Shāh Gharīb Mīrzā*).[55] It begins, "This exemplar is by the king of kings, lord of the faithful, guide of the seekers, master of the unitarian believers, sovereign of time and space, king of the saints, sovereign of the pious, master of authority" and seems to be addressed primarily to the dignitaries of the rank of muʿallim (teacher). The content is concerned largely with the mystical significance of letters and other esoteric matters. This prose work is followed by a poem, also by Shah Gharib, on similar matters.

One of the most enduring legacies of this period is a highly revered book entitled *The Counsels of Chivalry* (*Pandiyāt-i Jawānmardī*). Compiled by an anonymous scribe, apparently at the Imam Mustansir bi'llah's behest, the text contains the aphorisms of the Imam and provides many insights into the situation of the community at this time. The work is widely disseminated and was long ago transliterated into Khojki, the communal script of South Asia's Ismaili community.[56] Ivanow has already mentioned the very early translation of the work into Sindhi, and its later Gujarati recension.[57] Khojki manuscript 110 at the Institute of Ismaili Studies also preserves a hitherto unknown anonymous Hindustani translation of the *Counsels*. The circumstances that led to the compilation of the work are intriguing and are alluded to in a preface found in many of the manuscript copies, including this one:

> When Pir Taj al-Din passed away, a number of people from the Sindhi Ismaili community went to the Imam (*āgā sāhebh*). Upon arrival, they pleaded, "Our pir, Taj al-Din, has passed away. Now we are in need of a pir." The Imam then had the *Counsels of Chivalry* compiled and gave it to them saying, "This is your pir. Act according to its dictates."[58]

As such, the work is always respectfully addressed as *Pir Pandiyat-i Jawanmardi*, and this is the form the title takes in many of its manuscripts.[59]

The circumstances in which the book was compiled are made clear at the very outset of the work:

> May it not be concealed from the sun-illuminated hearts of those who tread the path of Murtada [ʿAli] that whenever this servant of the heavenly threshold of the Imam of the Age, Mawlana Shah Mustansir bi'llah

> was ennobled by attendance at the luminous gatherings when the Imam uttered the *Counsels of Chivalry* in every assembly, meeting, and congregation, he recorded the counsels and guidance that the Imam addressed to the disciples and followers concerning commands and prohibitions; moral principles, qualities, speech and conduct incumbent in the way of humanity; as well as faithfulness, worship and duties leading to bounty in the life of this world and felicity in the life of the next. This servant recorded all this in writing that it may be a means to salvation for those who listen and act upon it. I have titled this book the *Counsels*, for it contains a greater counsel, a shorter counsel and twelve principles of chivalry.[60]

That the *Counsels* contain the teachings of an Imam named Mustansir bi'llah is quite clear from this. However, there were two Imams at Anjudan with the name Mustansir bi'llah, the first being the grandfather of the second, as can be see in table 4.1. The latter was also known as Gharib Mirza. All scholars who have dealt with the question have accepted the *Counsels* as the work of the first of these two.[61] However, with the exception of Ivanow, none have considered the question in any detail. The problem is compounded by two brief passages mentioning another Imam by the name of ʿAbd al-Salam Shah. The first of these two passages alludes to a famous prophetic tradition found in both Shiʿi and Sunni collections: انما مثل اهل بيتي فيكم كمثل سفينة نوح، من ركبها نجا و من تخلف عنها هلك, "Verily, among you my family is like the Ark of Noah, he who embarks on it is saved and he who lags behind is destroyed."[62] The passage reads:

> Take hold of the hand of your leader and guide and sit in the house of truth, boarding the Ark of the Noah of the time so that you may safely reach the shore. That leader and Noah of the time is the Imam of your age, Shah ʿAbd al-Salamshah. Recognize him and board the Ark of Noah, that is, the path of his summons (*ṭarīqa-yi daʿwat-i ū*) that your faith may be perfected and your spirit preserved from calamities.[63]

The second passage is indicative of the continued need for caution:

> O faithful believers, Hadrat Mawlana Shah Mustansir bi'llah says: Never mention my name nor that of your Imam Shah ʿAbd al-Salamshah in the presence of the faithless, ignorant ones who harbor an innate enmity for the offices of prophecy and imamate.[64]

In light of these two passages, Ivanow proposes the following:

> The only solution in the case is the simplest: that the book, or its greater part, was compiled under Shah ʿAbdu's-Salam who succeeded Imam Mustansir bi'l-lah, and thus really was the Imam of the time when the compiler was engaged in writing. The enigmatic passage on p. 56 [i.e., the second passage] may be easily explained if we suggest that Mustansir bi'l-lah told his followers not to disclose his own identity to outsiders, nor of the Imam of one's time generally. And as the Imam of the time at the moment when the compiler was writing was Shah ʿAbdu's-Salam, he "automatically" mentioned his name.[65]

The scenario that Ivanow suggests is highly unlikely. The compiler clearly states that he wrote in the lifetime of the Imam Mustansir bi'llah, noting whatever he said in an assembly. The *Counsels* could therefore not have been compiled under Mustansir's successor, ʿAbd al-Salam. This latter option, favored by Ivanow, would also be quite against the tradition recorded at the beginning of the work in many manuscripts, that Mustansir himself dispatched the work to India.

In one sense, the quandary is easy enough to resolve. There is no reason that some of the sermons recorded in *Counsels of Chivalry* could not have been made at a time when the author's father was alive. Thus, assuming that Mustansir bi'llah acted as pir during the imamate of his father, some of his sermons would have been recorded while his predecessor (not successor), ʿAbd al-Salam, was the Imam. Ordinarily, this would help us solve the question of to which of the two Mustansir bi'llahs the teachings of the *Counsels* are to be ascribed. The only problem is that the predecessors of both Mustansirs were known as ʿAbd al-Salamshah. Fidaʾi Khurasani, however, quotes a long passage that he attributes to the Imam Gharib Mirza that exactly parallels in style and content similar segments in *Counsels of Chivalry*.[66] Unfortunately, he does not tell us the source of his quotation. The circumstances surrounding the dispatching of the *Counsels* to South Asia also suggest that it may have been the second of the two Mustansirs, as these events occurred after the death of one of the leading exponents of Ismailism, Pir Hasan Kabir al-Din, who died most likely toward the end of the fifteenth century.[67]

Events in South Asia Leading to the Dispatch of the Counsels

Hasan Kabir al-Din's death precipitated a tempestuous conflict among his offspring that rocked the local Ismaili community. According to testimony ascribed to his grandson, Nur Muhammadshah, the needs of the various Nizari congregations were neglected as the community was convulsed by the quarrels of Kabir al-Din's eighteen sons in Uch.[68] Nanji writes, "It is not clear if this disagreement was over the succession to the position of Pīr."[69] However, the Ismaili Ginans and the *Stations of the Spiritual Poles* (*Manāzil al-Aqṭāb*) seem to indicate that the dispute was about the division of Kabir al-Din's fortune.[70] It appears that Imamshah, being absent at the time of his father's death, was deprived of his rightful share of the inheritance[71] and that the religious dues destined for Persia were absconded by some of the other offspring.[72] The tumultuous situation alluded to in the Ginans and the *Stations* is further corroborated by the very early source *Reports of the Pious* (*Akhbār al-Akhyār*), which indicates that there was great turmoil among the descendants of Hasan Kabir al-Din.[73] As a result of this dissension, Kabir al-Din's younger brother, Taj al-Din, left to see the Imam in Kahak[74] where he was invested with the "turban" (*sirband*) of spiritual authority and appointed the Imam's representative.[75]

Taj al-Din faced formidable obstacles in heading the daʿwa. After returning to Uch, he was continuously harassed by his nephews, several of whom he may have excommunicated (*bāher dhareāṃ*).[76] It appears that some of the children of Hasan Kabir al-Din became Sunnis and took a leading role in the Sunni community.[77]

After five years of preaching in Uch and Lahore, Taj al-Din traveled to Persia to deliver the religious dues collected in this period, a sum amounting to forty thousand *mohors*[78] and ten *gaj* (approximately seven meters) of cloth.[79] Nur Muhammadshah tells us that the Imam bestowed a gift of some of the cloth on Taj al-Din, which the pir fashioned into a garment. This caused a sensation when he returned to Uch and his followers accused him of misappropriating the dues destined for Persia.[80] The shock of these accusations procured his early demise. Such was the uproar among his former disciples that they would not allow him to be buried in Uch, and it was only twenty years after his death that a proper mausoleum was constructed by his repentant followers.[81] According to Nur Muhammadshah's narrative, after an intense but fruitless effort to attract the followers who had been swayed to Sunnism by some of Kabir al-Din's brothers, his father, Imamshah, was discouraged, gave up his activities, and remained in seclusion.[82] Meanwhile, the Imam in Persia, apprised of the situation after Taj al-Din's death and aware of the desertion of several of Hasan Kabir al-Din's children, summoned Imamshah.[83] The name of the Imam is mentioned by Nur Muhammadshah as "Bhudar Ali," i.e., Abu Dharr ʿAli b. Gharib Mirza, who succeeded his father in 904/1498. As this Imam was also known as Nur al-Din, the reference ties in very well with Imamshah's testimony in the *City of Paradise* (*Janatpurī*) about his visit to the Imam Nurshah.[84]

It is very likely that the summoning of Imamshah from India and the dispatching of *The Counsels*, all in reaction to the death of Taj al-Din and the crisis precipitated by the earlier death of his brother, Hasan Kabir al-Din, occurred at a period after the death of the first Mustansir bi'llah.[85] This is further supported by the scribe's preamble to the work in the manuscript used by Ivanow in which it is written, "This book, the source of gnosis and repository of mercy, *The Counsels of Chivalry*, is composed completely of the clemency adorned pronouncements of Hadrat Mawlana Mustansir bi'llah the Second."[86] As Ivanow has indicated, it is Gharib Mirza who is known as Mustansir bi'llah the Second, his grandfather being the first. The Fatimid caliph of the same name had lived centuries earlier and was therefore not included in the enumeration.[87] We can therefore speculate, subject to correction in the event that further evidence comes to light, that the *Counsels* contain the teachings of the second Mustansir bi'llah, also known as Gharib Mirza.

Bu Ishaq Quhistani

One of the most interesting texts to come down to us from the period of Gharib Mirza is a work entitled simply *Seven Chapters* (*Haft Bāb*). It was written by an Ismaili proselyte, Bu Ishaq Quhistani, i.e., Abu Ishaq, the initial vowel, as is common, having been lost through a process of aphesis. A reference in his work to Mu'minabad in Quhistan suggests that he was from that locale.[88] Thankful for his new religious affiliation, Bu Ishaq felt beholden to his new co-religionists and wrote the work as a means of expressing his gratitude:

> When this most insignificant servant of the servants of the Rightly Guiding Summons—may God strengthen it in both the East and the West of the earth!—Bu Ishaq, by everlasting divine favor and sempiternal guidance, dissociated himself from those who were astray and the community of lost ones who are the devils of our days and the imposters of our time, that is to say those who remain with (only) the exoteric aspect of the words of the prophets and summoners and, in the manner of beasts, are content with straw and leaves, having fallen far from the status of humanity, [as the Qur'an 25:44 says]: "Nay! Like cattle, rather, even further from the path," he deemed it necessary to express his thanks and praise in this matter in whatever imperfect manner he was able to, containing his own story and that which he had learned about the path of the community of the bearers of truth (*muḥiqqān*) of our time. Thus, the meek among the respondents to the daʿwa may be helped and perchance may remember this most insignificant servant in their prayers, seeking help and success from the threshold of the lord of the worlds and the creator of men and jinn—may his power be exalted and his word be ennobled! Indeed, he is the best to assist and abet. We consider only him our lord, he alone, the sufficient![89]

In his third chapter, Bu Ishaq names the Imam at the time of his writing in his enumeration of all the Imams from ʿAli onward as "Mawlana, the lord of the present time, master of the resurrection, the commander of the faithful and the Imam of the pious, Mawlana Mustansir—prostration and glorification upon the mention of his name."[90] Similarly, when dwelling on the mystical importance of the number twelve, he writes:

> The glorious name of the Qa'im, the lord of eighteen thousand worlds—prostration and glorification be due on his mention—Mawlana *ʿala dhikri-hi al-salam*—consists of twelve letters. Blessings be upon the name of that saint by whom all that exists is kept alive:
>
> Even if I wash my mouth with musk and rose water a thousand times
> Still it would be utterly improper for me to pronounce thy name![91]

He is not, of course, referring to the name of Hasan *ʿala dhikrihi al-salam*, the Imam of Alamut, but to the Imam of his own time, Mustansir bi'llah, whose name, in Arabic, consists of twelve letters. The passage is also revealing in another sense. As a matter of deference, the proper name of an Imam was rarely used. This is a universal form of etiquette throughout much of the East. To refer to a distinguished personage by his or her proper name is considered a sign of disrespect. Even today, Ismailis of a traditional bent will rarely use the given name of the Imam, preferring instead to say Mawlana (our lord), Hadir Imam (the present Imam), Khudawand (lord), or other titles that vary depending on language and region. It is for this very reason that we find numerous Ismaili works that, while they repeatedly refer to the Imam, never explicitly name him, making the task of the historian particularly difficult.

Ivanow had searched in vain for copies of Bu Ishaq's *Seven Chapters* in Iran. He thus hypothesized that the work was preserved only in Badakhshan.[92] However, during the course of her research in Iranian Ismaili villages, Maryam Moezzi did, in fact, find a copy of the treatise preserved, which she adjudges to be superior to the copy available to Ivanow. An important portion of a sentence, absent in Ivanow's edition, mentions another work on spiritual exegesis written by the author. The missing fragment is contained in square brackets:

> In this epistle is but a scent of the spiritual exegeses (*taʾwīlāt*) of the religious laws (*sharāʾiʿ*). [We have written an epistle on the spiritual exegeses of the religious laws] and the exoteric aspects of the Qur'an from which should be sought a complete treatment of this subject. Nevertheless, here we will also mention a bit of the spiritual exegesis of the Qur'an.[93]

In addition to *The Seven Chapters* and this epistle on spiritual exegesis, we also know that Bu Ishaq conceived of writing a treatise on the proclamation of the Great Resurrection that occurred at Alamut during the imamate of the Imam Hasan *ʿala dhikrihi al-salam*:

> With the help of Mawlana, the lord of the resurrection, I hope to pen a few epistles on the history (*taʾrīkh*) of the great resurrection (*qiyāmat-i qiyāmāt*), which the prophets and sages have predicted, all of them indicating it and heralding its joyful tidings. The epistles will include a mention of the blessed address as well as its translation and explanation, to the best of the ability of this most insignificant of the servants of the rightly guiding summons, God willing, Mawlana![94]

It is not known if this desire was ever fulfilled. Ivanow, however, associates this book with a certain *History of Quhistan* (*Taʾrīkh-i Quhistān*) that is mentioned twice, without citing an author, by a slightly later figure, Khayrkhwah Harati (d. after 960/1553). Poonawala suggests that this planned epistle and *History of Quhistan* are two separate works, but he ascribes both to Bu Ishaq.[95] If they are not the same work, though, there is no reason to attribute *History of Quhistan* to him. In any case, the fact that the subject matter of the *History*, as described by Khayrkhwah, differs from what Bu Ishaq intended to write in his *Epistles* makes the identification of the two implausible.

The first reference to the contents of *History of Quhistan* in Khayrkhwah's writing occurs in a passage describing how the devotees (*fidāʾīs*) gave up their lives at the command of Sayyidna, i.e., Hasan-i Sabbah. He then states that this is described at length in *History of Quhistan*.[96] The second occurrence is in a very similar context but adds the names of Raʾis Muzaffar and Raʾis Hasan to that of Hasan-i Sabbah, both of these being prominent leaders in Alamut times.[97] There is nothing in either of these two citations that mentions the author of *History of Quhistan*. Moreover, the subject matter has nothing to do with the declaration of the great resurrection, which is the topic about which Bu Ishaq intended to write. Hence, there is no compelling reason to adopt the attribution of Ivanow and Poonawala. We do know, however, of a now lost *History of Quhistan* written by a certain Abu al-Mahamid Rubakhti. This history was cited by ʿAli b. Muhammad Yasiri Husami, a student of the aforementioned Ismaili poet Ibn Husam Khusfi. Rubakht, from where Abu al-Mahamid apparently came, is an old village situated between Qaʾin and Birjand, both major Ismaili centers. It is quite conceivable that this is the book referred to by Khayrkhwah Harati.[98]

Khwaja ʿAbd Allah Ansari, Husayn, Zamani, and Other Poets

In one version of *The Seven Chapters* available to him, as well as in *The Sage's Discourse*, Ivanow came across an interesting poetic quotation:

> Betimes an aged man, a child or a fair youth he becomes, betimes he rises to the heavens for the ascension (*miʿraj*)[99] or descends into a dark well. If he appears in a hundred different forms, why should those of spiritual insight be anxious? Betimes he becomes Mustansir betimes Salam Al-lah![100]

We can now positively identify the author of these verses as Khwaja ʿAbd Allah Ansari, an Ismaili poet who should not be confused with the Sufi poet of the same name. This Ismaili poet was first identified by Faquir M. Hunzai.[101] When read in its entirety, translated in chapter 8, it can be seen that the verses as found in the manuscript that Ivanow designates HBAB-B as well as in *The Sage's Discourse* are somewhat out of order. The verse on the possibility of the Imam being a child, a youth, or an elderly person is intriguing, particularly so because two other contemporary poets not mentioned in the bibliographies of Ivanow and Poonawala, with the pen names Husayn and Zamani, repeat this sentiment in their verses. Husayn writes: "We make the exalted name of the sovereign of faith, Gharib Mirza, the litany of our tongues. Betimes he's a child, betimes a youth, betimes an aged man. 'Tis incumbent we make the prophetic tradition our sign."[102] And we find virtually the same passage in Zamani:

> Betimes you come in the form of a child, betimes a youth or aged man. In every garb you've come with different attributes. By name you are Mustansir, for you are the Imam of the time. You've come luminous, like the sun in its noble constellation [Aries]. Betimes you appear with the name of Shah Gharib. The king with the countenance of Canopus and visage of the moon has come![103]

Yet again, in the *Seven Chapters* of Bu Ishaq, we find the same sentiment, "All the Imams are Mawlana ʿAli, all are one. Though sometimes he may appear as a youth, sometimes as an aged man and sometimes as a child, this is done in order that the world and creation may remain stable."[104] Is this perhaps an indication that the Imam was unusually young or old when he succeeded to the office? The latter seems quite likely as he had a very short period of imamate. In addition, he has left a few works, which would have been less likely had he died young. It is even possible that the Imam himself mentioned the inconsequence of age in the matter of the imamate, and hence it became a poetic trope used by contemporary Ismaili poets. The second hemistich of the couplet of Husayn might suggest that a prophetic tradition to this effect exists.[105] Of course, this idea was not at all new to Ismailism. Juwayni had already noted the belief that the "Imam is basically the same, whether an infant, a youth or an old man."[106] Nevertheless, the insistence on the concept during the reign of this Imam evokes curiosity.

With regard to the short extract of Khwaja ʿAbd Allah Ansari's poem in the HBAB-B and *The Sage's Discourse* that contains the "succession verses," Ivanow rightly observed:

> This may refer to the succession of the first Mustansir of Anjudan, "Shah Qalandar," by his son, Salamu'l-lah (or ʿAbdu's-Salam). Or should it be, counting back, Mustansir the second of Anjudan, "Shah Gharib," the present, who succeeded Salamu'l-lah?[107]

The appearance of similar verses in the poems of Husayn and Zamani, however, strongly suggests that Ansari, too, refers to the second Mustansir, known as Shah Gharib and Gharib Mirza. Husayn's poem is particularly noteworthy because it mentions the residence of the Imam as Anguwan (i.e., Anjudan), thus confirming the epigraphic evidence. He also quotes a verse of another poet, apparently Ismaili, who wrote under the pen name ʿAzizi. In addition to Husayn, Zamani, and ʿAbd Allah Ansari, two other poets, one anonymous and one with the pen name Darwish, some of whose verses will be discussed in the next chapter, wrote in the time of the Imam Gharib Mirza. Similarly, a reference to this Imam turns up unexpectedly in the old prayer (*duʿā*) formerly recited by the South Asian Ismailis, in which the believers utter a litany (*taṣbīḥ*) in the name of Shah Gharib Mirza.[108]

Within a few years of this Imam's death, Shiʿism was to emerge politically triumphant in Iran, brought to power by the Safawid revolution. His mausoleum, known locally as that of "Shah Gharib," is found at Anjudan.[109] The wooden casket that was once in the mausoleum is no longer in existence.[110] It was, however, virtually identical to that in the mausoleum of his grandfather.[111] The date recorded reads Muharram 904/August 1498, which means that the Imam Gharib Mirza must have passed away shortly before that time.

The Kaʿba of Reality

Gharib Mirza's disciple, the poet Husayn, had written of the Imam's residence, "We make Anjudan our Kaʿba of reality."[112] This was not simply a poetic trope, but an allusion to Ismaili spiritual hermeneutics (*taʾwīl*). To the community, unless the spiritual meanings of physical rites and practices were understood, these rituals were hollow. Bu Ishaq, a contemporary of this Imam, pointedly asked why a person of any religion makes a *qibla*, a direction of prayer, of the sky, or of a house.[113] Hasan-i Mahmud, writing during Alamut times, is even more explicit. He reflects:

> In worshipping God they set their faces toward a particular physical body, such as toward the heavens, or the sun, moon and stars, or toward a fire, or a house that is famous and well-known among the buildings of the world. They make that an intermediary between themselves and God, and imagine that through that *qibla* they will arrive at God. But in this regard God says, "They are like cattle, or even further astray" (7:179). A wise person ought to think and reflect upon this issue: In the matter of the recognition of God, which is the root of religion, how can those who take their own whims and suppositions as a guide, and in the matter of worshipping God, which is a branch of religion, make a stone, a house, a tree or something else a *qibla* as an intermediary, reach the lord? How can they recognize God?[114]

Unless a Muslim understood the spiritual significance of bowing in prayer toward the Kaʿba, how was this worship any different from that of the idolaters? Bu Ishaq's Ismaili predecessor and one of the greatest luminaries of Persian poetry and thought, Nasir-i Khusraw, insisted that the basis of religious law and ritual must be the God-given intellect. "I never accepted following along blindly (*taqlīd*)," he declares, "for this is not how truth becomes known."[115] "Thus did I travel from this town to that, asking questions, wandering, in search of truth, over land and sea." He charges:

> With my own eyes I see that it is day, yet you claim it's night, and when I ask for proof, all you can do is draw your sword. You claim, "In such and such a place, there is a stone most holy, all who undertake a pilgrimage there shall be ennobled. What?! Azar, father of Abraham, called us to an idol, you summon to a stone? I say, in my eyes you're nothing but today's Azar![116]

Without a spiritual exegesis, the blind following of rites was considered to border on gross idolatry. Nasir-i Khusraw's contemporary al-Mu'ayyad fi al-Din Shirazi had posed the same question and urged the believers to consider why God had commanded them to take as their *qibla* the "inviolable place of prostration" (2:144), the Kaʿba.[117] Logically speaking, the Kaʿba was an inanimate house, made of the same lifeless materials as any other house. That a human being, endowed with life and intellect, should bow in prayer toward unthinking, inert matter was a travesty. However, for people of spiritual understanding, this was a symbol (*mathal*). It is not the human soul that prostrates before the lifeless Kaʿba, but the human body, itself created from dust. As dust eventually returns to dust, the human body prostrates toward that to which it must ultimately return. The human soul, however, prostrates toward the purified spirit of the Imam of the time, who is the supreme sign of God, the luminous epiphany of his will and the *qibla* of truth.[118] In this way, the corporeal part of humanity bows toward that which is corporeal (*kathīf*), to which it must return; and the spiritual part of humanity bows toward that which is spiritual and sublime (*laṭīf*), to which it must return. Only by merging oneself in God's will, represented by the Imam, could the ultimate return to God be realized. The Imam is the one symbolized (*mamthūl*) by the Kaʿba, for he is the spiritual house of God, the living repository of the divine command. As al-Mu'ayyad explains in thought-provoking verses, "What the Almighty has said in the Book is a symbol, beneath which there is someone symbolized,"[119] "Strive toward the sanctuary of the symbolized beyond the symbol. The latter is the sting of a bee, the former is pure honey!"[120]

The inanimate Kaʿba is thus a physical sign of God's house (*bayt Allāh*), while the Imam is its living reality. The physical prostration toward the Kaʿba is a constant reminder of the spiritual prostration toward the bearer of God's command, the Imam of the time. The apparent meaning (*ẓāhir*) of the revelation and the practice of the faith is brought to life and made intelligible only through spiritual exegesis.[121] Thus, al-Mu'ayyad writes in verses addressed to the Fatimid Imam al-Mustansir, who coincidentally bore the same name as the last Imam discussed in this book:

> O most glorious *qibla* of Truth
> And most sublime Kaʿba of the living
> If the pilgrimage of the hajj is undertaken to the inanimate house
> So much more fitting, so much more worthy, that we betake ourselves
> unto you![122]

How apt it is that on the lower portion of the casket of the Imam Mustansir bi'llah of Anjudan, known as Gharib Mirza, is inscribed the following couplet:

> O King, certainly, in the way of the path
> The threshold of your court became the *qibla* of the world[123]

SEVEN

The Way of the Seeker

I was overcome with grief that my entire life had been thrown to the winds. Sometimes my soul, torn by sorrow, would be ready to escape my body in its longing for help. At other times my bleeding heart would burst into tears in its search for respite, forcing me to seek solitude from the company of others.

Bu Ishaq Quhistani in *Seven Chapters*

Nasir-i Khusraw lived a carefree life in his younger days. He was a lover of wine, women, and the company of friends, and enjoyed a comfortable position in government service.[1] Nevertheless, behind this façade was a man in deep pain who felt empty and hollow inside. Recalling the Prophet's words, "Speak the truth, even if it be against yourself," in his *Travelogue* (*Safarnāma*), he ruefully admits being constantly drunk during his month-long stay in Juzjanan.[2] It was in this place, however, that something extraordinary was to happen. He had a vision that was to transform his life forever:

> One night I was approached in a dream by someone who chided me, "How long will you drink this brew that destroys human intellect? 'Tis better to be sober." I responded, "The sages have failed to find a better elixir to drive away the sorrows of the world." He said, "Never has drunkenness brought peace of mind. Can one who leads people to stupor be called a sage? Seek that which increases intellect and wisdom."

> I asked, "Where can I find such a thing?" He replied, "Those who seek shall find." And then, pointing in the direction of the *qibla*, he fell silent.[3]

Nasir rose abruptly, the vision still vivid in his mind. He lamented, "I have woken up from last night's dream; but now I must awaken from a dream that has lasted forty years!"[4] He resolved to forswear his blithe ways, knowing that he would never attain true happiness until he did so. Resigning from government service, he set out on his famous journey in search of truth. In a poem in which he recounts what plagued him, he writes:

> Awake from your complacent sleep, O you who have slumbered forty years! Can't you see that not one of your friends remains here? . . . The year was three hundred and ninety-four of the hijra, that's when my mother brought me into this dusty world. So like a plant sprung from black soil and pure water grew I, without knowledge. From the state of plants I reached that of animals, and for a time was like a little birdie without wings. In the fourth stage the signs of humanity manifested as the faculty of speech somehow found its way into this turbid body.[5] When the celestial spheres measured out forty-two years for me, my enquiring soul began to seek wisdom. I listened to the learned expound the sciences of the spheres, time and elements, read book after book. I found myself more learned than those around me, but said, "There must certainly be someone superior!"[6] Like the hawk among birds, the camel among beasts, the date palm among trees, the ruby among jewels, the Quran among books, the Kaʿba among houses, like the heart in the human body, the sun among stars. My spirit was vexed with such ponderings and thoughts, this pensive soul enquired of every thinker: I sought from Shafiʿite, Malikite, and the words of the Hanafites the path to God's chosen one, the ruler of the world, the guide. Each one indicated a different path—one summoned to Tartary, one to the folk of Barbary. When I asked "why" and "wherefore" and desired strong proofs, they squirmed in helplessness, this one blind, the other deaf. Till one day I read the "Verse of the Covenant" (*bayʿat*) in the Quran, in which God says, "My hand is upon their hands" (48:10). Ah yes! These were the ones who swore the covenant, pledging allegiance beneath the tree, the likes of Jaʿfar, Miqdad, Salman and Abu Dharr. I asked, "Whereof that tree? That hand on which to pledge? Where can I find that hand, that covenant, that company?" They replied, "There remains neither that tree, nor that hand, for that assembly has now dispersed, that hand has disappeared." What?! All of them were friends of the

> Prophet, the best among mankind, rewarded with paradise, singled out for having pledged the oath! I asked, "Is it not stated in the Quran that Ahmad is the bearer of glad tidings, the warner, and a luminous lamp?" (33:45–46), and that if the infidels wish to extinguish that light God will keep it shining despite their intention? (9:32) How is it possible that today that assembly is no more? Are Almighty God's words not true? Whose hand shall we take to pledge our oath? Are those who came later to be deprived of what was given formerly? What sin of ours is it that we were not born at that time? Why should we be deprived of the Prophet, distressed?[7]

Nasir-i Khusraw was incredulous that God could be unjust. The Quran declared, "God was delighted with the believers when they swore the covenant to you (Muhammad) under the tree, and he knew what was in their hearts, sent down tranquility upon them, and rewarded them with victory close at hand" (48:18), and also, "Indeed, those who pledge the covenant to you (Muhammad), they swear it but to God himself. The hand of God is upon their hands. Then he who breaks the oath, breaks it against his own soul; but on those who fulfill what they have pledged to God, he will bestow a magnificent reward!" (48:10). "Why should later believers be deprived of this reward?" asked Nasir. "What fault was it of theirs that they were not born in the time of the Prophet?" God, in his justice, had not allowed that hand to disappear, nor that assembly to disperse. According to Nasir, there must always be someone at whose hand the covenant to God could be pledged. This, he decided, was the Imam descended from the Prophet, al-Mustansir of Cairo, the sovereign of a mighty empire. He attributed his spiritual transformation to the Imam, writing in limpid verses:

> When the light of the Imam of the time shone upon my soul
> Even though I was dark as night, I became the glorious sun
> The supreme name is the Imam of the time
> By which I ascended, Venus-like, from the earth to heaven[8]

Centuries later, a Muslim by the name of Bu Ishaq Quhistani was to face a crisis of faith similar to that of Nasir-i Khusraw. His search for truth eventually led him to pledge his fealty to the Imam al-Mustansir of Anjudan. However, unlike al-Mustansir of Cairo, to whom Nasir-i Khusraw owed his allegiance, al-Mustansir of Anjudan lived in a period of concealment and was forced by his enemies to leave his home, which, Pir Shihab al-Din Shah tells us, led to his being known as Gharib Mirza, "the Exiled Prince."[9] In this chapter we accompany Bu Ishaq on his spiritual search to explore the conduct of the daʿwa in this period, and examine the concept and context of taqiyya in greater depth.

VEILING AND UNVEILING: THE WORKINGS OF TAQIYYA

In chapter 6, abstention from the use of the Imam's proper name was discussed in the context of deference and respect. However, we should not overlook the fact that in addition to being a sign of reverence, the avoidance of naming the Imam was a means of preventing others from discovering his whereabouts. This reason is explicitly mentioned in a homily of the Imam in his *Counsels of Chivalry* (*Pandiyāt-i Jawānmardī*) in which he cautions the faithful not to mention his name in the presence of the enemies of the faith.[10] This was nothing new in Shiʿi Islam. In order to conceal the Imam's identity he was sometimes referred to in an oblique manner, as when the Imam Jaʿfar al-Sadiq is called simply "the man of knowledge" (*al-ʿālim*).[11] From a different angle, the Muʿtazili author Abu Jaʿfar al-Iskafi (d. 240/854) states that during the period of Umayyad rule, transmitters of traditions from ʿAli would never dare to refer to him by name and hence merely related from "a man from the Quraysh" (*rajul min quraysh*).[12]

The writings of Husayn, the poet of Imam Gharib Mirza's time, clearly point to the need for continued caution. However, while indicative of the ongoing practice of taqiyya, the verses also suggest that esoteric discussion within the community flourished and was encouraged:

> The time has come to express love openly, we expound the secrets of faith to the lovers. After this we shall sit together in probity, concealing the path of the summons from the enemies of faith.[13]

Some indications in Ibn Husam's poetry indicate that the Imam, whatever his policy with non-Ismailis, was now openly available to all of his followers. The full text of his composition, a verse of which, as we saw earlier, was favored by the author of *The Sage's Discourse* (*Kalām-i Pīr*), is as follows:

> Brothers, by God, it's the season of orisons; seek your desires, for it's the time of needs. It's the resurrection that manifests every six thousand years. Now, as it's the seventh, there's the lord of the resurrections. If you don't recognize the Imam of the time in truth, you will head for hellfire, despite your hundred thousand devotions. All who recognized not their lord are certainly plunged in infidelity and darkness. How can the secret remain hidden between God and his servant? For God is the knower of mysteries and master of hidden things. Abandon your caprice and fleshly thoughts, keep your eye steady on the goal, for naught but nonsense is all in your heart, save him. All I said from my own imaginings and

analogies was but a fable and delusion in his presence. Say the name of Mawlana with the innermost heart of sincerity, for he has become manifest, and his summons is the talk of the town. From east and west the comrades have manifested, but all of this is bound by a single indication. In your grace, cast a glance upon your humble slaves, for among the people there is much discourse. Give the wine of yearning from the brimful goblet of Mawlana, for all of this is due to the mercy of the congregations. Forgive Ibn Husam, your humble slave, for he is imprisoned in the well of darkness.[14]

The Seven Days of Creation

The second couplet of Ibn Husam's poem is a reference to the Ismaili belief concerning the seven days of creation,[15] premised, among other indications, on the Quran's declaration "Lo! Your lord is God who created the heavens and the earth in six days. Then he ascended the throne" (7:54).

The Abrahamic faiths share a belief in the completion of creation in six days, with the seventh day, or Sabbath, having a hallowed aura of particular veneration and sanctity. The Bible had also affirmed, "And God blessed the seventh day and made it holy" (Genesis 2:3). Reflecting on this notion, al-Mu'ayyad fi al-Din Shirazi observed that those who seek to explain this exoterically are completely befuddled. By confounding scriptural statements that, in his view, are clearly symbolic, with crude speculations about the creation of the physical universe in six twenty-four hour periods, the exotericists have completely misunderstood the sacred texts. Al-Mu'ayyad reasons that time itself is marked by the movement of the celestial spheres, with the rising and setting of the sun indicating to human beings the passing of the days. Now, if creation had yet to occur, if God had yet to fashion the sun, the earth, and the planetary bodies, how then could these verses refer to the passage of time as it is conventionally understood? The sage is even less impressed by those who claim, citing a Quranic verse, that the creation of the heavens and the earth takes God six days, each spanning a thousand years.[16] Certainly, he opines, the Creator, whose power is infinite, is not limited by time in his creation; as God says in the Quran, "Ours is but a single command, like the twinkling of an eye" (54:50).[17] There must therefore be a deeper meaning to the six days of creation, he asserts, and it is the place of esoteric exegesis (*ta'wīl*) to unveil that meaning.[18]

In his masterpiece of spiritual hermeneutics, *The Face of Religion* (*Wajh-i Dīn*), Nasir-i Khusraw expounds on the spiritual concept of the Sabbath as follows:

> It is mentioned in the traditions that God, may he be exalted, commenced the creation of the world on Sunday, completed it on Friday and rested

> on the Sabbath. The import of this tradition has been hidden from the people since the dawn of time. All have accepted it according to the capacity of their intellects. The Jews revere the Sabbath and do not work on it because God rested on this day. However, they are unaware that when the Prophets said this, they meant for people to know that, by the command of God, six Prophets would come to this world to direct people to work. When the seventh came, he would not direct in this manner. Rather, he would reward them for their labors. They called it the Sabbath and declared it sacred.[19]

Thus, these days do not concern the creation of the physical universe. They refer to the creation of a spiritual cosmos, a creation that commenced with Adam, who represented the first day of the week, Sunday, and continued with Noah, Abraham, Moses, and Jesus, who represented Monday, Tuesday, Wednesday, and Thursday respectively. This creation was brought to its completion by Muhammad, who is represented by Friday.[20] Yet to come was the last and final day, which would consummate the entire spiritual creation; a day not meant for the commandment of work, but rather for the allocation of reward and retribution. This was the Sabbath, or lord of the resurrection (*qāʾim-i qiyamat*).[21]

> People await the advent of the Sabbath, for there will be repose on that day for those who have recognized the reality of these days and who labored in fulfillment of (the Prophets') command and with knowledge. Those who toil physically in this physical world and know the esoteric meaning of this with their souls today will be rewarded for it tomorrow in the spiritual world.[22]

The days of creation, in Ismaili thought, were thus considered the great cycles of prophecy. God's intention in the verses concerning the creation of the world was not the dense world of earthly phenomena, but a world of far greater import, that of religion. In the former, time is marked by the movement of the celestial spheres, while in the latter, it is marked by the coming of God's messengers, the lords of the cycles (*ṣāḥibān-i adwār*). The structure of these cycles of prophecy was of tremendous interest to the Ismaili savants. In particular, Ibn Husam may have had in mind a dictum quoted and elaborated upon by the Imam *ʿAla dhikrihi al-salam*. The benedictory formula "*ʿala dhikrihi al-salam*" meaning "on whose mention be peace" was often used by Ismaili authors for their Imams. However, it was most commonly associated with the Imam of Alamut Hasan *ʿala dhikrihi al-salam* and it is likely that the following words are his:

> If mankind knew what the imamate was, no one would have entertained doubts such as these. If only they had realized that mutability cannot

> exist without some immutable [central] point, just as the circumference of a circle [cannot exist] without the center point. Everything that rotates or moves requires a cause for its rotation and movement, and the moving force in relation to the object which rotates or moves must be stable and perfect, in order to be able to spin or move it. This is why it has been said [in the Gospels]: "Heaven and earth will change, but the commandment of the Sabbath will never be altered."[23] This means that while the Prophets and the hujjats may change—at one time this one, at another time that one, at one time in this community, at another time in that—the Imam will never change: *We are the people of eternity.*[24]

The Paradise of Submission elaborates on this theme by commenting that in "the creation of the heavens and the earth," "heaven" refers to the exoteric physical laws and "earth" means the hidden spiritual laws that were completed and further perfected in each cycle by the prophets of revelation. The cycle of Muhammad is the beginning of the cycle of the resurrection, and hence his exoteric and esoteric laws were to attain their perfection on the advent of the seventh day, that of the lord of the resurrection.[25] According to Ibn Husam's verses, the seventh cycle was at hand and the lord of the resurrections was among his people.

The anonymous author of *The Epistle on the Recognition of the Imam*, who possibly lived sometime after Ibn Husam, also elaborates on this doctrine.[26] Only on the day of the Sabbath (i.e., the cycle of the lord of the resurrection) can the Imam be recognized in his essence. The Sabbath is the "day of faith" while the remaining six days are, by comparison, the "nights of faith" during which people are guided by the moon (the *ḥujjat*), which reflects the light of the sun (the Imam).[27]

Ibn Husam's allusion in his poem to his time being the seventh cycle suggests that the Imam was openly available to all of his followers, and not just to the higher ranks of the daʿwa hierarchy. We know from the anonymous *mathnawi*, cited earlier, that the four Imams after 'Ala' al-Din Muhammad were hidden.[28] By this time, though, the Imams had moved to the relative safety of Anjudan. Thus, Ibn Husam indicates that not only the comrades (*rafīqān*) (i.e., members of the daʿwa), but even the Imam himself was available to all the believers.

The Cloak of Twelver Shiʿism

In this period, we also witness the transformation of the types of religious pressures that were being exerted on the Ismailis. While earlier we find evidence of the community's dissimulation as Sunni Muslims, we now find proof of their adopting the cover of Twelver Shiʿism.[29] In fact, some of Ibn Husam's verses are in praise of the Imams of the Twelvers, indicating that by this time at least some of the Ismailis were dissimulating as Ithna ʿasharis.[30] D. O. Morgan, on the subject of the religious environment of fifteenth–century Iran, writes, "During this period, which was one of considerable religious flux, the expression of a reverence for ʿAlī and even for the later Shīʿī *imāms* does not seem to have been thought incompatible with a more or less orthodox Sunnism."[31] Such sentiments would have allowed the Ismailis to blend in more easily in both Twelver Shiʿi and Sunni milieus.

Particularly intriguing as evidence of this phenomenon, and its inherent danger, is testimony in *The Counsels of Chivalry*. Composed, as it was, on the eve of the Safawid revolution, and in the vicinity of the most important centers of Twelver learning, the text constantly reminds the believers that the Imam is present (*ḥāḍir*), not occulted (*ghāʾib*):

> A house with no windows remains dark. The house of the heart of someone who has no access to the Imam of the time, who is the sun of the age, remains dark and gloomy, having no enlightenment. It constantly remains in the obscurity of enmity and rancor. Darkness gives rise to calamity, straying from the path, and finding oneself lost. Those who have no access to the present (*ḥāḍir*) Imam, considering the Imam to be occulted (*ghāʾib*), are the people of discord and are lost. As they have no Imam they have split into numerous sects and are always quarrelling, opposing each other and at each other's throats.[32]

The Counsels of Chivalry explains that to find the Imam of the time is just as incumbent in the present age as finding the prophet of the time was in the past. Those who acted in accordance with the law (*sharīʿa*) of a previous prophet, not following the prophet of their own time, were in error. This was regardless of the fact that the older law may have been divinely ordained in its own age. A newer law always supersedes an older one. Now that the period of prophecy is over, that of imamate is in effect. It is therefore essential for people to recognize and follow the Imam of their time.[33] Those who don't seek out the Imam of the time and unthinkingly hold to the ways of their forefathers are the people of blind imitation (*ahl-i taqlīd*). Their leaders are most severely reproached, as can be seen in the Imam's powerful riposte to the priestcraft of the 'ulama':

> Beware! Beware of the people of blind imitation. Don't follow the oppressive 'ulama', by whom I mean the exoteric 'ulama'. They deny the very existence of the Imam, (the possibility of) finding the path to him and of being ennobled by proximity to the Imam of the time. If someone says, "The Imam is alive and present. It is incumbent to find a way to him," they declare that poor wise man an infidel and heretic, stoning him

> to death. They say, "The Imam is in occultation (*ghā'ib*). Whenever God wills, he will manifest." They continue, "If someone appoints a time for his manifestation, he is a liar." Take refuge in God from such self-worshipping 'ulama'. What a wonderful tale they have spun for themselves! What a wonderful well of water they've stored up for themselves! They silence people by threatening to declare them infidels. (The masses) set up such foolish commoners as their leaders. Meanwhile, the pure hearted who become aware of the Imam dare not breathe a word for fear of these obstinate self-worshippers![34]

The Imam Mustansir bi'llah continues with his criticism of the exoteric 'ulama', affirming that such people have existed in every period of history. Because they were greedy for power, they persecuted and fought the Imams of their time, seeking to "extinguish the light of God." This is a direct allusion to the Qur'an 9:32, also cited by Nasir-i Khusraw, "Fain would they extinguish the light of God with their mouths. But God disdains aught, save that he shall perfect his light, however much the disbelievers are averse." Unable to succeed in their evil designs, the 'ulama' resort to intrigue and lies, teaching that the Imam has disappeared (*ghā'ib shuda*). They stone to death all who dare assert that the Imam is present, issuing *fatwas* to this end.[35] In his *World Adorning ʿAbbasid History*, Iskandar Beg Munshi records an incident that sheds further light on the situation. Some three years after the suppression of the Nuqtawis, Shah ʿAbbas I had embarked on a symbolic pilgrimage on foot to the shrine of the eighth Ithna ʿashari Imam al-Rida in Mashhad. On the way he encountered two Nuqtawis, one of whom was Dervish Kamal. Dervish Kamal asked the mightiest of Safawid monarchs the logic of such a pious journey to the grave of a dead man. "Seek the living Imam," he advised. When Shah ʿAbbas asked him who that may be, Dervish Kamal responded, "me." The Shah taunted the dervish, taking aim at him and saying, "Let me see if you can survive a bullet then," to which Dervish Kamal responded sarcastically, "Your Imam Rida died eating a grape, and you expect me to survive a bullet?"[36]

The polemics of the clerics and reaction of the Safawid shah not only demonstrate the power of pharisaical condemnation, but also exhibit the passion and paranoia of a challenge to the established authorities. Clearly, this censure by the 'ulama' and the very real physical threats that accompanied it were something that must have plagued the Ismaili community at that time, this being the context of the speech of the Imam cited above. The Ismailis were certainly not alone in their wariness of the clerical class. Chardin records for us a popular medieval folk saying from Isfahan, "Keep a wary eye in front of you for a woman, behind you for a mule, and from every direction for a mullah!"[37]

Nizari Quhistani writes in the deliciously mordant lines of one of his poems:

> The world has been devastated by clerics who skim off charitable donations for themselves! Go, Nizari, and dress yourself in the garments of obtuse ignorance. Do not idly sow away the seed of your life in this world's farmlands, putting stock in the thought you'll reap any harvest from such brackish marshland. Why should a reasonable mind incline to hear the sermon preached by a hypocrite? When does a doctor of intellect ever prescribe opium to a madman? The perfidy and vice of the so-called "folk of virtue" has reached such a point that it is *de rigueur* that we commend and acclaim anybody who is a knave! Indeed, what have they learned from studying jurisprudence but the art of imposture, fraud and humbug? What have they profited from pursuit of knowledge and learning but enmity and hostility? Alas! If it weren't for the fact that they feared it might rouse popular agitation against them, these learned divines skilled in jurisprudence would themselves consume wine in public from on high in their pulpits! Go (just try it out for yourself): invite a jurist to a banquet: you'll see how like a cat he'll show up for lunch also when you invite him to dinner![38]

Centuries later, Pir Shihab al-Din Shah was to write:

> Brother, for the righteous, darkness has seized the world, the long arm of the enemies has stretched out, the place of tribulation has come in between. The people have changed. All take their own path and conceive their own ideas. A group rushed after the ignorant, who are nothing more than highway robbers. Wherever there was the right (of the true guides) the enemies seized it as best they could. Gradually hearts became dark, ears became deaf and the tongues of those who had the right to speak fell silent. After all, how can one address a crowd of the deaf who do not understand? But now, O brother, there is someone who has the right to speak. If you have the ears to listen, come hither! Or else you will not be able to understand this reality.[39]

The Cover of Sufism

It has been posited that to escape the persecution of such authorities, the Ismailis took the cover of Sufism. Groundbreaking research by the late French orientalist Henry Corbin and his Russian contemporary Wladimir Ivanow established as axiomatic the symbiotic relationship between Sufism and Ismailism in the aftermath of the Mongol invasions. This Ismaili-Sufi association was believed to have continued relatively uninterrupted from the middle of the thirteenth century until modern times. Later authors, including Hamid Algar, Nasrollah Pourjavady, Peter Lamborn Wilson, and Farhad Daftary, have repeated and further elaborated upon the basic hypothesis advanced by the two earlier scholars. While the validity of this thesis in a few recorded instances is clear, some of the presumptions used as evidence for the universal application of such a theory in the two centuries immediately following the destruction of the Ismaili state must be called into question and the hypothesis must be refined. Though the association of the two schools of thought can be well substantiated in the later period, evidence to argue for a blanket application of this thesis in the period immediately following the Mongol invasion is much more scant.

In a personal letter dated Bombay, July 30, 1947, Ivanow, dubbed the father of modern Ismaili studies, wrote to the eminent French Orientalist, Henry Corbin:

> I am much interested in your Institut Franco-Iranien, and shall be glad if you let me know what other departments, in addition to that of Iranology, studying mysticism, it contains? I believe the study of mysticism, unless it is merely silly talk, can only be done by qualified psychiatrists, by clinical methods. It is a pity that while the East is changing with such tremendous speed, and many old forms decay and pass away almost uncessantly [sic], no more urgent and important matter is found meriting study than mystic nonsense. Pity to waste time on this.

Perhaps somewhat taken aback by Ivanow's dismissive arraignment of a subject that he held so dear, the French savant replied simply: "The virulent attack on mysticism at the end of your letter gives me the impression that when using this word we do not mean exactly the same thing."[40]

This exchange between the two scholars most responsible for proposing the symbiotic relationship thesis perhaps typifies one of its central problems—the fact that there exists no universally accepted definition of the word "mysticism," nor of "Sufism." Carl Ernst writes, "How is it possible to tell what Sufism is, and who is a Sufi? In Arabic and Persian, there are dozens of terms for Muslim mystics with distinct and sometimes conflicting meanings, all of which are subsumed by the English word Sufism. As with other terms coined during the Enlightenment to describe religions, Sufism has now become a standard term, whether we like it or not."[41] We must therefore be cognizant of the fact that often scholars have accepted a very broad definition of the word Sufism, certainly much more all-encompassing than the way that the word *tasawwuf* is used in Arabic or Persian. With such broad brushstrokes, not only the Ismailis but also many other religious communities could be simplistically included in such a definition. Undoubtedly, there is a need for greater precision.

The writings of the thirteenth-century Ismaili poet Nizari Quhistani have frequently been forwarded as evidence to support the symbiotic relationship thesis.[42]

There can be little doubt that many of the themes upon which he elaborates and his form of expression mirror those of Sufi poets. However, as discussed in chapter 3, by Nizari's time, the Persian poetic canon was infused with such topoi. It would have been much more noteworthy if Nizari had *not* composed in this idiom. Lewisohn argues that "it is incorrect to say that Nizārī used the vocabulary of Sufism to express Ismāʿīlī ideas; rather it seems more accurate to say that he integrated Sufi spirituality into Ismāʿīlī theosophy."[43] The proposition that Sufism and Ismailism in this period shared many elements of an esoteric vocabulary is incontrovertible, even outside of the Persianate cultural sphere. We have seen evidence of this in the Syrian text by Shihab al-Din Abu Firas entitled *The Ladder of Ascent to the House of Eternity* (*Kitāb Sullam al-Ṣuʿūd ilā Dār al-Khulūd*). The significance of such terms in an Ismaili milieu, though, is sometimes quite unique and distinct from the meaning in other esoteric systems, including Sufism. For example, it has been noted that "the different Nizārī communities in Persia and adjoining regions as well as in India, had gradually come under the authority of their local leaders, who were often referred to by the Sufi term *pīr*, the Persian equivalent of *shaykh*."[44] However, what is more important than the fact that the Sufi term pir is the Persian equivalent of shaykh is the fact that the Ismaili term pir is not the equivalent of the Sufi term pir and differs in many ways from the Sufi concept. A pir is a specific dignitary in the Nizari hierarchy. As an Indic Ismaili poetic text proclaims:

> The true guide is the philosopher's stone
> His disciple, copper
> That will be transformed into gold
> By his touch
>
> In this shadowy age
> There are many
> Who declare themselves pirs
> But they dispel not misgivings
> Know that the true pir
> Is from the house of the Imam
> He will guide you
> Across the ocean of existence
>
> The pir has shown you
> The indescribable, exalted Imam
> The lord ʿAli
> Who has come in the West[45]

Clearly, then, in Ismailism the pir was appointed and his purpose was to lead the adepts to the Imam. This is further emphasized in *The Counsels of Chivalry*:

> O believers, if you wish to perfect your knowledge of God and attain gnosis of him, accept the commandments of the pir of your time. Do whatever he tells you, never straying from his order. Remain forever within his command, that you may be among the people of spiritual unveiling. The pir is someone upon whom the Imam of the time bestows this position, which makes him the noblest being of all creation. Whenever he has appointed and established a pir, the pir must explain the matters of gnosis in detail. Through his mediation, you must perfect your recognition of the Imam.[46]

Nizari Quhistani's elaboration of the position of the pir in his *Resplendent and Luminous* (*Azhar wa-Mazhar*) is equally telling:

> You must have a pir who is the master of mysteries, who will hold your hand and lead you to Someone. Entrust yourself and submit to him, to completely forsake all fear and desire. No station is higher than submission (*taslīm*), so long as you do not flee from spiritual teaching (*taʿlīm*). Through submission, one abandons one's self. Without abandoning the self, how can it be submission?[47]

The purpose of the pir is to lead the seekers to someone who will accept their submission (i.e., to the Imam himself). The seeker then progresses in the path of spiritual edification and teaching, or taʿlim. Hence, while the meanings of the word pir may overlap in the contexts of Sufism and Ismailism, they are certainly not identical. This sharing of a pervasive vocabulary is not at all unusual. The Jewish-Persian poet ʿImrani's work is similarly suffused with such words. He refers to the Jewish elders (Hebrew, *hazeqenim*) to whom the Torah was handed by Joshua as pirs and to Moses as a dervish; but one would hardly conclude from this that they were Sufis.[48]

The use of other such terms in the Nizari texts of this time have also been put forth to argue the Sufi connection. It has been noted that "the Nizārīs are referred to in the *Pandiyāt* by Sufi terms such as *ahl-i ḥaqq* and *ahl-i ḥaqīqat*, the people of the truth."[49] It is unclear, however, why these terms must be considered specifically Sufi. In al-Ghazali's *The Deliverer from Error* (*al-Munqidh min al-Ḍalāl*), for example, he uses the term *ahl al-ḥaqq* to refer to the ʿAsharite Sunnis. It is also the name of a sect in western Persia, not to mention the Hurufis, who may have had distinct Ismaili connections. Most important, the Ismailis had long used such terms to refer to their own community. Writing more than five hundred years before the author of *The Counsels of Chivalry*, in his *Book of Correction* (*Kitāb al-Iṣlāḥ*), the Ismaili daʿi Abu Hatim Razi characterized his co-religionists as the "people of truth" (*ahl al-ḥaqīqa*) in contrast to the "reproachable sects" (*al-firaq al-madhmūma*).[50]

Shortly thereafter, in his *Book of Glory* (*Kitāb al-Iftikhār*), Abu Yaʿqub Sijistani referred to his community as the "people of truths" (*ahl al-ḥaqāʾiq*).[51]

Similar is the argument that the fifteenth-century Ismaili Imams began to "adopt Sufi names, like Shāh Qalandar and Shah Gharīb, often also adding the Sufi terms Shāh and ʿAlī to their names."[52] Concerning the first part of the assertion, the title Shah Qalandar, which refers specifically to the mausoleum (rather than the proper name) of the first Imam of Anjudan named Mustansir bi'llah,[53] never occurs in any extant Ismaili source from this period yet discovered. Likewise, as mentioned earlier, the name Shah Gharib, in the Nizari tradition, has been taken as referring to the exile of the Imam from his home, not necessarily to any Sufi activities. With regard to the second argument, that the Ismaili Imams often added the Sufi terms *Shah* and *ʿAli* to their names, the *non sequitur* of the conclusion need scarcely be pointed out. It is difficult to see how Shah and, above all, ʿAli, can be construed to be exclusively Sufi designations. In fact, the use of such terms can be taken as indicative of rising ʿAlid loyalism among the Sufis, rather than increasing Sufi sympathies among the Shiʿa. Shared vocabulary may certainly encourage cross-fertilization, and it is entirely likely that it did. However, in and of itself this does not indicate the elision of boundaries. If we were to make an analogy, one could mention that the word *Imam* is used in both Shiʿism and Sunnism, but to conclude that it means the same thing in both communities would be a grave error. In most modern contexts, the Imam in Sunnism is nothing more than the person who leads the ritual prayer, whereas when this word is used in Shiʿism, the first definition that springs to mind is nothing less than the divinely appointed successor to the Prophet.

We are on much firmer ground when we speak of participation in Sufi orders. Even here, though, the evidence provided has been questionable. Hamid Algar asserts that the association of the Ismaili Imams with the Niʿmat Allahi Sufi order was "almost continuous from the time of al-Mustansir II onwards,"[54] that is to say, from the fifteenth century. However, this claim is not supported by any of the three sources cited by the author, nor have I come across any source from this period that suggests this. Algar's supposition is later repeated by Nasrollah Pourjavady and Peter Lamborn Wilson in their "Ismāʿīlīs and Niʿmatullāhīs"[55] and again by Farhad Daftary who, however, wisely cautions that "concrete evidence is lacking."[56] In fact, it is not until two centuries later that we have solid evidence of Ismaili-Niʿmat Allahi collaboration.[57] While this does not preclude the possibility of an earlier association (indeed, as mentioned earlier, Shah Niʿmat Allah Wali himself vaunted his descent from the Imam Ismaʿil), firm evidence to confirm such a hypothesis has never been presented. One scholar, exploring the life of Nizari Quhistani, writes that the poet "admits that both his friend and he 'had worn the same Sufi mantle from the same Sufi master,' that is, were fellow disciples of the same spiritual guide, demonstrating beyond all doubt his direct affiliation to a Sufi *tarīqa*."[58] This is a rather bold claim drawn from an extract of a poem that never even mentions the word *Sufi*. The reference to the cloak (*khirqa*), could possibly refer to a Sufi affiliation, but this is not a foregone conclusion. In fact, Ibn Khaldun wrote that the Sufis borrowed the practice of the bestowal of such cloaks from the Shiʿa.[59] It is quite possible that both communities maintained similar ritual practices. The same scholar's statement that a certain Amin al-Din, to whom Nizari dedicated his *Travelogue* (*Safarnāma*), was a "Sufi master" is simply an assumption.[60] The fact is we know next to nothing about the biography of this Amin al-Din, let alone that he was the master of a particular Sufi order. The epithets given to him in Nizari's *Travelogue* would certainly be appropriate for a Sufi master, and this may indeed be the case, but they are hardly unequivocal.[61]

The assertion that the Ismaili Pir Shams "adopted the garb of a poor ṣūfī" is similarly flawed.[62] This statement is based on a misreading of the source text, which does not say *ṣūfī*, but rather *sufet*, a fairly common medieval Hindi word derived from the Persian *safed* and its Sanskrit cognate *shveta*, meaning "white." Nor is the reference to Pir Shams, but it is rather his instruction to a disciple, advising the devotee to adopt poor white garb, not the vestments of a Sufi.[63] One of Pir Shams' descendants, Pir Hasan Kabir al-Din, however, was indeed a leading figure in the Suhrawardi Sufi order of South Asia, and this is far more fecund evidence for the symbiotic relationship thesis, albeit from the fifteenth century.[64] Equally significant is the remarkable contemporary testimony of Jalal-i Qaʾini, overlooked by most scholars, which explicitly mentions the community taking the cover of Sufism in order to avoid persecution.

When Ismaili dissimulation under the guise of Sufism is suggested because figures are mentioned in Ismaili texts whom Western scholars have classified as Sufis, we must remember that many of these "Sufis" never identified themselves by this term, nor is it used in the primary sources.[65] Even the redoubtable Ibn al-ʿArabi, who is invariably classified as a Sufi in Western writings, criticized Sufism for not attaining the highest ranks of spirituality and would hardly have used this term for his own mystical system.[66] The preservation of a text such as ʿAziz-i Nasafi's (d. ca. 661/1263) *Quintessence of Realities* (*Zubdat al-Ḥaqāʾiq*) by the Ismailis of the Upper Oxus region holds promise for providing clues of connections that may have existed.[67] But again, even here, it must be determined when this book entered an Ismaili milieu and when, or even if, it came to be considered the product of an Ismaili author, or simply "a good book that was worth copying." It should also be emphasized that Nasafi did not consider himself a Sufi in the technical sense of that term. In his writings, he consistently places the people of the law and the Sufis at a rank lower than those whom he refers to as "the people of unity," a term also used in Ismaili sources.[68] Hermann Landolt perceptively notes that following a dream in which Nasafi was cautioned not to reveal esoteric doctrines, he decided to omit three important chapters from his *Unveiling of Truths* (*Kashf al-Ḥaqāʾiq*). As it happens, these very chapters were on subjects that were of great significance in Ismaili thought, including the concept of the lord of the resurrection (*qā'im-i qiyāmat*).[69] The *Rose-Garden of Mystery* (*Gulshan-i Rāz*) by another mystic, Shabistari (d. after 740/1339), certainly shares many features with Ismaili works and has been called to evidence the symbiotic relationship thesis. Interestingly, there exists an anonymous commentary on the text by an Ismaili author. However, this commentary cannot be dated with certainty; and while there is some speculation that it may have been written by Shah Tahir in the 10th/16th century, it may even be as late as the date of its transcription in 1312/1895.[70]

While there was undeniable synergism of thought and expression between Sufism and Ismailism in the immediate post-Mongol period, formal affiliation can only be verified in a few instances. It must be admitted that even the word Sufi rarely appears in the extant Nizari literature of the time. The case must therefore not be overstated on the basis of specious evidence, nor generalized to all geographic regions. An awareness of all these issues can contribute a great deal to our understanding of the relationship between Sufism and Ismailism and a more nuanced conception of the symbiotic relationship thesis.

THE WORKINGS OF THE DAʿWA

Bu Ishaq

The fifteenth-century Ismaili author Bu Ishaq wrote simply, in an unassuming style, and with no attempt at literary artifice. However, his words display profound conviction and deep sincerity. The first of his *Seven Chapters* gives us great insight into what it was that attracted people to the Ismaili daʿwa in that age. When he reached maturity, Bu Ishaq was overcome with a desire to know God and attain his recognition. This longing was so overwhelming that from time to time he would escape to the mountains and deserts to contemplate. When he inquired about such questions of his intimate companions, they directed him to study the exoteric sciences (*ʿulūm-i ẓāhirī*), which he did with gusto, becoming a master of that field. However, it proved fruitless for his aim and failed to quench his thirst. In his own words:

> For a time I endeavored to acquire that (which they had recommended) as every breath of mine boiled in my heart's fire, but in no way did I find the path to what I was in search of, nor did I find any trace of the Adored. This continued until I had trod the path of the exoteric sciences and

> acquired them to the extent that the people of the time required. Yet my soul, not having acquired anything, cried out, "Alas, I am miserable!" and my heart lamented, "Alas, I am in anguish!" I was overcome with grief that my entire life had been thrown to the winds. Sometimes my soul, torn by sorrow, would be ready to escape my body in its longing for help. At other times, my bleeding heart would burst into tears in its search for respite, forcing me to seek solitude from the company of others.[71]

He found the exoteric sciences of formal religious worship ineffective in attaining his ultimate goal, the recognition of God. Time and again, questions harassed him:

> In every respect I was bewildered, wondering: Why did the prophets come? About whom did they inform us? Whom had they entrusted us to know? Whose were the seeds of love that they sowed in our hearts? Who is the Creator of the created things and the Manifestor of what exists? What is the ultimate purpose of bringing into being the engendered existences?[72]

Racking his brains in search of a solution, he finally realized that such questions could not be answered by the individual intellect (*ʿaql-i juzwī*). Similarly, he found subjective opinion (*raʾy*) and deductive analogy (*qiyās*), two methods devised by exoteric Islam for responding to these questions, repugnant. He reasoned that those who applied deductive analogy did so using their own, imperfect intellects. In this objection, he was joined by many other Muslims. The Sunni Hanbalis and the Shiʿis in general completely rejected qiyas, as all practitioners were liable to come up with differing conclusions. Similarly, the Sunni Ahl al-Hadith spoke deprecatingly of their opponents, including especially Abu Hanifa, Malik and the schools founded by them, as the Ahl al-Raʾy, "the people of subjective opinion."[73]

Bu Ishaq was plagued by the dissonant beliefs in Islam regarding the recognition of God. All people proposed conceptions of God based on their own fanciful opinions. This inconsistency gave rise to numerous and mutually contradictory paths, completely at odds, he argued, with the fundamental Islamic conception of unity (*tawḥīd*). Such a scenario was, in fact, what he saw all around him. He observes:

> Thus, the path taken by one intellect towards the god that it had conceptualized would lead to a god different from that conceptualized by another intellect which would follow its own path, and so many different gods would be found. The depravity of this is so patent as to dispense with any need for further discussion.[74]

He concluded that there must be a supreme intellect to which all imperfect intellects should submit, just as in the time of the Prophet. This would be an intellect that God, the pure and exalted, had himself indicated to his creatures, who would lead them to his recognition. No imperfect, individual intellect could attain gnosis of God except by submission to the perfectly realized intellect, the Universal Intellect (*ʿaql-i kull*), who was God's proof (*ḥujjat*) to his creatures. This proof would convey the gnosis of God by teaching (*taʿlīm*).

It is also in this sense that the title of the well-known Ismaili treatise of Alamut times, *The Paradise of Submission* (*Rawḍa-yi Taslīm*), should be understood. It appears to be inspired by the Quranic verse, "But no, by your lord, they will not believe until they make you (O Muhammad) the judge concerning the disagreement between them, and they find no dislike for what you decide, and they submit completely (*taslīm*)" (4:65).

An ingenious poem of Nizari Quhistani highlights the stages of Bu Ishaq's spiritual search:

> Truth and falsehood are separated by absolute contrariness, a sword suspended by a hair's thread. O friend, here's a piece of friendly advice: (In crossing this bridge) don't follow frail opinion (*raʾy*), don't listen to the chatter of fools! Strike the "h" of *ḥayrat* (perplexity) on the "q" of *qurb* (proximity). (That gives you Haqq, the Ultimate Truth), so that from the letter *ʿayn* of *ʿurf* (what is known), the "m" of the bearer of truth (*muḥiqq*), the Imam, is ascertained. . . .[75] Every exoteric form you see is not bereft of esoteric reality. Heed the call of the summons (*daʿwat*) from this trustworthy daʿi. With time, create a spiritual state, so that I may take the covenant from you. Let not your hand be bereft of this chalice of limpid wine. I am the pir of a cloister, a tavern. Simple cotton and wool is all I want, not silk and gold brocade. My soul is filled with love of someone, who when displaying a miracle, cleft asunder the moon in the sky with a single indication (54:1). The love of the master of authority (*walī*) is kneaded in my very flesh and blood. Do you know of whom I speak? ʿAli, the lion at the Battle of the Trench! Naturally, the ignorant will censure Nizari, but if the blind imitators oppose my words, who cares?[76]

How, asked Nizari incredulously, could imperfect human opinion (*raʾy-i nāqiṣ*) be capable of grasping the ultimate truth? It was incomprehensible that God had left his recognition to so deficient a device. After all, every person's opinion differed from that of every other and varied according to the capacity of his or her intellect. As human beings are imperfect, human speculation about the Creator had to be imperfect. This realization led to perplexity (*ḥayrat*). Only when an intellect, reaching this furthest stage of its development, recognized that it was incapable, on its own, of attaining its desired goal, proximity to God (*qurb*), would it seek out the one who could lead it to that goal. The first letters of *hayrat* and *qurb* combined to give truth (*ḥaqq*). But to find the truth, one had to locate its bearer, the Imam (*muḥiqq*), who could teach about such matters of the soul. As Ibn Husam had written, "All I said from my own imaginings and analogies (*khayāl wa-qiyās*) was but a fable and delusion in his presence."[77] Hamid al-Din Kirmani discusses this concept in his *Solace of the Intellect* (*Rāḥat al-ʿAql*):

> It is not possible for the human soul, imperfect and in potentiality as it is, to be actualized in the physical world. This can only happen through something that is actual in itself, perfect in its essence and action. Since, among human beings, only the souls of the Prophets, the Legatees (*awṣiyā*) and the Imams and those guided by them are actualized . . . the actualization [of the soul] is impossible except through them.[78]

The seekers had to realize that behind every exoteric form is an esoteric reality pointing to the recognition of God. Preparation for submission to God's guidance would make them hasten to pledge the covenant of God at the hand of a daʿi, thus accepting the chalice of the wine of spiritual gnosis. Nizari claims to be such a daʿi, a pir of the cloister, who is completely unconcerned with worldly show and trappings, indifferent to silk and gold brocade. Like the Sufis, he is content with simple cotton and wool (*ṣūf*). However, his soul is also filled with love of those who, because of the favor of God, are unlike any other human beings or ordinary shaykhs. They are the Prophet and ʿAli, who summon to the recognition of God by his grace and favor of their lineage, not by the frailty of human opinion. As in the poem cited in chapter 3, Nizari couldn't care less about the disapproval of the blind imitators (*muqallid*). They were, after all, ignorants (*juhhāl*). He likely alludes here to the well-known prophetic tradition, given prominence by the Shiʿa, but also common in Sunni works, "Whoever dies without recognizing the Imam of his time dies the death of the ignorant."[79]

In the Quranic story of Adam, Eve, and Satan, Bu Ishaq saw proof of his convictions of the need for a teacher and spiritual edification (*taʿlīm*), rather than personal opinion (*raʾy*) or analogy (*qiyās*):

> And when your lord told the angels: "Lo! I am placing a caliph in the earth," they replied, "Will you place therein one who causes mischief and sheds blood while we hymn your praise and sanctify you?" He said, "Surely, I know that which you do not know." And he taught Adam the

> names, all of them. Then he showed them to the angels, saying, "Inform me of the names of these if you are truthful." They replied, "Glory to you! We have no knowledge save what you have taught us, for indeed you, only you, are the knower, the wise!" He said, "O Adam, inform them of their names." And when he had informed them of their names, he said, "Did I not tell you that I know the secret of the heavens and the earth? And I know what you reveal and what you hide?" (2:31–33)

Hadn't God *taught* (*ʿallama*) Adam the names, then showed them to the angels (2:31)? Didn't the angels reply, "We have no knowledge (*ʿilm*) save that which you have *taught* us (*ʿallamtanā*)" (2:32)? Then Adam conveyed the knowledge of the names to the angels by way of teaching when God commanded him, "inform them of their names" (2:33). Thus, teaching (*taʿlīm*) is the way of God and his angels. The way of Satan, however, is different:

> And we created you, then gave you a form and then told the angels, "Fall prostrate before Adam!" Then they fell prostrate, except Iblis. He was not among those who bowed. He said, "What prevented you such that you did not prostrate when I commanded you?" He replied, "I am better than him. You created me from fire while you created him from clay. He said, "Then get down hence! It is not for you to show pride here. So get out from here! Lo, you are among the degraded." (7:11–13)

Thus, deductive analogy (*qiyās*) is the way of Satan, who reasoned when speaking to God, "You created me from fire while you created him from clay" (7:12). His analogy made him challenge God, and he refused to prostrate, saying, "I am of the genus of fire and he is of the genus of clay. The substance of fire is superior to the substance of clay and that which is superior does not submit to that which is inferior."[80] Hence it is said, "the first to use qiyas was Satan." Yet, this was one of the very pillars of the epistemology of exoteric Islam. Qiyas was the reason for Satan's eternal punishment, and God responded to it, saying, "Get out from here. Indeed you are accursed, and lo, upon you is my damnation until the Day of Judgment!" (38:77–78).

According to Nizari Quhistani, in matters of faith, the bearer of truth (*muḥiqq*) is the reliable guide, not qiyas:

> One who has realized the truth speaks words of a different sort, so don't rest upon something shaky and wobbly. Follow nobody save the Man of God (*mard-i khudā*).[81] Your own analogical reason (*qiyās*) is a ghoul, not a guide! First you will find the Imam, the bearer of truth (*muḥiqq*), through God (*ḥaqq*), then you will find God confirmed through the Imam.[82]

Bu Ishaq was now convinced that God would not leave humanity at the mercy of imperfect human intellects. There must be someone who could teach about God through taʿlim, just as Adam had taught the angels. But he was at a loss, wondering:

> Today, who is the noblest of all human beings? How can one gain knowledge of him? By whose teachings can one escape from the stranglehold of ignorance—which is the real hell—to the spacious expanse of knowledge—which is the eternal paradise? From whom can one enquire about this thing which is a stranger to the whole world but a friend to him?
>
> A thousand of one's own people who are strangers to God
> Should be sacrificed for a single stranger who is his friend![83]

Bu Ishaq describes the thoughts that occupied his mind, and then continues:

> Let us return to our story. I then knew that we (human beings) know nothing. But when my wretchedness and plight reached such an extent and resulted in such an extreme, the following (verse from the Quran) kept repeating itself on my tongue and reverberating in my heart and soul: "Is God not the one who responds to the afflicted one when he cries out to him?" (27:62) Then the sun of benevolence and the mercy of Hadrat-i Mawlana—upon whose mention be prostration and exaltation!—shone from the horizon of bounty and perceived this bewildered atom in the zephyr of its love:
>
> A sun shone upon my soul from the throne of its majesty
> Taking up my soul like an atom in its own gentle winds

One day, I was seated among others at an assembly, observing all in attendance. Everyone said a few words about gnosis (*maʿrifa*) and each discussed this subject in his own way and manner. My anguished heart let out a cold sigh as hot tears streamed down my cheeks. I thought, "Alas! Why are they smiting cold iron? What do they chase after? Why do they not seek for the true goal? How long will they pursue their own fancies and not turn to the instruction of the truthful one (*taʿlīm-i ṣādiq*), not going in quest of him?"

> My intellect is baffled, my heart bewildered, and my
> patience has been put to flight

Suddenly a man entered and sat among this company. Although I did not know him by face, his conduct gave evidence of his secret. When my glance fell upon him I set about investigating his state and listened attentively to what he was saying.

Truly, the few words that he uttered signaled his possession of the water of life and informed me of eternal existence. My heart said to me, "When you find the end of the string, do not let go of it. Set foot on the path of the quest and catch hold of the skirt of his good fortune."

> Hold fast to the belt of the fortunate ones
> Don't turn away from the company of the courageous[84]

Bu Ishaq was determined not to lose this opportunity. He confided his sorrows and anxieties to this learned person, who turned out to be an Ismaili dignitary.

> When he rose from the assembly I caught hold of his skirt, not raising my head from submission at his feet. I said, "O man of angel-like disposition! Who are your people? What is your way? I am ill and heartbroken, in need of a remedy. I long for a cure for my grief."
>
> I am afflicted by a strange illness, 'tis neither headache nor fever
> I find no cure for it on earth, for it has come from heaven
>
> When he saw the signs of illness on my pale face, he alleviated my grief by saying, take heart, for:
>
> We are divine physicians and do not desire fees from anyone
> We are pure souls, undefiled by greed
>
> "But tell me, what causes your illness?"
>
> I replied, "My illness is caused by the fact that God is one, the Prophet is one and God's Word is one, therefore the true Imam, the true religion and the true hujjat must also be one. These other imams and their religions must be false and untrue. He said, "Yes, it is so. The true Imam, the true religion and the true hujjat are one. I have been appointed in this 'island' (*jazīra*) to lead the confused ones out of the desert of deviation and to make them see the gnosis of the true Imam—may his mention be exalted!—and the supreme hujjat and to deliver all of them to the eternal paradise in the abode of the afterlife."[85]

While we do not know the name of the individual whom Bu Ishaq met in this assembly, we can say confidently that his position in the Ismaili hierarchy was that of a muʿallim, also known as lahiq.[86] As the author informs us, it was the muʿallim who was appointed over one of the twelve districts (*jazīra*, pl. *jazāʾir*), the next higher rank, daʿi, not being restricted to any particular region.[87] According to Bu

Ishaq, the muʿallims were a special class among the senior ma'dhuns who totaled twelve in number. Those of the status of ma'dhun-i akbar and higher were given permission to preach to anyone whom they deemed worthy. The ma'dhun-i asghar, however, was only allowed to preach among those whom the muʿallim had indicated. The anonymous muʿallim must have taken the new mustajib, "respondent" to the daʿwa, under his wing. As Bu Ishaq tells us, when the mustajib had learned enough and was capable of giving instruction (*taʿlīm*), he was given permission to preach among people whom the muʿallim had permitted and was given the title of ma'dhun-i asghar, the junior licentiate. Upon successfully fulfilling the duties of this rank, he could be promoted to the status of ma'dhun-i akbar, the senior licentiate.[88] However, this was a rank that the anonymous muʿallim was not permitted to grant. It could only be bestowed by the supreme hujjat who, we are informed, was a certain Khwaja Qasim at that time. Bu Ishaq explains that periods of manifestation (*ẓuhūr*) and unveiling (*kashf*) are like day. At this time, the Imam is like the sun and can be seen directly. However, periods of concealment (*satr*) and dissimulation (*taqiyya*) are like night and the believers must be guided by the hujjat, who is like the moon, and the daʿis, who are like stars. During the day, the moon and stars are not necessarily visible, but at night they are the sources of guidance.[89] Bu Ishaq describes his encounter with the hujjat in the following words:

> I remained with him [the anonymous muʿallim] for a time until felicity was auspicious and I (was able to) kiss the threshold of the just lord of the world, the supreme hujjat and the cherisher of the children of Adam, about whose glory the Speaker (*nāṭiq* = the Prophet) said, "The first thing that God created was the Intellect" and sometimes he explained, "The first thing that God created was the Pen."
>
> Someone who is the gate to the mercy of lordship
> Someone who is the gate to the distinction of our lord's knowledge
> Someone who is the distributor (*qāsim*) of sustenance to the servants
> Who sees the state of all his servants
>
> I reached the marvel of truth, the world and faith, Khwaja Qasim—may God be pleased with him[90]—and became the object of his exalted gaze. By his mercy I arrived and was permitted (ma'dhun) to write and discourse on that which concerned the people of the time and expanded this rightly guiding summons. What God wills happens and that which he does not will does not happen. May only those words be spoken with which Hadrat-i Mawlana—may his power be exalted—inspires the tongue of his servant. Indeed, he is the best of abettors and helpers. We consider only him our lord, he alone, the sufficient![91]

The benedictory formula used with Khwaja Qasim's name suggests that this person had already passed away at the time of writing.

Bu Ishaq was not alone in being distressed by the lack of unity in Islam. Kashani recounts an argument that occurred between the Shafiʿis and the Hanafis, two of the four major Sunni schools of law, in the reign of the Mongol sovereign Uljaytu. Exasperated with their bickering, Qutlughshah, Uljaytu's commander in chief, addressed his fellow Mongols, saying:

> What is this that we have done, abandoning the new *yasaq* and *yusun* of Genghis Khan, and taking up the ancient religion of the Arabs, which is divided into seventy-odd parts? The choice of either of these two rites (i.e. Hanafi or Shafiʿi) would be a disgrace and a dishonorable act. . . . We seek refuge in God from both of them! Let us return to the *yasaq* and *yusun* of Genghis Khan.[92]

Contradictions arising from the use of personal opinion in matters of religion had been criticized by Ismailis throughout their history. This issue is extensively dealt with by al-Qadi al-Nuʿman in a section of *The Pillars of Islam* (*Daʿāʾim al-Islām*) concerning "those from whom Knowledge should be Acquired and those from whom it should be Loathed and whose Pronouncements should be Rejected."[93] Against the use of subjective opinion in forming legal precedents, the Ismaili jurist decries the internal contradictions of the foremost practitioners of this juristic procedure. He cites as an example the case of Malik, the founder of one of the four Sunni schools of law, who was asked about irrevocable divorce (*al-batta*). Malik replied that it is the third utterance of the word "divorce" (*ṭalāq*). One of his foremost disciples, Ashhab b. ʿAbd al-ʿAziz, immediately seized his tablet to inscribe the verdict on the basis of the jurist's authority. Seeing this, Malik asked him what he was doing. When he discovered that Ashhab was recording this pronouncement, he told him to desist, as his opinion may change by evening.[94]

A similar instance is related with regards to Abu Hanifa, the founder of another Sunni school of law. One of his Khurasani disciples who had earlier recorded his opinions met Abu Hanifa again when he was performing the pilgrimage. He once again questioned Abu Hanifa regarding those issues. This time the jurist gave opinions completely in contradiction to what he had said merely a year ago. The man raised a hue and cry, and people gathered around. He then addressed them saying that Abu Hanifa had given legal opinions to him for which he could produce documents. On the basis of these opinions he had permitted marriages to be consummated, pronounced capital punishment for certain crimes, and reappointed property to new owners. However, on the basis of Abu Hanifa's new opinions, all of this was unlawful. At this point, Abu Hanifa defended himself, saying that those were once his opinions, but now he had reconsidered. The Khurasani rebuked him, charging that if he were to accept these new opinions, he may well return the following year and find that they had been reversed once again. The jurist conceded this possibility, to which the Khurasani hotly replied, "upon you lies the curse of God and the angels and all mankind."[95]

Al-Qadi al-Nuʿman thus charges that blind imitation (*taqlīd*) of the opinions of those whom God himself had not appointed was repugnant. They had no sanction to speak on their own authority nor to judge on the basis of their own faulty human intellects. Arguing forcefully, al-Nuʿman declares that if there were anyone who would have been permitted to give free rein to his opinion, it was the Prophet himself. But in fact, concerning even his situation, God had declared, "Nor does he speak of his own desire. It is naught save an inspiration that is inspired" (53:3–4).[96] To admit the need for subjective opinion (*raʾy*) and deductive analogy (*qiyās*) in matters of religion was to admit that Islam had been revealed incomplete and to reject God's pronouncement: "This day I have perfected your religion for you and completed my favor unto you and have chosen for you submission (*islām*) as your religion" (5:3).

Religion thus consists not in following one's own opinions, but in submitting (*taslīm*) to the command of God, as expressed through the Prophet and the Imams. If Islam is truly a perfect religion, it is not possible for anything to have been omitted in God's guidance. This is illustrated in an incident related by al-Nuʿman about one of Jaʿfar al-Sadiq's young companions, ʿAmr b. Udhayna. ʿAmr visited the celebrated judge of Kufa, ʿAbd al-Rahman b. Abi Layla, and requested permission to ask some questions. The learned qadi granted his consent. ʿAmr proceeded to depict a hypothetical scenario in which a legal case was brought forth regarding property or other matters that the judge decided upon according to his own opinion. The same case arises before the judge of Mecca who decides differently. The matter goes successively before the judges of Basra, Yemen, and Medina, where the judgments are again contradictory. Finally, all of the judges gather at the court of the caliph who appointed them, informing him of the discrepancy of opinions, but he approves of each of the decisions. ʿAmr's feigned astonishment and ingenuousness serve only to thinly veil his damning observations:

> Now your God is one, your Prophet is one, and your religion is one. If God has ordered you to differ amongst yourselves, then you have indeed obeyed his command; but if he has forbidden you that, you have disobeyed him. Or else you have become associates of God in his decision, wherein it is for you to make pronouncements and for him to agree! Or, possibly, God has revealed an imperfect religion and has asked your help in its completion. Or, perhaps, God has revealed a perfect religion, but it was his Messenger who was imperfect in its articulation.[97]

The learned judge was taken aback by these scathing questions. However, impressed by ʿAmr's favorable ancestry, he offers to clarify the situation, explaining that when a case comes before a judge in which a principle is found in the Quran or the practice of the Prophet, he cannot go beyond the rules laid down therein. However, if the case revolves around a question not contained in these two sources, the judge deduces a principle based on his own opinion.

ʿAmr disdains this line of reasoning, claiming it to be invalid, for the exalted God had declared, "We have neglected nothing in the Book" (6:38), and with regard to the same issue, "We have sent the Book down to you making clear everything" (16:89).

Ibn Abi Layla is amazed and asks if ʿAmr really asserts that everything is to be found in the Book of God. ʿAmr replies that this is not his claim, but that of God himself. However, only one who recognizes this fact will find these things in the Book. The jurist enquired from whom such knowledge was to be found and was led by ʿAmr to the conclusion that it could only be with the Imams of the Prophet's progeny.[98]

The similarity between Bu Ishaq's statements and those of ʿAmr b. Udhayna quoted here is striking. They are uncomfortable with discord and deficiency in a faith that should be one of unity and perfection, as it was in the time of the Prophet. By this same logic, Bu Ishaq became convinced of the necessity of submitting to the daʿwa of the Imam.

Similarly, Bu Ishaq's entire line of argument concerning the use of deductive reasoning (*qiyās*) mirrors a famous exchange that occurred between the Imam Jaʿfar al-Sadiq and Abu Hanifa who supported *qiyas*. Abu Hanifa asserted that when there was no explicit text in the Quran or report from the Prophet, he relied on deductive analogy. So the Imam countered by posing three questions. He asked Abu Hanifa whether semen or urine was purer, to which Abu Hanifa replied that semen was purer. Jaʿfar al-Sadiq responded that if such was the case, then why did God prescribe merely ablutions after urination, but a ritual bath in the case of semen. According to *qiyas*, the opposite should have been so. He then asked whether murder or unlawful sexual intercourse was the greater crime. Abu Hanifa replied that murder was. To this Jaʿfar replied that God had decreed two witnesses in the case of murder and four in that of unlawful intercourse. If *qiyas* were valid, four witnesses would have been required for murder, which is a greater offense. Finally, the Imam asked Abu Hanifa whether prayer or fasting was nobler in the eyes of God, to which the jurist replied prayer. The Imam rejoined that a menstruating woman was required by God's messenger to fulfill the obligation of fasting later on, but not that of prayer, contrary to what one would expect. In all three instances, the dictates of analogical reasoning contradicted authoritative statements of the Quran and the Prophet. The Imam thus made his well-known statement, citing the aforementioned Quranic story of the creation of Adam, "The first to use *qiyas* was Satan."[99] These very words of the Imam were then repeated by Bu Ishaq.

The efficient administration of the daʿwa organization that Bu Ishaq describes is quite impressive. We learn of a well-structured and effective hierarchy of devoted individuals, each with a specific duty and responsibility. The respondents to the summons (mustajīb), that is, the commonality of the believers, were guided by those who, because of their knowledge, had been authorized (ma'dhūn) to preach by the higher ranks in the daʿwa. The ma'dhuns were divided into two classes, the junior (*aṣghar*) and the senior (*akbar*). Among the senior ma'dhuns there was a special class known as muʿallim or lahiq. The muʿallims could authorize the junior ma'dhuns to conduct daʿwa among a specific group of people. A promotion to the rank of senior ma'dhun, however, required the authorization of the hujjat. A senior ma'dhun could conduct daʿwa activities at his discretion. The special class of twelve senior ma'dhuns, known as muʿallims or lahiqs, were appointed by the supreme hujjat to be in charge of an entire region. Above the muʿallims were the daʿis, who were not limited to any region. They may also have been known as hujjats in their own right. The supreme hujjat, however, was only one. In the daʿwa hierarchy, he was appointed by the Imam himself and was second only to the Imam. The structure of the daʿwa hierarchy as elaborated by Bu Ishaq may be seen in figure 7.1.

Counsels of Chivalry

Regardless of which of the two Mustansirs *The Counsels of Chivalry* belongs to, the text sheds a great deal of light on the contemporary situation of the daʿwa and the content of its teachings. It seeks to define the characteristics of a true believer (*mu'min*) and exhorts the followers of the Imam to aspire to this ideal. Those who are addressed in these homilies appear to have been primarily the faithful who were not enrolled in the higher echelons of the daʿwa, most likely the mustajibs and the ma'dhuns. This can be deduced from the frequent encouragement to follow the muʿallims.[100] Quite enlightening is the fact that both men and women were present at these gatherings, and some of the Imam's instructions are addressed specifically to the women in the group.[101] Such attendance must be considered as unusual in the context of fifteenth-century Iran. Nevertheless, the presence of women in such intellectual fora had its precedents in Ismailism. Nasir al-Din Tusi, for example, dedicated one of his treatises, *The Goal of the Faithful* (*Maṭlūb al-Mu'minīn*), to an Ismaili woman of high rank,[102] and women were also present at the Fatimid "sessions of wisdom" (*majālis al-ḥikma*).[103] This participation had been noted by non-Ismaili historians.[104]

Many of the sermons are focused on matters of piety, of constantly preparing for death and the afterlife, and especially of remembering God at all times:

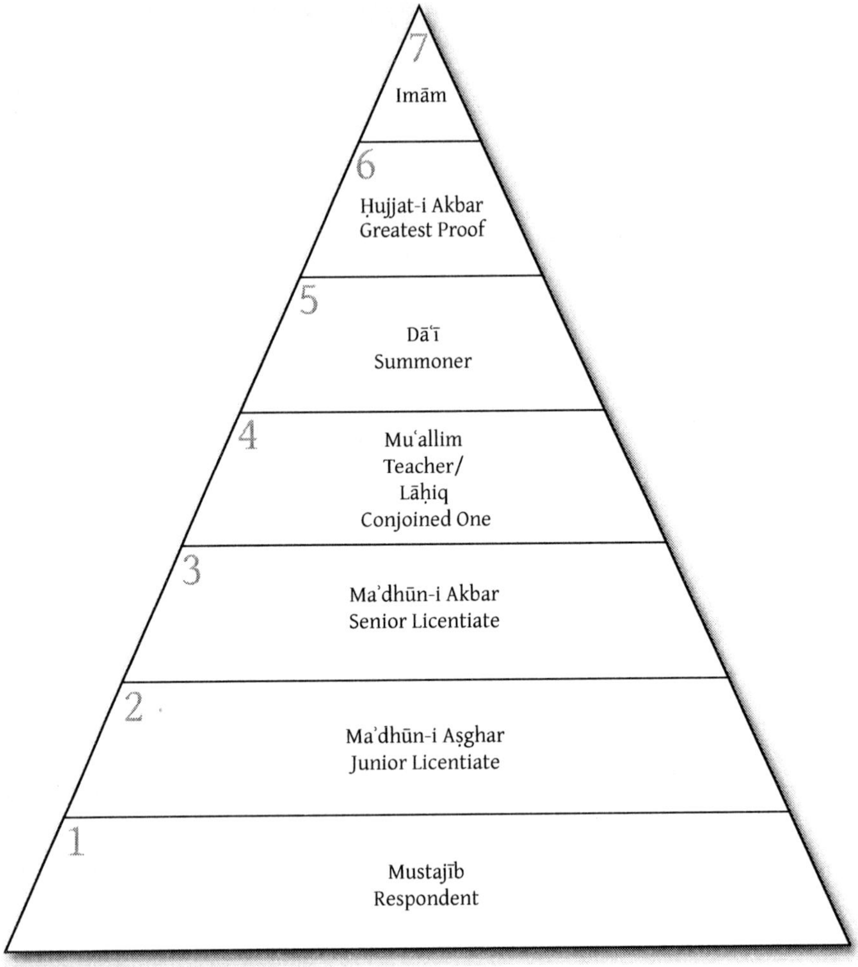

FIGURE 7.1 The Seven Heavens of the *Ḥudūd-i Dīn* in the time of Bū Isḥāq

True believers do not harbor hatred in their hearts and are constantly thinking of God. What is in their hearts and what springs from their tongues is the same. They associate with and express affection for all their fellow believers. They think of the afterlife and remember the words of knowledge. Day by day they progress on the path of truth. They don't find the path of the exalted lord to be constricting, and are never grieved by what befalls them on the path of truth, nor are they ever ungrateful or lazy in matters of faith. Rather, because of their ardent longing they busy themselves with pious works. Day by day their love and longing increase.

> Day by day their morals, qualities, speech and conduct improve and their faith is perfected, just like an ailing patient whose health improves until he is healed. They are always vigilant on the path of truth, their eyes are constantly filled with tears. They seldom laugh, guarding themselves from the laughter of heedlessness and devilishness, always keeping their gaze focused on God. They always remember the exalted God, remember the day of the resurrection, weep much and fear that day.[105]

It is clear, though, that what was sought here was not some type of austere asceticism. The text quite clearly advocates a type of spirituality that is in consonance with a productive and full life. The following passage, for example, suggests that the true chivalrous youths (*jawānmardān*) will be such that their tasks will always be completed, and that they will earn well, be successful, and have a good family life. However, the foundation for their accomplishments in these endeavors will be their faith:

> The chivalrous youths are always able to accomplish their work in a timely manner. Calamities remain distant from them and their adversaries remain blind. The gateway of plenty is opened wide for them and they are blessed with good fortune. All their tasks are completed successfully and their children will be virtuous and well. Their homes will flourish and they will have the occasion to complete all their endeavors as the oft-forgiving lord will help them. The lord's help consists of polishing the mirror of their hearts to a shine. Their faith will be strengthened, their earnings lawful. From these lawful earnings they will spend in the way of God. Their goodness will extend to the pure believers and the faithful, righteous ones. Lawful earnings are not the lot of the hypocrites and never reach their defiled spirits. Only lawful earnings reach the court of the blessed threshold and the presence of the present lord of the faithful believers with certainty. The lord of the world will be pleased with those servants and they will be well and blessed. The mighty and powerful lord will be overjoyed with those servants and their faith will be unshakeable, their souls and spirits luminous, their understanding and comprehension enlightened and in the next world the lord of majesty will bestow on them his beatific vision.[106]

The chivalrous youths must never allow piety to degenerate into an ostentatious show. The Imam advises that their devotion to God must be greater in reality than in appearance, and that they must rejoice in the joy of their fellows and be aggrieved at their losses.[107] The need to be united as a community and to help one's fellows is constantly repeated, a reflection of sentiments expressed in the Imam Islamshah's *Seven Aphorisms* described earlier:

> O believers, the truly religious people are those who long for salvation in the hereafter. Thus, they must befriend their brethren who are religious in truth, so that they may be among the people of deliverance. Believers must also help their brethren in faith, assisting them. They must share their food, their joys and their sorrows. Never should malice or spite enter their hearts. They must be united in both appearance and at heart. If one's hunger is satisfied, so should the other's. If one remains hungry, so should the other. One should eat what the other eats. They will be united in this world and in the hereafter in the presence of their lord.[108]

True believers are like an ocean that does not diminish if some water is taken away, nor change if water is added. This means they do not grieve if their property experiences a loss, nor exult at the gain of wealth. Whether they are reviled, spoken harshly to, robbed, or abused, their hearts are at peace with their lord.[109] These moral injunctions should be particularly cultivated by youngsters, who are encouraged:

> Strive to perfect your devotion and faith while you are still young that you may arrive at the coveted fountainhead, for in your old age greed may become overwhelming and intellect enfeebled. At that time, you may become greedy for the world and languish in heedlessness. So understand this and fulfill it right away while you can.[110]

This emphasis on inculcating virtue from a young age is a recurring theme in Ismaili literature. In his *Pillars of Islam*, al-Qadi al-Nuʿman quotes the following tradition of the Prophet narrated on the authority of the Imam Jaʿfar al-Sadiq, "When a man instructs himself in his youth, it is as if the knowledge he acquires is engraved on stone; but when a man sets out to do the same when he is old, it is like something written on the surface of water."[111]

Ivanow, followed by others, believed that *The Counsels of Chivalry* represented an attempt by the Imam to rein in the powers of the local pirs.[112] Some have even gone as far as to postulate that the dispatching of the text "probably indicates a change in the structure of the daʿwa whereby appointments of pīrs were suspended and a book was dispatched to take their place."[113] This cannot be supported by the contents of the book. Quite to the contrary, *The Counsels* are replete with exhortation to follow the pirs, never wavering in obedience to them. It lays immense emphasis on respecting the dignitaries of the Ismaili hierarchy. The fact that the *Pandiyat* itself is considered a pir, and is hence referred to as *Pir*

Pandiyat-i Jawanmardi, is further evidence of the importance of the office and in no way suggests that such appointments were discontinued after it was issued. That these appointments continued is fully supported by contemporary and later texts, all of which insist on the importance of following one's pir. Khayrkhwah (d. after 960/1553), writing in the succeeding generation, is emphatic about this.[114] The necessity of following the pir is also clear from various passages in *Counsels of Chivalry* itself, including the following:

> O believers, if you wish to perfect your knowledge of God and attain gnosis of him, accept the commandments of the pir of your time. Do whatever he tells you, never straying from his order. Remain forever within his command, so that you may be among the people of spiritual unveiling (*kashf*). The pir is someone upon whom the Imam of the time bestows this position, which makes him the noblest being of all creation. Whenever he has appointed and established a pir, the pir must explain the matters of gnosis in detail. Through his mediation, you must perfect your recognition of the Imam.[115]

It is clear from the text of *The Counsels* that the pirs were the most respected and esteemed dignitaries of the Ismaili hierarchy, to whom the muʿallims of every region were responsible.[116] While *Counsels of Chivalry* mentions that there were occasions when the Imam would not appoint a pir, this in no way suggests that such appointments were permanently discontinued, especially as the text indicates that even when no pir was appointed, the Imam would commission others for the guidance of the community.[117] The Imam further indicates the organization of the daʿwa in this regard, explaining that funding for the daʿwa was provided by the Imam himself and that the pirs would accept no fees from the believers.[118]

The Counsels of Chivalry also reveals that there were regular assemblies (*majlis*) being held in the community, in which the muʿallims and others would impart knowledge to the congregations.[119] This piece of information is significant, as it indicates the extent to which a formal structure was maintained. At such assemblies, esoteric matters were discussed:

> Everything concerned with the absolute truth is a hidden mystery that the Prophet, upon whom be peace, brought as a tremendous gift for the unitarian believers from his heavenly ascension (*miʿrāj*). Among these matters are a thousand unutterable things about which the lord proclaimed, "Reveal not our secrets to the unworthy." These are the counsels that the Prophet brought from the ascension for the people of truth. Those counsels which were for the people of the law were a thousand things that had to be said, all of which are known. However,

> none but the unitarian believers are aware of this discourse. The prophet entrusted it to the believers and commanded, "Speak not of it, and conceal it from the unworthy, just as I myself kept it concealed." It is about those same hidden matters that he said, "sit in the assemblies of truth (in which these matters are discussed)."[120]

While externally taqiyya kept the community safe from detractors by effectively concealing it, internally the daʿwa organization kept the community identity intact and provided for the edification (*taʿlīm*) of the believers. The elaborate structure and efficiency of the daʿwa as described in *Counsels of Chivalry* and the writings of Bu Ishaq are indeed impressive. All members of the hierarchy had clear and well-defined roles. Members of the daʿwa hosted assemblies of the believers in which esoteric truths were taught. These assemblies seem to have been frequented by both men and women, as well as by youths. The contents of *The Counsels* clearly indicate that in the Imam's own assemblies all these three groups were present and addressed specifically. The daʿwa agency was also responsible for receiving the religious dues from the believers, which it submitted to the Imam, thus ensuring the smooth functioning of the community. The financial needs of the daʿis were provided for by the Imams, and they received no funds for their own use from the believers. As Bu Ishaq indicates, the daʿwa was most active in periods of dissimulation.

One section of the *Counsels of Chivalry* is particularly apt to conclude this chapter, "The Way of the Seeker," and introduce the final chapter, "Salvation and Imamate." The passage explains that the religious law (*sharīʿa*) is comparable to a candle that lights the path (*ṭarīqa*), leading to the ultimate destination, the truth (*ḥaqīqa*). The truth, which is the esoteric meaning and ultimate purpose of the religious law, is recognition of the Imam, for only through the recognition of the Imam of one's time could one attain recognition of God.[121]

EIGHT

Salvation and Imamate

Were the world to be bereft of the Imam for but an instant, it would be convulsed with all its inhabitants.

The Prophet Muhammad

"YOU HAVE DONE THIS, AND YET YOU HAVE NOT DONE IT"

When the Prophet Muhammad passed away, his daughter Fatima asserted her claim to inherit the estate of Fadak, a garden oasis near Khaybar. Despite her declaration that her father had bequeathed this land to her, she was denied ownership and the plot was appropriated by the ruling authorities.[1] The Ismaili author of *The Sage's Discourse* (*Kalām-i Pīr*) tells of how several of the later caliphs regretted the injustice inflicted on Fatima and the Prophet's family and tried to make amends:

> Know that the crime of taking away the garden of Fadak and the injustice to Fatima were so glaring and outrageous that some of the Umayyad and ʿAbbasid caliphs, who felt that it was wrong, wanted to restore her rights by returning the garden to her descendants. The first of them was ʿUmar b. ʿAbd al-ʿAziz (d. 101/720), who was the most pious among the Umayyads. After him, among the ʿAbbasid caliphs were Ma'mun (d. 218/833), Muʿtasim (d. 227/842), and Wathiq (d. 232/847). They handed over the garden to the descendants of Fatima. When it came to the turn of

> Mutawakkil (d. 247/861), he took it back from them, but Muʿtadid (d. 289/902) handed it over. However, Muktafi (d. 295/908) took it back, and Muqtadir (d. 320/932) again returned it.[2]

Narratives of the dispute soon reached mythic proportions and offer us tremendous insight into Shiʿi conceptions of the inheritance of the Prophet's family. Quoting *The Subtleties of Peoples* (*Laṭāʾif al-Ṭawāʾif*), a work written in 933/1527 either by ʿAli b. Husayn al-Waʿiz al-Kashifi or his son Fakhr al-Din ʿAli Safi, *The Sages' Discourse* recounts the following tale.[3]

Harun al-Rashid, the celebrated caliph of *Arabian Nights* fame, felt remorse at his predecessors' oppression of the Prophet's family. He therefore summoned one of Fatima's descendants to ask the boundaries of the garden of Fadak so that he could restore it to its proper owners.[4] The sayyid warned him, "If I define the boundaries of Fadak, you won't feel like returning it." The caliph swore that he would not renege on his promise, so the sayyid began, "The first boundary of the garden of Fadak is Aden." Hearing this, Harun went pale, but said, "Go on." The sayyid continued, "The second boundary is Samarqand." The caliph's face turned yellow, but he bade him to continue. The sayyid declared, "The third boundary is the African Maghrib." The face of the caliph now changed from yellow to red. Enraged, he fumed, "And then?" The sayyid concluded, "The fourth boundary is the sea of Armenia." At this point, the color of Harun al-Rashid's face went from red to black. He exploded, "You have outlined the boundaries of my entire empire! In other words, everything within our realm belongs by right to the descendants of Fatima, and thus the descendants of ʿAbbas have usurped the rights of the kinsfolk of the Prophet." The sayyid chided the indignant caliph, "O Harun, didn't I warn you right at the outset that you would not agree with these boundaries? But you didn't listen to me."[5]

The anecdote is illuminating. While the totality of the caliph's possessions are said to be the inheritance of the Prophet's family, the claim is not pressed nor even cared for. In fact, the sayyid himself cautions the caliph against asking about the boundaries of Fadak. The implication is that it is the Islamic world that needs the Prophet's family, not the reverse. On another level, the narrative can be read as subtly alluding to the Prophet's farewell sermon at Ghadir Khumm, which was discussed in the Introduction. After a pulpit was erected, the Prophet mounted it and asked his followers whether he was not possessed of greater authority over them (*awlā*) than they over themselves. The gathering responded, "It is so, O Apostle of God." He then declared, "ʿAli is the lord (*mawlā*) of those whose lord I am." In the Shiʿi reading of this event, once the believers swear the covenant (*ʿahd*), the Prophets and Imams, as those appointed by God and at whose hand his pledge (*bayʿa*) is taken, have greater title over them than they have over themselves. The Quran declares that God has purchased from the believers their lives and wealth in exchange for paradise and that they have certainly dealt wisely in selling these (*bayʿa*) to him, "Rejoice then in your bargain (*bayʿ*) that you have made, for that is the supreme triumph" (9:111). In chapter 7, Nasir-i Khusraw's personal struggle to understand the Quranic "Verse of the Covenant" was discussed, "Indeed, those who pledge the covenant to you (Muhammad), they swear it but to God himself. The hand of God is upon their hands. Then he who breaks the oath, breaks it against his own soul; but on those who fulfill what they have pledged to God, he will bestow a magnificent reward" (48:10). The implication is clear. Breaking the oath is to the believer's own detriment, not the detriment of God or his appointees. In the above account, Harun al-Rashid's submission to the descendants of Fatima would have benefited only him, and his rejection of their authority didn't harm them in the least. It only hurt himself.

This sentiment is highlighted even more clearly in a famous narrative also contained in *The Epistle on the True Meaning of Religion* (*Risāla dar Ḥaqīqat-i Dīn*) by Pir Shihab al-Din Shah al-Husayni. The author writes that on the day that Abu Bakr was, "in appearance" (*ẓāhir*), recognized as caliph, Salman al-Farisi, the ardent supporter of ʿAli, declared in Persian, "You have done this, and yet you have not done it" (*kardīd wa-nakardīd*).[6] In other words, Abu Bakr's election to the caliphate, in reality (*ḥaqīqat*), was meaningless. External recognition and worldly power are of no consequence in matters of prophethood or imamate, for the primary function of the Prophets and Imams is to lead the believers to a recognition of the Creator. Muhammad was not a lesser prophet at Mecca because the people rejected him, nor a greater prophet at Medina because the people accepted him. Solomon and Jesus were equally prophets, though the former was a mighty king and the latter a humble shepherd. Salman's "You have done this, and yet you have not done it" indicates that the election of Abu Bakr really meant nothing, for ʿAli was the Prophet's successor, whether recognized by the people or not.[7] In such attitudes, explored further and elaborated in this chapter, we discover a spiritual worldview that contributed significantly to the survival of the Ismailis as a community after the Mongol invasions. The primacy of the belief in the soteriological necessity of the imamate and, in particular, the current Imam eclipsed other considerations commonly associated with the office. Doubtless, this conviction had existed throughout Ismaili history as it was a theme even in the earliest Imami Shiʿi literature. For example, in opposition to the Jarudiyya and other Shiʿi groups that insisted that the Imam must rebel against usurpers, the Imam al-Baqir insisted that uprising (*khurūj*) had nothing to do with the essential nature of the imamate.[8] Though this concept was basic to Shiʿism, it was expressed even more forcefully during the Alamut period, and particularly after the Mongol invasions. Earlier elaborations of the imamate had generally given a place to the Imam's political role and his right to rule the Muslim polity. This feeling was rife in the tumultuous milieu that led to the founding of the Ismaili state of the Fatimids.

Throughout their reign, the Fatimid caliph-imams and the members of the daʿwa boldly claimed the leadership role bestowed by God on the Prophet's descendants through ʿAli and Fatima. However, increasingly such sentiments became subsumed by the Imam's spiritual and soteriological functions. These are repeatedly emphasized in the extant "Blessed Epistles" (*Fuṣūl-i Mubārak*) of the Imams of Alamut.

SEEKERS OF UNION

In documents spanning the entire period of two hundred and fifty years after Alamut's fall to the Mongols, we find an emphasis on the absolute and uncompromising necessity for a present (*ḥāḍir*) and living (*mawjūd*) Imam, the manifest guide without whom the universe would simply cease to exist. God's very purpose in creating the world was that humankind recognize him. However, in Ismaili belief, God *qua* God is beyond any idea that the human intellect, in its imperfection, could possibly conceive. Only the perfect intellect could lead the human intellect to recognize its Creator. Hence, throughout the works of this period we find a common thread of utter and total devotion, affection, love, and submission to the perfect intellect, the "ʿAli of the age," who would guide souls to the recognition of their lord. Thus, the Imam's lack of political authority became inconsequential and insignificant. Contrary to what one would expect, there is not a single extant Ismaili document from this period that dwells on or bewails in any significant manner the loss of the Ismaili state. The de-emphasis of the political role of the imamate made such considerations immaterial and the ebb and flow of worldly fortune irrelevant. Hence, the community avoided the danger, in its own consciousness, of becoming peripheral to the Islamic world, merely a minor Muslim sect among others. The political marginalization of the Ismailis was of little consequence to their belief that their Imam was the spiritual center of the universe. This belief in the Imam of the time gave the community a sense of lofty mission. Khayrkhwah Harati writes, "At the onset it must be known that the purpose of the coming of the mustajibs (respondents) to this world is the recognition of the Exalted One (may his name be exalted)."[9] The Ismailis were thus the people of truth (*ahl-i ḥaqq*), whose ultimate purpose was a recognition of God through the person of the Imam. This is perhaps nowhere more apparent than in the poetry of the Imam ʿAbd al-Salam, whose powerful and evocative ode (*qaṣīda*) is quoted in Ismaili sources contemporary with its composition and is still read, recited, and studied with reverence.[10] It is written in the "shaking meter" (*hazaj sālim muthamman*), one of the simplest and most popular verse forms, used for such admired compositions as Jami's *Yusuf and Zulaykha* and Nizami's *Khusraw and Shirin*. Based on a collation of manuscripts, the first few verses of the ode are reproduced here in translation:

> Harken ye who quest for union, who boasts that he seeks. Heed my words, for I am the Book of God that speaks! If you desire that I open for you the door of mysteries, then enroll in the school of submission and attend to my teachings with all your heart. If you desire the Commander in this world of divinity, then gird yourself with my command and harken to my words![11]

The opening verse (*maṭlaʿ*) immediately addresses itself to those who quest for spiritual union (*waḥdat*). The ultimate purpose of creation is recognition of God, and those who attain this recognition are the people of unity (*ahl-i waḥdat*). They are the hujjats who hold the highest rank in the esoteric sodality. Those who aspire to this gnosis are summoned in the poem to listen to the words of the Imam, the speaking book of God.

The Book of God That Speaks

Shiʿi Islam recognizes two dimensions of the divine writ, one speaking and one silent. This is, in fact, the distinguishing characteristic Mahmoud Ayoub highlights in titling his contribution on Twelver Shiʿism in *Approaches to the History of Interpretation of the Qurʾān* "The Speaking Qurʾān and the Silent Qurʾān."[12] He writes, "Inasmuch as the Imams possess the true and limitless meaning of the Qurʾān, they keep alive the sacred Book as a moral and spiritual guide. They are the 'speaking' (*nāṭiq*) Qurʾān, while the Qurʾān after the death of Muhammad remains the 'silent' (*ṣāmit*) Qurʾān."[13] The same author maintains that the concept of the speaking and silent Quran is most clearly expressed in Ismaili literature.[14]

Al-Mu'ayyad fi al-Din Shirazi (d. 470/1078), a Fatimid luminary who was referred to by the Imam of his time as a towering mountain of knowledge before which climbers were helpless, elaborates this concept lucidly in his writings.[15] In considering the beginning of the "Chapter of the Cow" (*Sūrat al-Baqara*), the longest chapter of the Quran, al-Mu'ayyad comments on the phrase *dhalika al-kitab la rayba fihi*, literally, "That is the book in which there is no doubt."[16] Arguing forcefully against those who propose that God speaks here of the Quran; i.e., that which is between the two covers (*bayna al-daffatayn*), he asserts that if such were the case, God would have said, "*This* is the book in which there is no doubt." In Arabic, the word *dhalika* is a distal demonstrative pronoun referring to what is absent, while the word *hadha* is proximal and refers to what is present. Had

God been referring to the book "between the two covers" he would not have said "*that* is the book." Al-Mu'ayyad then proceeds to recall an incident when the Commander of the Faithful, ʿAli b. Abi Talib, was reading the Quran. When he arrived at the passage, "This book of ours speaks the truth against you" (45:29), the Imam interrupted his reading, placed the text on his head and said, "Speak, O book of God!" He repeated this three times, but received no answer. By this action, al-Mu'ayyad maintains, ʿAli wished to demonstrate that he himself was the speaking book of God, while the text of the Quran was the silent book.

By calling himself the speaking book of God, the Imam ʿAbd al-Salam declares that he is none other than ʿAli, the repository of all the Quran's secrets and the sole source for leading humankind to an understanding of its esoteric meaning. Because of his status as the speaking Quran, he can guide the seekers of union to their ultimate goal.

The School of Submission

In order for the Imam to "open the door of mysteries," the believers must enter the school of submission, (*maktabkhāna-yi taslīm*). *The Paradise of Submission* (*Rawḍa-yi Taslīm*) discusses this concept and its divisions in its twenty-third section.[17] Every existent is drawn toward perfecting itself by submitting to what transcends it. Thus, when soil submits itself to the domination of plants, the plants draw the minerals into themselves, growing and transforming the soil into a vegetative state. When plants submit themselves to the domination of animals, the animals convert them into food and the plants are raised to the status of animal life. The same process occurs when animals give themselves over to the domination of human beings. At each step, the entity comes closer and closer to perfection. In the same manner, when ignorant and imperfect human beings submit themselves to the wise, completely entrusting their wills to them, the wise transform them. Merging with the will of the wise and perfect, they are drawn out of the pit of ignorance and delivered to the degree of knowledge. Those who can draw the imperfect out of their imperfection must themselves be guided by the one who is absolutely perfect, the bearer of truth of the age (*muḥiqq-i waqt*). They are thus the teachers of the rightly guiding summons (*daʿwa-yi hādiyya*). At the head of this summons is the Universal Intellect. The preeminence of this intellect over the entire creation lies in its absolute and complete submission to the Sublime Word (*kalima-yi aʿlā*).

However, submission that is not accompanied by insight (*baṣīra*) is not really submission, but mere imitation (*taqlīd*). This is the lot of the people of discord (*ahl-i taḍādd)* who do not belong to the Imam's summons. They fall into error because their submission is not based on insight, their action is not based on knowledge, and their religious endeavor is not based on trust in God. Giving up their own desire, they merely submit to someone else who follows his own opinion and desire, not to one appointed by God for their perfection.[18] Meanwhile, those who belong to the summons, the people of ranks (*ahl-i tarattub*), have both spiritual insight and submission. Because of this, they derive benefit from both knowledge and action, and results are accrued by both religious endeavor and trust in God. Through submission to their superiors in the daʿwa, they ascend rank after rank, drawing ever closer to perfection.

In chapter 17 of his *Commencement and Culmination* (*Āghāz wa-Anjām*), Tusi elaborates his idea of how human attributes eventually become annihilated in the divine attributes. To begin with, the human will must completely lose itself in the absolute will. This is known as the rank of contentment (*riḍā*). The custodian of the gates of heaven is thus known as "Ridwan" because the delights of paradise cannot be enjoyed until someone arrives at the stage of contentment, which is evoked by the Quranic verse, "And the greatest bliss is contentment that comes from God" (9:72). After the dissolution of will, one's power must become annihilated in God's power. This is the rank of trust in God (*tawakkul*), in accordance with the verse, "And whosoever puts his trust in God, he shall suffice him. God attains his purpose. God has appointed a measure for everything" (65:3). However, when one's knowledge becomes annihilated in God's knowledge, so that he knows nothing on his own, he attains the rank of submission (*taslīm*), which is alluded to by the verse, "And submitting with fullest conviction" (4:65). Only one rank outstrips that of submission, and this is the rank of the people of unity (*waḥdat*), whose very existence is annihilated in God's existence, so that they are nothing on their own. It is the seekers of this very unity who are addressed in the opening lines of the ode of the Imam ʿAbd al-Salam and who are exhorted to enter the school of submission with heart and soul. Tusi concludes his discussion by stating that annihilation in God's power, knowledge, and existence necessitates infinite power, essential knowledge, and eternal existence.[19]

The most important element distinguishing the so-called submission, or what is in reality imitation, of the people of discord, and the submission of the people of ranks, is insight. Insight is described by Tusi as awareness and awakening to the fact that human beings are imperfect and in spiritual need of a fully realized master who would lead them to perfection. This consciousness leads them to seek out such a perfected master to whom they will submit themselves completely and absolutely. This reminds us of Nizari Quhistani's verse quoted in chapter 3: "Reflect on all the sciences, then come hither, that I may lead you to God's Proof, the perfector of the imperfect."[20] This same sentiment is repeated in a Ginan of Pir Shams, which asserts that one may have studied all fourteen branches of learning, art, and science, but without the guide, the spiritual path can never be found.[21]

A very poignant illustration of this process of realization is contained in Tusi's own spiritual autobiography, *The Journey* (*Sayr wa-Sulūk*). Recognizing that the frail human intellect was not capable of recognizing God on its own, he concluded:

> When this humble servant reached this station, I realized that the result of my efforts, the culmination of my search, was submission (*taslīm*)—that very submission that is required by the religion of the followers of *taʿlim* [i.e., the Ismailis]. [As the Quran 4:65 states:] "But no, by your lord, they will not believe until they make you (O Muhammad) the judge concerning the disagreement between them, and they find no dislike for what you decide, and they submit completely (*taslīm*)." Hitherto, as this seeker was at the station of individual judgment (*taḥakkum*), I was searching for the original teacher (*muʿallim-i aṣlī*) by intellectual deduction, by thought, reflection and reasoning. I sought the bearer of truth (*muḥiqq*) by means of the truth (*ḥaqq*). Now that I have come to know that unique person, the man of the epoch, the Imam of the age, the teacher of the followers of *taʿlim*, the epiphany of the Word (*maẓhar-i kalima*), he who enables one to recognize God—glory be to him—and now that I have acknowledged that he is the teacher, the bearer of truth and the ruler (*ḥākim*), and have arrived at the station of submission, entrusting the entirety of my will to him, I have arrived at the realm of learning and subjection. Gnosis and knowledge are what the teacher says are [true] gnosis and knowledge, all else is absolute ignorance and benightedness. . . . Whatever comes from him is the straight path, true faith and guidance, and whatever comes from myself, from my personal opinion, whim, speculation, intellect, learning and insight [and which is contrary to his teachings], is deviation (*ḍalālat*).[22]

The discussion of *taslim* in *The Paradise of Submission* concludes with a moving passage quoted from the Imam Zayn al-ʿAbidin's *Scroll of the Worshipful* (*ṣaḥīfat al-Sajjādiyya*), illustrative of absolute submission to the Creator:

> O God, you created us from frailty, built us up from feebleness, and originated us from a *mean water*.[23] We have no strength save through your power and no power except through your help. Help us to succeed, guide us the right way, blind the eye of our hearts toward everything opposed to your love and do not give any of our limbs an opportunity to disobey you.[24]

The theme of absolute submission to the Imam, as elaborated in the ode of the Imam ʿAbd al-Salam, is echoed in a composition of Husayn:

> We cut off our hearts from attachment to the world, regaling our souls by the light of God's mercy. Having liberated ourselves from the clutches of the demon of ego we serve the Imam of the time with sincerity. We free our hearts from the fraud of the internal devil, sacrificing our lives in the name of the lord of *jinn* and men. We make the exalted name of the sovereign of faith, Gharib Mirza, the litany of our tongues. Sometimes he's a child, sometimes a youth, sometimes an aged man.
>
> 'Tis incumbent we make the prophetic tradition our sign. May my life be sacrificed for ʿAzizi who has uttered what follows. I present to you a single couplet from his noble discourse: "Without doubt he is ʿAli himself. In serving him, 'tis not comely to lean an atom towards "why" or "wherefore." While the folk of the law turn their faces toward the Kaʿba, we make Anjudan our Kaʿba of reality; for in the annihilation of the life of this world is everlasting life in that one—so hasten to long for life eternal! By sinning and disobedience all of us have aged. We become youths once again by the light of obedience to him. When our spirit is liberated from the insinuation of the body, we will make our nests in the neighborhood of divine mercy. If we remember our origin with probity, in the manner of lovers, we will turn our faces towards the place of return.[25]

Husayn avows that the believers must liberate themselves from the clutches of carnal desires in order for life to be truly dedicated to the path of the faith. The Ginans, too, portray the ego (*huṃ khudī, ahaṃkāra*), the capricious self or mind (*man*), as the greatest deterrent to the soul's submitting to the guidance of God's appointees and achieving gnosis.[26] A composition of Pir Shams wryly remarks, "What can the guide do if, despite holding the lamp of gnosis in hand, the intrigues of the capricious self cause the believer to tumble into a dark well?"[27] Thus, absolute and unconditional love for the Imam must conquer the self. Only this can render it submissive and amenable to receive gnosis: "Love the beloved in such a way that divine gnosis arises from within. Slay the self and make it your prayer carpet. Brother, remain steadfast in contemplation."[28] And again in the Ginan *Awake! For the True Guide has Arrived*, in a verse that displays an ingenious play on words: "The Guide says: Slay the self (*man ne māro*) that you may meet me (*mane maṛo*). I shall hold you close, for indeed, a precious diamond has come into your grasp. Behold it, O chivalrous one, contemplate on these words of gnosis."[29] Only when the obstinate self's inane excuses are cast afar can the guide exercise his transforming effect and the soul acquire divine recognition.[30] This effect is picturesquely compared to that of a fragrant sandalwood tree in a forest filled with margosa trees. Just as the presence of the sandalwood tree makes the surrounding margosas redolent, so does the perfume of the guide's knowledge transform the disciples.[31] However, simple contact with the Imam does not guarantee the transfer of knowledge. Unless the self has first submitted to the Imam, the believer is no better than the bamboo trees that neighbor the sandalwood tree but are not affected in the least by its scent.[32]

The Eternal Imam: Truth and Its Bearer

The verse of ʿAzizi, quoted by the poet Husayn in the above composition, urges the believers to consider the present Imam to be none other than ʿAli himself and not to waver in their obedience to him. In this vein, we find poems such as that of Daʿi Anjudani, introduced in chapter 6, who lauds all the Imams from the time of ʿAli onward, naming them in turn. When he comes to his own time, Daʿi praises the Imam in the following verses, rhyming in "you find" (*yābī*):

ʿAli of the age, lord of the time, master of the epoch
From whose pleasure all your desires you find

Commander of the epoch, the lord at whose court
A hundred kings like Alexander and Caesar you find

Seated on the throne of *Whose is the Kingdom*, by God[33]
Whatever you seek from the light of his friendship you find

Shah Mustansir bi'llah, the bearer of truth (*muḥiqq*) of both the worlds
In the felicity of whose glance the garden of Ridwan you find

Treasurer of knowledge divine, king of the throne by whom
With ease the key to the mysteries of both this world and that you find

The one signified by the parables of the verses of God's word
From him, the interpretation of the hidden meaning of the
Quran you find . . .

Day and night, by the nobility of his mighty name
Weeping and composing his glories, the holy spirit you find

Doubtless, the trusted spirit inspires such that
My heart hastening on the path to the inspirer you find

From a single hallowed lineage, from ʿAli till present times
All, over both worlds, the lords of the command you find

So long as existed the world, 'twas never bereft of one of them
So long as it shall exist, till the end of time, the very same you find

Traversing the path of naming the Imams of truth
Daʿi! The jewel of your speech is a verity that from the mine you find[34]

The expression of the poem clearly bears the impress of Ismaili thought of the Alamut period. The Imam Mustansir bi'llah is referred to as the bearer of truth (*muḥiqq*), a term that most commonly refers to the Imam as the legitimate source of truth. The concept is apparently an elaboration of three Prophetic traditions: "Recognize the truth and you shall recognize the one who possesses it," "ʿAli is with the truth and truth is with him," and "[O God!] Make the truth turn with him wheresoever he turns."[35] In these three phrases, *The Paradise of Submission* sees three stages of recognition. At first, the believers realize that truth must exist. They therefore seek the one who possesses it. This leads them to the Imam. In the intermediate stage they recognize the Imam through the truth and the truth through him. Recognition is consummated in the final stage when they recognize ultimate truth through its possessor (the *muḥiqq*), because wherever the possessor of truth turns, that is where truth lies.[36] Nasir al-Din Tusi further elaborates the concept of the Imam as the bearer of truth (*muḥiqq*) using an example. Knowledge (*ʿilm*) is an abstract idea with no external existence. If asked to speak about knowledge in an external form, the best thing one can do is to indicate someone who possesses knowledge (*ʿālim*). By conceiving of a knowledgeable person, one can realize what knowledge is. Likewise, intellect (*ʿaql*) is an abstract concept that can only be witnessed when it is embodied in an intellectual (*ʿāqil*). Similarly, truth (*ḥaqq*)—and by this Tusi means ultimate truth—is an abstract idea. The only way to conceive of truth is to indicate one who is its embodiment, the bearer of truth (*muḥiqq*). Just as a knowledgeable person is the soul (*jān*) and form (*ṣūrat*) of knowledge, the bearer of truth (*muḥiqq*) is the soul and form of truth (*ḥaqq*).[37]

To the poet Daʿi, the Imam is the personification of God's command (*amr*), and the world cannot exist without him, for how can truth be found without its bearer?

So long as existed the world, 'twas never bereft of one of them
So long as it shall exist, till the end of time, the very same you find

These same themes are echoed in the composition of another poet with the pen name Darwish, a few of whose stirring verses, rhyming in "arise" (*bar khīz*), are translated here:

O heart, from your home in this shadowy container of dust, arise!
From caring for head, wealth, property and life, like the lovers, arise!

You're trapped in the snare of the world's bait
Cut away greed, from thoughts of this and that, arise!

Be not seduced by devilish colors
In the cause of servitude to the lord of the age, arise!

Leave to infidels the deceits and blandishments of the world
In this age of trial, like a chivalrous knight, arise!...

Do you desire salvation, O brother of mine?
Then with affection for the King of Anjudan, arise!...

Imam of the age, ʿAli of the time, Shah Gharib
Gird your loins in his service and from your soul, arise!...

It's time to decamp from this world, time to depart
Why do you tarry while your companions have left? O Darwish, arise![38]

In the continuation of his ode, the Imam ʿAbd al-Salam elaborates the concept of the spiritual recognition of the imamate.

Know that in this nine-roofed treasury of porticos four and faces six, the talisman of meaning's treasure is naught but my existence, world adorning. If you long to behold my face then open the eyes of your heart; for naught see these earthly, fleshly eyes save my appearance, time eroding. Whither can you behold me in this dusty realm, with these eyes? For I am in a place yet placeless, beyond place and habitation. If you desire to recognize me then first recognize your self, for I recognize those who recognize me. Quaff this cup, the goblet of love; be drunk, that you may fathom this secret: sometimes I'm wine, sometimes the goblet, sometimes the fair cupbearer. Thus naught but me do you see from Alpha to Omega; because of this meaning arcane I've manifested eternally. Changes not the meaning, yet in the way of appearances, sometimes I change, setting out in every form. Know me not to be the body, nor even subtle soul. Count me not to be this, consider me not that; for in the world of ineffability, I am beyond body, even soul. Neither am I existent, nor non-existent, neither perceptible, nor comprehensible to the mind; neither ineffable, nor effable, neither in a place, nor placeless. That world-illuminating candle am I, around which the world-adorning sun, circles distraught like a moth, longing for my orb, resplendent. My fashioning, so wondrous, that when I divulge meanings divine, both the worlds are set ablaze, by my light, refulgent. In essence I am absolute simplicity, the universal of universals; yet consider the particles of the existents to be but a particle of my particles. Know that I am sulfur red; call me elixir supreme. Call me not a pearl, for I am the ocean that gives birth to pearls. While I may resemble but a drop, from the sea fallen afar, when you

recognize that drop you'll know, the mighty sea to be naught but me. You behold many like me, because you're looking as you squint.
If you'd look straight then you'd see, I'm peerless and extraordinary. I have homes and places in the thousands, and yet my place is traceless. Names have I, thousands—more, yet the named is none but me. Now I am ʿAbd al-Salam, but if with this company I am grieved, to this assembly I'll bid adieu, once again to return to it.
ʿAbd al-Salam is my name, these heavens without pillars that you see, bearing the nine glass-like azure vaults, supporting, sustaining them, none but me![39]

The poem gives the impression of having been composed by a personality of overwhelming spiritual presence.[40] Its verses reverberate with esoteric Ismaili thought about the soteriological role of the Imam. The universe is described as a nine-roofed treasury, shimmering azure-hued crystalline vaults representing, in classical style, the seven heavens, the sphere of the fixed stars, and the sphere of spheres. The trove has six faces, symbolizing the six directions (north, south, east, west, up, and down) and thus encompassing the realm of space; and four porticos, these being the four primary elements (earth, air, fire, and water), which were considered the roots of physical existence. In other words, all of creation is a treasure, not of gold and precious gems, but rather of spiritual meaning. The Fatimid chief judge in Egypt, al-Maliji (fl. 5th/11th c.), distilling the words of the Imam al-Mustansir bi'llah, alludes to this in one of his addresses in *The Assemblies of al-Mustansir* (*al-Majālis al-Mustanṣiriyya*):

> Follow the clearest path—may God grant you success in bringing together what we recite to you from the exoteric (*ẓāhir*) and the esoteric (*bāṭin*)—and whenever you face difficulties, return to the one whom God chose as the best guardian for your guidance. As the exoteric and the esoteric are like body and soul, when they come together benefits are accrued, goals are realized and, by means of the senses the soul comprehends the marvels of the world and deduces gnosis of the Creator from the existence of the creation.[41]

The Quran urged those with the capacity to think to ponder upon the heavens and the earth, the alternation of the night and day and the entirety of the physical creation, as all of these are signs (*āyāt*) of God (2:164). Studying the signs of God in the creation would lead to a recognition of the Creator. As the ode of the Imam ʿAbd al-Salam tells us, the talisman that can open this treasure trove of spiritual meaning is the Imam. The Imam cannot be recognized with earthly, fleshly eyes, for these can only see his physical form, perishing like all else with the passage of time. His true face is to be perceived with the eyes of the heart, which witness him "in a placeless place, beyond place and habitation." He has thousands of physical habitations, but his true home is traceless; he has had a thousand names, but all of them refer to one reality. Today he is known as ʿAbd al-Salam, but tomorrow the physical body will be gone and the name will change, yet the essence will remain in the next Imam of the lineage. Those who look at the Imam as they squint will consider him like any other human being, but as soon as the eyes of the heart perceive correctly, his true status is discovered. In form the Imams change, but in meaning they are changeless. Human language cannot attain to the majesty of the Imams, for they are the epiphany of God's command, which is itself beyond the Universal Intellect (*ʿaql-i kull*) and Universal Soul (*nafs-i kull*). This accounts for the apophatic nature of the poem, which seems almost ready to burst for carrying a burden it cannot bear—"Count me not to be this, consider me not that." The earthly sun itself whirls moth-like around the even more overwhelming spiritual light of the Imam. The power of his very words can set both worlds ablaze. The Imam is the most precious ingredient in the supreme elixir of eternal life—red sulfur. He is not simply a pearl, but the ocean that gives birth to pearls. The existence of the Imam, who leads humankind to a recognition of God, is the very pinnacle of creation. Thus the heavens and earth would crumble without his presence. As the Prophetic hadith declared, لو خلت الأرض من إمام ساعةً لمادتْ باهلها "Were the world to be bereft of the Imam for but an instant, it would be convulsed with all its inhabitants."[42] Pir Shihab al-Din Shah writes:

> Outwardly (*dar ẓāhir*) [the Imam] has all the characteristics of an ordinary human being. However, you cannot envision him in your heart with these (ordinary) eyes. The gnosis of the heart differs from this path. This indeed is the meaning of luminosity (*nūrāniyyat*). About this, neither have I the power to divulge its mystery and speak more, nor have you the capacity to hear more.[43]

To Behold Your Face

If the sun itself sought the proximity of the light of the Imam, much more so were the faithful inclined to do so. A poem from the time of the Imam Gharib Mirza exists, whose author, unfortunately, must remain unknown, as the latter half of the copy available to me is illegible. The verses are revealing, however, as they were written by an Ismaili pilgrim from Khurasan who had trekked to Anjudan to see the Imam. Some of the verses seem to suggest that he came as a representative of the Ismailis of his region, and hence sought blessings on their behalf:

> Greetings! O Emperor of the realm of faith and world; I come from Khurasan to behold your face. No worship accompanies me as a companion that I may be worthy of pardon. All I have is a soul imperfect, sins and transgressions galore. Despite such worthless goods, I long for your grace, hoping that through me you may forgive the trespasses of your servants—one and all. As you are the sovereign and governor of all creation, this being testified to by the Quran itself, your proper name has been made manifest to all the faithful. You are Shah Gharib and Mustansir, the inheritor of Shah Salam![44]

The contents of Khwaja ʿAbd Allah Ansari's supplicatory verses, introduced in chapter 6, strongly suggest that they too were composed by a pilgrim who had traveled to Anjudan specifically to receive the beatific vision (*dīdār*) of the Imam, perhaps on the occasion of his succession to the imamate.

> Those who caught the scent of wisdom divine, with heart and soul became slaves of Mustansir bi'llah. In love, those who became dust at this threshold surpass even the portico of the throne on the basis of their eminence. I became the slave of a sovereign so magnificent and glorious that all who become his slaves become kings of both worlds. I became a slave so fortunate that all who beheld me declared: "What a lucky slave is he whose name is ʿAbd Allah, 'the slave of God.' " The longing of this forlorn one was but to behold the face of the friend. Praise be to God—the heart gained what it desired! Save for your essence, in the universe you have no like. Indeed, those who recognize you are peerless. How wonderful! In every age he appeared in a different form. Sometimes he's Mustansir, sometimes Salam Allah. Sometimes an aged man, a child or a fair youth he becomes. Sometimes he ascends to the heavens for the ascension (*miʿrāj*) or descends into a dark well. If he appears in a hundred different forms, why should those of spiritual insight be anxious? Those who see with the eye of the heart are guided to him aright. Those who trod not this path following your command, indeed, though they be ma'dhuns of your court, are wayward and astray. By God Almighty! He who disobeys your order, though he may appear an elder of your court, is naught but a babe on the path. O lord! In this lowly world, you know years and months passed by. I lived my life in heedlessness. O lord! In this world for the sake of that one, I sowed not a seed; now the season's passed. Then suddenly from the invisible world an oracle whispered in the inner recesses of my heart, "Grieve not! For an unexpected felicity has been conferred upon you!" Though I be bereft of worship, I take joy in the

> certainty that all who became beggars at this court become lords of majesty. O lord! Though I've been mighty impudent I shall not grieve, for your mercy is my companion. I also ended with your name, since in the realms of faith and world the beginning of all tasks commences with *In the Name of God*.[45]

Ansari places immense emphasis on submitting to the command of the Imam. The mighty who fail to do so are reduced to babes on the path, while the meek who become dust at his threshold are exalted to dizzying heights. The poet is comforted that despite the weight of his transgressions, his love, affection, and submission to the Imam, identified as God's "name," will lighten the burden. This identification is in consonance with the age-old Shiʿi belief that the Imams are the supreme name of God (*ism Allāh al-aʿẓam*), through whom God is invoked and recognized.[46] While the Imams differ in form, in essence they are the same. Thus Mustansir and Salam Allah are but two names of one reality.

Ansari explains that his longing was "but to behold the face of the friend." The importance of this act is described at length by the Imam Mustansir in the *Counsels of Chivalry*. *The Counsels* considers patience a virtue in all but two instances. The first is that the believer must always be impatient to fulfill the commands of God and never tarry in discharging his orders, while the second is to be impatient for the beatific vision, which is the most urgent of all matters. To be patient in this regard is a heinous crime and the cause for eternal remorse.[47] In this regard, a very touching story is narrated, which concludes one section of *The Counsels*:

> O believers, listen to the story of the Prophet Yahya. He shed tears day and night, never relenting. One day the angel Gabriel descended from the presence of the majestic lord, saying, "O Prophet Yahya, the lord of the two worlds has asked: 'Why do you weep so much? I feel immense pity for you. If you weep for paradise, it is granted to you. If you sob from fear of hell, I forbid it to touch you.' " The Prophet Yahya replied, "I weep neither desiring paradise nor fearing hell, but to behold you, to receive your beatific vision!" At that moment the lord said, "If you weep to behold me, then weep much that you may attain your purpose! May you remain safe in this mortal world and weep much."[48]

In a plaintive entreaty to the Imam al-Mustansir, al-Mu'ayyad typifies the impatience to behold the face of the Imam of one's time and the urgency of this beyond any possible worldly consideration:

> I swear, were you to crown me with the diadem of Khosroes, King of the East, and were you to grant me dominion over the world entire, of

> those who have passed on and those who remain, but say, "Let our meeting be postponed but an hour;" I would reply, "O my Mawla, let us meet instead! For your delay of but an hour has turned my hair gray.[49]

The beatific vision is of two kinds: one a physical meeting with the Imam and the other a spiritual recognition of his essence, through which God is recognized. Speaking of the second of these, Pir Sadr al-Din writes:

> Friend! None but a few know of the exalted station. Indeed, they alone recognize it who have found the true guide.
>
> Friend! Within the heart, at the confluence of the three spiritual rivers, there is an imperishable light. There—a shimmering effulgence, pearls are showered.
>
> Friend! I completely lost consciousness of my physical self when my meditation mounted the empyrean, bursting forth.
>
> Friend! I beheld the place of the lofty throne, I saw the seven islands, the nine continents.
>
> Friend! The religious scriptures and books cannot fathom this, for there is neither day there, nor night, neither sun, nor shade.
>
> Friend! My lord is not such that he can be spoken of. He is to be seen—for he is indescribable, and nameless.
>
> Friend! How sweet is that lord, indescribable, nameless. Says Pir Sadr al-Din, truly, with my own eyes, I have seen him![50]

The Counsels of Chivalry enumerates the immense trials and tribulations undertaken by the faithful to attain this vision of the Imam, a vision that ultimately leads to a recognition of God.[51] They have given up their property, and even their lives. All of them have faithfully submitted their religious dues, which is incumbent on them. Others have traveled long distances through arduous conditions by land and sea, braving storms and incurring great expense. Some attend religious assemblies to increase their knowledge while others, without any worldly motive, perform acts of charity to benefit the poor. Some have imposed upon themselves austerities, pious acts, righteousness, and all manner of noble actions in the cause of faith, including special devotions, worship and especially remembrance (*dhikr*), continually invoking the lord throughout the night, never neglecting God for even a moment, and worshipping him out of passionate devotion. All believers are urged to come into the presence of the Imam and to see him with their own eyes.[52] Thus, the esoteric (*bāṭinī*) vision, realized through pious works and the constant rememberance of God during the nightly vigil, as well as the exoteric (*ẓāhirī*) vision, achieved by traveling to the Imam's residence and beholding the gateway of God's mercy, become the ultimate purpose of human life. Piety should not be for fear of hell or desire of paradise, but for the purpose of recognizing and beholding God, which is achieved through the recognition and vision of the one who is the epiphany of his command (*amr*), the Imam of one's time.

CONCLUSION

None of the known Ismaili works of the two and a half centuries following the Mongol conquest of Alamut place any emphasis on the concept, so common in early Shiʿism, that the Imam must rule the Muslim world. The role of the imamate is completely depoliticized, and emphasis is placed on its esoteric dimensions. Prominence is given to the age-old belief that all the Imams are one in essence, and hence they are referred to as "ʿAli of the time." It is vital that the Imam always be present (*hāḍir*), as he is the bearer of truth (*muḥiqq*), through whom truth itself (*ḥaqq*) is recognized. The universe would perish if the Imam were not in it, for God's sole purpose in creating the world was that humankind achieve his recognition. In the ode of the Imam ʿAbd al-Salam, he refers to the ancient concept of the Imam as the speaking Quran. Seekers of union must thus heed the Imam's words to attain their ultimate goal and must completely submit themselves to his will. The Imam is the only source through whom God can be recognized. It is therefore the highest goal of human existence to attain his beatific vision. We thus witness poetry written by believers who trekked to Anjudan for this very purpose. The spiritualized conception of the imamate allowed the faithful to maintain a lofty sense of purpose and mission, despite the absence of an Ismaili state. They could see themselves as the People of Truth (*ahl al-ḥaqq*), as they are referred to in *The Counsels of Chivalry* and elsewhere. The right and duty of the Prophet's family to govern the Islamic polity, which was stridently proclaimed in Fatimid times, ceased to be of major importance. The ultimate aim and aspiration of the believers was explicitly to recognize the divine through the beatific vision of the Imam of their time.

Afterword

The Word of Divine Unity (*kalima-yi tawḥīd*)
is inherited and transmitted in the hallowed
lineage and blessed progeny (of the Imams)—a
single lineage, a single essence—(As the Quran
3:34 proclaims), *descendants, one after the
other.* Never will (this chain) be broken,
even unto the end of time!

Nasir al-Din Tusi and Hasan-i Mahmud in *The
Paradise of Submission*

In his contribution on the state of Alamut to *The Cambridge History of Iran*, the erudite Islamicist, Marshall Hodgson, marveled at the dogged resilience and ardent spirit of the Ismailis. He mused:

> That this handful of villagers and small townsmen, hopelessly outnumbered, should again and again reaffirm their passionate sense of grand destiny, reformulating it in every new historical circumstance with unfailing imaginative power and persistent courage—that they should be able so to keep alive not only their own hopes but the answering fears and covert dreams of all the Islamic world for a century and a half—this in itself is an astonishing achievement.[1]

If the successes of the Ismaili state centered at Alamut were an achievement, the continued survival of the community after the dramatic fall of their network of fortresses was an extraordinary feat. Genghis Khan had decreed that the Ismailis should be utterly annihilated: "None of that people should be spared, not even the babe in its cradle."[2] However, the community refused to die a martyr's death with the destruction of its political power in 654/1256 and, over the course of the ensuing centuries, never succumbed to the forces arrayed against it.

Inquiry into this period of Ismaili history is still in its infancy, most of the manuscript works being as yet uncatalogued or even uncollected, much less critically edited and translated. I therefore have neither the temerity nor the Quixotic optimism to suggest that *The Ismailis in the Middle Ages* is more than a prefatory reconstruction of the events and doctrines of the time. The book draws on whatever sources have weathered the ravages of centuries to examine the history of the Ismailis during the two hundred and fifty years following the destruction of their political power at Alamut, to analyze the methods of their survival and to study the matrix of their thought.

We can now effectively put to rest the venerable canard first promulgated by Juwayni about the complete annihilation of the community and its leaders after the Mongol irruption—in that historian's triumphant words, "He [the Imam Rukn al-Din Khwurshah] and his followers were kicked to a pulp and then put to the sword; and of him and his stock no trace was left, and he and his kindred became but a tale on men's lips and a tradition in the world."[3] In fact, it becomes clear from the sources that the region of Daylam, and the fortress of Alamut itself, continued to be a center of the Ismaili community for over a century after the Mongol invasion, albeit with disruptions, before the Imams moved to Anjudan shortly before the Safawid Revolution.

Three factors, in particular, emerge as having been crucial to the survival of the Ismailis in the inhospitable circumstances following the loss of their political power: taqiyya or precautionary dissimulation, the activities of the daʿwa or summons, and the centrality in Ismaili thought of the soteriological dimension of the imamate and, in particular, the role of the living Imam of one's time in leading the adepts to gnosis and a mystical understanding of God.

As mentioned in the Introduction, it was really the pioneering efforts of the Russian scholar Wladimir Ivanow that brought the continued existence of the Ismaili community to the attention of Western scholarship. In an uncharacteristically tender reminiscence, the usually acrid Ivanow thoughtfully reflected on the astonishment of his peers at the continued existence of the Ismailis and shares his own ruminations about the tenacity of this persecuted minority:

> My learned friends in Europe plainly disbelieved me when I wrote about the community to them. It appeared to them quite unbelievable that the most brutal persecution, wholesale slaughter, age-long hostility and suppression were unable to annihilate the community. . . . Only later on, however, when my contact with them grew more intimate, was I able to see the reasons for such surprising vitality. It was their quite extraordinary

> devotion and faithfulness to the tradition of their ancestors, the ungrudging patience with which they suffered all the calamities and misfortunes, cherishing no illusions whatsoever as to what they could expect in life. . . . They with amazing care and devotion kept through ages burning that Light, mentioned in the Koran, which God always protects against all attempts of His enemies to extinguish It. I rarely saw anything so extraordinary and impressive as this ancient tradition being devoutly preserved in the poor muddy huts of mountain hamlets or poor villages in the desert.[4]

As Ivanow observed, it is indeed extraordinary that through the gleeful requiem of the Mongol chroniclers exulting at the immolation of their foes and the litany of condemnations pronounced against the Ismaili community by extremist opponents, this voice of esoteric Islam remained alive, sometimes as a whispered vesper song, sometimes as a resounding rhapsody chanted in fortissimo tones, but never silenced.

Glossary

Many of the terms below have a variety of connotations in differing contexts. The definitions given here are those that have the greatest bearing on the contents of this book. Arabic words and phrases are often presented as they would appear in Persian as a reflection of usage in the sources. The plural forms of words are also provided if these appear in the text of the book.

ʿAbbāsids ⇁ A dynasty descended from the Prophet's uncle al-ʿAbbās b. ʿAbd al-Muṭṭalib. The ʿAbbāsids ruled from 132/749 to 656/1258, when the last ʿAbbāsid caliph was killed by the Mongols.

ahl al-bayt ⇁ "People of the house," "family," or "household" of the Prophet Muḥammad, including, in particular, the Prophet himself, his cousin and son-in-law ʿAlī, his daughter Fāṭima, his grandchildren al-Ḥasan and al-Ḥusayn, and their offspring.

ahl-i taḍādd ⇁ The people of discord; those who are not members of the Ismaili hierarchy and who therefore disagree among themselves; the lowest level of the tripartite division consisting of *ahl-i taḍādd*, *ahl-i tarattub* (q.v.), and *ahl-i waḥdat* (q.v.).

ahl-i tarattub ⇁ The people of ranks; those who have entered the Ismaili daʿwa and who receive *ʿilm* (q.v.) by *taʿlīm* (q.v.); the second level of the tripartite division consisting of *ahl-i taḍādd* (q.v.), *ahl-i tarattub*, and *ahl-i waḥdat* (q.v.).

ahl-i waḥdat ⇁ The people of unity; those in the very highest ranks of the *ḥudūd-i dīn* (q.v.) who have achieved gnosis of the Creator by *taʾyīd* (q.v.); the highest level of the tripartite division consisting of *ahl-i taḍādd* (q.v.), *ahl-i tarattub* (q.v.), and *ahl-i waḥdat*.

ʿAlids ⤻ The descendants of ʿAlī b. Abī Ṭālib. The progeny of ʿAlī and the Prophet's daughter Fāṭima who represent the Prophet Muḥammad's only blood descendants. The Shīʿa uphold the belief that the Imāms of the Muslim community must be ʿAlids. One branch of the ʿAlids went on to found the Fāṭimid (q.v.) caliphate.

ʿālim (pl. *ʿulamāʾ*) ⤻ Lit., a learned man. The term often refers especially to a specialist in the Islamic religious sciences. The *ʿulamāʾ* later formed a type of "clergy" in Islamic societies.

amr ⤻ Command, especially the divine command or logos. Often used with reference to the *kalima* (q.v.). In Nizari Ismailism, the Imām, as the expression of God's will, is the locus of manifestation of the *amr*. The Imāms are said to be the possessors of the command (*ulū al-amr*) mentioned in the Quran.

bāb ⤻ Lit., gate. The rank in the religious hierarchy or *ḥudūd-i dīn* (q.v.) immediately below that of the Imām (q.v.). It is often considered equivalent to the ḥujjat-i aʿẓam (q.v.). The bāb must always be in touch with the Imām, even in times of *satr* (q.v.).

bāṭin ⤻ The inward, spiritual, or esoteric meaning of, in particular, sacred texts and religious practices, as contrasted with the *ẓāhir* (q.v.).

bayʿa (or *bayʿat*) ⤻ The oath of allegiance pledged to God through his representative, such as the Prophet or the Imām in their respective cycles. The term connotes a transaction whereby, in exchange for right guidance, God "purchases" from the believers all that belongs to them (Quran 9:111).

dāʿī ⤻ Lit., a summoner. One of the high ranks in the religious hierarchy or *ḥudūd-i dīn* (q.v.).

daʿwa ⤻ Lit., summons. The invitation or summons of God, the Prophets, the Imāms, and the religious hierarchy to recognize God's supreme authority. The term, or its more specific form *al-daʿwa al-hādiya*, "the rightly guiding summons," sometimes connotes the entire system of the *ḥudūd-i dīn* (q.v.) or the Ismaili community as a whole.

dīwān ⤻ The omnibus or collected works of a poet.

farmān ⤻ An edict or commandment, particularly one issued by the Imām.

Fāṭimids ⤻ The Prophet's descendants through his daughter Fāṭima and his cousin ʿAlī b. Abī Ṭālib. One line of the Fāṭimids went on to found the dynasty of the same name, which separated into two branches after the death of the Imām Mustanṣir bi'llāh, the adherents of one branch centered in Egypt and those of the other centered at Alamūt.

fatwā ↪ A legal pronouncement.

fidā'ī (or *fidāwī*) ↪ Someone willing to sacrifice his life for a cause. In the case of the Ismailis, the term *fidā'ī* most specifically refers to those who, in the face of Saljuq massacres against the community, risked their lives to protect their fellows.

fiqh ↪ The term used for Islamic jurisprudence; the method by which the *sharī'a* (q.v.) is elaborated and codified.

Ginān ↪ Lit., gnostic or inspired knowledge; a general term used for the corpus of compositions attributed to the Ismaili pīrs (q.v.) of South Asia.

ḥadīth ↪ A report or tradition relating a statement, action, or tacit judgment of the Prophet and, in the case of the Shī'a, of the Imāms (q.v.).

ḥajj ↪ The annual pilgrimage to the Ka'ba (q.v.) in Mecca, performed in the month of Dhu al-Ḥijja.

ḥaqīqa (or *ḥaqīqat*) ↪ Truth; the inner reality of the message of Islam. *Ḥaqīqa* corresponds with *bāṭin* (q.v.) as *sharī'a* (q.v.) corresponds with *ẓāhir* (q.v.).

ḥudūd-i dīn ↪ Lit., the ranks of faith, sometimes simply referred to as the *ḥudūd*. The esoteric hierarchy of the Ismailis that receives religious knowledge either by *ta'yīd* (q.v.) or *ta'līm* (q.v.). Those in the very highest ranks of the *ḥudūd* are referred to as the *ahl-i waḥdat* (q.v.), while those who follow them are referred to as the *ahl-i tarattub* (q.v.).

ḥujjat (or ḥujja) ↪ Lit., proof. Among the Shī'a, this refers to the concept that humankind must always have a proof or evidence of God's will. The Prophets and Imāms are hence commonly referred to by this term. In the context of the *ḥudūd-i dīn* (q.v.), the ḥujjat is also a high-ranking dignitary in the hierarchy. There were believed to be twelve such ḥujjats (sometimes referred to as ḥujjats of the day) who were in charge of the twelve islands of the da'wa (q.v.), known as *jazā'ir* (sg. *jazīra*) (q.v.). Some texts also refer to the twelve ḥujjats of the night, bringing the total to twenty-four. In some contexts, the term ḥujjat denotes the chief representative of the Imām, also known as the bāb (q.v.) or ḥujjat-i a'ẓam (q.v.). The Ismaili texts maintain that the ḥujjats are in constant contact with the Imām, even in times of *satr* (q.v.).

ḥujjat-i aʿẓam (or ḥujjat-i akbar) ⤻ Lit., the supreme proof. The rank in the religious hierarchy or *ḥudūd-i dīn* (q.v.) immediately below that of the Imām (q.v.). It is often considered equivalent to the bāb (q.v.). The ḥujjat-i aʿẓam must always be in contact with the Imām, even in times of *satr* (q.v.).

ilḥād ⤻ Heresy or desertion; a heretic or deserter being referred to by the term *mulḥid* (pl. *malāḥida*). An accusation commonly leveled against religious and other groups that opposed the ruling authorities. Under the Umayyads (q.v.), the term was synonymous with rebel (*bāghī*) and one who breaks ranks (*shāqq al-ʿaṣā*), denoting the desertion (*ilḥād*) of the community of the faithful and rebellion against the ruling caliph. The Ottomans commonly used this term for the Ṣūfīs (q.v.) and the Shīʿa. Particularly in Alamūt times and later, the term was commonly applied to the Ismailis.

ʿilm ⤻ Knowledge, especially sapiential knowledge. The Shīʿa held that the Prophets and Imāms were the possessors of sapiential knowledge of God, transmitted by *naṣṣ* (q.v.). This knowledge was conveyed to the believers by way of *taʿlīm* (q.v.) and *taʾyīd* (q.v.).

Imām (pl. *aʾimma*) ⤻ Leader, anglicized as Imam. Among the Shīʿa, the term Imām most commonly refers to the divinely appointed successors of the Prophet who are blessed with *ʿilm* (q.v.). In a more general sense, an Imām may simply be a prayer leader or, particularly among the Sunnīs, any prominent leader, such as a founder of a legal school.

Ithnā ʿasharī ⤻ Lit. Twelver; a community of Shīʿī Muslims who believe in twelve Imāms (q.v.), the last of whom is said to be in occultation and who will emerge as the *mahdī* (q.v.) before the end of time.

jamāʿat (or *jamāʿa*) ⤻ A religious congregation or the members of a community.

jamāʿat-khāna ⤻ A house of assembly or congregation used by members of the community for religious and communal activities.

jazīra (pl. *jazāʾir*) ⤻ Lit., island. The Imām's *ʿilm* (q.v.) is depicted as an ocean, in which there are traditionally said to be twelve islands, each under the jurisdiction of a ḥujjat (q.v.) or, in the time of Bū Isḥāq, perhaps a muʿallim (q.v.).

Kaʿba ⤻ The famous cube-shaped sanctuary located at the center of the great mosque in Mecca. It is referred to as the house of God and is the primary destination of the pilgrimage known as the *ḥajj* (q.v.). During the lifetime of the Prophet Muhammad, it replaced Jerusalem as the Muslim *qibla* (q.v.).

kalima ⥽ Word, especially the divine word or logos; often used as a synonym for *amr* (q.v.). In Nizārī (q.v.) Ismailism, the Imām, as the expression of God's will, is the locus of manifestation of the *kalima*.

Khojā ⥽ See *khwāja*.

khudāwand ⥽ Lord, master; a Persian title commonly used in official documents of the Saljūqs and Khwarazmshāhs to address the sultan, but among the Ismailis used to address the Imām. Cf. mawlā (q.v.), mawlānā (q.v.), and shāh (q.v.).

Khwāja, also pronounced *khojā* ⥽ Master; a word having many connotations, but in the context of Nizārī (q.v.) Ismailism, the designation of one of the Ismaili communities of South Asia, primarily of Sindhi and Gujarati origin, which attributes its acceptance of the Imām to, in particular, Pīr Ṣadr al-Dīn and Pīr Ḥasan Kabīr al-Dīn.

lāḥiq ⥽ Lit. the conjoint one. A member of the *ḥudūd-i dīn* (q.v.). In Bū Isḥaq's elaboration, the equivalent of a muʿallim (q.v.).

ma'dhūn ⥽ Lit., licentiate; a lower rank in the *ḥudūd-i dīn* (q.v.), commonly divided into senior (*akbar*) and junior (*aṣghar*) ma'dhūns. The ma'dhūns were "licensed" to impart religious instruction.

mahdī ⥽ The rightly guided one; the Imām of the *ahl al-bayt* (q.v.) who will fill the world with justice. Sunni and Ithnā ʿasharī Islam generally use this term as an attribute for a leader who will appear at the end of time. In Nizārī (q.v.) Ismailism, it is also common for all the Imāms to be referred to collectively as *mahdī*. The *mahdī* is also frequently referred to as the *qā'im* (q.v.)

malāḥida (sg. *mulḥid*) ⥽ See *ilḥād*.

manṣūṣ ⥽ See *naṣṣ* (q.v.).

mawlā ⥽ Lord, master. Title commonly applied to ʿAlī b. Abī Ṭālib and all of the Imāms, cf. khudāwand (q.v.), mawlānā (q.v.), and shāh (q.v.).

mawlānā ⥽ Our lord, our master. Title commonly applied to the Imāms. When used without a name following, it generally refers to the present Imām, cf. khudāwand (q.v.), mawlā (q.v.), and shāh (q.v.).

muʿallim A teacher, one who transmits *taʿlīm* (q.v.). A rank of the *ḥudūd-i dīn* (q.v.), which may have been used in a general sense at some times, and in the specific sense of someone in charge of a *jazīra* (q.v.) at others.

mulḥid (pl. *malāḥida*) See *ilḥād.*

mustajīb A respondent to the daʿwa (q.v.); the lowest rank of the *ḥudūd-i dīn* (q.v.). The mustajīb can receive knowledge from his superiors but is not sufficiently advanced in the hierarchy to convey it to others.

Mustaʿlians The followers of Mustaʿlī and those descended from him, as opposed to the Nizārīs (q.v.). The most prominent branch is known as the Ṭayyibis (q.v.).

mustaqarr Lit. permanently established; an Imām (q.v.) possessed of all the prerogatives of the imamate whose progeny can also be *mustaqarr* Imāms. Contrasted with *mustawdaʿ* (q.v.).

mustawdaʿ Lit. temporarily lodged; an Imām (q.v.) possessed of all the prerogatives of the imamate, but whose progeny would not be *mustaqarr* (q.v.) Imāms. According to some sources, the *mustawdaʿ* imamate could continue for several generations before reverting to the *mustaqarr* line.

naṣṣ Explicit designation of a successor. One who receives this designation is called *manṣūṣ*.

nāṭiq (pl. *nuṭaqāʾ*) Lit., speaker, annunciator. A rank in the *ḥudūd-i dīn* (q.v.) designating the lords of the six cycles, Adam, Noah, Abraham, Moses, Jesus, and Muḥammad, who articulated a *sharīʿa* (q.v.) for humankind. The lord of the seventh cycle is the *qāʾim* (q.v.), who does not bring a new *sharīʿa* (q.v.), but rather reveals the *bāṭin* (q.v.) and spiritual meaning of the canon laws.

Nizārīs The followers of the Imām (q.v.) Nizār b. al-Mustanṣir and those descended from him, as opposed to the Mustaʿlians (q.v.), who recognized his younger brother Mustaʿlī and his descendants as Imāms.

Nuṣayrīs A Shīʿī sect that is widely represented in Syria, with pockets of adherents in Turkey and Lebanon. They are sometimes referred to as ʿAlawīs.

pīr A sage or spiritual preceptor. In Ismailism, a rank in the religious hierarchy or *ḥudūd-i dīn* (q.v.), generally considered equivalent to the ḥujjat (q.v.), though sometimes used in a more general sense for any high-ranking appointee of the Imām. In Ṣūfism (q.v.), a spiritual master or shaykh.

qāḍī (pl. *quḍāt*) ↪ A Muslim judge who administers justice based on an interpretation of the *sharīʿa* (q.v.).

qāʾim ↪ The Imām (q.v.) who would be the lord of the seventh cycle. He would inaugurate the *qiyāma* (q.v.) and reveal the spiritual purport, or *bāṭin* (q.v.), of the canon laws.

qaṣīda ↪ A poetic genre that is frequently panegyric in content; an ode.

qibla ↪ The direction to which believers face in prayers. Among the early Muslims, the *qibla* was Jerusalem before being fixed as the Kaʿba (q.v.) in Mecca.

qiyāma (or *qiyāmat*) ↪ The resurrection; the last of the seven cycles, it is inaugurated by the *qāʾim* (q.v.). The spiritual ascensions of the believers from rank to rank of the *ḥudūd-i dīn* (q.v.) are also referred to as *qiyāma*.

risāla (pl. *rasāʾil*) ↪ Treatise, epistle.

Ṣafawids ↪ A predominantly Ithnā ʿasharī (q.v.) dynasty that ruled Persia from 907/1501 until 1135/1722, but which had claims to power even after that.

Saljūqs ↪ A Turkish dynasty in the central Islamic lands that reached the peak of its power during the 5th–6th/11th–12th centuries; often considered defenders of Sunnī Islam.

satr ↪ Concealment. *Satr* is a technical term having different connotations at different times and in different contexts. It is often used in reference to a period, the *dawr-i satr*, during which the Imāms are concealed from the general public, but not from the highest ranks of the *ḥudūd-i dīn* (q.v.). It can also refer to the concealment of the *bāṭin* (q.v.) from those who are not prepared to receive it, cf. *taqiyya* (q.v.).

sayyid (pl. *sādāt*) ↪ Lord, master; a title frequently used for the Prophet's descendants through his daughter Fāṭima and his cousin and son-in-law ʿAlī b. Abī Ṭālib.

shāh ↪ A Persian regal title, commonly used when referring to the Imām (q.v.), cf. khudāwand (q.v.), mawlā (q.v.), and mawlānā (q.v.).

sharīʿa (or *sharīʿat*) ↪ The canon law of Islam, the details of which were developed and elaborated in the centuries following the Prophet's death. There exist diverse schools of *sharīʿa* in both Shīʿī and Sunnī Islam. In the thought of the Ismailis, along with other esoteric schools of Islam, *sharīʿa* corresponds with *ẓāhir* (q.v.) as *ḥaqīqa* (q.v.) corresponds with *bāṭin* (q.v.).

Ṣūfī ⥽ In a general sense, especially in Western languages, a Muslim mystic; in a more specific sense, a follower of a particular Ṣūfī order.

Ṣūfism ⥽ The practice of being a Ṣūfī (q.v.).

taʿlīm ⥽ Teaching, spiritual edification; authoritative instruction by which *ʿilm* (q.v.) is gradually conveyed to the lower ranks of the *ḥudūd-i dīn* (q.v.), as distinct from *taʾyīd* (q.v.).

taqiyya ⥽ Precautionary dissimulation of one's true religious beliefs, especially in times of danger; also, not revealing the *bāṭin* (q.v.) to those who are not yet prepared to receive it, cf. *satr* (q.v.).

taʾwīl ⥽ Lit. to take something back to its origin; the method by which spiritual meaning, the *bāṭin* (q.v.), was educed from divine revelation, the *sharīʿa* (q.v.), the world of physical phenomena or the progress of history; a type of spiritual hermeneutics.

taʾyīd ⥽ Inspiration, spiritual support; the method by which *ʿilm* (q.v.) is directly inspired in the higher ranks of the *ḥudūd-i dīn* (q.v.), as distinct from *taʿlīm* (q.v.).

Ṭayyibīs ⥽ The most prominent branch of the Mustaʿlians (q.v.). They recognized al-Ṭayyib, an infant son of one of their Imāms, as his successor. This was in opposition to another branch of the Mustaʿlians that recognized a cousin of the Imām. In South Asia, the Ṭayyibīs are commonly known as Bohras.

ʿulamāʾ ⥽ See *ʿālim* (q.v.).

Umayyads ⥽ The first dynasty of Muslim caliphs, they were descended from Umayya b. ʿAbd Shams. ʿUthmān was the first Umayyad to become caliph. He was criticized for favoring his clan with political positions, but as he did not declare an heir, he is generally not considered the dynasty's founder, that title belonging to Muʿāwiya I. The Umayyads ruled from Damascus, and a later branch of the family ruled from Cordoba.

ẓāhir ⥽ The outward, apparent, or exoteric form of, in particular, divine revelation, the *sharīʿa* (q.v.), the world of physical phenomena, or the progress of history, as contrasted with the *bāṭin* (q.v.).

Zaydīs ⥽ A Shīʿī community that, unlike the Ithnā ʿasharīs (q.v.) and the Ismailis, demanded a political role for the Imām (q.v.). They are named after the Imām al-Bāqir's half-brother, Zayd b. ʿAlī.

Abbreviations

The following abbreviations are used in the notes and bibliography.

BRISMES	*Bulletin of the British Society for Middle Eastern Studies*
BSO(A)S	*Bulletin of the School of Oriental (and African) Studies*
EI2	*Encyclopaedia of Islam*, 2nd ed.
Iran	*Iran: Journal of the British Institute of Persian Studies*
IC	*Islamic Culture*
JASB	*Journal and Proceedings of the Asiatic Society of Bengal*
JA	*Journal Asiatique*
JAOS	*Journal of the American Oriental Society*
JBBRAS	*Journal of the Bombay Branch of the Royal Asiatic Society*
JRAS	*Journal of the Royal Asiatic Society*
NS	New Series
SI	*Studia Islamica*

Notes

NOTE ON THE TEXT

1. Lamb, *The Works of Charles and Mary Lamb: Elia and The Last Essays of Elia,* ed. Lucas (Project Gutenberg, http://www.gutenberg.org/author/Charles_Lamb, accessed March 15, 2006). Hume, of course, was David Hume (d. 1776), the English philosopher and historian, and William Robertson (d. 1793) was a historian of America.

2. Cited in Sharpe, *Comparative Religion: A History*, 2nd ed. (La Salle, IL, 1986), 115–116.

INTRODUCTION

1. Quoted in Fernández-Armesto, "Steppes Towards the Future" (March 12, 2004), (Independent News and Media, http://www.independent.co.uk/, accessed March 13, 2004). Cf. Man, *Genghis Khan: Life, Death and Resurrection* (London, 2004), 251.

2. Juwaynī, *Taʾrīkh-i Jahāngushāy*, ed. Qazwīnī, 3 vols. (Leiden, 1912–1937), vol. 1, 81, trans. Boyle, *The History of the World-Conqueror*, 2 vols. (Cambridge, MA, 1958), vol. 1, xxxiii, 105.

3. Browne, *A Literary History of Persia*, 4 vols. (Cambridge, 1902–1924), 426–427. While the number of victims recorded by the chroniclers is incredible, "these figures should be taken seriously, not as statistics but as evidence of the chroniclers' state of mind," Morgan, *Medieval Persia, 1040–1797* (London, 1988), 79–80.

4. Juwaynī, *Jahāngushāy*, ed. vol. 3, 275, trans. vol. 2, 723. This edict was repeated by his grandson Mongke, who sent his brother Hūlāgū to destroy the Ismailis.

5. One of the most influential explanations of this crime is found in "Convention on the Prevention and Punishment of the Crime of Genocide" (December 9, 1948), (Office of

the United Nations High Commissioner for Human Rights, http://www.unhchr.ch/html/menu3/b/p_genoci.htm, accessed February 2, 2006).

6. For a discussion of Juwaynī's possible motivations for this unusual treatment, see Hillenbrand, "The Power Struggle Between the Saljuqs and the Ismaʿilis of Alamūt, 487–518/1094–1124: The Saljuq Perspective," in *Mediaeval Ismaʿili History and Thought*, ed. Daftary (Cambridge, 1996), 214; Morgan, *The Mongols* (Oxford, 1986), 17–18; and chapter 2 of this book.

7. Fuller details of the early Islamic milieu and the development of Shīʿism can be found in Halm, *Shiʿism*, trans. Watson and Hill, 2nd ed. (New York, 2004); Jafri, *The Origins and Early Development of Shiʿa Islam* (London, 1979); Madelung, *The Succession to Muhammad* (Cambridge, 1997); Momen, *An Introduction to Shiʿi Islam: The History and Doctrines of Twelver Shiʿism* (New Haven, 1985), all of which contain further references.

8. See, for example, the massive Laknawī, *ʿAbaqāt al-Anwār fī Imāmat al-Aʾimma al-Aṭhār*, 10 vols. ([Qumm], 1983–1990), which has been published repeatedly in both Persian and Arabic, and the equally voluminous al-Amīnī, *al-Ghadīr fī al-Kitāb wa-al-Sunna wa-al-Adab*, 2nd ed., 11 vols. (Tehran, 1372/1952), which provides full references to over one hundred companions of the prophet who narrated the incident of Ghadīr. The author also provides a chronological account of historians, traditionalists, exegetes, and poets who mention the ḥadīth of Ghadīr Khumm from the beginning of Islam until modern times. See also Jafri, *Shiʿa Islam*, 19–22; Vaglieri, "Ghadīr Khumm," in *EI2*, vol. 2 (Leiden, 1960–2004; reprint, CD-ROM v. 1.0).

9. See Virani, "Ahl al-Bayt," in *Encyclopedia of Religion*, ed. Jones, vol. 1 (New York, 2005).

10. See Levi Della Vida and Khoury, "ʿUthmān b. ʿAffān," in *EI2*, vol. 10 (Leiden, 1960–2004; reprint, CD-ROM v. 1.0).

11. Jafri, *Shiʿa Islam*, 87, and sources cited at 99 n28.

12. Crone, "ʿUthmāniyya," in *EI2*, vol. 10 (Leiden, 1960–2004; reprint, CD-ROM v. 1.0).

13. See Lammens, *Étude sur la règne du calife omaiyade Moʿāwiya Ier* (Paris, 1908), 180ff.

14. The prominence of al-Ḥusayn's descendants in this line is highlighted in a letter of al-Manṣūr, the second ʿAbbāsid caliph, to Muḥammad b. ʿAbd Allāh al-Nafs al-Zakiyya of the Ḥasanid line: "No one born from among you [the ʿAlids] after the death of the Prophet was more virtuous than ʿAli b. al-Husayn. . . . After him, no one among you was like his son, Muhammad b. ʿAli . . . , nor like his [Muhammad b. ʿAli's] son, Jaʿfar." Cited with references in Modarressi, *Crisis and Consolidation in the Formative Period of Shīʿite Islam: Abū Jaʿfar ibn Qiba al-Rāzī and His Contribution to Imāmite Shīʿite Thought* (Princeton, NJ, 1993), 5 n5.

15. Jafri, *Shiʿa Islam*, 273. For a very brief biography of ʿAbd Allāh al-Maḥḍ, which does not mention this incident, see Zettersteen, "ʿAbd Allāh b. al-Ḥasan b. al-Ḥasan," in *EI2*, vol. 1 (Leiden, 1960–2004; reprint, CD-ROM v. 1.0).

16. See Moscati, "Abū Salama Ḥafs b. Sulaymān al-Khallāl," in *EI2*, vol. 1 (Leiden, 1960–2004; reprint, CD-ROM v. 1.0). When the first ʿAbbāsid caliph, Abū al-ʿAbbās, was inaugurated, his uncle Dāʾūd b. ʿAlī proclaimed that his nephew was the only caliph apart

from ʿAlī b. Abī Ṭālib not to have usurped the position. Jafri, *Shiʿa Islam*, 274; Zaman, *Religion and Politics Under the Early ʿAbbāsids: The Emergence of the Proto-Sunnī Elite*, (Leiden, 1997), 43–44. Cf. Crone, *God's Rule: Government and Islam*, (New York, 2004), 87. The rebellion, at least in Khurasan, had called people to return to the Book of God and the tradition of Muḥammad and ʿAlī. See *Akhbār al-dawla al-ʿAbbāsiyya wa-fīhi akhbār al-ʿAbbās wa-waladihi*, ed. al-Dūrī and al-Muṭṭalibī (Beirut, 1971), 284; and the discussion in Zaman, *Religion and Politics*, 43ff.

17. On Jaʿfar al-Ṣādiq see al-Ṭūsī, *Ikhtiyār maʿrifat al-rijāl, al-maʿrūf bi-rijāl al-Kashshī*, ed. al-Muṣṭafawī (Mashhad, Iran, 1348 HS/1969), index, s.v.; Halm, *Shīʿism* (Edinburgh, 1991), 29f.

18. On Jaʿfar al-Ṣādiq's father, Muḥammad al-Bāqir, see Lalani, *Early Shīʿī Thought: The Teachings of Imam Muḥammad al-Bāqir* (London, 2000).

19. See, for example, Amir-Moezzi, *The Divine Guide in Early Shiʿism: The Sources of Esotericism in Islam*, trans. Streight (Albany, NY, 1994), index, s.v., "ilm;" Clarke, "Early Doctrine of the Shiʿah, According to the Shīʿī Sources" (PhD dissertation, McGill University, 1994), 76–176. See also Madelung and Tyan, "ʿIṣmā," in *EI2*, vol. 4 (Leiden, 1960–2004; reprint, CD-ROM v. 1.0).

20. Buhl, "Muḥammad b. ʿAbd Allāh b. al-Ḥasan al-Muthannā b. al-Ḥasan b. ʿAlī b. Abī Ṭālib, called al-Nafs al-Zakiyya," in *EI2*, vol. 7 (Leiden, 1960–2004; reprint, CD-ROM v. 1.0); Kennedy, *The Early ʿAbbāsid Caliphate* (London, 1981), 200 ff; Modarressi, *Crisis*, 6–8, 53; Vaglieri, "Ibrahīm b. ʿAbd Allāh," in *EI2*, vol. 3 (Leiden, 1960–2004; reprint, CD-ROM v. 1.0). Zaman, *Religion and Politics*, 73 n11 provides additional bibliographic references.

21. The majority of Mūsā's followers initially accepted the claims of Jaʿfar al-Ṣādiq's son, ʿAbd Allāh al-Afṭāḥ. However, his death soon after his father's demise led to their acknowledgment of Mūsā al-Kāẓim. See Daftary, *The Ismāʿīlīs: Their History and Doctrines* (Cambridge, 1990), 94; Hodgson, "Djaʿfar al-Ṣādiḳ," in *EI2*, vol. 2 (Leiden, 1960–2004; reprint, CD-ROM v. 1.0); Ibn al-Haytham, *Kitāb al-Munāẓarāt*, ed. Madelung and Walker, trans. Madelung and Walker, *The Advent of the Fatimids: A Contemporary Shiʿi Witness* (London, 2000), ed. 35–37, trans. 90–92; Modarressi, *Crisis*, 53ff.

22. This designation was seldom used by the early sectarians themselves and was applied to them by the heresiographers. Cf. Daftary, *Ismāʿīlīs*, 93. This group has been referred to by a plethora of names in the early literature. Niẓām al-Mulk (d. 485/1092), for example, mentions ten geographically specific designations, Ismāʿīlī (Aleppo and Cairo), Qarmaṭī (Baghdad, Transoxiana, and Ghazna), Mubārakī (Kufa), Rāwandī and Burquʿī (Basra), Khālafī (Rayy), Muḥammira (Jurjān), Mubayyiḍa (Syria), Saʿīdī (Maghrib), Janābī (Lahsa and Bahrain), and Bāṭinī. See Niẓām al-Mulk, *Siyar al-Mulūk or Siyāsatnāma*, trans. Darke, 2nd ed. (London, 1978), 231. Ghazālī (d. 505/1111) mentions Bāṭiniyya, Qarāmiṭa, Khurramiyya or Khurramdīniyya, Bābakiyya, Muḥammira, Sabʿiyya, Ismāʿīliyya, and Taʿlīmiyya. Cited in Corbin, "The Ismāʿīlī Response to the Polemic of Ghazālī," in *Ismāʿīlī Contributions to Islamic Culture*, ed. Nasr, trans. Morris (Tehran, 1977), 74. The name of a branch of the community that had become particularly infamous, the Qarāmiṭa, was often applied derogatorily, and incorrectly, to the entire community. In addition, hostile historical sources frequently refer to the Ismailis abusively as *malāḥida*, the apostates or heretics.

Various Muslim groups commonly referred to their foes by this derogatory name, but by Alamūt times it seems to have been most widely directed toward the Ismailis. See Madelung, "Mulḥid," in *EI2*, vol. 7 (Leiden, 1960–2004; reprint, CD-ROM v. 1.0). Mīrkhwānd, for example, states that the term was particularly applied to this community. See Mīrkhwānd, *Rawḍat al-Ṣafā'*, 10 vols. (Tehran, 1338–1339 HS/1959–1960); 114, Mīrkhwānd, *Rawḍat al-Ṣafā'*, ed. Am. Jourdain, trans. Am. Jourdain, *"Histoire de la dynastie des Ismaéliens de Perse," Notices et Extraits des Manuscrits*, vol. 9 (1813), 155.

Many of these names are inaccurate, some clearly polemical, and others a conflation of the group under study with others that had nothing to do with it. In the early period, the community commonly referred to itself as *al-daʿwat al-hādiya*, "the Rightly Guiding Summons," or simply as *al-daʿwa*, "the Summons." We also find such names as *ahl-i ḥaqq* or *ahl-i ḥaqīqat*, "the people of truth," used in Persian-speaking regions; *Mawlāʾī*, "the partisans of the lord," in Hunza, Gilgit, and Chitral; *Panjtanī*, "the partisans of the five," i.e., Muḥammad, ʿAlī, Fāṭima, al-Ḥasan, and al-Ḥusayn, in parts of Central Asia; and *Satpanthī*, "follower of the path of truth"; *Khwāja* (*Khojā*), "the venerable," *Shamsī*, "the followers of Pīr Shams" and *Muʾmin* (*Momnā*), "the faithful" in South Asia.

The name currently employed in academia, Ismāʿīliyya, seems to have been used by the early community only occasionally. It appears to have originated with the early heresiographers, notably al-Nawbakhtī and al-Qummī.

The term "Ismaili," however, has a number of advantages, not least of which is its currency in academia. Moreover, it was not rejected among the Ismailis themselves. In a riposte to al-Ghazālī's virulent attack on the Ismailis in his *Infamies of the Bāṭinīs and the Virtues of the Mustaẓhirīs* (*Kitāb Faḍāʾiḥ al-Bāṭiniyya wa Faḍāʾil al-Mustaẓhiriyya*), ʿAlī b. Muḥammad b. Walīd (d. 612/1215), the fifth dāʿī of the Ṭayyibī Ismailis, comments on the names Ghazālī ascribed to the community. With regards to the term "Ismāʿīliyya," he vaunts:

> This name designates those whose [spiritual] ancestry goes back to Mawlāna [sic, Mawlānā] Ismāʿīl ibn Jaʿfar al-Ṣādiq, ibn Muḥammad al-Bāqir, ibn ʿAlī Zayn al-ʿĀbidīn, ibn al-Ḥusayn al-Taqī, ibn ʿAlī al-Murtaḍā al-Waṣī. This is our inherent name. It is our honour and our glory before all of the other branches of Islam, because we stand on the Path of the Truth, in following our guides the Imāms. We drink at an abundant fountain, and we hold firmly to the guiding lines of their walāya. Thus they cause us to climb from rank to rank among the degrees of proximity [to God] and excellence.

Translated in Corbin, "Ismāʿīlī Response," 74–75. See also Poonawala, "An Ismāʿīlī Refutation of al-Ghazālī," in *Middle East 130th International Congress of Human Sciences in Asia and North Africa 1976*, ed. Lama (Mexico City, 1982), 131–134.

Significantly, this name is now current in the community that considers itself the inheritor of the traditions of the descendants of the Imam Ismāʿīl and that presently owes its allegiance to Prince Karim Aga Khan, the forty-ninth Imam. Thus, despite the drawbacks outlined above and the fact that some other groups, including the Druze and the Ṭayyibī community (commonly called the Bohrās in South Asia), are equally Ismaili, this term will be used to refer to the Nizārī Ismaili community.

23. On the Fāṭimids, see Daftary, *Ismāʿīlīs*, 144–255; Halm, *Die Kaliefen von Kairo: Die Fatimiden in Ägypten, 973–1074* (Munich, 2003); Halm, *The Empire of the Mahdi: The Rise of the Fatimids*, trans. Bonner (Leiden, 1996).

24. For an overview of this episode, see Daftary, *Ismāʿīlīs*, 205–206; Makdisi, *Ibn ʿAqīl et la Résurgence de l'Islam traditionaliste au XIe Siècle* (Damascus, 1963), 90–102; Qutbuddin, *Al-Muʾayyad al-Shīrāzī and Fatimid Daʿwa Poetry* (Leiden, 2005), 67–76.

25. al-Baghdādī, *al-Farq bayna al-Firāq*, trans. Seelye, *Moslem Schisms and Sects: (al-Farḳ bain al-firāḳ) Being the History of the Various Philosophic Systems Developed in Islam* (New York, 1966), part II, 107–108.

26. His contemporary, Abū al-Maʿālī writes in 485/1092 that both Ḥasan-i Sabbāḥ and Nāṣir-i Khusraw were distinguished as *ṣāḥib-i jazīra*, i.e., as *ḥujjats* in the Ismaili hierarchy. See Abū al-Maʿālī, *Bayān al-Adyān*, ed. Āshtiyānī and Dānishpazhūh (Tehran, 1376 HS/1997), 55.

27. Ibn al-Athīr, *Taʾrīkh al-Kāmil [a.k.a. al-Kāmil fī al-Taʾrīkh]* (Cairo, 1303/1885), vol. 10, 112.

28. Juwaynī, *Jahāngushāy*, ed. vol. 3, 269–270, trans. vol. 2, 719. Cf., however, Daftary, *Ismaili Literature* (London, 2004), 46, in which the author does not follow Juwaynī's testimony, but the list of preserved items recorded in Ivanow, *Ismaili Literature: A Bibliographical Survey*, 2nd amplified ed. (Tehran, 1963), 127–136; Poonawala, *Biobibliography of Ismāʿīlī Literature* (Malibu, CA, 1977), 251–263.

29. Cited in Daftary, *Ismāʿīlīs*, 8–9.

30. Juwaynī, *Jahāngushāy*, ed. vol. 3, 269–270, trans. vol. 2, 719.

31. Ibid, ed. vol. 3, 186–187, 269–270, trans. vol. 2, 666, 719.

32. Ibid, ed. vol. 3, 139–142, trans. vol. 2, 639–640, translation slightly modified.

33. Juwaynī, *Jahāngushāy*, ed. vol. 3, 277, trans. vol. 2, 724–725.

34. This is a reference to the forty-fifth Imam of the Ismailis, Shāh Khalīl Allāh, who, in 1206/1792, succeeded his father (not uncle) Abū al-Ḥasan ʿAlī, who was also known as Sayyid Kahakī. See Daftary, *Ismāʿīlīs*, 503–504.

35. Sacy, "Mémoire sur la dynastie des Assassins," *Mémoirs de l'Institut Royal de France* 4 (1818). The selection quoted is translated by A. Azodi as "Memoir on the Dynasty of the Assassins and on the Etymology of Their Name by Silvestre de Sacy" in Daftary, *The Assassin Legends: Myths of the Ismailis* (London, 1994), 182, translation emended slightly. Soon after this notice, another report about the continued existence of the Ismailis in Persia, Syria, and India appeared in Hammer-Purgstall, *Die Geschichte der Assassinen aus Morgenländischen Quellen* (Stuttgart and Tübingen, 1818), translated into English as Hammer-Purgstall, *The History of the Assassins, Derived from Oriental Sources*, trans. Wood (London, 1835) 210–212. In 1906, E. G. Browne wrote of the community's continued existence in Syria, though he seems to have been unaware that they survived in Persia as well. See Browne, *Literary History*, vol. 2, 206–207.

36. Cited in Dumasia, *The Aga Khan and His Ancestors* (Mumbai, 1939), 38, and Picklay, *History of the Ismailis* (Mumbai, 1940), 73. The Baron C. A. De Bode, during his travels, had earlier noted Aga Khan I's appointment as governor of Kirman and his confrontation with government forces from the citadel of Bam. In so doing, he remarks:

> On my right hand, to the east, was the mountainous district of Mahalat, where a remnant of the Ismaeli sect, the descendants of the followers of Hasān-Sabāh [sic], or Sheikh-Jabal (the old man of the mountain), are said still to exist. It is currently believed that their Chief, Aga-Khan, is likewise looked upon by the Ismaeli sectarians of India as their head.

De Bode, *Travels in Luristan and Arabistan*, vol. 2 (London, 1845), 317.

37. See, for example, Majerczak, "Les Ismaéliens de Choughnan," *Revue du Monde Musulman* 24 (1913), Menant, "Les Khodjas du Guzarate," *Revue du Monde Musulman* 12 (1910), Semenov, "Iz oblasti religioznikh verovaniy gornikh tadzhikov [On the Religious Beliefs of the Mountain Tajiks]," *ätnograficheskoe obozrenie (Moscow)* 47, no. 4 (1900), Semenov, "Iz oblasti religioznikh verovaniy shughnanskikh ismailitov [On the Religious Beliefs of the Ismailis of Shughnān]," *Mir Islam (St Petersburg)* 1, no. 44 (1912), Semenov, "Opisanie ismailitskikh rukopisey, sobranikh A. A. Semyonovim [Description of Ismāʿīlī manuscripts, A. A. Semenov's collection]," *Izvestiya Rossiyskoy Akademii Nauk/Bulletin de l'Académie des Sciences de Russie (Petrograd)* 6 série, no. 12 (1918). Decades before these studies were published, a speech on the subject was delivered by E. I. Howard, one of the counsels for the defense in the "Aga Khan Case" of 1866. Howard, *The Shia School of Islam and Its Branches, Especially That of the Imamee-Ismailies: A Speech Delivered by E. I. Howard, Esquire, Barrister-at-Law, in the Bombay High Court, in June, 1866* (Mumbai, 1866). This was later reprinted by the Bombay Education Society in 1895, and again in 1906. These reprints may be added to the reference in Daftary, *Ismaili Literature*, 297.

38. Ivanow, "My First Meeting with the Ismailis in Persia," *Ilm* 3, no. 3 (December 1977): 16–17. This is a reprint of an article that originally appeared as Ivanow, "My First Meeting with Ismailis of Persia," *Read and Know* 1 (1966): 11–14. The original is not available to me. See Daftary, *Ismaili Literature*, 306. "Great World War I" in the text has been emended to read "Great War."

39. See Daftary, *Ismaili Literature*, 73; Daftary, *Ismāʿīlīs*, 547.

40. Daftary, *Ismaili Literature*, 59; Daftary, *Ismāʿīlīs*, 30–31.

41. Daftary, *Ismāʿīlīs*, 435. He is preceded in this regard by Algar, "The Revolt of Āghā Khān Maḥallātī and the Transference of the Ismāʿīlī Imamate to India," *SI* 29 (1969): 55; Ali, *The Origin of the Khojāhs and Their Religious Life Today* (Würzburg, 1936), 55; Howard, *Shia School*, 57–59.

42. Daftary, *Ismāʿīlīs*, 443. See also Daftary, *Ismaili Literature*, 59.

43. Ivanow, *A Guide to Ismaili Literature* (London, 1933); Ivanow, *Ismaili Literature;* Poonawala, *Biobibliography*. The more recent study, Daftary, *Ismaili Literature*, is a very useful guide for published Ismaili works.

44. See Daftary, "Persian Historiography of the Early Nizārī Ismāʿīlīs," *Iran* 30 (1992): 97.

45. The following narrative is from Kūchak, *Silk-i Gawhar Rīz*, ed. Qudertullah (Dushanbe, Tajikistan, nd), 100–101.

46. See, for example, his "Introduction" to Mustanṣir bi'llāh (=Gharīb Mīrzā?), *Pandiyāt-i Jawānmardī*, ed. Ivanow, trans. Ivanow, *Pandiyat-i Jawanmardi or "Advices of Manliness"* (Leiden, 1953), 018.

47. Khayrkhwāh Harātī, *Taṣnīfāt-i Khayrkhwāh-i Harātī*, ed. Ivanow (Tehran, 1961).

48. *Biblia Sacra: iuxta Vulgatam versionem*, ed. Fischer and Weber (Stuttgart: Deutsche Bibelgesellschaft, 1983, http://www.thelatinlibrary.com/bible/prologi.html, accessed February 2, 2006).

CHAPTER 1

1. Josephine Tey, *The Daughter of Time*, new edition, (New York, 1970), 84–85.

2. Juwaynī, *Ta'rīkh-i Jahāngushāy*, trans. Boyle, *The History of the World-Conqueror*, 2 vols. (Cambridge, MA, 1958), Juwaynī, *Ta'rīkh-i Jahāngushāy*, ed. Qazwīnī, 3 vols. (Leiden, 1912–1937).

3. Cited in Daftary, *The Ismāʿīlīs: Their History and Doctrines* (Cambridge, 1990), 8–9.

4. Adae, *Directorium ad passagium faciendum, in RHC: Documents Arméniens*, vol. 2 (Paris, 1869–1906), 496–497.

5. Jūzjānī, *Ṭabaqāt-i Nāṣirī*, trans. Raverty, *The ṭabaḳāt-i-Nāṣirī: A General History of the Muhammadan Dynasties of Asia* (London, 1881–1899); Jūzjānī, *Ṭabaqāt-i Nāṣirī*, ed. Ḥabībī, 2nd ed. (Kabul, 1342–1343 HS/1963–1964). On this author, see Bazmee Ansari, "al-Djūzdjānī," in *EI2*, 2nd ed., vol. 2 (Leiden, 1960–2004; reprint, CD-ROM v. 1.0).

6. Rashīd al-Dīn, *Jāmiʿ al-Tawārīkh*, trans. Thackston, *Jamiʿu't-tawarikh: Compendium of Chronicles*, 3 vols. (Cambridge, MA, 1998); Rashīd al-Dīn, *Jāmiʿ al-Tawārīkh*, ed. Karīmī (Tehran, 1338 HS/1959).

7. A third source for the immediate aftermath of the destruction of Alamūt is the *Zubdat al-Tawārīkh* of Jamāl al-Dīn Abū al-Qāsim ʿAbd Allāh b. ʿAlī Kāshānī (d. ca. 738/1337), a Persian Shīʿī historian who was associated with the Īlkhānid administration. His narrative is very close to Rashīd al-Dīn's, with whom he worked and whom he accused of appropriating his research. While there are some minor differences and additional details in his work, these are not particularly significant, and so have not been taken account of in the present study. See Kāshānī, *Zubdat al-tawārīkh: bakhsh-i Fāṭimiyān wa-Nizāriyān (partial edition)*, ed. Dānishpazhūh, 2nd ed. (Tehran, 1366 HS/1987).

8. Qazwīnī, *Ta'rīkh-i Guzīda*, ed. Browne, trans. Browne, *The Ta'rīkh-i Guzīda: or, "Select History"* (Leiden, 1910–1913).

9. Qazwīnī, *Nuzhat al-Qulūb*, ed. Le Strange, trans. Le Strange, *The Geographical Part of the Nuzhat al-Qulūb* (Leiden, 1915–1919).

10. Ms. British Library Or. 2833, fols. 712vo-717ro. Qazwīnī, *Ẓafarnāma*, ed. Pūrjawādī and Rastigār, facsimile ed., 2 vols. (Tehran, 1377 HS/1999). The work has been translated in Ward, "The Ẓafarnāma of Ḥamd Allāh Mustaufī and the Il-khan Dynasty of Iran" (PhD dissertation, University of Manchester?, 1983), vol. 3, 567–587. The translation, however, has been judged "helpful in a general sense . . . [but] too unreliable to be used with confidence" by Melville, "The Īlkhān Öljeitü's Conquest of Gīlān (1307): Rumour and Reality," in *The Mongol Empire and Its Legacy*, ed. Amitai-Preiss and

Morgan (Leiden, 1999), 75. Appraisals of the *Ẓafarnāma* include Melville, "Ḥamd Allāh Mustawfī's Ẓafarnāmah and the Historiography of the Late Ilkhanid Period," in *Iran and Iranian Studies: Essays in Honor of Iraj Afshar*, ed. Eslami (Princeton, 1997), 1–12; and Soudavar, "Ẓafarnāma wa-Shāhnāma-yi Mustawfī," *Īrānshināsī* 7, no. 4 (1996): 752–761.

11. Ḥāfiẓ Abrū, *Dhayl-i Jāmiʿ al-Tawārīkh* (Tehran, 1317 HS/1938).

12. Kāshānī, *Taʾrīkh-i Ūljāytū*, ed. Hambly (Tehran, 1348 HS/1969), particularly 55–73.

13. Sayf b. Muḥammad b. Yaʿqūb, *Taʾrīkh Nāma-yi Harāt*, ed. Ṣiddīqī (Calcutta, 1944).

14. Faṣīḥ Khwāfī, *Mujmal-i Faṣīḥī*, ed. Farrukh, 2 vols. (Mashhad, 1339–1340 HS/1960–1961).

15. Marʿashī, *Taʾrīkh-i Gīlān wa-Daylamistān*, ed. Rabino (Rasht, 1330/1912); Marʿashī, *Taʾrīkh-i Gīlān wa-Daylamistān*, ed. Sutūda (Tehran, 1347 HS/1968).

16. See Rabino, "Les Dynasties locales du Gīlān et du Daylam," *JA* 237 (1949): 314.

17. Gīlānī, *Taʾrīkh-i Māzandarān*, ed. Sutūda (Tehran, 1352 HS/1973).

18. Qāʾinī, "Naṣāʾiḥ-i Shāhrukhī," in *Österreichische Nationalbibliothek*, Monastic Microfilm Project Number 22 249, University Microfilms, Codex Vindobonensis Palatinus. A.f. 112 (Flügel 1858) (Vienna, 1970).

19. Ibn Baṭṭuta, *Riḥla*, trans. Gibb, *The Travels of Ibn Battuta*, 4 vols. (Cambridge, 1971); Ibn Baṭṭūṭa, *Riḥla*, ed. Defrémery and Sanguinetti, trans. Defrémery and Sanguinetti, *Voyages d'Ibn Battūta* (Paris, 1853–1859).

20. al-Dimashqī, *Nukhbat al-Dahr fī ʿAjāʾib al-Barr wa-al-Baḥr* (Copenhagen, 1874); al-Dimashqī, *Nukhbat al-Dahr fī ʿAjāʾib al-Barr wa-al-Baḥr*, ed. Mehren, *Cosmographie de Chems-ed-Din Abou Abdallah Mohammed Ed-Dimichqui* (St. Petersburg, 1866); al-Dimashqī, *Nukhbat al-Dahr fī ʿAjāʾib al-Barr wa-al-Baḥr (Persian translation)* (Shayryūr, 1357 HS/1978).

21. Dihlawī, *Akhbār al-Akhyār fī Asrār al-Abrār* (Delhi, 1891).

22. Quoted in Ivanow, "The Sect of Imam Shah in Gujrat," *JBBRAS* 12 (1936).

23. Idrīs, *ʿUyūn al-Akhbār wa-Funūn al-āthār*, ed. Sayyid, trans. Walker and Pomerantz, *The Fatimids and the Successors in Yaman: The History of an Islamic Community, Arabic Edition and English Summary of Volume 7 of Idrīs ʿImād al-Dīn's ʿUyūn al-Akhbār*, vol. 7 (London, 2002).

24. Shāmī, *Ẓafarnāma*, ed. Tauer, trans. Tauer, *Histoire des Conquêtes de Tamerlan, Intitulée Ẓafarnāma* (Prague, 1937–1956).

25. Yazdī, *Ẓafarnāma*, ed. ʿAbbāsī (Tehran, 1336 HS/1957); Yazdī, *Ẓafarnāma* (Delhi, 1972).

26. Mīrkhwānd, *Rawḍat al-Ṣafāʾ*, 10 vols. (Tehran, 1338–1339 HS/1959–1960).

27. Khwāndamīr, *Ḥabīb al-Siyar*, ed. Humāʾī (Tehran, 1333 HS/1954); Khwāndamīr, *Ḥabīb al-Siyar*, ed. Thackston, trans. Thackston, *Habibu's-Siyar, Tome Three. The Reign of the Mongol and the Turk* (Cambridge, MA, 1994).

28. Turkumān, *Taʾrīkh-i ʿĀlamārā-yi ʿAbbāsī*, 2 vols. (Tehran, 1971); Turkumān, *Taʾrīkh-i ʿĀlamārā-yi ʿAbbāsī* (Tehran, 1314/1897).

29. Dawlatshāh, *Tadhkirat al-Shuʿarāʾ*, ed. Browne (London, 1901).

30. Sām Mīrzā, *Tuḥfa-yi Sāmī*, ed. Humāyūn-Farrukh (Tehran, nd).

31. Shushtarī, *Majālis al-Mu'minīn* (Tehran, 1299/1882); Shushtarī, *Majālis al-Mu'minīn* (Tehran, 1375–1376/1955–1956).

32. Ādhar, *Ātishkada*, ed. Nāṣirī (Tehran, 1337–1338 HS/1958–1959).

33. Muḥammad Zardūz, "Alfāẓ-i Guharbār wa-Durr Nithār," in *Institute of Ismaili Studies Library*, unnumbered Persian ms (London); Shams al-Dīn Muḥammad?, "Alfāẓ-i Guharbār," in *Institute of Ismaili Studies Library*, Persian ms 15092 (London); Shams al-Dīn Muḥammad?, "Guharbār—15071"; Shams al-Dīn Muḥammad?, "Guharbār—15077."

34. Shams al-Dīn Muḥammad?, "[No Title]," in *Institute of Ismaili Studies Library*, Persian ms 814 (London, 1313/1895); 105.

35. Islāmshāh, "Haft Nukta," in *Institute of Ismaili Studies Library*, Persian ms 43 (London); Islāmshāh, "Haft Nukta," in *Kitāb-i Mustaṭāb-i Haft Bāb-i Dā'ī Abū Isḥāq*, ed. Beg (Gilgit, Pakistan, 1962).

36. [Imām 'Abd al-Salam?], "Panj Sukhan kih Ḥaḍrat-i Shāh Islām Farmūda and," in *Kitāb-i Mustaṭāb-i Haft Bāb-i Dā'ī Abū Isḥāq*, ed. Beg (Gilgit, Pakistan, 1962).

37. See Ivanow, *Ismaili Literature: A Bibliographical Survey*, 2nd amplified ed. (Tehran, 1963), 140–141.

38. 'Abd al-Salām, "Alā ay ṭālib-i waḥdat hamī lāfī kih jūyāyam," in *Institute of Ismaili Studies Library*, Persian ms 15033 (London); 'Abd al-Salām, "Alā ay ṭālib-i waḥdat kih mī lāfī kih jūyāyam," in *Kitāb al-Manāqib*, ed. Hiz Hā'īnes Prins Āghā Khān Shī'a Imāmī Ismā'īliya Esūsī'eshan barā'e Pākistān (Karachi, 1406/1986); 'Abd al-Salām, "Alā ay ṭālib-i waḥdat kih mī lāfī kih jūyāyam," in *Institute of Ismaili Studies Library*, Persian ms 14704 (London); 'Abd al-Salām, "Alā e ṭālib-i waḥdat hamī lāfī kih jūyāyam," in *Qasidas: Great Ismaili Tradition of Central Asia*, ed. The Shia Imami Ismaili Tariqah and Religious Education Board for Pakistan, vol. 1 ([Karachi], nd). Another work of this Imam, entitled simply *Bandī az Shāh 'Abd al-Salām [bin] Shāh Mustanṣir bi'llāh*, is found in a microfilm from the Vazīrī collection and the Tehran-Markazī library. See Poonawala, *Biobibliography of Ismā'īlī Literature* (Malibu, CA, 1977), 269. This work was not available to me.

39. Mustanṣir bi'llāh (=Gharīb Mīrzā?), *Pandiyāt-i Jawānmardī*, ed. Ivanow, trans. Ivanow, *Pandiyat-i Jawanmardi or "Advices of Manliness"* (Leiden, 1953).

40. Gharīb Mīrzā, "Min Kalām-i Shāh Gharīb Mīrzā," in *Institute of Ismaili Studies Library*, Persian ms 123 (London).

41. Quhistānī, *Dīwān-i Ḥakīm Nizārī Quhistānī*, ed. Muṣaffā (Tehran, 1371 HS/1992); Quhistānī, "Safarnāma," in *The Continuity of the Nizari Ismaili Da'wa*, ed. Jamal (PhD dissertation, New York University, 1996).

42. Quhistānī, *Haft Bāb*, ed. Ivanow, trans. Ivanow, *Haft Bab or "Seven Chapters"* (Mumbai, 1959).

43. 'Āmir b. 'Āmir al-Baṣrī, *Tā'iyya*, ed. Marquet, trans. Marquet, *Poésie ésoterique Ismailïenne: La Tā'iyya de 'Āmir b. 'Āmir al-Baṣrī* (Paris, 1985).

44. [pseudo-Shihāb al-Dīn Abū Firās], *al-Qaṣīda al-Shāfiya*, ed. Makarem, trans. Makarem, *Ash-Shāfiya (The Healer): An Ismā'īlī Poem Attributed to Shihāb ad-Dīn Abū Firās* (Beirut, 1966); [pseudo-Shihāb al-Dīn Abū Firās], *al-Qaṣīda al-Shāfiya*, ed. Tāmir (Beirut, 1967).

45. "Risāla-yi Ṣirāṭ al-Mustaqīm," in *Institute of Ismaili Studies Library*, Persian ms 15034 (London); "Risāla-yi Ṣirāṭ al-Mustaqīm," in *Seekers of Union: The Ismailis from the Mongol Debacle to the Eve of the Safavid Revolution*, ed. Virani, trans. Virani, *The Epistle of the Right Path* (PhD dissertation, Harvard University, 2001).

46. Qāsim Tushtarī (Turshīzī?), "[Risāla dar Maʿrifat-i Khāliq]," in *Institute of Ismaili Studies Library*, Persian ms 15048 (London); Qāsim Tushtarī (Turshīzī?), "Maʿrifat—814."

47. "Risāla-yi Munāẓara" in *Institute of Ismaili Studies Library*, Persian ms, accession number unknown, London.

48. Badakhshānī, *Sī wa-Shish Ṣaḥīfa*, ed. Ujaqi (Tehran, 1961); Badakhshānī, *Tuḥfat al-Nāẓirīn*, ed. Beg (Gilgit, Pakistan, 1960).

49. See Ivanow, *A Guide to Ismaili Literature* (London, 1933), 98; Poonawala, *Biobibliography*, 352. Ivanow inadvertently omits the work from his later publication *Ismaili Literature*. The texts and manuscripts used for this elaboration are as follows, "Sharḥ-i Marātib," in *Tuḥfat al-Nāẓirīn*, ed. Beg (Gilgit, Pakistan, 1960); "Sharḥ al-Marātib," in *Institute of Ismaili Studies Library*, Persian ms 15077 (London); "Marātib—15092"; "Marātib—15093."

50. There appear to have been two Syrian Ismaili authors of this name, but both lived in the period under study.

51. Khayrkhwāh Harātī, *Taṣnīfāt-i Khayrkhwāh-i Harātī*, ed. Ivanow (Tehran, 1961).

52. [Khayrkhwāh Harātī?], *Faṣl dar Bayān-i Shinākht-i Imām*, trans. Ivanow, 2nd rev. ed. (Mumbai, 1947); [Khayrkhwāh Harātī?], *Faṣl dar Bayān-i Shinākht-i Imām*, ed. Ivanow, 3rd rev. ed. (Tehran, 1960).

53. [pseudo-Nāṣir-i Khusraw: Khayrkhwāh Harātī?], *Kalām-i Pīr*, ed. Ivanow, trans. Ivanow (Mumbai, 1935).

54. The Institute of Ismaili Studies possesses a few manuscript copies of this work, including Kūchak, *Silk-i Gawhar Rīz*, ed. Qudertullah (Dushanbe, Tajikistan, nd), which the editor appears to have intended for publication. This latter manuscript has the accession number 16048.

55. Ivanow, "Tombs of Some Persian Ismaili Imams," *JBBRAS* NS 14 (1938).

56. al-Ḥusaynī, *Kitāb-i Khiṭābāt-i ʿĀliya*, ed. Ujāqī (Mumbai, 1963).

57. Muḥammad Taqī b. ʿAlī Riḍā b. Zayn al-ʿĀbidīn, *Āthār-i Muḥammadī* (Maḥallāt, Iran, 1893). The author was apparently not an Ismaili, but his family was attached to that of the Imams. In this regard, see Ivanow, *Ismaili Literature*, 152–153. I would like to express my gratitude to Mumtaz Ali Tajdin Sadik Ali, who kindly sent me a copy of this book from the Ismaili Tariqah and Religious Education Board Library of Karachi, Pakistan.

58. Fidāʾī Khurāsānī, *Hidāyat al-Muʾminīn al-Ṭālibīn*, ed. Semenov (Moscow, 1959). Regarding this work and the later additions, see Daftary, *Ismaili Literature* (London, 2004), 112; Ivanow, *Ismaili Literature*, 153–154.

59. Fidāʾī Khurāsānī, "Hidāyat al-Muʾminīn al-Ṭālibīn," in *Institute of Ismaili Studies Library*, Khojki ms KH29 (London, 1960 vs/[1903] Shrāvaṇ 22), 1–290. Cf. Moir, *A Catalogue of the Khojki MSS in the Library of the Ismaili Institute* (London, 1985), [306–307].

60. Fidāʾī Khurāsānī, "Hidāyat," 290.

61. See Muʿizzī, "Ismāʿīliyyān-i Īrān" (MA thesis, Dānishgāh-i Firdawsī, 1371–1372 HS/1992–1993), 50.

62. Chunārā, *Nūram Mobīn: yāne Allāhanī pavitra rasī [English Title: Noorum-Mobin or The Sacred Cord of God]*, ed. Sufī, 4th ed. (Mumbai, 1961); Chunārā, *Nurun Mobīn: athavā Allāhanī pavitra rasī*, 1st ed. (Mumbai, 1935).

63. Boghā, *Isamāilī Darpaṇ* (Mumbai, 1323/1906).

64. Nānajīāṇī, *Khojā Vṛttānt* (Ahmadabad, India, 1892).

65. Rematulā, *Khojā Kom no Itihās* (Mumbai, 1905).

66. Mulukshāh and ʿĪsanshāh, *Gulzār-i Shams* ([Multan], 1334/1916). This is a work by a non-Ismaili, but one who seems to have had a close relationship with the Ismaili community.

CHAPTER 2

Large sections of this chapter are drawn from the previously published Virani, "The Eagle Returns: Evidence of Continued Ismāʿīlī Activity at Alamūt and in the South Caspian Region following the Mongol conquests," *JAOS* 123 (2003), to which the reader may refer for further details. I am greateful to the *Journal of the American Oriental Society* for allowing me to reprint these sections.

1. Ibn al-Athīr, *Taʾrīkh al-Kāmil* [a.k.a. *al-Kamil fī al-Taʾrīkh*] (Cairo, 1303/1916), vol. 10, 110–113. Cf. for example, Juwaynī, *Taʾrīkh-i Jahāngushāy*, ed. Qazwīnī, 3 vols. (Leiden, 1912–1937), ed. vol. 3, 194, trans. vol. 2, 670; Mīrkhwānd, *Rawḍat al-Ṣafāʾ*, ed. Am. Jourdain, trans. Am. Jourdain, *"Histoire de la dynastie des Ismaéliens de Perse," Notices et Extraits des Manuscrits*, vol. 9 (1813); Mīrkhwānd, *Rawḍat al-Ṣafāʾ*, 10 vols. (Tehran, 1338–1339 HS/1959–1960); Qazwīnī, *Nuzhat al-Qulūb*, ed. Le Strange, trans. Le Strange, *The Geographical Part of the Nuzhat al-Qulūb* (Leiden, 1915–1919), ed. 61, trans. 66. Juwaynī, Mīrkhwānd, and many others give an alternative translation of Alamūt as "the eagle's nest" (*āshyāna-yi ʿuqāb*); see, for example, Juwaynī, *Jahāngushāy*, ed. vol. 3, 193, trans. vol. 2, 669–670. Browne, *A Literary History of Persia*, 4 vols. (Cambridge, 1902–1924), vol. 2, 203 considered "the eagle's teaching" to be etymologically more convincing. Wladimir Ivanow felt that these medieval attempts were "absurd" and that it was impossible to reconstruct the etymology of a word from an unknown language. See Ivanow, *Alamut and Lamasar* ([Tehran], 1960), 1. Rashīd al-Dīn's dating is different from the above, being based on the chronogram of Alamūt, rather than the older variation of the name. See Rashīd al-Dīn, *Jāmiʿ al-Tawārīkh*, ed. Karīmī (Tehran, 1338 HS/1959), ed. vol. 2, 697, trans. vol. 2, 486.

2. This was first suggested by Hyacinth Louis Rabino (d. 1950), the British vice consul in Rasht, whose writings contributed significantly to scholarship on the region. See, for example, Rabino, "Les Dynasties du Māzandarān," *JA* 228 (1936): 472–473; Rabino, "Les Dynasties locales du Gīlān et du Daylam," *JA* 237 (1949); Rabino, *Les Provinces Caspiennes de la Perse: Le Guīlān* (Paris, 1917), 281, 402–405, 409–410; Rabino, "Rulers of Gīlān," *JRAS* (1920): 293–295. Little use was made of Rabino's findings until Farhad Daftary revisited the issue briefly in his work, Daftary, *The Ismāʿīlīs: Their*

History and Doctrines (Cambridge, 1990), 448–451. Slightly later, Maryam Muʿizzī contributed new insights in Muʿizzī, "Ismāʿīliyyān-i Īrān" (MA thesis, Dānishgāh-i Firdawsī, 1371–1372 HS/1992–1993), 193–237.

3. See, for example, Jūzjānī, *Ṭabaqāt-i Nāṣirī*, ed. Ḥabībī, 2nd ed. (Kabul, 1342–1343 HS/1963–1964); Jūzjānī, *Ṭabaqāt-i Nāṣirī*, trans. Raverty, *The Ṭabaḳāt-i-Nāṣirī: A General History of the Muhammadan Dynasties of Asia* (London, 1881–1899).

4. Ibn al-Athīr, *al-Kāmil*, vol. 12, 358 translated in "Preface" to Rashīd al-Dīn, *Jāmiʿ*, trans. xi.

5. Morgan, *The Mongols* (Oxford, 1986), 17–18.

6. In fact, Hillenbrand, "The Power Struggle Between the Saljuqs and the Ismaʿilis of Alamūt, 487–518/1094–1124: The Saljuq Perspective," in *Mediaeval Ismaʿili History and Thought*, ed. Daftary (Cambridge, 1996), 214, suggests that Juwaynī intentionally inflated the number of failed Saljūq forays against the Ismāʿīlīs in order to bring into relief the Mongol success.

7. See Ayalon, "The Great Yāsa of Chingiz Khān: A Re-examination," *SI* 33 (1971): 133; Morgan, "Persian Historians and the Mongols," in *Medieval Historical Writing in the Christian and Islamic Worlds*, ed. Morgan (London, 1982), 114.

8. Browne, *Literary History*, vol. 2, 473.

9. This is the most generally credited account. See Boyle, "The Death of the Last ʿAbbāsid Caliph: A Contemporary Muslim Account," *Journal of Semitic Studies* 6 (1961): 160. Another equally uncomplimentary, though perhaps less creditable version, is that of Marco Polo and others, which has the caliph shut up in a tower surrounded by his treasures and starved to death. See Marco Polo, *The Travels of Marco Polo*, trans. Ricci (New York, 1931), 27.

10. He appends this document to one of the chapters. See Juwaynī, *Jahāngushāy*, vol. 3, 114, trans. vol. 2, 622. We must wonder, though, if Juwayni's immense distaste for the Ismailis was shared to the same degree by his patron. In fact, Hulagu's attitude toward them is ambiguous at times. There are instances in which he seems to have treated their Imam with great deference, viewing him with "attention and kindness," and even bestowing lavish gifts on him. Juwaynī, *Jahāngushāy*, vol. 3, 274, trans. vol. 2, 722. This surprisingly warm reception was also noted by Lewis, *The Assassins: A Radical Sect in Islam* (London, 1967), 93. However, any favor shown was soon withdrawn.

11. Juwaynī, *Jahāngushāy*, vol. 3, 276, trans. vol. 2, 723.

12. Ibid, vol. 3, 277, trans. vol. 2, 724–725. Cf. Rashīd al-Dīn, *Jāmiʿ*, ed. vol. 2, 697, trans. vol. 2, 486, whose testimony suggests that this massacre was limited to "his kith and kin, including men and women down to babes in cradles" who accompanied him on the journey between Abhar and Qazwīn.

13. Ibn Isfandiyār and anonymous continuator, cited by Hodgson, *The Order of Assassins* (New York, 1980), 270.

14. Juwaynī, *Jahāngushāy*, ed. 225, 228, 235, trans. 688, 690, 694. Noticing the odd use of the verbal tense, Boyle decided to change it to the past in his translation of Juwaynī's work.

15. Rashīd al-Dīn, *Jāmiʿ*, ed. vol. 2, 695, 766, trans. vol. 2, 485, vol. 3, 535–536. See also Jūzjānī, *Ṭabaqāt*, vol. 2, 186, trans. vol. 2, 1206–1211. Here he states that the garrison of Girdkūh, reduced to one or two hundred men, was still holding out against the Mongols

in 658/1260, at the time he was writing. Also cited in Daftary, *Ismāʿīlīs*, 429, 698 n242. Daftary provides some of his own observations concerning the situation of Girdkūh.

16. Browne, *Literary History*, vol. 3, 25.

17. Faṣīḥ Khwāfī, *Mujmal-i Faṣīḥī*, ed. Farrukh, 2 vols. (Mashhad, 1339–1340 HS/ 1960–1961), vol. 2, 344; Lockhart, "Alamūt," in *EI2*, vol. 1 (Leiden, 1960–2004; reprint, CD-ROM v. 1.0), vol. 1, 352; Qazwīnī, *Taʾrīkh-i Guzīda*, ed. Browne, trans. Browne, *The Taʾrīkh-i Guzīda: or, "Select History"* (Leiden, 1910–1913), 592. Lockhart mistakenly gives the date as 673. The name of the son is given as Bū Dawlat or Naw Dawlat, the difference in the names being easily explained as Naw and Bū (the apocopated form of Abū) are written in the same way in the Arabic script with the exception of a single dot, بو vs. نو. The two Persian words, in order of appearance, are as follows: نو بو.

18. Rabino, "Rulers of Gīlān," 293–294, "Ismaʿīlī" emended to "Ismāʿīlī."

19. Juwaynī, *Jahāngushāy*, ed. vol. 3, 139, trans. vol. 2, 639. The word *ibāḥa*, left untranslated by Boyle, is here rendered as libertinism.

20. "Afghans' Attack to Alamut Fortress Confirmed" (August 28, 2005), (Cultural Heritage News Agency, http://www.chn.ir/en/news/?id=5512&section=2, accessed February 5, 2006). Juwaynī himself was suitably impressed by the fortifications of the castle and describes the immense difficulty of destroying it:

> The ascents and approaches had been so strengthened by plastered walls and lead-covered ramparts (*bunyān*) that when it was being demolished it was as though the iron struck its head on a stone, and it had nothing in its hand and yet still resisted. . . . The King appointed an emir with a large force of soldiers and levies to demolish the castle. Picks were of no use: they set fire to the buildings and then broke them up, and this occupied them for a long time.

Juwaynī, *Jahāngushāy*, ed. vol. 3, 272–273, trans. vol. 2, 720–721.

21. Juwaynī, *Jahāngushāy*, vol. 3, 267, trans. vol. 2, 717, emphasis added.

22. Ibid, vol. 3, 111, trans. vol. 2, 620.

23. Rashīd al-Dīn, *Jāmiʿ*, ed. vol. 2, 694, trans. vol. 2, 484. This is also noted in Hodgson, *The Order of Assassins*, 267.

24. Juwaynī, *Jahāngushāy*, vol. 3, 264, trans. vol. 2, 715. It is equally inexplicable how he was somehow able to positively identify as false a child whom even the Imam's most intimate associates thought to be his son.

25. This seems in keeping with the fact that Rukn al-Dīn Khwurshāh was also quite young at this time, his youth being mentioned in the *Fatḥnāma* of Alamūt. See ibid, vol. 3, 106, 116, 124, trans. vol. 2, 617, 624, 628.

26. Ibid, vol. 3, 133, trans. vol. 2, 634.

27. Ibid, vol. 3, 267, trans. vol. 2, 717; Rashīd al-Dīn, *Jāmiʿ*, ed. vol. 2, 685, trans. vol. 2, 485.

28. Rashīd al-Dīn, *Jāmiʿ* ed. vol. 2, 685, trans. vol. 2, 485.

29. Juwaynī, *Jahāngushāy*, vol. 3, 276, trans. vol. 2, 723. At another place, he also refers to the Imam's "brothers, children, domestics and dependents," Juwaynī, *Jahāngushāy*, vol. 3, 134, trans. vol. 2, 635.

30. Qazwīnī, *Guzīda*, vol. 1, 583, vol. 2, 143.

31. Hamd Allāh Mustawfī, *Ẓafarnāma*, British Library ms Or. 2833, fol. 712vo; Aḥmad-i Tabrīzī, *Shāhanshāhnāma*, ms. British Library Or. 2780, fol. 116ro, both cited in Melville, "The Īlkhān Öljeitü's Conquest of Gīlān (1307): Rumour and Reality," in *The Mongol Empire and Its Legacy*, ed. Amitai-Preiss and Morgan (Leiden, 1999), 84. See also Minorsky and Bosworth, "Māzandarān," in *EI2*, vol. 6 (Leiden, 1960–2004; reprint, CD-ROM v. 1.0).

32. Melville, "Conquest of Gīlān," 117.

33. Rashīd al-Dīn, *Jāmiʿ*, ed. vol. 2, 984, trans. vol. 3, 676.

34. Melville, "Conquest of Gīlān," 105. See also Spuler, "Gīlān," in *EI2*, vol. 2 (Leiden, 1960–2004; reprint, CD-ROM v. 1.0).

35. Melville, "Conquest of Gīlān," 105.

36. Boyle, "Dynastic and Political History of the Il-Khans," in *The Cambridge History of Iran*, ed. Boyle, vol. 5 (Cambridge, 1968), 401.

37. Māzandarān, too, was largely governed by minor fiefdoms. See Minorsky and Bosworth, "Māzandarān."

38. Qazwīnī, *Nuzhat al-Qulūb*, 60–61, trans. 65–67.

39. Gīlānī, *Taʾrīkh-i Māzandarān*, ed. Sutūda (Tehran, 1352 HS/1973), 66–68; Marʿashī, *Taʾrīkh-i Gīlān wa-Daylamistān*, ed. Rabino (Rasht, 1330/1912), 64–67. See also Rabino, "Les Dynasties locales," 316–317; Rabino, *Les Provinces Caspiennes*, 281, 403–404; Rabino, "Rulers of Gīlān," 295.

40. Calmard, "Marʿashīs," in *EI2*, vol. 6 (Leiden, 1960–2004; reprint, CD-ROM v. 1.0); Minorsky and Bosworth, "Māzandarān."

41. Bosworth and Minorsky, "Lāhīdjān," in *EI2*, vol. 5 (Leiden, 1960–2004; reprint, CD-ROM v. 1.0); Calmard, "Marʿashīs."

42. See Rabino, "Les Dynasties locales," 314.

43. Ibid, Rabino, "Rulers of Gīlān"; Rabino, "Rulers of Lahijan and Fuman, in Gilan, Persia," *JRAS* (1918); Spuler, "Gīlān." The names "Malāṭī," "Kārkiyāʾī," and "Amīrkiyāʾī" all apparently refer to the same dynasty.

44. Marʿashī, *Taʾrīkh-i Gīlān wa-Daylamistān*, ed. Sutūda (Tehran, 1347 HS/1968), 67; Rabino, "Rulers of Gīlān," 295.

45. Marʿashī, *Gīlān wa-Daylamistān*, 67.

46. Qazwīnī, *Nuzhat al-Qulūb*, 58–59, trans. 64.

47. Marʿashī, *Gīlān wa-Daylamistān*, 69–70.

48. Marʿashī, *Taʾrīkh-i Ṭabaristān wa-Rūyān wa-Māzandarān*, ed. Tasbīḥī (Tehran, 1361 HS/[1983]), 147.

49. Mīrkhwānd, *Rawḍat al-Ṣafāʾ*, vol. 6, 207; Shāmī, *Ẓafarnāma*, ed. Tauer, trans. Tauer, *Histoire des Conquêtes de Tamerlan, Intitulée Ẓafarnāma* (Prague, 1937–1956), vol. 1, 168; Yazdī, *Ẓafarnāma*, ed. ʿAbbāsī (Tehran, 1336 HS/1957), vol. 1, 412. This attack occurred in 794/1392, when Nizām al-Dīn Shāmī was actually present; see Shāmī, *Ẓafarnāma*, vol. 1, 128.

50. Khwāndamīr, *Ḥabīb al-Siyar*, ed. Thackston, trans. Thackston, *Habibu's-Siyar, Tome Three. The Reign of the Mongol and the Turk* (Cambridge, MA, 1994); Mīrkhwānd, *Rawḍat al-Ṣafāʾ*, vol. 6, 211–212; Shāmī, *Ẓafarnāma*, vol. 1, 136; Yazdī, *Ẓafarnāma*, vol. 1, 443–444. With regard to the *Ḥabīb al-Siyar*, reference should be made to the section quoted

in Dihgān, *Kārnāma yā dū bakhsh-i dīgar az ta'rīkh-i Arāk* ([Tehran], 1345 HS/1966), 47–49, which includes passages that do not appear in Thackston's critical edition and translation. The attack on the Ismāʿīlīs in Anjudān occurred just a year after the attack in Māzandarān.

51. Marʿashī, *Gīlān wa-Daylamistān*, 54.

52. Apparently a reference to the downturn of Ismaili political fortunes.

53. Marʿashī, *Gīlān wa-Daylamistān*, 54.

54. Ibid, 56, 58.

55. Ibid, 58.

56. Ibid, 59.

57. On this dynasty, see Smith, "Djalāyir, Djalāyirid," in *EI2*, vol. 2 (Leiden, 1960–2004; reprint, CD-ROM v. 1.0).

58. Marʿashī, *Gīlān wa-Daylamistān*, 60–61.

59. Ibid, 63–64. With regard to the actions of a certain Sayyid Fakhr al-Dīn against Alamūt, see Calmard, "Marʿashīs"; Marʿashī, *Ṭabaristān wa-Rūyān wa-Māzandarān*, 290ff.

60. Marʿashī, *Gīlān wa-Daylamistān*, 65. Muʿizzī, "Ismāʿīliyyān-i Īrān," 229 n28, while also forwarding this interpretation, correctly comments that the meaning of the phrase *wa-awlād-i ān jamāʿat aknūn nīz īnjā and* [this reads *ānjā and* in Sutūda's edition] is equivocal.

61. Marʿashī, *Gīlān wa-Daylamistān*, 89, 121.

62. Ibid, 123. Cf. Daftary, *Ismāʿīlīs*, 450. On the dynasty to which this ruler belonged, see Bosworth, "Kāwūs, Banū," in *EI2*, vol. 4 (Leiden, 1960–2004; reprint, CD-ROM v. 1.0); Minorsky, "Rūyān," in *EI2*, vol. 8 (Leiden, 1960–2004; reprint, CD-ROM v. 1.0); Nikitine, "Bādūsbānids," in *EI2*, vol. 1 (Leiden, 1960–2004; reprint, CD-ROM v. 1.0). The reappearance of Khudāwand Muḥammad, who must have been quite old by this time, and his participation in yet another battle, seems unusual. While it is not impossible, we must also consider the prospect that Marʿashī has reported the incident incorrectly, or that this was a successor to the first Khudāwand Muḥammad. Maryam Muʿizzī expresses the same reservations in Muʿizzī, "Ismāʿīliyyān-i Īrān," 199 and considers the possibility of there having been more than one Khudāwand Muḥammad.

63. Marʿashī, *Gīlān wa-Daylamistān*, 129. See also Bosworth and Minorsky, "Lāhīdjān"; Minorsky, "Daylam," in *EI2*, vol. 2 (Leiden, 1960–2004; reprint, CD-ROM v. 1.0).

64. Rabino, *Mazandaran and Astarabad* (London, 1928), 60; Sutūda, *Az Āstarā tā Astarābād*, 10 vols. (Tehran, 1366 HS/1987), vol. 2, 343, 346–348.

65. Gīlānī, *Ta'rīkh-i Māzandarān*, 88–89, 99–100. Maryam Muʿzzī, while admitting the possibility that these rulers were Ismāʿīlī, expresses some reservations as they are referred to simply as *malāḥida* in our sources. See Muʿizzī, "Ismāʿīliyyān-i Īrān," 212–214. While this derogatory epithet does indeed have broader applications, it is most commonly used of the Ismāʿīlīs, particularly in the South Caspian region, though certainly elsewhere as well. See, for example, Madelung, "Mulḥid," in *EI2*, vol. 7 (Leiden, 1960–2004; reprint, CD-ROM v. 1.0). Gīlānī's statement in reference to Sulṭān Muḥammad b. Jahāngīr, that "he renewed the influence of the deviation (*ilḥād*) of [the Ismāʿīlī Imām Ḥasan] ʿAlā Dhikrihi al-Salām in the land of Rustamdār," is very explicit about the religious leanings of this ruler.

66. Khākī Khurāsānī, *Dīwān*, ed. Ivanow, *An Abbreviated Version of the Diwan of Khaki Khorasani* (Mumbai, 1933), 69.

67. Hammer-Purgstall, *The History of the Assassins, Derived from Oriental Sources*, trans. Wood (London, 1835), 210–211. Cf. also Ivanow, "Ismailitica 1 and 2," *Memoirs of the Asiatic Society of Bengal* 17 (1922): 53, which, however, does not seem to be based on any personal knowledge of the area.

68. Cf. Madelung, "Ismāʿīliyya," in *EI2*, vol. 4 (Leiden, 1960–2004; reprint, CD ROM v. 1.0).

69. Marʿashī, *Gīlān wa-Daylamistān*, 86–87, 216. Recent archaeological data suggests other uses for the fortress; see "Alamut Fortress, No Prison" (August 29, 2005), (Cultural Heritage News Agency, http://www.chn.ir/en/news/?Section=2&id=5522, accessed February 5, 2006).

70. Ivanow, "A Forgotten Branch of the Ismailis," *JRAS* (1938).

71. Tāmir, "Furūʿ al-shajarat al-Ismāʿīliyya," *al-Mashriq* 51 (1957).

72. Tāmir, *al-Imāma fī al-Islām* (Beirut, [1964]), 157–158, 169–178, 192ff.

73. See, for example, Cortese, "Eschatology and Power in Mediaeval Persian Ismailism" (PhD dissertation, University of London, 1993), 204; Daftary, *Ismāʿīlīs*, 449.

74. This work is not mentioned in Ivanow, *A Guide to Ismaili Literature* (London, 1933); Ivanow, *Ismaili Literature: A Bibliographical Survey*, 2nd amplified ed. (Tehran, 1963); Poonawala, *Biobibliography of Ismāʿīlī Literature* (Malibu, CA, 1977).

75. See, for example, al-Ḥusaynī, *Kitāb-i Khiṭābāt-i ʿĀliya*, ed. Ujāqī (Mumbai, 1963), 45.

76. Tāmir, *al-Imāma*, 199.

77. Ibid, 158.

78. As will be seen in chapter 3, there exists a manuscript of the *Pearl Scattering Words* (*Alfāẓ-i Gawharbār*) that apparently pertains to the Imam Shams al-Dīn Muḥammad who is identified simply as Khudāwand Muḥammad in some manuscripts. In light of this, while it may seem tempting to identify the Khudāwand Muḥammad of the Daylam battles with the Imam Shams al-Dīn Muhammad, chronologically this is impossible, as the clash with Kiyā Malik took place in 776/1374, at which time this Imām would have been well over one hundred years old. However, it is possible, though unlikely, that the *Pearl Scattering Words* are the utterances of Khudāwand Muḥammad of the Daylam battles and their attribution to Shams al-Dīn Muḥammad is a later interpolation.

79. Adae, *Directorium ad passagium faciendum, in RHC: Documents Arméniens*, vol. 2 (Paris, 1869–1906), 496–497.

80. My observations on this text are based on the research conducted in 1997 by a candidate for a master's degree in history at the Université de Montréal. Repeated attempts to obtain the thesis were unsuccessful, though large extracts were available at the following URL: *Le projet de croisade de Philippe VI de Valois* (1997), (http://www.geocities.com/Area51/Corridor/7872/croisade.htm, accessed February 2, 2002). Unfortunately, the author of the thesis did not provide his name on his website. See also Daftary, *Ismāʿīlīs*, 14.

81. Qāʾinī, "Naṣāʾiḥ-i Shāhrukhī," in *Österreichische Nationalbibliothek*, Monastic Microfilm Project Number 22 249, University Microfilms, Codex Vindobonensis Palatinus. A.f. 112 (Flügel 1858) (Vienna, 1970), 301a.

82. Ibid, 303a.

83. In this regard, see Daftary, "Persian Historiography of the Early Nizārī Ismāʿīlīs," *Iran* 30 (1992).

84. Nanji, *The Nizārī Ismāʿīlī Tradition in the Indo-Pakistan Subcontinent* (Delmar, NY, 1978) remains a useful introduction to the history of Ismāʿīlism in South Asia. The later history should be supplemented by Virani, "The Voice of Truth: Life and Works of Sayyid Nūr Muḥammad Shāh, a 15th/16th Century Ismāʿīlī Mystic" (MA thesis, McGill University, 1995). The earlier period has been studied in Kassam, *Songs of Wisdom and Circles of Dance: Hymns of the Satpanth Ismaili Muslim Saint, Pir Shams* (Albany, NY, 1995).

85. See Virani, "Symphony of Gnosis: A Self-Definition of the Ismaili Ginān Literature," in *Reason and Inspiration in Islam: Theology, Philosophy and Mysticism in Muslim Thought*, ed. Lawson (London, 2005).

86. In this connection, see Nanji, *Nizārī Ismāʿīlī Tradition*, 10–11.

87. See Moir, *A Catalogue of the Khojki MSS in the Library of the Ismaili Institute* (London, 1985), 1.

88. This unique artifact reflects the architectural features of the equally ancient tombs of Bahāʾ al-Dīn Zakariyyā and Shadnā Shahīd. See Mumtaz, *Architecture in Pakistan* (Singapore, 1985), 42–43.

89. See Nanji, *Nizārī Ismāʿīlī Tradition*, 70. A late lithograph source gives the death of Naṣīr al-Dīn as 682/1283, and the death of Shihāb al-Dīn as 750/1349. See Mulukshāh and ʿĪsanshāh, *Gulzār-i Shams* ([Multan], 1334/1916), 366, 377.

90. Imāmshāh, *Janatpurī*, 2nd ed. (Mumbai, 1976 vs/1920), v. 83; Naṣīr al-Dīn, "Huṃ balahārī tame shāhā rājā," in *100 Ginān nī Chopaḍī*, 5th ed., vol. 2 (Mumbai, 1993 vs/1936), #66; Nūr Muḥammadshāh, *Sat Varaṇī Moṭī* ([Mumbai?], nd), cc. 190–197. See also Nanji, *Nizārī Ismāʿīlī Tradition*, 70.

91. Jūzjānī, *Ṭabaqāt*, 518, trans. 1205–1206. Bernard Lewis feels this number to be rather high. See Lewis, *Assassins*, 94.

92. The system of dispatching religious dues through the *rāhīs* continued into the early 1800s. See Howard, *The Shia School of Islam and Its Branches, Especially That of the Imamee-Ismailies: A Speech Delivered by E. I. Howard, Esquire, Barrister-at-Law, in the Bombay High Court, in June, 1866* (Mumbai, 1866), 88.

93. Willey, *Eagle's Nest: Ismaili Castles in Iran and Syria* (London, 2005), 165; see also 35, 163, 272. A picture of this particular fort can be seen in Daftary, *The Ismāʿīlīs*, 347.

94. Mustanṣir bi'llāh (=Gharīb Mīrzā?), *Pandiyāt-i Jawānmardī*, ed. Ivanow, trans. Ivanow, *Pandiyat-i Jawanmardi or "Advices of Manliness"* (Leiden, 1953), ed. 2, 11, 17, 21, 34, 60, 63–64, 70, 78, 82, 88–89, trans. 2, 8, 11, 13, 21, 37, 39, 43–44, 48–49, 51, 54–55.

95. Such references are found scattered in Khayrkhwāh Harātī, "Qiṭʿāt," in *Taṣnīfāt-i Khayrkhwāh Harātī*, ed. Ivanow, *Taṣnīfāt-i Khayrkhwāh Harātī* (Tehran, 1961), see, for example, 105–107; Khayrkhwāh Harātī, "Risāla," in *Taṣnīfāt-i Khayrkhwāh Harātī*, ed. Ivanow, *Taṣnīfāt-i Khayrkhwāh Harātī* (Tehran, 1961), see, for example, 23, 39, 55, 60–61.

96. Ṣāhib al-Dīn, "Āo gatīure bhandhe," in *100 Ginānanī Chopaḍī*, 5th ed., vol. 3 (Mumbai, 1991 vs/1935), #74, vv. 1–10. The translation of *turā* in verse 5 as "raft" is tentative. This word is not found in any of the various dictionaries consulted. The translation is

based on the semblance of this word to the word *tulahāri* in Shams, "Bhulo: bhulotebhulo: bhamaraḍore: lol," in *28 Garabī: pīr: samas nī*, ed. Devarāj, 2nd ed. (Mumbai, 1913), v. 8, in which it seems to mean a boatman or an oarsman, and on verse 7 of Ṣadr al-Dīn, "Bhāīr bhāṅā ma ṭaḍo," in *100 Ginānanī Chopaḍī*, 5th ed., vol. 3 (Mumbai, 1991 vs/1935), #81. All these words appear to be based on the Sanskrit word *tarī*, meaning any seafaring vessel.

97. These are Ṣadr al-Dīn, "Aj sahi māhādin bujo bhev," in *100 Ginānanī Chopaḍī*, 5th ed., vol. 1 (Mumbai, 1990 vs/1934); Ṣadr al-Dīn, "Āshājī sacho tuṃ alakh nirījan agam agochar," in *102 Ginānajī: Chopaḍī*, 3rd ed., vol. 4 (Mumbai, 1968 vs/[1912]), #4; Ṣadr al-Dīn, "Des delamame shāhā harī avatareo," in *100 Ginānanī Chopaḍī*, 4th ed., vol. 6 (Mumbai, 1989 vs/1933), #29; Ṣadr al-Dīn, "Dhan dhan ājano dāḍalore ame harīvar pāyājī," in *100 Ginānanī Chopaḍī*, 4th ed., vol. 5 (Mumbai, 1990 vs/1934), #42; Ṣadr al-Dīn, "Jugā jug shāhā avatāraj dhareā [a.k.a. Sen Akhāḍo]," in *100 Ginānanī Chopaḍī*, 5th ed., vol. 2 (Mumbai, 1993 vs/1936), #26; Ṣadr al-Dīn, "Payalore nām sāhebajo vado līje," in *102 Ginānajī: Chopaḍī*, 3rd ed., vol. 4 (Mumbai, 1968 vs/[1912]), #82; Ṣadr al-Dīn, "Sansār sāgar madhe vān āpaṇā satagure noriyāṃre," in *100 Ginānanī Chopaḍī*, 5th ed., vol. 1 (Mumbai, 1990 vs/1934), #68; Ṣadr al-Dīn, "Shāhāke hek man āṃhī sirevo," in *102 Ginānajī: Chopaḍī*, 3rd ed., vol. 4 (Mumbai, 1968 vs/[1912]), #48; Ṣadr al-Dīn, "Thar thar moman bhāī koī koī rahesejī," in *100 Ginānanī Chopaḍī*, 4th ed., vol. 5 (Mumbai, 1990 vs/1934), #50; Ṣadr al-Dīn, "Yārā anat kiroḍie vadhāīuṃ," in *102 Ginānajī: Chopaḍī*, 3rd ed., vol. 4 (Mumbai, 1968 vs/[1912]), #29.

98. Hundreds of Gināns attributed to Pīr Ṣadr al-Dīn are found both in published form as well as in Ismāʿīlī manuscripts. See Asani, *The Harvard Collection of Ismaili Literature in Indic Languages: A Descriptive Catalog and Finding Aid* (Boston, 1992); Moir, *Khojki MSS of the Ismaili Institute*; Nooraly, *Catalogue of Khojki Manuscripts in the Collection of the Ismailia Association for Pakistan (draft copy)* (Karachi, 1971).

99. The *shajara* discovered by Wladimir Ivanow gives his dates as 1290–1380, Ivanow, "The Sect of Imam Shah in Gujrat," *JBBRAS* 12 (1936): 34. Both Mulukshāh and ʿĪsanshāh, *Gulzār*, 378 and Daragāhavālā, *Tavārīkhe Pīr*, 2 vols. (Navasārī, India, 1914–1935), vol. 2, 90 give the dates 650–770/1252–1368. It is interesting that Ivanow does not mention any dates from the *Manāzil al-Aqṭāb* in connection with this pīr. See Ivanow, "Sect of Imam Shah." On Pīr Ṣadr al-Dīn, see Nanji, *Nizārī Ismāʿīlī Tradition*, 72–77.

100. This compelling consistency is important to note in light of the theory advanced in Asani, "The Ismaʿili Ginān: Reflections on Authority and Authorship," in *Mediaeval Ismaʿili History and Thought*, ed. Daftary (Cambridge, 1996), 265–280. See also Nanji, "The Ginān Tradition among the Nizārī Ismāʿīlīs: Its Value as a Source of Their History," in *Actes du XXIXe Congrès international des Orientalistes* vol. 3 (Paris, 1975), 143–146. All Gināns in the six-volume set published by Mukhī Lālajībhāī Devrāj were consulted. The class of Gināns known as *granths*, however, was not used to investigate this question and should be examined as it may contain valuable information. There is a reference to Daylam in Imāmshāh, "Velā pohotī ne ved vīchāro," in *100 Ginānanī Chopaḍī*, 4th ed., vol. 1 (Mumbai, 1990 vs/1934), #14, v. 7, by the later Ismāʿīlī savant, Sayyid Imāmshāh, but this is merely a statement that in the fourth aeon, the Imam appeared in Daylam, not that he was residing there in the author's time. Another Ginān, Muḥammadshāh, "Sācho tuṃ moro sāṃhīā," in *102 Ginānajī: Chopaḍī*, 3rd ed., vol. 4 (Mumbai, 1968 vs/[1912]),

#67, v. 8, asserts that the Imām has established his throne in the land of Daylam. However we do not know the dates of this Sayyid Muḥammadshāh. The fact that this composition is in Sindhi largely precludes the possibility of his being any of the figures named Muḥammadshāh who lived after Imāmshāh and are known to have composed Gināns, as their compositions are very influenced by Gujarati and Hindustani.

101. Ṣadr al-Dīn, "Shāhāke hek man āṃhī sirevo," vol. 4, #48, vv. 15–16.

102. The expression *bār gur* refers to Pīr Ṣadr al-Dīn as the leader of twelve crore (a sum of 120,000,000) souls who are to be saved in the last age of the world. On this concept, see Shackle and Moir, *Ismaili Hymns from South Asia: An Introduction to the Ginans* (London, 1992), 89, 169.

103. The word *shāh*, translated here as Imam, is one of the most commonly occurring terms in the Gināns used to refer to the Imam. Gulshan Khakee notes that *shāh* is the most frequently used noun in the tenth chapter of Sayyid Imāmshāh's *Das Avatār*, occurring an astounding 147 times. See Khakee, "The Dasa Avatara of the Satpanthi Ismailis and the Imam Shahis of Indo-Pakistan" (PhD dissertation, Harvard University, 1972), 14. Similarly, the word *shāh* is one of the most common appellations for the Imam in the *dīwān* of Khākī Khurāsānī (and, we may extrapolate, for Persian speaking Ismāʿīlīs in the mid-1600s). See Ivanow's introduction to Khākī Khurāsānī, *Dīwān*, 10.

104. Ṣadr al-Dīn, "Dhan dhan ājano dāḍalore ame harīvar pāyājī," vol. 5, #42, vv. 1–5.

105. Ṣadr al-Dīn, "Sīrīe salāmashāhā amane malīyā," in *100 Ginānanī Chopaḍī*, 4th ed., vol. 5 (Mumbai, 1990 vs/1934), #10, v. 1. The second line may also be translated as "Who bestowed the kingdom of religion upon us."

106. Ṣadr al-Dīn, "Ālamot gaḍh pāṭaṇ delam des bhāire," in *100 Ginānanī Chopaḍī*, 5th ed., vol. 2 (Mumbai, 1993 vs/1936), #39.

107. The twelve splendors (*bār kaḷā*) refer to the sun, perhaps because it passes through twelve signs of the Zodiac on its celestial rounds. It is contrasted with the moon of sixteen splendors (*soḷ kaḷā*), which has sixteen digits and is representative of the pīr. The term, admittedly a difficult and infrequently used Ginānic concept, is mistranslated in Shackle and Moir, *Ismaili Hymns*, 89, 169, where the notion of *bār kaḷā* is confused with that of *bār karoḍ*, mentioned above, which refers to the twelve crore (120,000,000) disciples who are initiated into the mysteries of the *Satpanth* in the last age of the world.

108. Ṣadr al-Dīn, "Jugame phīre shāhājī munerī," in *102 Ginānajī: Chopaḍī*, 3rd ed., vol. 4 (Mumbai, 1968 vs/[1912]), #3, vv. 1–4.

109. Marʿashī, *Gīlān wa-Daylamistān*, 129.

CHAPTER 3

1. al-Nuʿmān, *Kitāb Iftitāḥ al-daʿwa*, ed. Dachraoui, *Les commencements du califat Fatimid au Maghreb: Kitāb Iftitāḥ al-daʿwa du Cadi Nuʿman* (Tunis, 1975), 30, 47–48; al-Nuʿmān, *Risālat Iftitāḥ al-Daʿwa*, ed. al-Qāḍī (Beirut, 1971), 59, 71–73. Cf. al-Nuʿmān,

Sharḥ al-Akhbār fī faḍā'il al-a'immat al-aṭhār, ed. al-Jalālī, 3 vols. (Qumm, 1409–1412/1988–1992), vol. 3, 416.

2. Related terms include *istitār, musātara, satr, isrār*, and *khabā'*. See Layish, "*Taqiyya* among the Druzes," *Asian and African Studies* 19 (1985): 246.

3. For taqiyya, the following sources are particularly useful: Amir-Moezzi, *The Divine Guide in Early Shi'ism: The Sources of Esotericism in Islam*, trans. Streight (Albany, NY, 1994), index, s.v. "taqiyya"; Clarke, "The Rise and Decline of *Taqiyya* in Twelver Shi'ism," in *Reason and Inspiration in Islam: Theology, Philosophy and Mysticism in Muslim Thought*, ed. Lawson (London, 2005); Corbin, *En Islam Iranien: Aspects Spirituels et Philosophiques*, 4 vols. (Paris, 1971), index, s.vv. "ketmān," "taqīyeh" Jafri, *The Origins and Early Development of Shi'a Islam* (London, 1979), index, s.v. "taqīya, principal of"; Kohlberg, "Some Imāmī-Shī'a Views on Taqiyya," *JAOS* 95 (1975): 395–402; Kohlberg, "Taqiyya in Shī'ī Theology and Religion," in *Secrecy and Concealment: Studies in the History of Mediterranean and Near Eastern Religions*, ed. Kippenberg and Stroumsa (Leiden, 1995), 345–380; Morris, "Taqīyah," in *Encyclopedia of Religion*, ed. Eliade, vol. 14 (New York, 1987), 336–337; Strothmann and Djebli, "Taḳiyya," in *EI2*, vol. 10 (Leiden, 1960–2004; reprint, CD-ROM v. 1.0), 135–136. See also Reckendorf, "'Ammār b. Yāsir," in *EI2*, vol. 1 (Leiden, 1960–2004; reprint, CD-ROM v. 1.0), 448.

4. Ibn Bābawayhi, for example, cites this verse in justification of the practice of taqiyya. See Ibn Bābawayh, *A Shī'ite Creed*, trans. Fyzee (Calcutta, 1942), 111. Similar explanations are given in exegetical works. See, for example, al-Ṭabarsī, *Majma' al-bayān fī tafsīr al-Qur'ān*, vol. 3 (Beirut, 1954–1957), 55–56.

5. See, for example, al-Majlisī, *Biḥār al-Anwār*, vol. 16 ([Iran], 1305–1315 HS/1926–1936), 224; Goldziher, "Das Prinzip der taḳijja im Islam," *Zeitschrift der Deutschen Morgenländischen Gesellschaft* 60 (1906): 214.

6. Hinds, "Miḥna," in *EI2*, vol. 7 (Leiden, 1960–2004; reprint, CD-ROM v. 1.0); Nawas, *al-Ma'mūn: Miḥna and Caliphate* (Nijmegen, 1992), 61. Cf. Zaman, *Religion and Politics Under the Early 'Abbāsids: The Emergence of the Proto-Sunnī Elite*, ed. Haarmann and Kadi (Leiden, 1997), 106–114. Other instances of non-Shī'ī taqiyya are discussed in Goldziher, "Das Prinzip der taḳijja"; Harvey, "The Moriscos and the Ḥajj," *BRISMES* 14, no. 1 (1987): 12–13; Wilkinson, "The Ibāḍī Imāma," *BSO(A)S* 39, no. 3 (1976): 537.

7. The political implications of taqiyya in early Shī'ism are discussed in McEoin, "Aspects of Militancy and Quietism in Imami Shi'ism," *BRISMES* 11, no. 1 (1984): 19–20, while judicial implications of this practice are examined in Calder, "Judicial Authority in Imāmī Shī'ī Jurisprudence," *BRISMES* 6, no. 2 (1979): 106–107. Shī'ī protective dissimulation in Afghanistan is discussed in Dupree, "Further Notes on Taqiyya: Afghanistan," *JAOS* 99, no. 4 (October–December 1979).

8. Numerous usages of this term are cited in Kohlberg, "Some Imāmī-Shī'a Views," 397 n13. See also the same author's later work, Kohlberg, "Taqiyya in Shī'ī Theology."

9. In this latter meaning, see especially Clarke, "Rise and Decline of *Taqiyya*"; and Steigerwald, "La dissimulation (*taqiyya*) de la foi dans le Shi'isme Ismaelien," *Studies in Religion/Sciences Religieuses* 27 (1988).

10. al-Qummī, *Baṣā'ir al-Darajāt fī Faḍā'il Āl Muḥammad*, ed. Kūcha Bāghī ([Tabrīz ?], [1960]), section 1, chapter 12, no. 4, 28.

11. See Virani, "Seekers of Union: The Ismailis from the Mongol Debacle to the Eve of the Safavid Revolution" (PhD dissertation, Harvard University, 2001), passim, and, for example, al-Nuʿmān, *Taʾwīl al-Daʿāʾim*, ed. al-Aʿẓamī, 3 vols. (Cairo, 1967–1972), vol. 1, 127, cf. 201, 349. See also Daftary, *The Ismāʿīlīs: Their History and Doctrines* (Cambridge, 1990), index, s.v. "taqiyya."

12. Citing the *Gulzār-i Shams*, the *Nūram Mobīn* suggests Makhdūmshāh as an additional name of the Imam. Chunārā, *Nūram Mobīn: yāne Allāhanī pavitra rasī [English Title: Noorum-Mobin or The Sacred Cord of God]*, ed. Sufī, 4th ed. (Mumbai, 1961), 305. This may be a misreading of the original text, though. See Mulukshāh and ʿĪsanshāh, *Gulzār-i Shams* ([Multan], 1334/1916), 288. The *Lamaʿāt al-Ṭāhirīn*, composed in 1108/1697, gives him the same name as his predecessor, Shāh Khwurshāh. See Ivanow, "An Ismailitic Pedigree," *JASB* NS 18 (1922): 406.

13. Ivanow, *Ismaili Literature: A Bibliographical Survey*, 2nd amplified ed. (Tehran, 1963), 152.

14. Muḥammad Taqī b. ʿAlī Riḍā b. Zayn al-ʿĀbidīn, *Āthār-i Muḥammadī* (Maḥallāt, Iran, 1893), 56.

15. Algar, "The Revolt of Āghā Khān Maḥallātī and the Transference of the Ismāʿīlī Imamate to India," *SI* 29 (1969): 78, Chunārā, *Nūram Mobīn*; Daftary, *Ismāʿīlīs*, 511; Khākī Khurāsānī, *Dīwān*, ed. Ivanow, *An Abbreviated Version of the Diwan of Khaki Khorasani* (Mumbai, 1933), 12; Muḥammad Taqī b. ʿAlī Riḍā b. Zayn al-ʿĀbidīn, *Āthār-i Muḥammadī*, 56. A number of other late sources also speak of the Imam Shams al-Dīn as *zardūz*. See, for example, Fidāʾī Khurāsānī, *Hidāyat al-Muʾminīn al-Ṭālibīn*, ed. Semenov (Moscow, 1959), 117, and the non-Ismāʿīlī Mulukshāh and ʿĪsanshāh, *Gulzār*, 289.

16. Firishta, *Taʾrīkh-i Firishta [a.k.a. Gulshan-i Ibrāhīmī]*, ed. Briggs (Mumbai, 1832), vol. 2, 213. See also Hosain, "Shāh Ṭāhir of the Deccan," *New Indian Antiquary* 2 (1939): 461; Muʿizzī, "Ismāʿīliyyān-i Īrān" (MA thesis, Dānishgāh-i Firdawsī, 1371–1372 HS/1992–1993), 94. A short extract in a Syrian manuscript, which the author refers to as the "blessed genealogical tree from Adam until al-Qāʾim," contains brief biographical notes about the Imams from ʿAlī b. Abī Ṭālib to the first of the Imams after the fall of Alamūt in 654/1256. Unfortunately the work, which may date from the second half of the 8th / 14th century, was not available to me. See Mirza, *Syrian Ismailism: The Ever Living Line of the Imamate* (Richmond, Surrey, 1997), 95.

17. Quhistānī, *Dīwān-i Ḥakīm Nizārī Quhistānī*, ed. Muṣaffā (Tehran, 1371 HS/1992), 105, 109. See also Jamal, *Surviving the Mongols: Nizari Quhistani and the Continuity of Ismaili Tradition in Persia* (London, 2002), 124, 126–127, 131–132, 134–135.

18. "Risāla-yi Ṣirāṭ al-Mustaqīm," in *Seekers of Union: The Ismailis from the Mongol Debacle to the Eve of the Safavid Revolution*, ed. Virani, trans. Virani, *The Epistle of the Right Path* (PhD dissertation, Harvard University, 2001). This work may date from the fourteenth to fifteenth century; see Virani, "Seekers of Union," 201–202.

19. See [pseudo-Shihāb al-Dīn Abū Firās], *al-Qaṣīda al-Shāfiya*, ed. Makarem, trans. Makarem, *Ash-Shāfiya (The Healer): An Ismāʿīlī Poem Attributed to Shihāb ad-Dīn Abū Firās* (Beirut, 1966), 158–159, 227–228 n254; [pseudo-Shihāb al-Dīn Abū Firās], *al-Qaṣīda al-Shāfiya*, ed. Tāmir (Beirut, 1967). Makarem states that Qusūr is now a little village six kilometers north of Riḍāʾiyya. See also I. K. Poonawala's criticism of the dating

of both these editors in his Poonawala, *Biobibliography of Ismāʿīlī Literature* (Malibu, CA, 1977), 350, which is based on Madelung, "Ash-Shāfiya—Review," *Oriens* 23–24 (1974): 517–518; Madelung, "Ash-Shāfiya—Review," *Zeitschrift der Deutschen Morgenländischen Gesellschaft* 118 (1968): 423–427.

20. Dawlatshāh, *Tadhkirat al-Shuʿarā'*, ed. Browne (London, 1901), 126–127. On Dawlatshāh, see Huart and Masse, "Dawlat-Shāh (Amīr) b. ʿAlā' al-Dawla Bakhtīshāh," in *EI2*, vol. 2 (Leiden, 1960–2004; reprint, CD-ROM v. 1.0).

21. Shushtarī, *Majālis al-Mu'minīn* (Tehran, 1299/1882), 300. See also Akhtar, "Shams Tabrizi: Was He an Ismailian," *IC* 10 (January 1936): 131–136.

22. Browne, *A Literary History of Persia*, 4 vols. (Cambridge, 1902–1924), vol. 2, 516–517.

23. Such a conflation is readily apparent in works such as Mulukshāh and ʿĪsanshāh, *Gulzār*, passim. See also Ivanow, "Shums Tabrez of Multan," in *Professor Muhammad Shafi Presentation Volume*, ed. Abdullah (Lahore, 1955); Ivanow, "Some Muhammadan Shrines in Western India," *Ismaili: Golden Jubilee Number* (1936 January 21); Kassam, *Songs of Wisdom and Circles of Dance: Hymns of the Satpanth Ismaili Muslim Saint, Pir Shams* (Albany, NY, 1995), 77–85 et passim.

24. Khayrkhwāh Harātī, "Risāla," in *Taṣnīfāt-i Khayrkhwāh Harātī*, ed. Ivanow (Tehran, 1961), 78. The question of the conflation of the two personalities is ably discussed in Muʿizzī, "Ismāʿīliyyān-i Īrān," 78–84.

25. The poem is the well-known *bāz āmadam bāz āmadam az pīsh-i ān yār āmadam*. It is, of course, possible that the poem was actually by a "Shams-i Tabrīz" and was accidentally incorporated into the *Omnibus*, but this is pure speculation. For a translation, see Lewis, *Rumi: Past and Present, East and West* (Oxford, 2000), 352–354.

26. "Risāla-yi Ṣirāṭ al-Mustaqīm," ed. 230, trans. 217–218.

27. Fidā'ī Khurāsānī, *Hidāyat*, 118.

28. On this figure, see al-Ḥusaynī, *Kitāb-i Khiṭābāt-i ʿĀliya*, ed. Ujāqī (Mumbai, 1963); al-Ḥusaynī, *Risāla dar Ḥaqīqat-i Dīn*, trans. Ivanow, *True Meaning of Religion or Risala dar Haqiqati Din*, 2nd ed. (Mumbai, 1933; reprint, Dar es Salam, Tanzania: Shia Imami Ismailia Association for Tanzania, 1970); Daftary, *Ismāʿīlīs*, 439, 518; Daftary, "Shihāb al-Dīn al-Ḥusaynī, Shāh," in *EI2*, vol. 9 (Leiden, 1960–2004; reprint, CD-ROM v. 1.0); Fidā'ī Khurāsānī, *Hidāyat*, 178–179; Sadik Ali, "Pir Shahabu'd Din Shah al-Husayni," in *The Great Ismaili Heroes* (Karachi, 1973).

29. al-Ḥusaynī, *Khiṭābāt*, 42.

30. al-Aflākī, *Manāqib al-ʿĀrifīn*, ed. Yazici, 2 vols. (Ankara, 1959), vol. 1, 614, Lewis, *Rumi*, 134. Annemarie Schimmel likewise gives this name, relying on the testimony of the much later *Breezes of Intimacy* (*Nafaḥāt al-Uns*) of Jāmī, who himself used Aflākī as a source. See Schimmel, "Shams-i Tabrīz(ī)," in *EI2*, vol. 9 (Leiden, 1960–2004; reprint, CD-ROM v. 1.0).

31. See Lewis, *Rumi*, 141, 250–251 et passim.

32. Ibid, 175, 177; Walad, *Mathnawī-yi Waladī*, ed. Humā'ī (Tehran, 1316/1937), 43.

33. al-Aflākī, *Manāqib*, 618. In this regard, see Lewis, *Rumi*, 154–155, and Schimmel, "Shams-i Tabrīz(ī)."

34. Rukn al-Dīn Khwurshāh's age at the time can be calculated as follows: ʿAlāʾ al-Dīn Muḥammad was nine years old when he succeeded to the imamate in 618; Juwaynī, *Taʾrīkh-i Jahāngushāy*, ed. Qazwīnī, 3 vols. (Leiden, 1912–1937), ed. vol. 3, 249, trans. vol. 2, 703; hence he was born in 609. He was eighteen years old when his son Rukn al-Dīn Khwurshāh was born; Juwaynī, *Jahāngushāy*, ed. vol. 3, 243, trans., vol. 2, 707. Hence, Rukn al-Dīn Khwurshāh was born in 627 and would have been about fifteen years old in 642/1244.

35. Daftary places the birth of the Ismāʿīlī Imam Shams al-Dīn Muḥammad in the late 640s/1240s. See Daftary, "Shams al-Dīn Muḥammad," in *EI2*, vol. 9 (Leiden, 1960–2004; reprint, CD-ROM v. 1.0). While this is certainly plausible, the author does not provide any source for his information, nor is it mentioned in his earlier work, Daftary, *Ismāʿīlīs*. Ivanow dates Shams al-Din Muḥammad's birth to 650/1252 but, again, without citing any source for his information. See Ivanow, "Shums Tabrez," 116.

36. Lewis, *Rumi*, 155; Muwaḥḥid, *Shams-i Tabrīzī* (Tehran, 1996); Shams al-Dīn Tabrīzī, *Maqālāt-i Shams-i Tabrīzī*, ed. Muwaḥḥid, 2 vols. (Tehran, 1990), vol. 1, 734.

37. This possibility is also suggested in Schimmel, "Shams-i Tabrīz(ī)." In Akhtar, "Shams Tabrizi," the author argues against Shams's descent from the Ismaili Imams.

38. See Hidāyat, *Majmaʿ al-Fuṣaḥāʾ*, ed. Muṣaffā (Tehran, 1336 HS/1957), vol. 1, 771; Ṣafā, *Taʾrīkh-i Adabiyāt-i Īrān* (Tehran, 1352 HS/1973), vol. 3, part 2, 1174. See also Muʿizzī, "Ismāʿīliyyān-i Īrān," 82–83.

39. van den Berg, "Minstrel Poetry from the Pamir Mountains: A Study on the Songs and Poems of the Ismāʿīlīs of Tajik Badakshan" (PhD dissertation, State University of Leiden, 1997), 47.

40. During, *Musique et mystique dans les traditions de l'Iran* (Tehran, 1989), 415–416; Shams-i Tabrīz, "Tā Ṣūrat-i Paywand-i Jahān būd ʿAlī būd," in *Gulzār-i Shams*, ed. Mulukshāh and ʿĪsanshāh ([Multan], 1334/1916), 350–351; Shams-i Tabrīz, "Tā Ṣūrat-i Paywand-i Jahān būd ʿAlī būd," in *Kitāb al-Manāqib*, ed. Pākistān (Karachi, 1406/1986); Shams-i Tabrīz, "Tā Ṣūrat-o Paywand-i Jahān būd ʿAlī būd," in *Majmūʿa-yi Ashʿār-i Madhhabī*, ed. Anjuman-i taʿlīm (Mashhad, Iran, 1995); van den Berg, "Minstrel Poetry," 487–488. The meter is *hazaj akhrab makfūf maḥdhūf.*

41. Shams-i Tabrīz, "Sāqīy-i bā wafā manam dam hama dam ʿAlī ʿAlī," in *Medā Lāl Qalandar*, ed. Parwīn. See also Hiz Hāʾīnes Prins Āghā Khān Shīʿa Imāmī Ismāʿīliya Esūsīʾeshan barāʾe Pākistān, ed., *Kitāb al-Manāqib* (Karachi, 1406/1986); Shams-i Tabrīz, "*Sāqi-yi bā wafā manam dam hama dam ʿAlī ʿAlī*," in *Qasidas: Great Ismaili Tradition of Central Asia*, ed. The Shia Imami Ismaili Tariqah and Religious Education Board for Pakistan, vol. 1 ([Karachi], nd); Shams-i Tabrīz, "*Sāqī-yi bā wafā manam dam hama dam ʿAlī ʿAlī*," in *Kitāb al-Manāqib*, ed. Hiz Hāʾīnes Prins Āghā Khān Shīʿa Imāmī Ismāʿīliya Esūsīʾeshan barāʾe Pākistān (Karachi, 1406/1986); Shams-i Tabrīz, "*Sāqiy-i bā wafā manam dam hama dam ʿAlī ʿAlī*," in *Manāqib: Surūda shuda dar huḍūr-i Mawlānā Ḥāḍir Imām dar dawrān-i bāzdīd-i Pākistān, Aktūbar 2000, bā tarjamāy-i Inglīsī*, ed. Pakistan ([Karachi], [Soon after October 2000]). The meter is *rajaz muthamman matwī wa-makhbūn*. The second hemistich of this couplet is صوفی با صفا منم دم همه دم علی علی which lacks a verb, as Hermann Landolt observes (personal communication, February 12, 2006). He therefore suggests the simple and elegant possibility that the second علی be replaced by زنم.

42. van den Berg, "Minstrel Poetry," 107; "Unsuccesful" corrected to read "unsuccessful."

43. Ibid, 111.

44. Mulukshāh and ʿĪsanshāh, *Gulzār*, 350. The name of the author of the *Gulzār-i Shams* is thus vocalized on p. 403 of the book, rather than as Malikshāh. It is unclear from which edition this author quotes, though it is possible that it is one of the older Lucknow lithographs. See Lewis, *Rumi*, 300–303 for a discussion of the printed editions of this text.

45. Shushtarī, *Majālis al-Muʾminīn*, 301.

46. Mulukshāh and ʿĪsanshāh, *Gulzār*, 324, for example, insists that there exists a corpus of Shams-i Tabrīz's poetry distinct from that composed in his name by Rūmī.

47. This somewhat resembles the prophecy augured in Ṭūsī and Ḥasan-i Maḥmūd, *Rawḍa-yi Taslīm*, ed. Badakhchani, trans. Badakhchani, *Paradise of Submission: A Medieval Treatise on Ismaili Thought* (London, 2005), ed. 194, trans. 156–157.

48. This is a saying of the Imam al-Bāqir, as quoted by the Imam al-Ṣādiq. See al-Nuʿmān, *Daʿāʾim al-Islām wa-Dhikr al-Ḥalāl wa-al-Ḥarām wa-al-Qaḍāyā wa-al-Aḥkām*, ed. Fayḍī (Cairo, 1951–1961), vol. 1, 59–60. The same tradition is found in al-Muʾayyad fī al-Dīn Shīrāzī, *al-Majālis al-Muʾayyadiyya*, ed. Ghālib, vols. 1 and 3 (Beirut, 1974–1984), vol. 3, 203 as well as in numerous Twelver sources, including Aḥmad b. Muḥammad al-Barqī, *Kitāb al-Maḥāsin*, ed. Jalāl al-Dīn al-Ḥusaynī al-Rasūlī al-Maḥallātī (Qumm: 1380–1), vol. 1, 255, no. 286; Abū Jaʿfar Muḥammad b. Yaʿqūb al-Kulaynī, *al-Kāfī* (Tehran: 1375–1377), vol. 2, 223–224, both cited in Kohlberg, "Taqiyya in Shīʿī Theology," 356, n61.

49. Shams al-Dīn Muḥammad?, "[No Title]," in *Institute of Ismaili Studies Library*, Persian ms 814 (London, 1313/1895), 105. Copied in Ishkashim. The date 1313/1895 occurs on pp. 97 and 104. Some of the passages are obscure and the reading is tentative in these places.

بر جمله بنده گان پوشیده نماناد که مولانا علی و مولانا حسین لذکره سلام [sic، لذکرهما السلام] چنانچه فرموده اند که ما را به جبلستان و دیلمان گذار افتاد که کربلای آخرین باشد که قصر قیصر و قلعه الموت به پیرزن دهند و قبول نکند و این جمله شد و خلایق عالم بدیدند و از آنچه گفته بودیم هیچ نه گردیدند اکنون از زمین ایران بطوران [sic، بتوران] رفتیم و بتماشاه [sic، بتماشا] ما در آن شهر [sic، شهرها؟] بگردیم [sic، بگردیدیم] و ثمرقند [sic، سمرقند] و بخارا و خطا و خطن [sic، ختا و ختن] و بلخ و چین و ماچین و تیبت و کشمیر بگردیم [sic، بگردیدیم] و بزمین فرنگ بگشتیم القصه از جابلسا [=جابرسا، جابلص، جابلصا .etc] تا بجابلقا در نظر آوردیم از روی ظاهر در شهر اوچه و ملتان ظهور کردیم و وعده که با محبان کرده بودیم بجا اوردیم و شفقتی که با محبان و رفیقان هندوستان بود بزمین ایران مراجعت نمودیم و درین ویلایتها [sic، ولایتها] که بگردیدیم همه جا تقیه کردیم که *التقیه دینی و دین آبائي* یعنی پنهان کنید [sic، کردن] دین من و دین پدر [sic، پدران] من و بهر مقامی خود را بشکل و بصورت باز نمودیم که مصلحت کار عالم در آن می دیدیم اما مصلحت کار ما بندگان ما بهتر دانند اگر کسی کاری و مصلحت بهتر داندپیشتر [sic، و اندیشتر؟] آید و در کل کاینات این دعوی کسی دیگر نرسد و اگر کسی در شك افتد از خیال فاسد و از وسواس شیطانی خود باشد خدای تعالی جمله بنده گان را در پناه خود بدارد بحق حقه.

50. The Press' anonymous reader suggests that this may be a reference to Constantinople. Indeed, that city did experience a disastrous capture and plunder early in the thirteenth century during the fourth Crusade.

51. al-Ḥusaynī, *Khiṭābāt*, 42; Fidā'ī Khurāsānī, *Hidāyat*, 117–118.

52. Fidā'ī Khurāsānī, *Hidāyat*, 118. An early twentieth-century book written by Khwāja Hāshim Laʿlū, a Sindhi Ismāʿīlī, also maintains that the Imam Shams al-Dīn Muḥammad was buried in Multan. The shrine in that city is now more commonly associated with the Ismāʿīlī pīr of the same name. See Laʿlū (Laʿl Muḥammad) [Khoja Hashim Lalloo], *[Ḥaqq-i Mawjūd ?]* (Hyderabad, Sindh, [after 1899: cover damaged]), 176.

53. Among the *garbīs* attributed to Pīr Shams, see Shams, "*Gur vachane chālea*," in *100 Ginānanī Chopaḍī*, 4th ed., vol. 4 (Mumbai, 1989 vs/1933), #60; Shams, "*Nar: kāsamanā: pharamānathī: gur: shamas: pīr: ||: ramavā nīsareāremā*," in *12 Girathane: 101 Ginān*, ed. Gulāmahusen (Mumbai, nd [before 1905?]), 572 v. 2. Somewhat more detailed itineraries are laid out in works such as Imāmshāh, "Mumaṇ: Chitāmaṇī," in *12 Girathane: 101 Ginān*, ed. Gulāmahusen (Mumbai, nd [before 1905?]), 205–207. Cf. Nanji, *The Nizārī Ismāʿīlī Tradition in the Indo-Pakistan Subcontinent* (Delmar, NY, 1978), 53.

54. al-Aflākī, *Manāqib*, 615; Lewis, *Rumi*, 182.

55. See Shackle and Moir, *Ismaili Hymns from South Asia: An Introduction to the Ginans* (London, 1992), 192–193, in which they have commented on another Ginān displaying the same elements.

56. Shams, "E sabhāgā har puchh nind [*sic*] niravāṇ pañjetan," in *100 Ginānanī Chopaḍī*, 5th ed., vol. 2 (Mumbai, 1993 vs/1936), vv. 9–10. The word used here is *mulasatān*, which is the ancient name of Multan. The word *sāheb* in verse 9 is a reference to the Imam.

57. Shams, "Jīv tuṃ jāvā de," in *100 Ginānanī Chopaḍī*, 5th ed., vol. 2 (Mumbai, 1993 vs/1936), v. 3. For the word *harī* as a reference to the Imam, cf. Shackle and Moir, *Ismaili Hymns*, 154, 168.

58. Shams, "Shāhānī sarevāe tame jāgajo," in *100 Ginānanī Chopaḍī*, 5th ed., vol. 1 (Mumbai, 1990 vs/1934), v. 1. Other Gināns of Pīr Shams that make reference to such a promise or to an arrival in India include Shams, "Evi: garabi: sampuraṇ: sār," in *28 Garabī: pīr: samas nī*, ed. Devarāj, 2nd ed. (Mumbai, 1913), v. 14; Shams, "Tiyāṃ thī ame āveā uñchamāṃ," in *100 Ginānanī Chopaḍī*, 4th ed., vol. 6 (Mumbai, 1989 vs/1933), v. 1. The anachronisms contained in the compositions attributed to Pīr Shams must be borne in mind in using these materials. See Mallison, "Les Chants *Garabi* de Pir Shams," in *Littératures Médievales de l'Inde du Nord*, ed. Mallison (Paris, 1991), 127.

59. The dates of this figure are extremely uncertain. A detailed discussion may be found in Kassam, *Songs of Wisdom*, 75–123. Daragāhavālā, *Tavārīkhe Pīr*, 2 vols. (Navasārī, India, 1914–1935), vol. 2, 83 provides a death date of 675/1277.

60. The name, however, may be a corruption of Dawlat Ṣifat. See Chunārā, *Nūram Mobīn*, 306, Chunārā, *Nurun Mobīn: athavā Allāhanī pavitra rasī*, 1st ed. (Mumbai, 1935), 496. That the Imams of Alamut were in close contact with their Indian devotees is suggested by the fact that one of the Imam ʿAlā' al-Dīn Muḥammad's companions, who was also wounded when the Imam was killed, was Indian. See Juwaynī, *Jahāngushāy*, ed. vol. 3, 255, trans. vol. 2, 709.

61. ʿAlī b. Abī Ṭālib, *Nahj al-Balāgha*, ed. al-Ṣāliḥ (Beirut, 1387/1967), 497.

62. Qazwīnī, *Nuzhat al-Qulūb*, ed. Le Strange, trans. Le Strange, *The Geographical Part of the Nuzhat al-Qulūb* (Leiden, 1915–1919), ed. 65, trans. 70.

63. Rashīd al-Dīn, *Jāmiʿ al-Tawārīkh*, trans. Thackston, *Jamiʿu't-tawarikh: Compendium of Chronicles*, 3 vols. (Cambridge, MA, 1998), vol. 2, 984, trans. vol. 3, 676.

64. "Risāla-yi Ṣirāṭ al-Mustaqīm," ed. 229–239, trans. 217–218.

65. Cf. Ivanow, *Alamut and Lamasar* ([Tehran], 1960), 23.

66. Ṭūsī and Ḥasan-i Maḥmūd, *Rawḍa-yi Taslīm*, ed. 146, trans. 118–119.

67. The appellation given to the Imam Khudāwand Muḥammad, *zardūz*, is suggestive of this. See, for example, Shams al-Dīn Muḥammad?, "Alfāẓ-i Guharbār," in *Institute of Ismaili Studies Library*, Persian ms 15077 (London), 58. If this is an interpolation, the text may pertain to the Imam Nūr al-Dīn Muḥammad [ʿAlāʾ Muḥammad] (d. 607/1210) or ʿAlāʾ al-Dīn Muḥammad (d. 653/1255). Cf. Ivanow, *Ismaili Literature*, 132–133. There is also a possibility, not suggested in the bibliographies of either Ivanow or Poonawala, that the document pertains to the Ismaili Imam Khudāwand Muḥammad, who recaptured Alamūt for a spell.

68. This is how the word is spelled in all mss, apparently for Qazwīn or Ghaznīn/Ghaznayn, i.e., Ghaznī. I would like to thank Wheeler Thackston and Sunil Sharma, both of whom suggested this latter alternative.

69. Copy of manuscript transcribed by Sayyid Muḥammad, dated 25 Ramadan, 1380. No accession number is recorded in the copy available to me. The places listed differ somewhat in various recensions, often omitting some locations. Cf. Shams al-Dīn Muḥammad?, "Guharbār—15077," 58; Shams al-Dīn Muḥammad?, "Guharbār—15092," 184; Shams al-Dīn Muḥammad?, "Guharbār—15071," 179–180. The manuscript used, though recent, seems to have been copied from a much older and more accurate exemplar than some of the others. While the title of the text is given as *Kitāb-i Pandiyāt wa-Mawʿiẓāt al-Naṣāʾiḥ*, it is clearly the same work as the *Alfāẓ-i Guharbār [wa Durr Nithār]*.

70. al-Ḥusaynī, *Khiṭābāt*, 19.

71. Faṣīḥ Khwāfī, *Mujmal-i Faṣīḥī*, ed. Farrukh, 2 vols. (Mashhad, 1339–1340 HS/1960–1961), vol. 2, 380.

72. Ibid, vol. 2, 343.

73. Lewis, *Rumi*, 199.

74. This work, apparently no longer extant, is cited in Rematulā, *Khojā Kom no Itihās* (Mumbai, 1905), 212–214. The family tree, transcribed here in Gujarati, ends with Jāfarshāh b. Kāsamalī, whose successor, Abū al-Ḥasan ʿAlī, passed away in 1206/1792, thus suggesting an eighteenth-century provenance for the source. See Daftary, *Ismāʿīlīs*, 500–503, 553. While the family tree makes Qāsim ʿAlī and Jaʿfarshāh two separate individuals, Daftary indicates that these are two names of the same person.

75. This is mentioned in Howorth, *History of the Mongols: From the 9th to the 19th Century* (London, 1876–1927), 92–93, in which he describes how the Imam ʿAlāʾ al-Dīn Muḥammad had sent an envoy to Khūy to negotiate with the Khwārazmshāh, Sulṭān Jalāl al-Dīn.

76. Quhistānī, "Safarnāma," in *The Continuity of the Nizari Ismaili Daʿwa*, ed. Jamal (PhD dissertation, New York University, 1996), 262.

77. Lewis, *Rumi*, 558–559.

78. Muwaḥḥid, *Shams-i Tabrīzī*, 209.

79. Amīn-Riyāḥī, *Ta'rīkh-i Khuy* (Tehran, 1372 HS/1993), 94.

80. See note 34. Franklin Lewis, to whose scholarship I am indebted for many of the above references, feels that despite the improbability of the death date recorded by Faṣīḥ-i Khwāfī, in the absence of reliable alternatives, Khūy may indeed be the burial place of Rūmī's preceptor. He details the debates on this issue in Lewis, *Rumi*, 198–200.

81. Daftary, *Ismāʿīlīs*, 446, 452, 553; Daftary, "Shams al-Dīn Muḥammad"; Madelung, "Ash-Shāfiya—Review," 424. Fida'i Khurasani gives 603/1207, which is certainly an error. Fidā'ī Khurāsānī, *Hidāyat*, 118. Perhaps 703/1304 is the year he intended.

82. Daftary, *Ismāʿīlīs*, 702 n21; Tāmir, *al-Imāma fī al-Islām* (Beirut, [1964]), 196.

83. Tāmir, *al-Imāma*, 196.

84. Chunārā, *Nūram Mobīn*, 296, 305; Chunārā, *Nurun Mobīn*, 477, 495.

85. Nūr Muḥammadshāh, *Sat Varaṇī Moṭī nī Vel [a.k.a. Sat Veṇī nī Vel]* (Mumbai, 1962 VS/1905). On this author and a further discussion of this Ginān, see Virani, "The Voice of Truth: Life and Works of Sayyid Nūr Muḥammad Shāh, a 15th/16th Century Ismāʿīlī Mystic" (MA thesis, McGill University, 1995). For the date of his death, see Qāḍī Raḥmatallāh b. Ghulām Muṣṭafā, *Manāzil al-Aqṭāb wa Basātīn al-Aḥbāb*, cited in Ivanow, "The Sect of Imam Shah in Gujrat," *JBBRAS* 12 (1936): 45, and Daragāhavālā, *Tavārīkhe Pīr*, vol. 2, 124.

86. Ivanow, "Shums Tabrez," 116.

87. Nūr Muḥammadshāh, "Sat Varaṇi Moṭi ni Vel," in *Personal Library of Mr Abdulrasool Mawji* (Calgary, Canada). For a description of the manuscript, see Virani, "Voice of Truth," 105–106.

88. In this regard, see Virani, "Voice of Truth," 28–29.

89. Nūr Muḥammadshāh, *Sat Varaṇī Moṭī nī Vel [a.k.a. Sat Veṇī nī Vel]*, 187.

90. Rematulā, *Khojā Kom no Itihās*, 212–214.

91. A brief biography of this personality is found in Sadik Ali, *101 Ismaili Heroes: (Late 19th Century to Present Age)*, vol. 1 (Karachi, 2003), 290–293.

92. Boghā, *Isamāilī Darpaṇ* (Mumbai, 1323/1906), 23.

93. Ibid.

94. Ibid.

95. Sadik Ali, *Ismaili Heroes*, 290.

96. See, for example, Rajabalī, ed., *Khojā Isamāilī Keleṇḍar ane Dīrekaṭarī: 1910* (Mumbai, 1910).

97. Kābā, *Khojā Kom nī Tavārīkh [English Title, The History of the Khojas]* (Amarelī, Kāṭhīyāvāḍ, India, 1330/1912), 202–205.

98. Ṭūsī and Ḥasan-i Maḥmūd, *Rawḍa-yi Taslīm*, ed. 163–164, trans. 131–132, *ḥujjat* rendered as hujjat.

99. A reference to Quran 3:34, which is understood to refer to the continuity of the succession of the Imams.

100. This poem is found in Quhistānī, *Dīwān*, 80–81 and in Baiburdi, *Zhizn' i Tvorchestvo Nizari—Persidskogo Poeta XIII–XIV vv.* (Moscow, 1966), translated into

Persian as Baiburdi, *Zindagī wa-Āthār-i Nizārī*, trans. Ṣadrī (Tehran, 1370 HS/[1991]), 65. The latter source gives a better reading, and it is from this that passage has been translated. Cf. Hunzai, *Shimmering Light: An Anthology of Ismaili Poetry* (London, 1996), 89–91; Jamal, "The Continuity of the Nizari Ismaili Daʿwa: 1256–1350" (PhD dissertation, New York University, 1996), 157–158; Jamal, *Surviving the Mongols*, 97.

101. This is expressed, for example, in [Khayrkhwāh Harātī?], *Faṣl dar Bayān-i Shinākht-i Imām*, ed. Ivanow, 3rd rev. ed. (Tehran, 1960), ed. 4, 7, 14, 19, 29, trans. 30–31, 33–34, 44; [pseudo-Nāṣir-i Khusraw: Khayrkhwāh Harātī?], *Kalām-i Pīr*, ed. Ivanow, trans. Ivanow (Mumbai, 1935), ed. 68, trans. 63. On the spiritual role of Salman, see Corbin, *Temple and Contemplation*, trans. Sherrard (London, 1986), 176–180; Ivanow, "Ismailitica 1 and 2," *Memoirs of the Asiatic Society of Bengal* 17 (1922): 11–12; Massignon, "Salmān Pāk et les prémices spirituelles de l'Islam Iranien," in *Opera Minora*, vol. 1 (Beirut, 1963).

102. Badakhshānī, *Sī wa-Shish Ṣaḥīfa*, ed. Ujaqi (Tehran, 1961), 62; cf. [pseudo-Nāṣir-i Khusraw: Khayrkhwāh Harātī?], *Kalām-i Pīr*, ed. 107, trans. 103.

103. "Risāla-yi Ṣirāṭ al-Mustaqīm," ed. 231, trans. 218.

104. Qazwīnī, *Nuzhat al-Qulūb*, ed. 144, trans. 143.

105. Browne, *Literary History*, vol. 3, 154.

106. Rāzī, *Haft Iqlīm*, ed. Fāḍil (Tehran, nd), vol. 2, 322–323, cited in Jamal, *Surviving the Mongols*, 59.

107. Quhistānī, *Dīwān*, vol. 1, 131. Translated in Jamal, *Surviving the Mongols*, 77; cf. Baiburdi, *Zhizn'*, 199. "Was" in line 11 emended to "were," and formatting modified.

108. Kramers, "Ḳūhistān," in *EI2*, vol. 5 (Leiden, 1960–2004; reprint, CD-ROM v. 1.0).

109. Lewisohn; *Beyond Faith and Infidelity: The Sufi Poetry and Teachings of Mahmud Shabistari* (Surrey, 1995), 56. Cf. Petrushevsky, "The Socio-Economic Conditions of Iran under the Il-Khāns," in *The Cambridge History of Iran*, vol. 5 (Cambridge, 1968), 484–488.

110. See Rypka, "Poets and Prose Writers of the Late Saljuq and Mongol Periods," in *The Cambridge History of Iran* (Cambridge, 1968), 604.

111. Qazwīnī, *Nuzhat al-Qulūb*, ed. 27, trans. 34, translation modified.

112. Jamal, *Surviving the Mongols*, 66, 70–72. Jamal gives 676/1278 as the date of Shams al-Dīn Kart's death, but cf. Haig and Spuler, "Kart," in *EI2*, vol. 4 (Leiden, 1960–2004; reprint, CD-ROM v. 1.0).

113. Rashīd al-Dīn, *Jāmiʿ al-Tawārīkh*, ed. Karīmī (Tehran, 1338 HS/1959), ed. vol. 2, 691, trans. 482.

114. Sayf b. Muḥammad b. Yaʿqūb, *Ta'rīkh Nāma-yi Harāt*, ed. Ṣiddīqī (Calcutta, 1944), 267–268.

115. Ibid, 302.

116. Jamal, *Surviving the Mongols*; Quhistānī, "Safarnāma," 257–298.

117. Cf., however, the views expressed in Muʿizzī, "Ismāʿīliyyān-i Īrān," 326.

118. Quhistānī, *Dīwān*, vol. 1, 732. Cf. Muʿizzī, "Ismāʿīliyyān-i Īrān," 84, 159 n32.

119. Baiburdi, *Zhizn'*, 179, translated in Jamal, "Continuity of the Nizari Ismaili Daʿwa," 142.

120. Cited in Baiburdi, *Zindagī wa-Āthār-i Nizārī*, 49. The meter is *ramal sālim makhbūn maḥdhūf*.

121. Qazwīnī, *Nuzhat al-Qulūb*, ed. 61, trans. 67.

122. Cited in Baiburdi, *Zindagī wa-Āthār-i Nizārī*, 48; cf. Jamal, *Surviving the Mongols*, 55–67, in which she describes the circumstances surrounding the composition of this poem. The line می کنم پشت دست is probably an error for می گزم پشت دست.

123. Quhistānī, *Dīwān*, 84.

124. Translated in Hunzai, *Shimmering Light*, 87, formatting modified. *Maʿrifa* is glossed as "a technical expression used primarily in Ṣūfism for spiritual knowledge derived through an intuitive and illuminative cognition of the divine. In Ismaili thought, the term also signifies the spiritual recognition of one's own soul, which is tantamount to the recognition of God." 144 n72.

125. Daftary, *Ismāʿīlīs*, 439. Ivanow, *Ismaili Literature*, 137–138.

126. Historically speaking, it could be argued that a figure such as al-Ḥallāj was as much a Qarmatian as he was a Sufi. See, for example, Massignon, *Hallāj: Mystic and Martyr*, ed. Mason, trans. Mason, abridged ed. (Princeton, NJ, 1994), 109–112.

127. Ibn Khaldūn, *The Muqaddimah: An Introduction to History*, trans. Rosenthal, 3 vols. (Princeton, 1967), trans. vol. 3, 94.

128. Thackston, *A Millennium of Classical Persian Poetry: A Guide to the Reading and Understanding of Persian Poetry from the Tenth to the Twentieth Century* (Bethesda, MD, 1994), xi, italics added.

129. See Lewisohn, "Sufism and Ismāʿīlī Doctrine in the Persian Poetry of Nizārī Quhistānī (645–721/1247–1321)," *Iran* 41 (2003): 243–244.

130. Cited in Baiburdi, *Zindagī wa-Āthār-i Nizārī*, 67–68 and in Muṣaffā's introduction to Quhistānī, *Dīwān*, 61; cf. Jamal, *Surviving the Mongols*, 98.

131. Nūrbakhsh, *Risāla al-Hudā*, ed. Bashir, *Between Mysticism and Messianism: The Life and Thought of Muhammad Nūrbakś (d. 1464)* (New Haven, 1997), 298–299. Cf. Bashir, "Between Mysticism and Messianism: The Life and Thought of Muhammad Nurbakś (d. 1464)" (PhD dissertation, Yale University, 1997), 190.

132. Ibn Khaldūn, *The Muqaddimah: An Introduction to History*, trans. 92–94.

133. Ibid, 93–94.

134. This couplet appears in the manuscript used by Baiburdi, *Zindagī wa-Āthār-i Nizārī*, 83, but not in Quhistānī, *Dīwān*.

135. Also cited in [Khayrkhwāh Harātī?], *Faṣl dar Bayān-i Shinākht-i Imām*, 26; [Khayrkhwāh Harātī?], *Faṣl dar Bayān-i Shinākht-i Imām*, trans. Ivanow, 2nd rev. ed. (Mumbai, 1947), trans. 42.

136. Quhistānī, *Dīwān*, 674–675 and Baiburdi, *Zindagī wa-Āthār-i Nizārī*, 83. Cf. Hunzai, *Shimmering Light*, 91–92, Jamal, *Surviving the Mongols*, 96–97; Lewisohn, "Nizārī Quhistānī," 241.

137. In this verse, Nizārī is, in fact, echoing an extract from the *Blessed Epistles* (*fuṣūl-i mubārak*) of the Imam Ḥasan *ʿalā dhikrihi al-salām*:

> A perfect man (*kāmilī*) must always exist amongst God's creatures in order to raise those who are incomplete and deficient to a state of perfection. Even if

> you assume that he [the Ismaili Imam] is not that person (the perfect man), there would still have to be someone else. For, if each imperfect soul needs a more perfect one [to perfect it], and the more perfect soul, (in its turn), needs an even more perfect one, and in the final case, (the chain) must terminate with the perfect man who does not need anybody else, and through whose instruction [all others] may reach perfection."

Ṭūsī and Ḥasan-i Maḥmūd, *Rawḍa-yi Taslīm*, ed. 151, trans. 123, cf. ed. 154–155, trans. 124–125.

138. This is a recognized Shīʿī tradition, reported in slightly different wordings in, for example, al-Kulaynī, *al-Uṣūl min al-Kāfī*, ed. Kamarāʾī (Tehran, 1392 HS/1972), vol. 1, 332–334; Ṭūsī and Ḥasan-i Maḥmūd, *Rawḍa-yi Taslīm*, ed. 148, trans. 120. See also Amir-Moezzi, *Divine Guide*, 43, 125, 229 n673–n675 for further references.

139. A description of these manuscripts is found in Muʿizzī, "Ismāʿīliyyān-i īrān," 38–39.

140. Sells, ed., *Early Islamic Mysticism: Sufi, Quran, Miraj, Poetic and Theological Writings* (New York, 1996), 75–89.

141. See F. M. Hunzai's Preface to Nāṣir-i Khusraw, *Gushāyish wa-Rahāyish*, ed. Hunzai, trans. Hunzai, *Knowledge and Liberation: A Treatise on Philosophical Theology* (London, 1998), ix–x.

142. Jamal, "Continuity of the Nizari Ismaili Daʿwa," 141 n340; Jamal, *Surviving the Mongols*, 100, 102–103.

143. Cf. al-Ḥusaynī, *Khiṭābāt*, 40; Fidāʾī Khurāsānī, *Hidāyat*, 117–118. Daftary, *Ismāʿīlīs*, 553 is inclined to accept this date.

144. From the *Dastūrnāma*. See Quhistānī, *Dīwān*, 263. Cf. Jamal, *Surviving the Mongols*, 98; Lewisohn, "Nizārī Quhistānī," 243.

CHAPTER 4

1. Images and further descriptions of these coins may be found in Walker, *Exploring an Islamic Empire: Fatimid History and Its Sources* (London, 2002), plates following 144.

2. In this regard, see Daftary, *The Ismāʿīlīs: Their History and Doctrines* (Cambridge, 1990), 93.

3. Quhistānī, *Haft Bāb*, ed. Ivanow, trans. Ivanow, *Haft Bab or "Seven Chapters"* (Mumbai, 1959), ed. 47, trans. 47.

4. On the term "*daʿwa*," see Canard, "Daʿwa," in *EI2*, vol. 2 (Leiden, 1960–2004; reprint, CD-ROM v. 1.0).

5. al-Ghazālī, *Faḍāʾiḥ al-Bāṭiniyya wa-Faḍāʾil al-Mustaẓhiriyya*, ed. Badawī (Cairo, 1383/1964). Translated in McCarthy, *Freedom and Fulfillment* (Boston, 1980), 175–286. The work is studied in Mitha, *Al-Ghazali and the Ismailis: A Debate on Reason and Authority in Medieval Islam* (London, 2001). Partially edited in al-Ghazālī, *Faḍāʾiḥ al-Bāṭiniyya wa-Faḍāʾil al-Mustaẓhiriyya*, ed. Goldziher, *Streitschrift des Gazālī gegen die*

Bāṭinīya-Sekte, (Leiden, 1910). The selections in this edition are criticized in Corbin, "The Ismāʿīlī Response to the Polemic of Ghazālī," in *Ismāʿīlī Contributions to Islamic Culture*, ed. Nasr, trans. Morris (Tehran, 1977), 69–70. An Ismaili response to al-Ghazālī's polemic was composed by one of the Ṭayyibī dāʿīs; see Ibn al-Walīd, *Dāmigh al-Bāṭil wa-Ḥatf al-Munāḍil*, ed. Ghālib, 2 vols. (Beirut, 1403/1982).

6. Niẓām al-Mulk, *Siyar al-Mulūk or Siyāsatnāma*, trans. Darke, 2nd ed. (London, 1978), 208–231.

7. See, for example, Eche, *Les Bibliothèques Arabes Publiques et Semi-Publiques en Mésopotamie, en Syrie et en Egypte au moyen âge* (Damascus, 1967); Lewis, "Some Observations on the Significance of Heresy in the History of Islam," *SI* 6 (1953): 49. Other scholars have disagreed with this interpretation. See, for example, Makdisi, *The Rise of Colleges: Institutions of Learning in Islam and the West* (Edinburgh, 1981), 308–311.

8. An overview of the *ḥudūd* is provided in Daftary, *Ismāʿīlīs*, 228–230, 475–476. For a study of the *ḥudūd* as explained by Nāṣir-i Khusraw, see Hunzāʾī, *Silsila-yi Nūr-i Imāmat* (Karachi, 1957); Virani, "The Days of Creation in the Thought of Nāṣir Khusraw," in *Nāṣir Khusraw: Yesterday, Today, Tomorrow*, ed. Niyozov and Nazariev (Khujand, Tajikistan, 2004) 74–83. For Kirmānī's elaboration in his *Rāḥat al-ʿAql*, see Makarem, *The Doctrine of the Ismailis* (Beirut, 1972), 29–31.

9. See Ivanow, *A Guide to Ismaili Literature* (London, 1933), 98; Poonawala, *Biobibliography of Ismāʿīlī Literature* (Malibu, CA, 1977), 352. Ivanow inexplicably omits the work from his *Ismaili Literature: A Bibliographical Survey*, 2nd amplified ed. (Tehran, 1963). The texts and manuscripts used for this elaboration are as follows: "Sharḥ-i Marātib," in *Tuḥfat al-Nāẓirīn*, ed. Beg (Gilgit, Pakistan, 1960), 88–95; "Sharḥ al-Marātib," in *Institute of Ismaili Studies Library*, Persian ms 15077 (London); "Marātib - 15092"; "Marātib - 15093."

10. Daftary, *Ismāʿīlīs*, 369.

11. Cf. [pseudo-Nāṣir-i Khusraw: Khayrkhwāh Harātī?], *Kalām-i Pīr*, ed. Ivanow, trans. Ivanow (Mumbai, 1935), ed. 68, trans. 63.

12. This text was brought to scholarly attention in Mirza, *Syrian Ismailism: The Ever Living Line of the Imamate* (Richmond, Surrey, 1997), 96–98. As the manuscript is not available to me, I depend on this author's description of its contents. Another work by Shihāb al-Dīn Abū Firās, written in a similar style, is *Sullam al-Irtiqāʾ ilā Dār al-Baqā*. See Ivanow, *Ismaili Literature*, 172; Mirza, *Syrian Ismailism*, 101.

13. Daftary, *Ismāʿīlīs*, 441–442.

14. Catafago, "Lettre de M. Catafago à M. Mohl," *JA* série 12, no. 12 (1848); Daftary, *Ismaili Literature* (London, 2004), 106, 146–147.

15. See, for example, Ivanow, "Sufism and Ismailism: Chiragh-Nama," *Revue Iranienne d'Anthropologie* 3 (1959): 026; Ivanow, *The Truth-Worshippers of Kurdistan* (1953), 011–013.

16. Daftary, *Ismāʿīlīs*, 444. See also Daftary, "The Medieval Ismāʿīlīs of the Iranian Lands," in *The Sultan's Turret: Studies in Persian and Turkish Culture*, ed. Hillenbrand, vol. 2 (Leiden, 2000), 43–81.

17. Quhistānī, *Haft Bāb*, ed. 43–44, trans. 43–44.

18. Ibn Khaldūn, *The Muqaddimah: An Introduction to History*, trans. Rosenthal, 3 vols. (Princeton, 1967), vol. 1, 412–413.

19. Ivanow, "A Forgotten Branch of the Ismailis," *JRAS* (1938). Cf. Chunārā, *Nurun Mobīn: athavā Allāhanī pavitra rasī*, 1st ed. (Mumbai, 1935), 496.

20. Ivanow, "Forgotten Branch," 64; Ivanow, *Ismaili Literature*, 165. I have been unable to locate this manuscript.

21. Ivanow, *Ismaili Literature*, 165.

22. Poonawala, *Biobibliography*, 270–271.

23. See, for example, Daftary, *Ismāʿīlīs*, 447.

24. See ibid, 554.

25. The feminine Muḥammadum (or Muḥammadam) is apparently constructed from the name Muḥammad in the same way as *khānam* is derived from *khān* and *begam* from *beg*.

26. "Irshād al-Ṭalibīn," in *Institute of Ismaili Studies Library*, Persian ms 15095 (London), 24–25.

27. See Daftary, *Ismāʿīlīs*, 447. Fidāʾī Khurāsānī conflates the two lines; see Fidāʾī Khurāsānī, *Hidāyat al-Muʾminīn al-Ṭālibīn*, ed. Semenov (Moscow, 1959), 123.

28. Nānajīāṇī, *Khojā Vṛttānt* (Ahmadabad, India, 1892), 121.

29. Dihgān, *Kārnāma yā dū bakhsh-i dīgar az taʾrīkh-i Arāk* ([Tehran], 1345 HS/ 1966), 14. He mistakenly makes Sharaf Khātūn the daughter of Mu'minshāh, apparently misreading a family tree in Chunārā, *Nūram Mobīn: yāne Allāhanī pavitra rasī [English Title: Noorum-Mobin or The Sacred Cord of God]*, ed. Sufi, 4th ed. (Mumbai, 1961), 306; Chunārā, *Nurun Mobīn*, 496. The table in this book seems to be based on the late Muḥammadshāhī tradition mentioned above. It makes Sharaf Khātūn the wife of Muʾminshāh II, the son of the first Mu'minshāh.

30. Dihgān, *Kārnāma*, 22. He refers simply to Shāh ʿAbbās. However, since there were no Ismaili Imams contemporary with the reigns of ʿAbbas II (r. 1052–1077/1642–1666) or ʿAbbas III (r. 1145–1148/1732–1736), who had the name Khalīl Allāh, it must be a reference to Shāh ʿAbbās I. Cf. Daftary, *Ismāʿīlīs*, 473; Khākī Khurāsānī, *Dīwān*, ed. Ivanow, *An Abbreviated Version of the Diwan of Khaki Khorasani* (Mumbai, 1933), 14.

31. Cited in Sykes, *A History of Persia*, 2 vols. (London, 1915), vol. 2, 268.

32. Daftary, *Ismāʿīlīs*, 458, 473.

33. The contents of this manuscript are analyzed in Badakhchani, "The Paradise of Submission" (PhD dissertation, Oxford University, 1989), 144–146. I am grateful to both Jalal Badakhchani and Faquir Hunzai who made a copy available to me. The pages on which the *mathnawī* is found may be a later addition to the manuscript. See Hermann Landolt's Introduction to Ṭūsī and Ḥasan-i Maḥmūd, *Rawḍa-yi Taslīm*, ed. Badakhchani, trans. Badakhchani, *Paradise of Submission: A Medieval Treatise on Ismaili Thought* (London, 2005), 4.

34. Lewis, *Rumi: Past and Present, East and West* (Oxford, 2000), 166.

35. Shams, "Bhulā: ma: bhule: bhamajore: hinduo," in *28 Garabī: pīr: samas nī*, ed. Devarāj, 2nd ed. (Mumbai, 1913), v. 11; Shams, "Cheto: cheto: te: chañchal: chetiyāre: lol," in *28 Garabī: pīr: samas nī*, ed. Devarāj, 2nd ed. (Mumbai, 1913), v. 13; Shams, "Gure: kāḍhichhe: pāvaḷ: hāthe," in *28 Garabī: pīr: samas nī*, ed. Devarāj, 2nd ed.

(Mumbai, 1913), v. 4; Shams, "Ke: tame: amiras: pijo: din: ne: rāt," in *28 Garabī: pīr: samas nī*, ed. Devarāj, 2nd ed. (Mumbai, 1913), v. 17; Shams, "Nar: kāsham nā: pharamān thī:," in *28 Garabī: pīr: samas nī*, ed. Devarāj, 2nd ed. (Mumbai, 1913), v. 1; Shams, "Satagur: samash: em: kahere: gāphalo: kem: utaraso: pār," in *28 Garabī: pīr: samas nī*, ed. Devarāj, 2nd ed. (Mumbai, 1913), v. 7. Cf. Kassam, *Songs of Wisdom and Circles of Dance: Hymns of the Satpanth Ismaili Muslim Saint, Pir Shams* (Albany, NY, 1995), 329, 345, 350, 352, 367, 342. See also Daftary, *Ismāʿīlīs*, 415; Mallison, "Les Chants *Garabi* de Pir Shams," in *Littératures Médievales de l'Inde du Nord*, ed. Mallison (Paris, 1991), passim; Nanji, *The Nizārī Ismāʿīlī Tradition in the Indo-Pakistan Subcontinent* (Delmar, NY, 1978), 63, 65. There is some indication that one of the Qāsimshāhs may also have been known as Anwar. See Nūr Muḥammadshāh, *Sat Varaṇī Moṭī* ([Mumbai?], nd), c. 176.

36. Shams, "Gur: āvatā: sarave: rāt," in *28 Garabī: pīr: samas nī*, ed. Devarāj, 2nd ed. (Mumbai, 1913), vv. 12–13. Cf. Kassam, *Songs of Wisdom*, 327. Kassam considered the name "Nizār" to be an anachronism in the composition, believing that it referred to an eighteenth-century Imam of the same name; Kassam, *Songs of Wisdom*, 105. In the light of evidence indicating that the Imam Qāsimshāh was also known as Nizār, however, the difficulty appears to be resolved. The Ginān s of Pīr Ṣadr al-Dīn also evoke the name Nizār, but this generally appears to be a reference to a name by which he himself was known. See Ṣadr al-Dīn, "Bhāīr bhāṅā ma ṭaḍo," in *100 Ginānanī Chopaḍī*, 5th ed., vol. 3 (Mumbai, 1991 vs/1935), 11; Ṣadr al-Dīn, "Jampu meṃ jampu meṃ var shāhā ache," in *100 Ginānanī Chopaḍī*, 5th ed., vol. 2 (Mumbai, 1993 vs/1936), v.16; Ṣadr al-Dīn, "Namo: te: shāhā: nur ke" in *102 Ginānajī: Chopaḍī:*, ed. Devarāj, 2nd ed., vol. 4 (Mumbai, 1961 vs/[1905]), v. 11; Ṣadr al-Dīn, "Pāchham: dese thi: parabhu: padhāreā," in *102 Ginānajī: Chopaḍī:*, ed. Devarāj, 2nd ed., vol. 4 (Mumbai, 1961 vs/[1905]), v. 34; Ṣadr al-Dīn, "Pāchham: dese: parabhu: paratak: beṭhā," in *102 Ginānajī: Chopaḍī:*, ed. Devarāj, 2nd ed., vol. 4 (Mumbai, 1961 vs/[1905]), vv. 26, 31, 52, 54. In Ṣadr al-Dīn, "Ejio: āeo: āeo: haṃsejo: var: rājā:," in *102 Ginānajī: Chopaḍī:*, ed. Devarāj, 2nd ed., vol. 4 (Mumbai, 1961 vs/[1905]), v. 4, the reference is to an Imam by the name of Shāh Nizār. The mention of Shāh Nizār in Ṣadr al-Dīn, "Āvo mārā munivar bhāiḍā hojī," in *100 Ginānanī Chopaḍī*, 5th ed., vol. 2 (Mumbai, 1993 vs/1936), v. 6 may, however, be a reference to the 5th/11th century Imam Nizār b. Mustanṣir bi'llāh, as the Imam Ismāʿīl's name is also mentioned.

37. Dawlatshāh, *Tadhkirat al-Shuʿarāʾ* ed. Browne (London, 1901), 231–234.

38. Jamal, *Surviving the Mongols: Nizari Quhistani and the Continuity of Ismaili Tradition in Persia* (London, 2002), 59, Khwāndamīr, *Ḥabīb al-Siyar*, ed. Humāʾī (Tehran, 1333 HS/1954), vol. 2, 457; Mīrkhwānd, *Rawḍat al-Ṣafāʾ*, 10 vols. (Tehran, 1338–1339 HS/1959–1960), vol. 4, 70, 193.

39. Browne, *A Literary History of Persia*, 4 vols. (Cambridge, 1902–1924), vol. 3, 154–155.

40. Nadia E. Jamal notes that while most of Nizārī's major works were composed after 680/1281, a scattering of earlier poetry is also present in his *Dīwān*; Jamal, *Surviving the Mongols*, 72.

41. Lewisohn, "Sufism and Ismāʿīlī Doctrine in the Persian Poetry of Nizārī Quhistānī (645–721/1247–1321)," *Iran* 41 (2003): 235–236 details the various opinions on this subject.

42. al-Qummī, *Kitāb al-maqālāt wa-al-firaq*, ed. Mashkūr (Tehran, 1963), 87. Cf. Daftary, *Ismāʿīlīs*, 94; Halm, *Shiʿism*, trans. Watson and Hill, 2nd ed. (New York, 2004), 29. For a more detailed discussion of the various brothers who were believed to have succeeded to the imamate, with a full account of the primary sources, see Modarressi, *Crisis and Consolidation in the Formative Period of Shīʿite Islam: Abū Jaʿfar ibn Qiba al-Rāzī and His Contribution to Imāmite Shīʿite Thought* (Princeton, NJ, 1993), passim.

43. Compare, however, the sentiment expressed in Yaghmāʾī's edition of the *Abū Muslimnāma,* in which the descendants of al-Ḥusayn are given precedence over those of his brother because they are the offspring of the Persian princess Shahrbānū, cited in Babayan, *Mystics, Monarchs, and Messiahs: Cultural Landscapes of Early Modern Iran* (Cambridge, MA, 2002), 134.

44. Daftary, *Ismāʿīlīs*, 96.

45. See, for example, Quhistānī, *Haft Bāb*, ed. 22, trans. 22, in which this verse is cited.

46. [Khayrkhwāh Harātī?], *Faṣl dar Bayān-i Shinākht-i Imām*, ed. Ivanow, 3rd rev. ed. (Tehran, 1960), 7; cf. [Khayrkhwāh Harātī?], *Faṣl dar Bayān-i Shinākht-i Imām*, trans. Ivanow, 2nd rev. ed. (Mumbai, 1947), trans. 23–24. The corresponding passage in the words of the Imam Ḥasan ʿalā dhikrihi al-salām is quoted in Ṭūsī and Ḥasan-i Maḥmūd, *Rawḍa-yi Taslīm*, ed. 150, trans. 122. The words *mustaqarr* and *mustawdaʿ* are not used here, however. Cf. Corbin, *Trilogie Ismaélienne* (Tehran, 1961), part 3, 55; Haji, "La Doctrine Ismaélienne d'après l'oeuvre d'Abū Isḥāq Qohestānī" (PhD dissertation, Sorbonne, 1975), 205–213.

47. The words replaced by the ellipsis, "the oldest, if there are several of them," seem to be a later addition. The author himself contradicts this condition in the following paragraph in which he makes Mūsā al-Kāẓim a *mustawdaʿ* Imam of the *mustaqarr* Imam, Ismāʿīl.

48. [pseudo-Nāṣir-i Khusraw: Khayrkhwāh Harātī?], *Kalām-i Pīr*, ed. 75, trans 70, cf. ed. 49–50, trans. 18, 41–42; "Imamat" modified to read "imamate."

49. Bū Isḥāq Quhistani elaborates that al-Ḥasan therefore occupied a position between the exoteric and the esoteric ḥujjat. Unfortunately, he does not elaborate on this theme and simply states that he is not using these expressions in their usual sense. Quhistānī, *Haft Bāb*, ed. 22, trans. 21–22.

50. In one of the *Blessed Epistles*, the Imam Ḥasan ʿalā dhikrihi's-salām also refers to al-Ḥasan as a trustee Imam. See Ṭūsī and Ḥasan-i Maḥmūd, *Rawḍa-yi Taslīm*, ed. 152, trans. 123. It seems that trustee imamate could continue for several generations. *Seven Chapters* and, in greater detail, *The Paradise of Submission* speak of the descendants of Abraham continuing in two lineages: an exoteric one of royalty and prophethood (*mulk wa-nubuwwat*), by which the trustee imamate of Isaac (Isḥāq) and his descendants is implied, and an esoteric one of religion and imamate (*dīn wa-imāmat*), by which the permanent imamate of Ishmael (Ismāʿīl) and his descendants is to be understood. The line of *mustawdaʿ* Imams descended from Isaac ended with the death of Jesus. See Quhistānī,

Haft Bāb, ed. 22, trans. 22; Ṭūsī and Ḥasan-i Maḥmūd, *Rawḍa-yi Taslīm*, ed. 170–171, trans. 137. Cf. Ghālib, *Aʿlām al-Ismāʿīliyya* (Beirut, 1964), table appended to the end of the book; Abū al-Maʿālī, "Risālat al-Uṣūl wa-al-Aḥkām," in *Khams Rasāʾil Ismāʿīliyya*, ed. Tāmir (Salamiyya, Syria, 1375/1956), 120; al-Bazāʿī, "Kitāb al-Tarātīb al-Sabʿa wa-hiya Sabʿa Tarātīb ʿalā al-Tamām wa-al-Kamāl," in *Akhbār al-Qarāmiṭa*, ed. Zakkār, 2nd ed. (Damascus, 1402/1982); al-Nuʿmān, *Kitāb Asās al-Taʾwīl*, ed. Tāmir (Beirut, [1960]), 176–177 n1; Hajnal, "On the History of the Ismāʿīlī 'Hidden Imāms' as Reflected in the Kitāb at-tarātīb as-sabʿa," *The Arabist, Budapest Studies in Arabic (Essays in Honour of Alexander Fodor on His Sixtieth Birthday)* 23 (2001), 101–116.

51. Quhistānī, *Haft Bāb*, ed. 22, trans. 21.

52. Later traditions, quite naturally, considered Qāsimshāh to have been the son of Shams al-Dīn Muḥammad. See, for example, al-Ḥusaynī, *Kitāb-i Khiṭābāt-i ʿĀliya*, ed. Ujāqī (Mumbai, 1963). It is, of course, possible that Qāsimshāh C in the genealogical tree corresponds to Qāsimshāh II of the genealogical registers, but this seems less likely as we have no indication that he had a descendant by the name of Salāmshāh who succeeded him. Moreover, the author of the *Guidance* states clearly that his opponents believed this Qāsimshāh, whose name was also Nizār, to be an Imam, claiming him to be the son of Qāsimshāh b. Mu'minshāh. However, the first Qāsimshāh named in our three registers may also be Nizārshāh, while the second was his son Qāsimshāh b. Nizārshāh. This is only possible if Qāsimshāh b. Nizārshāh had a lineal descendant named Salāmshāh who succeeded him as Imam, but again, we have no evidence of this having been the case.

53. Ṭūsī and Ḥasan-i Maḥmūd, *Rawḍa-yi Taslīm*, ed. 157, trans. 126.

54. But cf. the situation in which Joshua (Yūshaʿ b. Nūn) was appointed as a guardian for the two young boys of Aaron (Hārūn), in which it is implied that he was a *mustawdaʿ* Imam. Ibid, ed. 170, trans. 137. This incident is also related by a Ṭayyibī dāʿī, see Idrīs, "Zahr al-Maʿānī," in *Ismaili Tradition Concerning the Rise of the Fatimids*, ed. Ivanow, trans. Ivanow (London, 1942), ed. 47, trans. 233. See also al-Ḥāmidī, *Kanz al-Walad*, ed. Ghālib (Wiesbaden, 1391/1971), 206–210. The later Ṭayyibīs elaborated a rather different conception of the *mustawdaʿ* Imams, which is discussed more extensively in Ivanow, *Ibn Al-Qaddah (The Alleged Founder of Ismailism)*, 2nd rev. ed. (Mumbai, 1957), 128–132; Ivanow, *Ismaili Tradition Concerning the Rise of the Fatimids* (London, 1942), 54–56, 153–154; Lewis, *The Origins of Ismailism: A Study of the Historical Background of the Fatimid Caliphate* (New York, 1975), 49–54; Vatikiotis, *The Fatimid Theory of State* (Lahore, [1957]), 59–60, 132–133.

55. Ṭūsī and Ḥasan-i Maḥmūd, *Rawḍa-yi Taslīm*, ed. 159–160, trans. 260 n125. This English translation is taken from the Persian translation of the original Arabic. Both al-Kulaynī and al-Majlisī attribute the saying to the Imam ʿAlī; cited in Ṭūsī and Ḥasan-i Maḥmūd, *Rawḍa-yi Taslīm*, 260 n125.

56. Ṭūsī and Ḥasan-i Maḥmūd, *Rawḍa-yi Taslīm*, ed. 157, trans. 126; translation slightly modified.

57. "Dhuā: vakhatji," in *The Harvard Collection of Ismaili Literature in Indic Languages*, Ms Ism K 22 (Cambridge, MA), f. 356. The folio numbering system of the cataloger differs from the scribe's page numbering here. See Asani, *The Harvard*

Collection of Ismaili Literature in Indic Languages: A Descriptive Catalog and Finding Aid (Boston, 1992), 127. The name Mu'minshāh also occurs in Khojki ms 25 and other older manuscripts now housed at the Institute of Ismaili Studies, London. See Nanji, *Nizārī Ismāʿīlī Tradition*, 65, 166 n. 153. Note, however, that the list of contents provided by the cataloguer of this collection differs from Nanji's citation; Moir, *A Catalogue of the Khojki MSS in the Library of the Ismaili Institute* (London, 1985), [1–33].

58. "Dhoā: sāji: somaṇi: subhuaji," in *The Harvard Collection of Ismaili Literature in Indic Languages, Houghton Library*, Ms Ism K 19 (Cambridge, MA), f. 53. The folio numbering system of the cataloger differs from the scribe's page numbering here. See Asani, *Harvard Collection*, 112. The scribe had copied this list from a book, perhaps no longer extant, published by Alādīn Gulāmi Husen in 1951 vs/1895; see ff. 34–35.

59. Dāʿī Anjudānī, "[Qaṣīda-yi dhurriyya]," in *Institute of Ismaili Studies Library*, Persian ms 15030 (London), 6.

60. This couplet was found in a manuscript available to Maryam Muʿizzī, see her "Ismāʿīliyyān-i Īrān" (MA thesis, Dānishgāh-i Firdawsī, 1371–1372 HS/1992–1993), 167–168 n76.

61. Boghā, *Isamāilī Darpaṇ* (Mumbai, 1323/1906), 21; Nūr Muḥammadshāh, *Sat Varaṇī Moṭī nī Vel [a.k.a. Sat Veṇī nī Vel]* (Mumbai, 1962 vs/1905), c. 96. The manuscript version of the same work gives 1331 vs/1275 CE, which seems far too early. The disparity in the Christian era dates cited above is due to the varying methods of calculation used by the authors of the sources. Again, there is ambiguity about which Qāsimshāh is being referred to.

62. The word used, *mutaqaddim*, is ambiguous. It may also be translated as "the late" Imam Qāsimshāh.

63. The word in the text is *balāghīn*, which makes no sense in this context. I have emended it to *malāʿīn* on the basis of the text in Islāmshāh, "Haft Nukta," in *Institute of Ismaili Studies Library*, Persian ms 43 (London).

64. *Ibn ʿamm*, the son of his father's brother.

65. Islāmshāh, "Haft Nukta," in *Kitāb-i Mustaṭāb-i Haft Bāb-i Dāʿī Abū Isḥāq*, ed. Beg (Gilgit, Pakistan, 1962), 121–123.

66. Ivanow apparently had access to another Qāsimshāhī work, a *farmān* of the Imam ʿAbd al-Salām dated 895/1490 that was addressed to the Ismailis of Badakhshan and Kabul who followed the Muḥammadshāhī line. It urged them to return to the fold of the Qāsimshāhīs. Unfortunately, I am not aware of any copy of this work in an institutional collection. See Ivanow, *Ismaili Literature*, 140–141.

67. Rematulā, *Khojā Kom no Itihās* (Mumbai, 1905), 212.

68. Ivanow, *Ismaili Literature*, 134. One instance in which such a quotation occurs is [Khayrkhwāh Harātī?], *Faṣl dar Bayān-i Shinākht-i Imām*, ed. 20, trans. 36. Poonawala, *Biobibliography*, 263 does not add any new information on this figure.

69. Ivanow may have been aware of this work but confused it with the *Panj Sukhan*, which perhaps preceded it in the manuscript available to him. His description reflects the contents of this work as well. See Ivanow, *Ismaili Literature*, 140. See also the discussion of the *Panj Sukhan* elsewhere in this book.

70. Qāsim Tushtarī (Turshīzī?), "[Risāla dar Maʿrifat-i Khāliq]," in *Institute of Ismaili Studies Library*, Persian ms 15048 (London).

71. Qāsim Tushtarī (Turshīzī?), "[Risāla dar Maʿrifat-i Khāliq]," in *Institute of Ismaili Studies Library*, Persian ms 814 (London).

72. Qazwīnī, *Nuzhat al-Qulūb*, ed. Le Strange, trans. Le Strange, *The Geographical Part of the Nuzhat al-Qulūb* (Leiden, 1915–1919), ed. 143, trans. 142.

73. Ibid, ed. 143, trans. 141–142.

74. See, for example, Daftary, *Ismāʿīlīs*, 344, 362. Ḥasan-i Ṣabbāḥ himself had preached Ismailism in Khuzistan, see Daftary, *Ismāʿīlīs*, 338.

75. Sanāʾī's dates are uncertain. J. T. P. de Bruijn feels that the most likely date for his death is 525/1131, which is mentioned in a notice on the last day of his life, attached as an appendix to a prose introduction of his *Ḥadīqat al-Ḥaqīqa*. Jāmī mentions the same date in his *Nafaḥāt al-Uns*. Bruijn, "Sanāʾī," in *EI2*, vol. 9 (Leiden, 1960–2004; reprint, CD-ROM v. 1.0).

76. The second volume has, in fact, been published. See Daftary, *Ismaili Literature*, 141. Numerous attempts to secure a copy from various Iranian booksellers were unsuccessful, however.

77. Qāsim Tushtarī (Turshīzī?), "Maʿrifat—15048."

78. Qāsim Tushtarī (Turshīzī?), "Maʿrifat—814."

79. Quhistānī, "Safarnāma," in *The Continuity of the Nizari Ismaili Daʿwa*, ed. Jamal (PhD dissertation, New York University, 1996), 259. Cf. Jamal, "The Continuity of the Nizari Ismaili Daʿwa: 1256–1350" (PhD dissertation, New York University, 1996), 171; Jamal, *Surviving the Mongols*, 127.

80. Translated by collating Qāsim Tushtarī (Turshīzī?), "Maʿrifat—15048," 6 and Qāsim Tushtarī (Turshīzī?), "Maʿrifat—814," 58.

81. See Daftary, *Ismāʿīlīs*, 339, 343–344.

82. Qāsim Tushtarī (Turshīzī?), "Maʿrifat—15048," 1–2.

جماعت مستجیبان و طالبان راه یقین و دوستان خاندان طیبین و طاهرین *احسن الله احوالهم* بدانند که بر رای ارباب بصیرت و اصحاب عقیدت چون آفتاب روشن است و [sic، که] احکام ناطقان شرایع و حجتان حقایق علیه السلام [sic، علیهم السلام] بهر دور و زمان این بوده و این خواهند بود که مقصود از آفرینش هژده هزار عالم ترکیب وجود انسان است و مقصود وجود انسان از آنکه معرفت خدای تعالی حاصل کند تا معنی *و لقد کرمنا بني آدم* در ذات انسان از قوت بفعل آمده باشد.

83. Badakhshānī, *Sī wa-Shish Ṣaḥīfa*, ed. Ujaqi (Tehran, 1961), 1; Badakhshānī, *Tuḥfat al-Nāẓirīn*, ed. Beg (Gilgit, Pakistan, 1960), 1. This is repeated almost verbatim in Quhistānī, *Haft Bāb*, ed. 2, trans. 1.

84. Qāsim Tushtarī (Turshīzī?), "Maʿrifat—15048," 5.

CHAPTER 5

1. As cited in Halm, *The Fatimids and Their Traditions of Learning* (London, 1997), 92. Cf. Walker, *Exploring an Islamic Empire: Fatimid History and Its Sources* (London, 2002), 43–44, 89.

2. al-Nuʿmān, *Kitāb al-Majālis wa-al-Musāyarāt*, ed. al-Faqī, Shabbūḥ, and al-Yaʿlāwī (Tunis, 1978), 533. See also Halm, *Traditions of Learning*, 91.

3. Al-Musabbiḥī as quoted in al-Maqrīzī, *Kitāb al-mawāʿiẓ wa-al-iʿtibār bi-dhikr al-khiṭaṭ wa-al-āthār*, 2 vols. (Būlāq, 1270/1854), vol. 1, 458ff. Cf. Halm, *Traditions of Learning*, 73–74.

4. al-Maqrīzī, *Ittiʿāẓ al-ḥunafāʾ bi-akhbār al-aʾimma al-Fāṭimiyīn al-khulafāʾ*, ed. al-Shayyāl and Aḥmad, 3 vols. (Cairo, 1967–1973), vol. 2, 295. Cf. Halm, *Traditions of Learning*, 77–78.

5. Juwaynī, *Taʾrīkh-i Jahāngushāy*, ed. Qazwīnī, 3 vols. (Leiden, 1912–1937), ed. vol. 3, 269–270, trans. vol. 2, 719.

6. Bernard, "Fear of Book Assasination [*sic*] Haunts Bibliophile's Musings" (December 15, 2003), (http://www.nyobserver.com/pages/story.asp?ID=8291, accessed January 28, 2004).

7. Orwell, *Nineteen Eighty-four* (New York, 1992), 37.

8. Ṭūsī, *Sayr wa-Sulūk*, ed. Badakhchani, trans. Badakhchani, *Contemplation and Action: The Spiritual Autobiography of a Muslim Scholar* (London, 1998), ed. 19–20, trans. 50–51.

9. Ibid, ed. 19, cf. trans. 50, translation slightly modified.

10. Shams al-Dīn Tabrīzī, *Maqālāt-i Shams-i Tabrīzī,* ed. Muwaḥḥid, 2 vols. (Tehran, 1990) 18. This passage is translated in Lewis, *Rumi: Past and Present, East and West* (Oxford, 2000) 136.

11. Ṭūsī and Ḥasan-i Maḥmūd, *Rawḍa-yi Taslīm*, ed. Badakhchani, trans. Badakhchani, *Paradise of Submission: A Medieval Treatise on Ismaili Thought* (London, 2005), ed. 86, trans. 74.

12. For the Imams as the Possessors of the Command, see al-Nuʿmān b. Muḥammad, *Ikhtilāf Uṣūl al-Madhāhib*, ed. Ghālib (Beirut, 1393/1973), 40.

13. See, for example, al-Ḥusaynī, *Kitāb-i Khiṭābāt-i ʿĀliya*, ed. Ujāqī (Mumbai, 1963), 45; Kūchak, *Silk-i Gawhar Rīz*, ed. Qudertullah (Dushanbe, Tajikistan, nd), 49, 97. Muḥammad Taqī b. ʿAlī Riḍā b. Zayn al-ʿĀbidīn, *Āthār-i Muḥammadī* (Maḥallāt, Iran, 1893), 58 also refers to this Imam as Aḥmad but makes him the son of Shams al-Dīn Muḥammad, omitting Qāsimshāh from his narrative. This confusion may have occurred because Shams al-Dīn Muḥammad did, in fact, have a son name Salāmshāh, who is mentioned in "Irshād al-Ṭalibīn," in *Institute of Ismaili Studies Library*, Persian ms 15095 (London). Cf. also Mulukshāh and ʿĪsanshāh, *Gulzār-i Shams* ([Multan], 1334/1916), 289, who gives these names on the basis of the *Malfūẓ-i Kamāliyya.*

14. Rājgīrī, *Madhumālatī*, trans. Behl and Weightman, *Madhumālatī: An Indian Sufi Romance* (Oxford, 2000), xii, 245. Fidāʾī Khurāsānī, *Hidāyat al-Muʾminīn al-Ṭālibīn*, ed.

Semenov (Moscow, 1959), 119 confuses Muḥammad b. Islāmshāh and Shāh Ṭāhir of the Deccan.

15. Chunārā, *Nūram Mobīn: yāne Allāhanī pavitra rasī [English Title: Noorum-Mobin or The Sacred Cord of God]*, ed. Sufī, 4th ed. (Mumbai, 1961), 320; Chunārā, *Nurun Mobīn: athavā Allāhanī pavitra rasī*, 1st ed. (Mumbai, 1935), 516.

16. "Risāla-yi Ṣirāṭ al-Mustaqīm," in *Seekers of Union: The Ismailis from the Mongol Debacle to the Eve of the Safavid Revolution*, ed. Virani, trans. Virani, *The Epistle of the Right Path* (PhD dissertation, Harvard University, 2001), ed. 222, trans. 210.

17. Ibid, ed. 222, trans. 210–211.

18. Islāmshāh, "Haft Nukta," in *Kitāb-i Mustaṭāb-i Haft Bāb-i Dāʿī Abū Isḥāq*, ed. Beg (Gilgit, Pakistan, 1962), 115–124.

19. Islāmshāh, "Haft Nukta," in *Institute of Ismaili Studies Library*, Persian ms 43 (London).

20. An allusion to Qur'ānic verses, such as, *Thus Allah made them taste humiliation in the life of the world and verily the doom of the Hereafter will be greater if they did but know* (39:26).

21. A reference to the people of the bench (*ahl al-ṣuffa*), who were believed to be a group of companions of the Prophet who typified the ideals of piety and poverty. Some commentators believe that Quran 2:273–274 and some other verses allude to the people of the bench.

22. Islāmshāh, "Haft Nukta," ed. Ḥājī Qudrat Allāh Beg, 120–121.

اهل این طایفه اگر بطریق دیگران حسد و کینه و عداوت بر سر دنیا بر یکدیگر بورزند یا داشته باشند لایق جماعت مولانا نباشند و در آخرت از مراد نجات باز مانند، و *خزی الدنیا* و *عذاب الآخرة*، و اصحاب صفه صفا نباشند...و جماعت که بر یک طریقه اند و باشند باید که خون و رگ و بدن و روح ایشان با یکدیگر اتفاق داشته باشند. و اگر بخلاف این باشند نام ایشان در مجموعه قایم ننویسند. و معلوم است که مخالفت اهل دنیا با یکدیگر بسبب حرص دنیا و مال و جاه است. اولاً آنکه این جماعت طلب حرص دنیا ننمایند و نفس خطیر و عمر عزیز را فدای برای مرداری بسیار خصم نگردانند. قطعه:

این جهان بر مثال مرداریست　　گرد او کرگسان هزار هزار
این مران را همین [sic، همی] زند مخلب　　وان مران [sic، مرین]را همین [sic، همی] زند منقار
آخر الامر بگذرند همه　　وز همه باز ماند این مردار

23. The word مقتصد has been translated here as "to strive," rather than the more common understanding of "people of the middle course," in accord with Suhrāb Walī Badakhshānī's Persian rendering, جهد کنندگان. See Badakhshānī, *Sī wa-Shish Ṣaḥīfa*, ed. Ujaqi (Tehran, 1961), 63.

24. Ibid.

25. Quhistānī, *Haft Bāb*, ed. Ivanow, trans. Ivanow, *Haft Bab or "Seven Chapters"* (Mumbai, 1959), ed. 21, cf. trans. 21. Cf. [pseudo-Nāṣir-i Khusraw: Khayrkhwāh Harātī?], *Kalām-i Pīr*, ed. Ivanow, trans. Ivanow (Mumbai, 1935), ed. 48–49, trans. 40–41.

26. Quhistānī, *Haft Bāb*, 21–22, cf. trans. 21. Cf. [pseudo-Nāṣir-i Khusraw: Khayrkhwāh Harātī?], *Kalām-i Pīr*, ed. 78, trans. 73.

27. Ṣadr al-Dīn, "Sāmi rājo āve jaṅgī ḍhol vajāve," in *100 Ginānanī Chopaḍī*, 5th ed., vol. 2 (Mumbai, 1993 vs/1936), v. 2.

28. al-Dimashqī, *Nukhbat al-Dahr fī ʿAjāʾib al-Barr wa-al-Baḥr* (Copenhagen, 1874), 233. Cf. Lewis, "Kamāl al-Dīn's Biography of Rashīd al-Dīn Sinān," *Arabica* 13, no. 3 (1966): 249.

29. Cited in Daftary, *The Assassin Legends: Myths of the Ismailis* (London, 1994), 93.

30. See Ivanow, *Ismaili Literature: A Bibliographical Survey*, 2nd amplified ed. (Tehran, 1963), 173.

31. See Ghālib, *Sinān Rashīd al-Dīn: Shaykh al-Jabal al-Thālith* (Beirut, 1967), 33; Mirza, *Syrian Ismailism: The Ever Living Line of the Imamate* (Richmond, Surrey, 1997), 101; Tāmir, ed., *Khams Rasāʾil Ismāʿīliyya* (Salamiyya, Syria, 1375/1956), 13. Also see Poonawala, *Biobibliography of Ismāʿīlī Literature* (Malibu, CA, 1977), 293. Tamir actually quotes this work in his "Ḥaqīqat Ikhwān al-Ṣafāʾ wa-Khullān al-Wafāʾ," *al-Mashriq* 51 (1957): 130ff. Cf. Mirza, *Syrian Ismailism*, 101, in which the author dates the *Fuṣūl wa-Akhbār* to the 8th/14th century.

32. See Tāmir, ed., *Khams Rasāʾil*, 89–97. This work is esoteric in nature and does not refer to the author's journey to visit the Imam. See also Ivanow, *Ismaili Literature*, 172.

33. These are the *Risāla fī al-radd ʿalā al-Badakhshānī* and *Risālat al-Shifāʾ min al-wabāʾ*; see Poonawala, *Biobibliography*, 294.

34. Ivanow, *Ismaili Literature*, 172; Mirza, *Syrian Ismailism*, 102.

35. Idrīs, *ʿUyūn al-Akhbār wa-Funūn al-Āthār*, ed. Sayyid, trans. Walker and Pomerantz, *The Fatimids and the Successors in Yaman: The History of an Islamic Community, Arabic Edition and English Summary of Volume 7 of Idrīs ʿImād al-Dīn's ʿUyūn al-Akhbār*, vol. 7 (London, 2002), ed. 211–212, trans. 78.

36. Crowe, "Samarḳand," in *EI2*, vol. 8 (Leiden, 1960–2004; reprint, CD-ROM v. 1.0); Manz, "Tīmūr Lang," in *EI2*, vol. 10 (Leiden, 1960–2004; reprint, CD-ROM v. 1.0); Manz, "Ulugh Beg," in *EI2*, vol. 10 (Leiden, 1960–2004; reprint, CD-ROM v. 1.0).

37. "Risāla-yi Ṣirāṭ al-Mustaqīm," ed. 229, trans. 217.

38. Juwaynī, *Jahāngushāy*, ed. vol. 3, 148, trans. vol. 2, 645. Cf. Stern, "The Early Ismāʿīlī Missionaries in North-West Persia and in Khurāsān and Transoxiana," *BSO(A)S* 23 (1960): 85–87, in which he expresses suspicion about this information.

39. Cited in Lewis, *The Origins of Ismailism: A Study of the Historical Background of the Fatimid Caliphate* (New York, 1975), 71.

40. Cited in ibid.

41. Casanova, "Un nouveau manuscrit de la secte des Assassins," *JA* 11 série, no. 19 (1922): 126–135; Qazwīnī, *Yāddāshthā-yi Qazwīnī*, ed. Afshār, vol. 8 (Tehran, 1332–1354 HS/1953–1975), vol. 8, 110–143. See also Daftary, *The Ismāʿīlīs: Their History and Doctrines* (Cambridge, 1990), 598 n36, 601 n61.

42. See, for example, the genealogy provided by Fayḍ Muḥammad b. Khwāja Amīr Muḥammad, *Shajara*, as recorded in Ivanow, "The Sect of Imam Shah in Gujrat," *JBBRAS* 12 (1936): 31. Cf. Nanji, *The Nizārī Ismāʿīlī Tradition in the Indo-Pakistan Subcontinent* (Delmar, NY, 1978), 139–140, in which the list is not based on genealogy, but on succession to the office of pīr. I myself have seen a number of these *shajaras* in manuscripts and scrolls preserved at the shrines.

43. al-Nuʿmān, *Risālat Iftitāḥ al-Daʿwa*, ed. al-Qāḍī (Beirut, 1971), 45, 47.

44. al-Nuʿmān, *Taʾwīl al-Daʿāʾim*, ed. al-Aʿẓamī, 3 vols. (Cairo, 1967–1972), vol. 2, 74, vol. 3, 48–49. Cf. Daftary, *Ismāʿīlīs*, 228.

45. al-Nuʿmān, *Iftitāḥ*, 45. Cf. al-Hamdani, *The Beginnings of the Ismāʿīlī Daʿwa in Northern India (now Pakistan)* (Cairo, 1956), 1; Nanji, *Nizārī Ismāʿīlī Tradition.*

46. al-Nuʿmān, *al-Majālis*, 405–411, 477–481. A letter from the Imam al-Muʿizz condemning the dāʿī's beliefs is found in the *ʿUyūn al-Akhbār* and is translated in Stern, "Heterodox Ismāʿīlism at the Time of al-Muʿizz," *BSO(A)S* 17 (1955): 11–12. The events are analyzed in Maclean, *Religion and Society in Arab Sind* (Leiden, 1989), 132–134.

47. Jalam and other variations on this name are also to be found.

48. An epistle sent by the Imam-Caliph al-Muʿizz to the victorious dāʿī is preserved in the ʿUyūn al-Akhbār and is quoted in Stern, "Ismāʿīlī Propaganda and Fatimid Rule in Sind," in *Studies in Early Ismāʿīlism* (Leiden, 1983), 181–182.

49. al-Maqdisī, *Aḥsan al-taqāsīm*, ed. deGoeje, 2nd ed. (Leiden, 1906), 485, see also 481–482. Cf. Halm, *The Empire of the Mahdi: The Rise of the Fatimids*, trans. Bonner (Leiden, 1996), 388; Stern, "Ismāʿīlī Propaganda," 183.

50. On the Ismaili state in Multan, see al-Jurbādhaqānī, *Tarjuma-yi Taʾrīkh-i Yamīnī*, ed. Shiʿār (Tehran, 1345 HS/1966), 278–280; *Ḥudūd al-ʿĀlam*, trans. Minorsky, *Ḥudūd al-ʿĀlam, the Regions of the World*, 2nd ed. (London, 1970), 178–180; Mīrkhwānd, *Rawḍat al-Ṣafāʾ*, 10 vols. (Tehran, 1338–1339 HS/1959–1960), vol. 4, 96–97.

51. al-Hamdani, *Beginnings*, 7.

52. al-Jurbādhaqānī, *Tarjuma*, 369–373; Gardīzī, *Zayn al-Akhbār*, ed. Ḥabībī (Tehran, 1347 HS/1968), 181. Ibn Taghrībirdī, *al-Nujūm al-Zāhira fī mulūk Miṣr wa-al-Qāhira* (Cairo, 1348–1391/1929–1972), vol. 4, 232. Cf. Daftary, *Ismāʿīlīs*, 194.

53. Stern, "Ismāʿīlī Propaganda," 303.

54. For details with citations of sources, see Daftary, *Ismāʿīlīs*, 210, 636 n121; Spuler, "Ḥasanak," in *EI2*, vol. 3 (Leiden, 1960–2004; reprint, CD-ROM v. 1.0).

55. Abu-Izzeddin, *The Druzes: A New Study of Their History, Faith and Society* (Leiden, 1984), 73, 108, 236; Daftary, *Ismāʿīlīs*, 198; Sacy, *Exposé de la religion des Druzes*, 2 vols. (Paris, 1838), vol. 2, 335–348.

56. al-Hamdani, *Beginnings*, 8.

57. See al-Hamdani, "Some Unknown Ismaili Authors and Their Works," *JRAS* (1933): 321, 324. An indication that al-Mustanṣir had received requests from ʿUmān and India to send deputies to fill vacancies left by the death of their dāʿīs is found in the letter dated 476/1083. His formal authorization for a certain dāʿī's appointment to a post in India is found in another letter dated 481/1088.

58. Jūzjānī, *Ṭabaqāt-i Nāṣirī*, ed. Ḥabībī, 2nd ed. (Kabul, 1342–1343 HS/1963–1964), trans. 363.

59. Ibid, trans. 365, transliteration modified.

60. Ibid, trans. 293.

61. Khayrkhwāh Harātī, "Risāla," in *Taṣnīfāt-i Khayrkhwāh Harātī*, ed. Ivanow, *Taṣnīfāt-i Khayrkhwāh Harātī* (Tehran, 1961), 28.

62. Imāmshāh, *Janatpurī* ([Mumbai?], nd), v. 83; Naṣīr al-Dīn, "Huṃ balahārī tame shāhā rājā," in *100 Ginān nī Chopaḍī*, 5th ed., vol. 2 (Mumbai, 1993 vs/1936); Nūr Muḥammadshāh, *Sat Varaṇī Moṭī* ([Mumbai?], nd), cc. 190–197.

63. Nanji, *Nizārī Ismāʿīlī Tradition*, 72.

64. Daftary, *Ismāʿīlīs*, 459.

65. See Nanji, *Nizārī Ismāʿīlī Tradition*, 72–73 and W. Ivanow's footnote to Hooda, "Some Specimens of Satpanth Literature," in *Collectanea*, ed. Ivanow, vol. 1 (Leiden, 1948), 106. The footnote is confused and should possible be read as "ʿAbdu's-Salam Shah, the *son* [not father] of Shah Mustanṣir bi'l-lah II."

66. al-Ḥusaynī, *Khiṭābāt*, khitab 23.

67. See, for example, Ṣadr al-Dīn, "Aj sahi māhādin bujo bhev," in *100 Ginānanī Chopaḍī*, 5th ed., vol. 1 (Mumbai, 1990 vs/1934), vv. 1, 3; Ṣadr al-Dīn, "Āshā: trī: trī: lokā :l: dhara-alī: hek: vado: sāmī," in *102 Ginānajī: Chopaḍī:*, ed. Devarāj, 2nd ed., vol. 4 (Mumbai, 1961 vs/[1905]), v. 5; Ṣadr al-Dīn, "Ejio: āeo: āeo: haṃsejo: var: rājā:," in *102 Ginānajī: Chopaḍī:*, ed. Devarāj, 2nd ed., vol. 4 (Mumbai, 1961 vs/[1905]), v. 6; Ṣadr al-Dīn, "Hame umāyā ne kāyam pāyā," in *100 Ginānanī Chopaḍī*, 4th ed., vol. 5 (Mumbai, 1990 vs/1934), v. 2; Ṣadr al-Dīn, "Jem jem jugatasuṃ pirīt karevā," in *100 Ginānanī Chopaḍī*, 5th ed., vol. 2 (Mumbai, 1993 vs/1936), v. 6; Ṣadr al-Dīn, "Jituṃ: lāl: sirie: e: sāraṅg: dhar-āshā: tribhovar: vado: sāmī:," in *102 Ginānajī: Chopaḍī:*, ed. Devarāj, 2nd ed., vol. 4 (Mumbai, 1961 vs/[1905]), v. 7; Ṣadr al-Dīn, "Jugā jug shāhā avatāraj dhareā [a.k.a. Sen Akhāḍo]," in *100 Ginānanī Chopaḍī*, 5th ed., vol. 2 (Mumbai, 1993 vs/1936), v. 1; Ṣadr al-Dīn, "Kāṃ bāndho māyā puravase ho kāyā pur," in *100 Ginānanī Chopaḍī*, 4th ed., vol. 6 (Mumbai, 1989 vs/1933), v. 8; Ṣadr al-Dīn, "Kiratā: jugeṃ: dhuār: utar: dise: huaḍā," in *102 Ginānajī: Chopaḍī:*, ed. Devarāj, 2nd ed., vol. 4 (Mumbai, 1961 vs/[1905]), v. 1; Ṣadr al-Dīn, "Pañchame [sic] āyā shāhā paratak pāyā," in *100 Ginānanī Chopaḍī*, 5th ed., vol. 3 (Mumbai, 1991 vs/1935), v. 1; Ṣadr al-Dīn, "Sāmi rājā jampuadipe umāeoji," in *100 Ginānanī Chopaḍī*, 5th ed., vol. 1 (Mumbai, 1990 vs/1934), v. 7; Ṣadr al-Dīn, "Shāhāke: hekamaṃn: āaṃhi: sirevo: jire: yārā: mumanājio," in *102 Ginānajī: Chopaḍī:*, ed. Devarāj, 2nd ed., vol. 4 (Mumbai, 1961 vs/[1905]), v. 13. Cf. Nanji, *Nizārī Ismāʿīlī Tradition*, 72.

68. Ṣadr al-Dīn, "Kiratā: jugeṃ: dhuār: utar: dise: huaḍā," v. 1.

69. See Nanji, *Nizārī Ismāʿīlī Tradition*, 74.

70. Schimmel, *Islam in the Indian Subcontinent* (Leiden, 1980), 73.

71. Qā'inī, "Naṣā'iḥ-i Shāhrukhī," in *Österreichische Nationalbibliothek*, Monastic Microfilm Project Number 22 249, University Microfilms, Codex Vindobonensis Palatinus. A.f. 112 (Flügel 1858) (Vienna, 1970), 299a, 300b. The description below is taken from pages 295a–304b of the manuscript. Specific pages are only indicated in the case of direct quotations.

72. A summary of the contents of the whole work is given in Flugel, *Die Arabischen, Persischen und Turkischen Handschriften der Kaiserlich-königlichen Hofbibliothek zu*

Wien (Wien, 1867), vol. 3, 289–291. See also Hammer-Purgstall, ed., *Codices Arabicos, Persicos, Turcicos, Bibliothecae Caesareo-Regio-Palatinae Vindobonensis* (Vindobonae, 1820), n. 163; *Naṣāʾiḥ-i Shāh Rukhī*, Persian ms. 1858 (cf. Flugel), folio 302a. Cf. Cortese, "Eschatology and Power in Mediaeval Persian Ismailism" (PhD dissertation, University of London, 1993), 195–197; Hammer-Purgstall, *The History of the Assassins, Derived from Oriental Sources*, trans. Wood (London, 1835), 204–210. Recently, much light has been shed on the author of this treatise in Subtelny, "The Sunni Revival under Shāh-Rukh and Its Promoters: A Study of the Connection Between Ideology and Higher Learning in Timurid Iran," in *Proceedings of the 27th Meeting of Haneda Memorial Hall Symposium on Central Asia and Iran: August 30, 1993* (Kyoto, 1994), 16–21; Subtelny and Khalidov, "The Curriculum of Islamic Higher Learning in Timurid Iran in the Light of the Sunni Revival under Shāh-Rukh," *JAOS* 115, no. 2 (1995): 217–222.

73. al-Ḥusaynī, *Risāla-yi Mazārāt-i Harāt (=Maqṣad al-Iqbāl-i Sulṭāniyya)*, ed. Saljūqī, vol. 1, part 1 (Kabul, 1967), 90 and other sources cited in Subtelny and Khalidov, "Curriculum of Islamic Higher Learning," 219 n94. The adherents of the Shāfiʿī school were considered acceptable.

74. Qāʾinī, "Naṣāʾiḥ-i Shāhrukhī," 298b.

75. Hodgson, *The Order of Assassins*, 111.

76. See ibid, 95–96. Hodgson draws his account from Rāwandī and Ibn al-Athīr, year 500 as well as Ibn al-Qalānisī.

77. Jūzjānī's testimony is not to be taken lightly. In 1224, he himself was sent to the Ismāʿīlī ruler Abū al-Fatḥ Shihāb al-Dīn Manṣūr on an embassy via Qāʾin. Despite his dim view of the community in general, he seems to have been quite taken by this Abū al-Fatḥ and praises him lavishly for his sagacity and wisdom, as well as for his courtesy to visitors, poor wayfarers, and refugees fleeing from the Mongols. See Bosworth, "The Ismaʿilis of Quhistān and the Maliks of Nīmrūz or Sīstān," in *Mediaeval Ismaʿili History and Thought*, ed. Daftary (Cambridge, 1996), 226.

78. Qāʾinī, "Naṣāʾiḥ-i Shāhrukhī," 303a. On Shahrukh's religious proclivities, see Morgan, *Medieval Persia, 1040–1797* (London, 1988), 95.

79. Daftary, *Ismāʿīlīs*, 454, 456; Manz, "Shāh Rukh," in *EI2*, vol. 9 (Leiden, 1960–2004; reprint, CD-ROM v. 1.0); Savory, "Ḳāsim-i Anwār," in *EI2*, vol. 4 (Leiden, 1960–2004; reprint, CD-ROM v. 1.0).

80. Qāʾinī, "Naṣāʾiḥ-i Shāhrukhī," 303a.

81. Cf. statements in the *Ḥadīqat al-Shīʿa* about a group known as the Shamrākhiyya who are considered heretics (*mulḥids*) and who use Sufism (*taṣawwuf*) to hide their beliefs; [pseudo-Aḥmad b. Muḥammad Ardabīlī], *Ḥadīqat al-Shīʿa* (Tehran, 1964), 580. See also Babayan, *Mystics, Monarchs, and Messiahs: Cultural Landscapes of Early Modern Iran* (Cambridge, MA, 2002), 420, 284 n27, in which further details are given and the authorship and dating of this seventeenth-century work is considered.

82. Qāʾinī, "Naṣāʾiḥ-i Shāhrukhī," 300a.

83. The final subjugation of the Syrian Nizārī fortresses is recorded in Abū al-Fidā, "al-Mukhtaṣar [fī] taʾrīkh [or akhbār] al-bashar (extracts with French translation)," in *Recueil des Historiens des Croisades: Historiens Orientaux*, vol. 1 (Paris, 1872–1906), vol. 1, 153–154; Ibn Shaddād, *Taʾrīkh al-Malik al-Ẓāhir*, ed. Ḥuṭayṭ (Wiesbaden, 1983),

37, 60, 323 and others. For full references and a summary of the information therein, see Daftary, *Ismāʿīlīs*, 430–434.

84. This is a reference to Quran 4:65.

85. The Arabic text of the letter is found in Lewis, "Sinān," 263. I have followed Lewis's translation, pp. 232–233, but have modified it in places.

86. See Daftary, *Ismāʿīlīs*, 433.

87. Ibn Baṭṭuta, *Riḥla*, trans. Gibb, *The Travels of Ibn Battuta*, 4 vols. (Cambridge, 1971), vol. 1, 106–109.

88. Ibn Kathīr, *al-Bidāya wa-al-Nihāya* (Beirut, 1977), vol 12, 208; cf. Saleh, "The Use of Bāṭinī, Fidāʾī and Ḥashīshī Sources in the Writings of the Arab Sunni Historians," *SI* 82 (1995): 40.

89. Ibn al-Qalānisī, *Dhayl Taʾrīkh Dimashq*, ed. Amedroz (Leiden, 1908), 213. Cf. Saleh, "Bāṭinī, Fidāʾī and Ḥashīshī," 38.

90. An interesting examination of the development of this literary trope is found in Guillaume, "Les Ismaéliens dans le Roman de Baybars: Genèse d'un type littéraire," *SI* 84 (1996).

91. Mirza, *Syrian Ismailism*, 65–66.

92. Chambers, "The Troubadours and the Assassins," *Modern Language Notes* 64 (1949). See also Daftary, *Assassin Legends*, passim.

93. This edition is described and used extensively by Yves Marquet who, however, does not list the work in his bibliography. See ʿĀmir b. ʿĀmir al-Baṣrī, *Tāʾiyya*, ed. Marquet, trans. Marquet, *Poésie ésoterique Ismailïenne: La Tāʾiyya de ʿĀmir b. ʿĀmir al-Baṣrī* (Paris, 1985).

94. Tāmir, ed., *Arbaʿ Rasāʾil Ismāʿīliyya* (Salamiyya, Syria, 1952).

95. ʿĀmir b. ʿĀmir al-Baṣrī, *Tāʾiyya*. While the learned editor is convinced of the Nizari character of this poem, there are verses that suggest that it may not be so, or else that Nizari doctrine in Syria differed in detail from Persian Nizarism.

96. Fidāʾī Khurāsānī, *Hidāyat*, 119.

97. Nūr Muḥammadshāh, "Sat Varaṇi Moṭi ni Vel," in *Personal Library of Mr Abdulrasool Mawji* (Calgary, Canada), c. 119, but cf. c. 157, which gives him an imamate of thirty years. Boghā, *Isamāilī Darpaṇ* (Mumbai, 1323/1906), 22; Nūr Muḥammadshāh, *Sat Varaṇī Moṭī nī Vel [a.k.a. Sat Veṇī nī Vel]* (Mumbai, 1962 vs/1905), c. 107. This tallies with a date associated with Islāmshāh in one of the Gināns, 1452 vs/1396 CE; Ḥasan Kabīr al-Dīn, "Saṃvat chaud so ne bāvan," in *100 Ginān nī Chopaḍī*, 4th ed., vol. 5 (Mumbai, 1990 vs/1934), v. 11. Other anachronisms, however, make it clear that there are later interpolations in this composition.

98. Boghā, *Isamāilī Darpaṇ*, 22; Nūr Muḥammadshāh, *Sat Varaṇī Moṭī nī Vel [a.k.a. Sat Veṇī nī Vel]*, c. 108.

99. Rematulā, *Khojā Kom no Itihās* (Mumbai, 1905), 212.

100. Muʿizzī, "Ismāʿīliyyān-i Īrān" (MA thesis, Dānishgāh-i Firdawsī, 1371–1372 HS/1992–1993), 123–126.

101. In South Asia, this ceremony is known as *ghaṭ-pāṭ*. Nanji, "Ritual and Symbolic Aspects of Islam in African Contexts," in *Islam in Local Contexts*, ed. Martin, vol. 17 (Leiden, 1982) is a cursory article on the subject. More details may be found in Dossa,

"Ritual and Daily Life: Transmission and Interpretation of the Ismaili Tradition in Vancouver" (PhD dissertation, University of British Columbia, 1985); Nazarali, *A Brief Outline of Ismaili Rites, Rituals, Ceremonies and Festivals* ([Edmonton, Canada?], nd); Kamāl al-Dīn and Kamāl al-Dīn, *Manāsik Majālis wa-Tasbīḥāt* (Karachi, 2004), 101–103.

102. See, for example, Ḥasan Kabīr al-Dīn, "Sarave jivuṃnā jāre lekhāṃ lese," in *100 Ginānanī Chopaḍī*, 5th ed., vol. 2 (Mumbai, 1993 vs/1936), vv. 44–46.

103. *Dhuā: gaṭ: pāṭ - sāñji: somaṇi: tathā subhuhaji: khās: imāmii: isamāili: khojā: jamātaje: vāsate*, (Mumbai, 1958 vs/1902), 18. See also, for example, Asani, *The Harvard Collection of Ismaili Literature in Indic Languages: A Descriptive Catalog and Finding Aid* (Boston, 1992), 665.

CHAPTER 6

1. Dughlāt, *Ta'rīkh-i Rashīdī*, ed. Thackston, trans. Thackston, *Mirza Haydar Dughlat's Tarikh-i Rashidi: A History of the Khans of Moghulistan* ([Cambridge, MA], 1996), trans. vol. 2, 3.

2. Ivanow, *Ismaili Literature: A Bibliographical Survey*, 2nd amplified ed. (Tehran, 1963), 168.

3. The information that follows is derived from discussions with a number of Afghan Ismaili refugees, with Dr. Latif Pedram, former director of this library, whom I had the opportunity to meet during the UNESCO-sponsored Nāṣir-i Khusraw millennial celebrations in Tajikistan, and Stavridès, "Ils ont massacré les livres au lance-roquette" (January 10, 2002), (Groupe Express-Expansion, http://www.lexpress.fr/info/monde/dossier/afghanistan/dossier.asp?ida=418403, accessed February 28, 2006).

4. My enquiries among Afghan Ismailis hailing from different regions found that this expression is common in Afghan Badakhshan, but not among the Hazāra Ismailis resident in Kabul.

5. Ḥusayn, "Āmad zamān ānkih maḥabbat ʿīyan kunīm," in *Institute of Ismaili Studies Library*, Persian ms 14698 (London).

ما کعبه حقیقت خود انگوان کنیم

6. Niʿmat Allāh Walī, *Kulliyāt-i dīwān*, ed. ʿIlmī (Tehran, 1333 HS/1954), 585–586. Daftary reports that the poem and genealogy are reproduced in near contemporary biographies written by ʿAbd al-Razzāq Kirmānī (d. after 911/1505) and ʿAbd al-ʿAzīz Wāʿiẓ (d. after 839/1436), edited in Aubin, *Matériaux pour la biographie de Shāh Niʿmatullāh Walī Kermānī* (Tehran, 1956), 21–23, 274–276. See Daftary, *The Ismāʿīlīs: Their History and Doctrines* (Cambridge, 1990), 78 and n58, where he also lists additional references.

7. See Algar, "Niʿmat-Allāhiyya," in *EI2*, vol. 8 (Leiden, 1960–2004; reprint, CD-ROM v. 1.0).

8. See Bashir, "Between Mysticism and Messianism: The Life and Thought of Muhammad Nurbakś (d. 1464)" (PhD dissertation, Yale University, 1997), 10 and Bashir, *Fazlallah Astarabadi and the Hurufis* (Oxford, 2005).

9. The account below is drawn from Shāmī, *Ẓafarnāma*, ed. Tauer, trans. Tauer, *Histoire des Conquêtes de Tamerlan, Intitulée Ẓafarnāma* (Prague, 1937–1956), vol. 1, 136; Yazdī, *Ẓafarnāma*, ed. ʿAbbāsī (Tehran, 1336 HS/1957), vol. 1, 443–444; Mīrkhwānd, *Rawḍat al-Ṣafā*ʾ, 10 vols. (Tehran, 1338–1339 HS/1959–1960), vol. 6, 211–212; and Khwāndamīr, *Ḥabīb al-Siyar*, as quoted by Dihgān, *Kārnāma*, 47–49. This passage from the *Ḥabīb al-Siyar* does not appear in the critical edition and translation Khwāndamīr, *Ḥabīb al-Siyar*, ed. Thackston, trans. Thackston, *Habibu's-Siyar, Tome Three. The Reign of the Mongol and the Turk* (Cambridge, MA, 1994). Dihgān, *Kārnāma, Yā dū bakhsh-i dīgar az taʾrikh-i Arāk* ([Tehran], 1345 HS/1966), 45–46. The leading quotation of this chapter is from p.1 of Dihgānʿs *Kārnāma*.

10. Marlowe, *Tamburlaine the Great: Part I*, ed. Dyce (Project Gutenberg, November 1997, accessed February 21, 2006).

11. Ibid.

12. Morgan, *Medieval Persia, 1040–1797* (London, 1988), 93.

13. Sharaf al-Dīn ʿAlī Yazdī, *Ẓafarnāma*, as translated in Davy, *Political and Military Institutes of Tamerlane* (Delhi, 1972), 66–68.

14. It should be noted, though, that while the Tehran edition of the *Rawḍat al-Ṣafā*ʾ reads *qalʿa-i Ānkuwān*, "the fort of Anjudān," another exemplar reads *qarya-yi Ānguwān*, "the village of Anjudān"; see Dihgān, *Kārnāma*, 49.

15. See, for example, Daftary, *Ismāʿīlīs*, 459; Muʿizzī, "Ismāʿīliyyān-i Īrān" (MA thesis, Dānishgāh-i Firdawsī, 1371–1372 HS/1992–1993), 107; Poonawala, *Biobibliography of Ismāʿīlī Literature* (Malibu, CA, 1977), 268.

16. Information on Ivanow's activities can be found in Daftary, "W. Ivanow: A Biographical Notice," *Middle Eastern Studies* 8, no. 2 (May 1972): 241–244.

17. Dihgān, *Kārnāma*, 45–46.

18. The eighteenth-century family tree cited in Rematulā, *Khojā Kom no Itihās* (Mumbai, 1905), 213 identifies this Imam's residence and burial place as Shahr Bābak. The second part of the assertion, at least, is incorrect.

19. Boghā, *Isamāilī Darpaṇ* (Mumbai, 1323/1906), 22; Nūr Muḥammadshāh, *Sat Varaṇī Moṭī nī Vel [a.k.a. Sat Veṇī nī Vel]* (Mumbai, 1962 VS/1905), 108. The manuscript version of Nūr Muḥammadshāh's work does not provide any dates.

20. Muḥammad Taqī b. ʿAlī Riḍā b. Zayn al-ʿĀbidīn, *Āthār-i Muḥammadī* (Maḥallāt, Iran, 1893), 63; Mulukshāh and ʿĪsanshāh, *Gulzār-i Shams* ([Multan], 1334/1916), 290, Rematulā, *Khojā Kom no Itihās*, 213. The family tree omits "bi'llāh." Confusing this Imam with one of the Muḥammadshāhī line, Fidā'ī Khurāsānī, *Hidāyat al-Muʾminīn al-Ṭālibīn*, ed. Semenov (Moscow, 1959), 132 gives the name al-Mustanṣir bi'llāh Ḥaydar ʿAlīshāh. The *Hidāyat al-Muʾminīn*, p. 133, also has the Imam send Bābā Shahīdī to Herat, Mullā ʿAbd al-Raḥmān to Jām, and Mīrẓā Abū al-Qāsim Āstarābādī to Amīr Muḥammad Ḥakīm in Rayy.

21. Mustanṣir bi'llāh (=Gharīb Mīrzā?), *Pandiyāt-i Jawānmardī*, ed. Ivanow, trans. Ivanow, *Pandiyat-i Jawanmardi or "Advices of Manliness"* (Leiden, 1953).

22. Dihgān, *Kārnāma*, 26. Dihgān's quotation of the second Quranic verse is inaccurate.

23. For some inexplicable reason, Ibrāhīm Dihgān makes this read *Mustanṣir bi'llāh-i duwwum*, i.e., the second. This reading is not to be found in the works of W. Ivanow, F. Daftary, or M. Muʿizzī. The carbon impression provided as plate 7 in Ivanow's Imam Mustanṣir bi'llāh, *Pandiyāt-i Jawānmardī*, while difficult to read, does not seem to contain this word. It must therefore be considered an error on the part of this Iranian scholar. The remnants of the *ṣandūq* are shown in Muʿizzī, "Ismāʿīliyyān-i Īrān," 104, and Mustanṣir bi'llāh (=Gharīb Mīrzā?), *Pandiyāt*, plate 6 (mislabeled plate 7); the mausoleum can be seen in Daftary, *Ismāʿīlīs*, 457 and the aforementioned edition and translation of the *Pandiyāt* by Ivanow.

24. It seems that W. Ivanow had become aware of the existence of this Ismaili poet as early as 1949. That he was familiar with the writings of Dāʿī is clear from a personal letter he sent to his French colleague, Henry Corbin, from Bombay on December 12, 1949. See Schmidtke, ed., *Correspondance Corbin-Ivanow: Lettres Échangés entre Henry Corbin et Vladimir Ivanow de 1947 à 1966* (Paris, 1999), 42. It is puzzling that he never mentions this author in academic writings such as in Ivanow, *Ismaili Literature*.

25. Turkumān, *Taʾrīkh-i ʿĀlamārā-yi ʿAbbāsī* (Tehran, 1314/1897), 182–183.

26. Cited in Muʿizzī, "Ismāʿīliyyān-i Īrān," 40. There is another poet with the *takhalluṣ* Dāʿī who seems to have prepared a popular selection of about one thousand couplets from Sanāʾī's *Ḥadīqat al-Ḥaqīqa* entitled *Laṭīfat al-ʿirfān*. His full name was Niẓām al-Dīn Maḥmūd Ḥusaynī Shīrāzī, and he died in 867/1463 or 870/1466, which may correspond with the imamate of Mustanṣir bi'llāh. The pen name "Dāʿī" is mentioned in the introductory lines of the selection. See Bruijn, "Sanāʾī," in *EI2*, vol. 9 (Leiden, 1960–2004; reprint, CD-ROM v. 1.0), 3; Bruijn, *Of Piety and Poetry: The Interaction of Religion and Literature in the Life and Works of Ḥakīm Sanāʾī of Ghazna* (Leiden, 1983), 121.

27. Turkumān, *ʿĀlamārā-yi ʿAbbāsī*, 182–183. In this passage, I have occasionally preferred the reading provided by Dihgān, *Kārnāma*, 64–65.

28. Ādhar, *Ātishkada*, ed. Nāṣirī (Tehran, 1337–1338 HS/1958–1959), vol. 3, 1248, 1316–1317.

29. Hidāyat, *Majmaʿ al-Fuṣaḥāʾ*, ed. Muṣaffā (Tehran, 1336 HS/1957), 289–290.

30. On Ibn Ḥusām, see Dawlatshāh, *Tadhkirat al-Shuʿarāʾ*, ed. Browne (London, 1901), 301; Muʿizzī, "Ismāʿīliyyān-i Īrān," 327–330; Aubin, "Un Santon Quhistani de l'Époque Timouride," *Revue des Études Islamiques* 35 (1967): 187–188, 195, 201 et passim; Khwāndamīr, *Ḥabīb al-Siyar*, ed. Humāʾī (Tehran, 1333 HS/1954), vol. 4, 336; Maʿṣūm ʿAlīshāh, *Tarāʾiq al-Ḥaqāʾiq*, ed. Maḥjūb (Tehran, 1345 HS/1966), vol. 3, 112; Shushtarī, *Majālis al-Muʾminīn* (Tehran, 1299/1882), 533.

31. Aḥmad Aḥmadī Bīrjandī, introduction to Khūsfī, *Dīwān-i Muḥammad b. Ḥusām Khūsfī: Shāmil-i qasīdahā, ghazalhā, tarkībbandhā, tarjīʿbandhā, musammaṭhā, mathnawīhā, qiṭʿahā, rubāʿīhā*, ed. Bīrjandī and Taqī (Mashhad, 1366 HS/1988), 11–12.

32. Dawlatshāh, *Tadhkirat al-Shuʿarāʾ*, 302; Khwāndamīr, *Ḥabīb al-Siyar*, vol. 4, 336. See also Aubin, "Un Santon Quhistani," 187–188 n3; Shushtarī, *Majālis al-Muʾminīn*, 536.

33. See Muʿizzī, "Ismāʿīliyyān-i Īrān," 329.

34. [pseudo-Nāṣir-i Khusraw: Khayrkhwāh Harātī?], *Kalām-i Pīr*, ed. Ivanow, trans. Ivanow (Mumbai, 1935), ed. 62, 63, 72, trans. 56, 57, 67.

35. A picture of the mausoleum can be seen in Muʿizzī, "Ismāʿīliyyān-i Īrān," 328.

36. The editor of Ibn Ḥusām's *Dīwān* quotes this verse in his introduction, p. 17. See also p. 359 n102 in the same work.

37. Khūsfī, *Dīwān*, 301–302; Muʿizzī, "Ismāʿīliyyān-i Īrān," 384, 416 n75. Qāsim-i Anwār's name is found in [Khayrkhwāh Harātī?], *Faṣl dar Bayān-i Shinākht-i Imām*, ed. Ivanow, 3rd rev. ed. (Tehran, 1960), 13; cf. [Khayrkhwāh Harātī?], *Faṣl dar Bayān-i Shinākht-i Imām*, trans. Ivanow, 2nd rev. ed. (Mumbai, 1947), trans. 29.

38. Ivanow, *Ismaili Literature*, 163.

39. See Badakhshānī, *Sī wa-Shish Ṣaḥīfa*, ed. Ujaqi (Tehran, 1961); Badakhshānī, *Tuḥfat al-Nāẓirīn*, ed. Beg (Gilgit, Pakistan, 1960), 1–85; Ivanow, *Ismaili Literature*; Poonawala, *Biobibliography*, 267.

40. Badakhshānī, *Sī wa-Shish Ṣaḥīfa*, 55. A copy of this work was possibly found by Semenov, "Opisanie ismailitskikh rukopisey, sobranikh A. A. Semyonovim [Description of Ismāʿīlī manuscripts, A. A. Semenov's collection]," *Izvestiya Rossiyskoy Akademii Nauk/ Bulletin de l'Académie des Sciences de Russie (Petrograd)* 6 série, no. 12 (1918): 2190 n2.

41. See note 54, chapter 1.

42. Cited in Muʿizzī, "Ismāʿīliyyān-i Īrān," 169–170 n91, who believes it is with regards to the Imam ʿAbd al-Salām. The meter is *ramal maḥdhūf muthamman*.

آمد آن عیسی دم مریم نجات او را سلام — از کجا از کعبه مستنصر بالله امام
زین بشارت هر که واقف گشت جانش تازه شد — هر که زان دوری کند والله اعلم بالسلام
چند اورا مرحبا زان مژده کامد بی خلاف — از سپهر عالم دین هر نفس در جان پیام
گردن از فرمان هرآنکس کو بپیچد بی گمان — در جهنم باشد اورا عاقبت جا و مقام...
سالکی گر چند بیتی گفته شد گستاخ وار — باشد اندر رشتهء اصلاح گردد با نظام

43. Muḥammad Taqī b. ʿAlī Riḍā b. Zayn al-ʿĀbidīn, *Āthār-i Muḥammadī*, 64. Mulukshāh and ʿĪsanshāh, *Gulzār*, 290 also refers to ʿAbd al-Salām as Muḥammadshāh; Salām is also a name of God in the Quran (59:23), and so the title has a double entendre.

44. Chunārā, *Nūram Mobīn: yāne Allāhanī pavitra rasī [English Title: Noorum-Mobin or The Sacred Cord of God]*, ed. Sufi, 4th ed. (Mumbai, 1961), 340.

45. The eighteenth-century family tree cited in Rematulā, *Khojā Kom no Itihās*, 213, states, probably incorrectly, that this Imam lived in Shahr Bābak.

46. [Imām ʿAbd al-Salam?], "Panj Sukhan kih Ḥaḍrat-i Shāh Islām Farmūda and," in *Kitāb-i Mustaṭāb-i Haft Bāb-i Dāʿī Abū Isḥāq*, ed. Beg (Gilgit, Pakistan, 1962), 125–126.

47. Ivanow, *Ismaili Literature*, 140. "Deallng" emended to "dealing," "ʿalā dhikri-hī's-salām" to "ʿalā dhikri-hi's-salām," and missing quotation mark before *Faṣl-i Fārsiyān* added.

48. Ibid, 140–141; "Mūḥammad-Shāhī" emended to "Muḥammad-Shāhī."

49. Poonawala, *Biobibliography*, 269.

50. Ibid, 353.

51. Boghā, *Isamāilī Darpaṇ*, 22; Nūr Muḥammadshāh, *Sat Varaṇī Moṭī nī Vel [a.k.a. Sat Veṇī nī Vel]*, c. 109. Cf. Daftary, *Ismāʿīlīs*, 459. The manuscript version of Nūr Muḥammadshāh's work, which makes ʿAbd Islām the successor of Islāmshāh and immediate predecessor of Gharīb Mīrzā, gives the date 1495 vs/1439 CE in one place, but 1550 vs/1494 CE in another; see Nūr Muḥammadshāh, "Sat Varaṇi Moṭi ni Vel," in *Personal Library of Mr Abdulrasool Mawji* (Calgary, Canada), cc. 119, 157.

52. This name is also given to him in al-Ḥusaynī, *Kitāb-i Khiṭābāt-i ʿĀliya*, ed. Ujāqī (Mumbai, 1963); Muḥammad Taqī b. ʿAlī Riḍā b. Zayn al-ʿĀbidīn, *Āthār-i Muḥammadī*, 64–65; Mulukshāh and ʿĪsanshāh, *Gulzār*, 290, 295; cf. Dihgān, *Kārnāma*, 31.

53. al-Ḥusaynī, *Khiṭābāt*, 42–43. Cf. Dihgān, *Kārnāma*, 31. The *Gawhar Rīz* of Kūchak also alludes to this incident. Muḥammad Taqī b. ʿAlī Riḍā b. Zayn al-ʿĀbidīn, *Āthār-i Muḥammadī*, 65 suggests that the name was a result of this Imam's frequent retreats to a secluded place where he would sit in contemplation. Mulukshāh and ʿĪsanshāh, *Gulzār*, 290 provides the close alternative Gharībshāh; and similarly Chunārā, *Nūram Mobīn*, 344 gives Gharībullāh.

54. Dihgān, *Kārnāma*, 31; Muḥammad Taqī b. ʿAlī Riḍā b. Zayn al-ʿĀbidīn, *Āthār-i Muḥammadī*, 64–65. Chunārā, *Nūram Mobīn*, 344 indicates that this is now a village near Anjudan that has a hospice called the ʿAbbās Shāhī Khānqa.

55. Gharīb Mīrzā, "Min Kalām-i Shāh Gharīb Mīrzā," in *Institute of Ismaili Studies Library*, Persian ms 123 (London).

56. See Nanji, "A Khojki Version of the Nizari Ismaili Works: The Pandiyat-i Javanmardi," in *[Proceeding of the] 30th International Congress of Human Sciences in Asia and North Africa: Middle East 1*, ed. Lama (Mexico, 1982), 122–125. For information on the Khojki script, see Asani, *The Harvard Collection of Ismaili Literature in Indic Languages: A Descriptive Catalog and Finding Aid* (Boston, 1992); Asani, "The Khojki Script: A Legacy of Ismaili Islam in the Indo-Pakistan Subcontinent," *JAOS* 107, no. 3 (1987).

57. See Introduction to Mustanṣir bi'llāh (=Gharīb Mīrzā?), *Pandiyāt*, 03–04.

58. Mustanṣir bi'llāh (=Gharīb Mīrzā?), "Pandiyāt-i Jawānmardī," in *Institute of Ismaili Studies Library*, Khojki ms KH110 (London).

59. See my "Pir Pandiyat-i Jawanmardi," http://www.iis.ac.uk/library_iis/collections/k_pir_pandiyat.htm.

60. Mustanṣir bi'llāh (=Gharīb Mīrzā?), *Pandiyāt*, ed. 1–2, cf. trans. 1–2.

61. Daftary, *Ismāʿīlīs*, 468–469; Ivanow, *Ismaili Literature*, 139–140; Muʿizzī, "Ismāʿīliyyān-i Īrān," 41; Nanji, *The Nizārī Ismāʿīlī Tradition in the Indo-Pakistan Subcontinent* (Delmar, NY, 1978), 81; Poonawala, *Biobibliography*, 268.

62. Sunni collections containing this tradition include al-Muttaqī, *Kanz al-ʿUmmāl* (Beirut, 1399/1979), ḥadīth 34169 as reproduced and translated in Hunzai and Hunzai, *The Holy Ahl-i Bayt in the Prophetic Traditions* (Karachi, 1999), 62. See also al-Tabrīzī, *Mishkāt al-Maṣābīḥ*, ed. al-Albānī (Beirut, 1961), vol. 3, 265. Ismaili sources include Abū al-Fawāris, *al-Risāla fī al-Imāma*, ed. Makarem, trans. Makarem, *The Political Doctrine of the Ismāʿīlīs (The Imamate)* (Delmar, NY, 1977), ed. 30, trans. 42; and al-Nuʿmān, *Daʿāʾim al-Islām wa-Dhikr al-Ḥalāl wa-al-Ḥarām wa-al-Qaḍāyā wa-al-Aḥkām*, ed. Fayḍī (Cairo, 1951–1961), vol. 1, 35.

63. Mustanṣir bi'llāh (=Gharīb Mīrzā?), *Pandiyāt*, ed. 47, cf. trans. 29.

64. Ibid, ed. 56, cf. trans. 35.

65. See Introduction to Ibid, 04.

66. Ibid, 134–135.

67. The date 875/1470 is recorded in the *Manāzil al-Aqṭāb*, a later source, but one dedicated primarily to the life of Kabīr al-Dīn's son, Imām al-Dīn, while the date 896/1490 is recorded by the generally reliable Shaykh ʿAbd al-Ḥaqq Dihlawī, who wrote just a century after this date. The former date has been given the most credence by scholars, generally following on Ivanow's conclusions. Ivanow, *Ismaili Literature*, 178. Cf. Daftary, *Ismāʿīlīs*, 480, Nanji, *Nizārī Ismāʿīlī Tradition*, 77. There is also a tradition preserved in the *Taʾrīkh-i Burhānpūr*, whereby Ḥasan Kabīr al-Dīn died in 851/1447. Cited in Ivanow, "The Sect of Imam Shah in Gujrat," *JBBRAS* 12 (1936): 51. If this is, in fact, true, then it is quite possible that the *Pandiyāt-i Jawānmardī* was written by the first Mustanṣir of Anjudān.

68. Nūr Muḥammadshāh, *Sat Varaṇī Moṭī* ([Mumbai?], nd), c. 272.

69. Nanji, *Nizārī Ismāʿīlī Tradition*, 79.

70. Nūr Muḥammadshāh, *Sat Varaṇī Moṭī*, c. 119, where the term used is *pātī*, which means "deed" or "share"; and Qāḍī Raḥmatallāh b. Ghulām Muṣṭafā, *Manāzil al-Aqṭāb wa Basātīn al-Aḥbāb*, cited in Ivanow, "Sect of Imam Shah," 40, where the *Manāzil* is quoted as using the term *niʿmat*, which may indicate wealth or fortune.

71. Ivanow, "Sect of Imam Shah," 39–40, paraphrasing the *Manāzil*. Imāmshāh, "Jirebhāīre pīr kabīradīn jomu sīpārīu," in *100 Ginānanī Chopaḍī*, 5th ed., vol. 1 (Mumbai, 1990 vs/1934), passim; and Imāmshāh and Buḍhāī, *Ekiyāsī: ginānajī: chopaḍī: jeṃmiñj: ginān: 71 pīr: emām: shāhi: ne: bāī: buḍhāījā tathā ginān: 10 gugarījā* (np, 1953 vs/1897), passim.

72. Nūr Muḥammadshāh, *Sat Varaṇī Moṭī nī Vel [a.k.a. Sat Veṇī nī Vel]*, c. 119.

73. Dihlawī, *Akhbār al-Akhyār fī Asrār al-Abrār* (Delhi, 1891), 207–208.

74. A village situated about thirty-five kilometers northeast of Anjudān and northwest of Mahallat. It seems that Kahak refers to the entire area surrounding the village, including Anjudān. See Nanji, *Nizārī Ismāʿīlī Tradition*, 73.

75. Nūr Muḥammadshāh, *Sat Varaṇī Moṭī*, c. 273.

76. Ibid, cc. 274–275.

77. Nūr Muḥammadshāh, *Sat Varaṇī Moṭī nī Vel [a.k.a. Sat Veṇī nī Vel]*, c. 123. It is difficult to determine which of Ḥasan Kabīr al-Dīn's offspring seceded. Imāmshāh, Raḥmat Allāh Shāh, and Bāī Buḍhāī all seem to have remained faithful to the Nizārī Imams. A Ginān composed by Kathīr al-Dīn is preserved in manuscript Ism K 22 of the Harvard collection, indicating that he, too, remained loyal. See Asani, *Harvard Collection*, 146. As a Ginān composed by Mīthā Shāh (=Muḥammad Nūrbakhsh II), the son of Awliyāʾ ʿAlī, is to be found in the corpus, it is likely that Awliyāʾ ʿAlī also adhered to the Nizārī doctrine. Jalālshāh, Dulā, Mast Qalandar, and Lāl Qalandar are specifically mentioned by Nūr Muḥammadshāh as having seceded, but as some of these appellations are titles rather than proper names, it is difficult to identify exactly which of Kabīr al-Dīn's children these may have been.

78. Apparently equivalent to sixteen rupees.

79. Nūr Muḥammadshāh, *Sat Varaṇī Moṭī*, c. 280; Nūr Muḥammadshāh, *Sat Varaṇī Moṭī nī Vel [a.k.a. Sat Veṇī nī Vel]*, c. 121.

80. Nūr Muḥammadshāh, *Sat Varaṇī Moṭī*, c. 282–283; Nūr Muḥammadshāh, *Sat Varaṇī Moṭī nī Vel [a.k.a. Sat Veṇī nī Vel]*, c. 122.

81. Nūr Muḥammadshāh, *Sat Varaṇī Moṭī*, cc. 284–285, 287.

82. Nūr Muḥammadshāh, *Sat Varaṇī Moṭī nī Vel [a.k.a. Sat Veṇī nī Vel]*, c. 124. Imāmshāh also describes his rejection by the *jamāʿat* of Sindh. See his Imāmshāh, *Janatpurī*, 2nd ed. (Mumbai, 1976 vs/1-8-20), vv. 15–26 translated in Hooda, "Some Specimens of Satpanth Literature," in *Collectanea*, ed. Ivanow, vol. 1 (Leiden, 1948), 122–137. See also Nanji, *Nizārī Ismāʿīlī Tradition*, 79–80.

83. Nūr Muḥammadshāh, *Sat Varaṇī Moṭī nī Vel [a.k.a. Sat Veṇī nī Vel]*, c. 124. The joy of Imāmshāh upon receiving this letter from the Imam is picturesquely described in Nūr Muḥammadshāh, *Sat Varaṇī Moṭī nī Vel [a.k.a. Sat Veṇī nī Vel]*, c. 112 as well as in Imāmshāh, "Shāhā nā khat āyā vīrā jampudīp māṃhe" in *100 Ginānanī Chopaḍī*, 4th ed., vol. 5 (Mumbai, 1990 vs/1934), 94–95, a Ginān that is, to this day, frequently recited upon receipt of letters from the Imam.

84. Thus, Ivanow's assumption that this is simply a title rather than a name seems to be incorrect. While the term "Nūrshāh" has occasionally been used in the Gināns as a general title (cf. Ṣadr al-Dīn, "More āshājī harovar sarovar," in *102 Ginānajī: Chopaḍī*, 3rd ed., vol. 4 (Mumbai, 1968 vs/[1912]), v. 6, where the Imam is termed Nūrshāh or "lord of light"), here it appears to be a specific reference to the thirty-fifth Nizārī Imam.

85. However, supporting its composition by the elder Mustanṣir is the Nūr Muḥammadshāh, *Sat Varaṇī Moṭī nī Vel [a.k.a. Sat Veṇī nī Vel]*, c. 108.

86. Mustanṣir bi'llāh (=Gharīb Mīrzā?), *Pandiyāt*, ed. 1, cf. trans. 1.

87. Ivanow's Introduction to Ibid, 08.

88. Quhistānī, *Haft Bāb*, ed. Ivanow, trans. Ivanow, *Haft Bab or "Seven Chapters"* (Mumbai, 1959), ed. 42, trans. 42.

89. Ibid, ed. 1–2, cf. trans., 1–2.

90. Ibid, ed. 24, trans. 24.

91. Ibid, ed. 63, trans. 63, slightly modified.

92. Ivanow's "Introduction" to Ibid, 03.

93. Muʿizzī, "Ismāʿīliyyān-i Īrān," 42. Ivanow's edition of Quhistānī, *Haft Bāb*, 55–56.

و در این رساله این مقدار شمه ای بود از تأویلات شرائع [و مارا رساله ایست در تأویلات شرائع] و ظاهر قرآن از آنجا تمامی آن باید جست، و شمه ای نیز از تأویلات قرآن اینجا یاد خواهیم کرد.

94. Quhistānī, *Haft Bāb*, ed. 42, cf. trans. 42.

95. Poonawala, *Biobibliography*, 270.

96. Khayrkhwāh Harātī, "Risāla," in *Taṣnīfāt-i Khayrkhwāh Harātī*, ed. Ivanow, *Taṣnīfāt-i Khayrkhwāh Harātī* (Tehran, 1961), 8.

97. Ibid, 21.

98. On this figure, see Aubin, "Un Santon Quhistani," 187–188, 188 n4.

99. An allusion to the Prophet's nocturnal journey to paradise, hinted at in Quran 17:1 and elsewhere. See Robinson, "Miʿrādj," in *EI2*, vol. 7 (Leiden, 1960–2004; reprint, CD-ROM v. 1.0).

100. See W. Ivanow's "Introduction" to Quhistānī, *Haft Bāb*, 04.

101. Hunzai, *Shimmering Light: An Anthology of Ismaili Poetry* (London, 1996), 93–95.

102. Ḥusayn, "Āmad zamān." The meter, technically speaking, may be classified as *muḍāriʿ makhbūn akhrab makfūf wa-sālim wa-akhrab wa-maḥdhūf* or even as *ramal makhbūn mushaʿʿas makfūf wa-ṣālim.* In reality, it is almost the same as *muḍāriʿ akhrab makfūf maḥdhūf.* On the difficulties of classification, see Thiesen, *A Manual of Classical Persian Prosody: With Chapters on Urdu, Karakhanidic and Ottoman Prosody* (Belgium, 1982), 153–156, 180.

سلطان دین که شاه غریب است نام او　　　نام بزرگ او همه ورد زبان کنیم
گاه [sic، گاهی] چو طفل و گاه جوانست و گاه پیر　　　باید که ما حدیث پیمبر نشان کنیم

103. Zamānī, "Ay dar miyān-i jān," in *Institute of Ismaili Studies Library*, Persian ms 14718 (London). The meter is the same as in Ḥusayn, "Āmad zamān."

گاهی بشکل طفلی گاه [sic، گاهی] جوان و پیر　　　در هر لباس هر[sic، در or بر] صفتِ دیگر آمده
مستنصری باسم که [تو] ای امام وقت　　　چون آفتاب برج شرف انور آمده
گاهی بنام شاه غریبی در ظهور　　　شاه سهیل طلعت و مه پیکر آمده

A metrical fault indicates that a single syllable word has been omitted in the first hemistich of the last couplet between the words غریبی and در.

104. Quhistānī, *Haft Bāb*, ed. 40, trans. 40.

105. I have, however, been unable to trace such a *ḥadīth.*

106. Juwaynī, *Taʾrīkh-i Jahāngushāy*, ed. Qazwīnī, 3 vols. (Leiden, 1912–1937), ed. vol. 3, 249, trans. vol. 2, 704.

107. See Ivanow's Introduction to Quhistānī, *Haft Bāb*, 04.

108. *Dhuā: gaṭ: pāṭ - sāñji: somaṇi: tathā subhuhaji: khās: imāmīi: isamāili: khojā: jamātaje: vāsate* (Mumbai, 1958 vs/1902), 87.

109. The eighteenth-century family tree cited in Rematulā, *Khojā Kom no Itihās*, 213 and Mulukshāh and ʿĪsanshāh, *Gulzār*, 290 maintain that it was this Imam who first left Shahr Bābak (Bībak or Bābek in their rendering) and took up residence in Anjudan.

110. Daftary, *Ismāʿīlīs*, 459; Muʿizzī, "Ismāʿīliyyān-i Īrān," 107.

111. Pictures of both the *ṣandūq* and the mausoleum can be seen in Ivanow's "Introduction" to Mustanṣir bi'llāh (=Gharīb Mīrzā?), *Pandiyāt*, plate 6 (mislabeled as plate 7); and the mausoleum can be seen in Daftary, *Ismāʿīlīs*, 457.

112. Ḥusayn, "Āmad zamān."

.ما کعبه حقیقت خود انگوان کنیم

113. Quhistānī, *Haft Bāb*, ed. 65, trans. 65.

114. This text, edited as [pseudo-Ḥasan-i Ṣabbaḥ], "Haft Bāb-i Bābā Sayyidnā," in *Two Early Ismaili Treatises*, ed. Ivanow (Mumbai, 1933), 7, was translated in Hodgson, *The Order of Assassins* (New York, 1980), 282–283. Since that time, a new manuscript has come to light that identifies the author as Ṣalāḥ al-Dawla wa-al-Dīn Ḥasan-i Maḥmud, who was also known as Ḥasan-i Ṣalāh Munshī and Ḥasan-i Maḥmūd Kātib. See S. J. Badakhchani's Preface to Ṭūsī and Ḥasan-i Maḥmūd, *Rawḍa-yi Taslīm*, ed. Badakhchani, trans. Badakhchani, *Paradise of Submission: A Medieval Treatise on Ismaili Thought* (London, 2005), xv–xvi, 244 n15 and Badakhchani, "The Paradise of Submission" (PhD dissertation, Oxford University, 1989), 58–59. Dr. Badakhchani kindly made available to me the text of the newly discovered manuscript. In a few passages, Ivanow's edition gives a better reading. I have reconstructed the text of this passage as follows:

و در خدا پرستی روی سوی جسمی از اجسام کنند، مثلاً به آسمان، یا خورشید و ماه و کواکب، یا آتش یا خانه ئی از خانه های عالم که معروف و مشهور است. آنرا میان خود و خدای واسطه سازند و چنان پندارند که به آن قبله به خدا خواهند رسید. از این جهت [خدا] می فرماید: *اولئك كالانعام بل هم اضلّ* (۷:۱۷۹).دراین حال خردمند باید که در این معنی تفکّر و تَأمّل نماید: کسی را که در خداشناسی که اصل دین است وهم و پنداشت راهبر باشد و در خداپرستی که فرع دین است سنگ و دار و درخت و غیره را هم بواسطه قبله سازند، چون به خداوند برسند؟ ویا چه طور خدای را توانند شناخت؟

115. Nāṣir-i Khusraw, *Dīwān-i Ashʿār-i Ḥakīm Nāṣir-i Khusraw Qubādiyānī*, ed. Mīnuwī and Muḥaqqiq (Tehran, 1357 HS/1978), 510; Nāṣir-i Khusraw, *Dīwān-i Ashʿār-i Nāṣir-i Khusraw Qubādiyānī: Mushtamil ast bar Rawshanāʾīnāma, Saʿādatnāma, Qasāʾid wa-Muqaṭṭaʿāt*, ed. Taqawī et al. (Tehran, 1380 HS/2001), 259.

116. Nāṣir-i Khusraw, *Dīwān—Mīnuwī & Muḥaqqiq*, 513; Nāṣir-i Khusraw, *Dīwān—Taqawī*, 260.

117. al-Mu'ayyad fī al-Dīn Shīrāzī, *al-Majālis al-Muʾayyadiyya*, ed. Ḥamīd al-Dīn, vols. 1 and 2 (Mumbai and Oxford, 1975–1986), vol. 1, 15–16. See also Qutbuddin, *Al-Muʾayyad al-Shīrāzī and Fatimid Daʿwa Poetry* (Leiden, 2005), 105–110, to which I am indebted for some of the following references on this subject.

118. al-Mu'ayyad fī al-Dīn Shīrāzī, *Dīwān*, ed. Ḥusayn (Cairo, 1949), 204, 229, 251, 292, 295, 297, 311, 314.

119. Ibid, 217, translated in Qutbuddin, *Al-Muʾayyad*, 108.

والذي قالَ في الكتاب تعالى　　　مثلٌ ذاك تحته ممثول

120. al-Mu'ayyad fī al-Dīn Shīrāzī, *Dīwān*, 203, translation modified from Qutbuddin, "al-Mu'ayyad fī al-Dīn al-Shīrāzī: Founder of a New Tradition of Fāṭimid Da'wa Poetry" (PhD dissertation, Harvard University, 1999), 108.

اِقصِدْ حِمَى ممثوله دون المثل ذا إبَرُ النَّحْلِ و هذا كالعَسَل

121. Cf. Nāṣir-i Khusraw, *Gushāyish wa-Rahāyish*, ed. Hunzai, trans. Hunzai, *Knowledge and Liberation: A Treatise on Philosophical Theology* (London, 1998), ed. 65, trans. 102–103.

122. al-Mu'ayyad fī al-Dīn Shīrāzī, *Dīwān*, 229.

يا قبلة الحقّ الاعزّ و كعبة الحيّ الأجَلا
إنْ حُجّ للبيت الجَماد فنَحْوَكم أولى وأولى

123. Dihgān, *Kārnāma*, 29. In recent times, the casket constructed for the grave of the Imam Gharīb Mīrzā was dismantled by intruders, who left only a few pieces in the mausoleum. See Daftary, *Ismā'īlīs*, 459. Fortunately, Dihgān recorded this information when it was still intact.

CHAPTER 7

1. Hunsberger, *Nasir Khusraw: The Ruby of Badakhshan* (London, 2000), 5.
2. Nāṣir-i Khusraw, *Safarnāma*, ed. Dabīr-i Siyāqī (Tehran, 1984), 2.
3. Ibid.
4. Ibid. On Nāṣir-i Khusraw's place within the Ismaili hierarchy and a detailed exposition of his thought, see Faquir M. Hunzai, *The Face of Religion: Nāṣir-i Khusraw's Spiritual Hermeneutics* (London: I.B. Tauris, forthcoming).
5. This refers to the stages of inert matter, vegetative soul, animal soul, and human soul through which a human being passes.
6. This couplet may also be understood as, "When I found my body better than everything, I said, 'There must be someone best in the creation.' "
7. Nāṣir-i Khusraw, *Dīwān-i Ash'ār-i Ḥakīm Nāṣir-i Khusraw Qubādiyānī*, ed. Mīnuwī and Muḥaqqiq (Tehran, 1357 HS/1978), 506–509; Nāṣir-i Khusraw, *Dīwān-i Ash'ār-i Nāṣir-i Khusraw Qubādiyānī: Mushtamil ast bar Rawshanā'ināma, Sa'ādatnāma, Qaṣā'id wa-Muqaṭṭa'āt*, ed. Taqawī et al. (Tehran, 1380 HS/2001), 258–259. Cf. Hunsberger, *Nasir Khusraw*, 55–58; Ivanow, *Problems in Nasir-i Khusraw's Biography* (Mumbai, 1956), 23–25; Schimmel, *Make a Shield from Wisdom: Selected Verses from Nāṣir-i Khusraw's Dīvān* (London, 1993), 45–46.
8. Nāṣir-i Khusraw, *Dīwān—Mīnuwī and Muḥaqqiq*, 139; Nāṣir-i Khusraw, *Dīwān—Taqawī*, 341. *Az īn* has been corrected to *zīn* to suit the meter, which is *muḍāri' akhrab makfūf maḥdhūf*.

بر جان من چو نور امام زمان بتافت	لیل السرار بودم و شمس الضحی شدم
نام بزرگ امام زمانست زین قبل	من از زمین چو زهره بدو بر سما شدم

9. al-Ḥusaynī, *Kitāb-i Khiṭābāt-i ʿĀliya*, ed. Ujāqī (Mumbai, 1963), 42–43.

10. Mustanṣir bi'llāh (=Gharīb Mīrzā?), *Pandiyāt-i Jawānmardī*, ed. Ivanow, trans. Ivanow, *Pandiyat-i Jawanmardi or "Advices of Manliness"* (Leiden, 1953), ed. 56, trans. 35.

11. Kohlberg, "Imām and Community in the Pre-Ghayba Period," in *Authority and Political Culture in Shiʿism*, ed. Arjomand (Albany, 1988), 26.

12. See *Naqḍ al-ʿUthmāniyya*, the excerpts appended to al-Jāḥiẓ's *ʿUthmāniyya*, 282, cited in Kohlberg, "Taqiyya in Shīʿī Theology and Religion," in *Secrecy and Concealment: Studies in the History of Mediterranean and Near Eastern Religions*, ed. Kippenberg and Stroumsa (Leiden, 1995), 348 n12.

13. Ḥusayn, "Āmad zamān ānkih maḥabbat ʿīyan kunīm," in *Institute of Ismaili Studies Library*, Persian ms 14698 (London).

آمد زمان آنکه محبت عیان کنیم	اسرار دین بنزد محبان بیان کنیم
با یکدیگر بصدق نشینیم بعد از این	و زدشمنان دین ره دعوت نهان کنیم

14. Ibn Ḥusām Khūsfī, "Birādarān ba-ḥaqq mawsim-i munājāt ast," in *Majmūʿa-yi Ashʿār-i Madhhabī*, ed. Anjuman-i taʿlīm (Mashhad, Iran, 1995), np; Muʿizzī, "Ismāʿīliyyān-i Īrān" (MA thesis, Dānishgāh-i Firdawsī, 1371–1372 HS/1992–1993), 358–359. The meter is *mujtathth muthamman makhbūn aṣlam*.

برادران بحق موسم مناجاتست	مراد خویش طلب کن که وقت حاجاتست
قیامت است که هر شش هزار سال ظهور	کنون چه [sic، که] هفت شود قائم القیاماتست
اگر امام زمان را بحق به نشناسی [sic، نه بشناسی]	روی به دوزخ اگر صد هزار طاعاتست
هرآنکس [sic، آنکسی] که خداوند خویش را نشناخت	محقّق است که در کفر و در ظلاماتست
میان بنده و حق راز کی نهان ماند	خدای عالم اسرار و ذوالخفایاتست
به ترك نفس هوا و مراد خویش نگر	که هر چه در دل تو غیر اوست طاماتست
بهرچه پیش خیال و قیاس خود گفتم	به نزد او همه افسانه و خیالاتست
بگوی از سر اخلاص نام مولانا	که آشکار شد و دعوتش مقالاتست
عیان شد است [sic، شدند] رفیقان ز مشرق و مغرب	و لیك این همه در بند یك اشاراتست
بفضل خود نظری کن به بندگان ضعیف	که درمیان خلایق بسی مقالاتست
شراب شوق لبالب ز جام مولانا	بده که این هم از رحمت جماعاتست
ببخش بندهء مسکین خویش ابن حسام	بدان سبب که گرفتار چاه ظلماتست

15. Regarding this notion, see Virani, "The Days of Creation in the Thought of Nāṣir Khusraw," in *Nāṣir Khusraw: Yesterday, Today, Tomorrow*, ed. Niyozov and Nazariev (Khujand, Tajikistan, 2004) 74–83.

16. The reference here is to Quran 32:5, "He regulates the affair from the heaven to the earth; then shall it ascend to him in a day the measure of which is a thousand years of what you count." Cf. 70:4.

17. Nāṣir-i Khusraw, *Jāmiʿ al-Ḥikmatayn*, ed. Corbin and Muʿīn, *Le Livre Réunissant les Deux Sagesses* (Tehran, 1953), 163–164 is equally critical of this interpretation.

18. al-Mu'ayyad fī al-Dīn Shīrāzī, *al-Majālis al-Mu'ayyadiyya*, ed. Ḥamīd al-Dīn, vols. 1 and 2 (Mumbai and Oxford, 1975–1986), vol. 1, 358–359; al-Mu'ayyad fī al-Dīn Shīrāzī, *al-Majālis al-Mu'ayyadiyya*, trans. Muscati and Moulvi, *Life and Lectures of the Grand Missionary al-Muayyad-fid-Din al-Shirazi* (Karachi, 1950), 123–124.

19. Nāṣir-i Khusraw, *Wajh-i Dīn*, ed. Aavani (Tehran, 1977), 65.

20. Nāṣir-i Khusraw, *Jāmiʿ al-Ḥikmatayn*, 163, 165; Nāṣir-i Khusraw, *Wajh-i Dīn*, 65. Cf. Corbin, *Cyclical Time and Ismaili Gnosis* (London, 1983), 97; Marquet, "Le Qāḍī Nuʿmān à propos des heptades d'imāms," *Arabica* 25, no. 3 (September 1978): 225–232.

21. The centrality of the Qā'im and his identification with the Sabbath is vividly illustrated by a diagram of concentric circles found in Nāṣir-i Khusraw, *Khwān al-Ikhwān*, ed. al-Khashshāb (Cairo, 1940), 155.

22. Nāṣir-i Khusraw, *Wajh-i Dīn*, 65.

23. Cf. Matthew 5:18; Luke 16:17.

24. Quoted by Ṭūsī and Ḥasan-i Maḥmūd, *Rawḍa-yi Taslīm*, ed. Badakhchani, trans. Badakhchani, *Paradise of Submission: A Medieval Treatise on Ismaili Thought* (London, 2005), ed. 151–152, trans. 123, translation slightly modified.

25. Ibid, ed. 174–175, trans. 140–141. Cf. Similar speculations of the Fatimid thinker Abū Ḥātim al-Rāzī in his *Kitāb al-Iṣlāḥ*, cited in Nomoto, "Early Ismāʿīlī Thought on Prophecy According to the Kitāb al-Islāḥ by Abū Hātim al-Rāzī (d. ca. 322/934–5)," (PhD dissertation, McGill University, 1999), 100.

26. Ivanow considers this a work of Khayrkhwāh Harātī. See his Introduction to [Khayrkhwāh Harātī?], *Faṣl dar Bayān-i Shinākht-i Imām*, ed. Ivanow, 3rd rev. ed. (Tehran, 1960) and Ivanow, *Ismaili Literature: A Bibliographical Survey*, 2nd amplified ed. (Tehran, 1963), 144; cf. Poonawala, *Biobibliography of Ismāʿīlī Literature* (Malibu, CA, 1977), 144. This attribution, however, is based on dubious premises.

27. [Khayrkhwāh Harātī?], *Faṣl dar Bayān-i Shinākht-i Imām*, trans. Ivanow, 2nd rev. ed. (Mumbai, 1947), trans. 18; [Khayrkhwāh Harātī?], *Faṣl dar Bayān-i Shinākht-i Imām*, ed. 2.

28. The author includes the *mustawdaʿ* Imams in this enumeration.

29. Poonawala, *Biobibliography*, 271, n2 postulates an even earlier resort to the cover of Twelver Shīʿism, but thus far no substantial evidence for this has been adduced. Jalāl-i Qā'inī, for example, suspected a number of the Khurāsānī Sunnis of Ismaili proclivities but makes no mention of a similar phenomenon among the Twelvers.

30. See Khūsfī, *Dīwān-i Muḥammad b. Ḥusām Khūsfī: Shāmil-i qasīdahā, ghazalhā, tarkībbandhā, tarjīʿbandhā, musammaṭhā, mathnawīhā, qiṭʿahā, rubāʿīhā*, ed. Bīrjandī and Taqī (Mashhad, 1366 HS/1988), 83–84, 239–240, 453–454. These poems were first cited by Muʿizzī, "Ismāʿīliyyān-i Īrān," 359 n103.

31. Morgan, *Medieval Persia, 1040–1797* (London, 1988), 103.

32. Mustanṣir bi'llāh (=Gharīb Mīrzā?), *Pandiyāt*, ed. 47, cf. trans. 29.

33. Ibid, ed. 48, trans. 30.

34. Ibid, ed. 67–68, trans. 42.

35. Ibid, ed. 68, trans. 42.

36. Turkumān, *Ta'rīkh-i ʿĀlamārā-yi ʿAbbāsī*, 2 vols. (Tehran, 1971), vol. 1, 476. Cf. Babayan, *Mystics, Monarchs, and Messiahs: Cultural Landscapes of Early Modern Iran* (Cambridge, MA, 2002), 106. It was believed that the Twelver Imam al-Riḍā died after eating a poisoned grape.

37. Chardin, *Voyages de monsieur le chevalier Chardin en Perse et autres lieux de l'orient*, 3 vols. (Amsterdam, 1709), vol. 3, 208.

38. Quhistānī, *Dīwān-i Ḥakīm Nizārī Quhistānī*, ed. Muṣaffā (Tehran, 1371 HS/ 1992), 83. Translated in Lewisohn, "Sufism and Ismāʿīlī Doctrine in the Persian Poetry of Nizārī Quhistānī (645–721/1247–1321)," *Iran* 41 (2003): 232. Translation slightly modified.

39. al-Ḥusaynī, *Risāla dar Ḥaqīqat-i Dīn*, ed. Ivanow, Facsimile of the autograph copy ed. (Mumbai, 1947), 28–29. Cf. Ivanow's translation in al-Ḥusaynī, *Risāla dar Ḥaqīqat-i Dīn*, trans. Ivanow, *True Meaning of Religion or Risala dar Haqiqati Din*, 2nd ed. (Mumbai, 1933; reprint, Dar es Salam, Tanzania: Shia Imami Ismailia Association for Tanzania, 1970), 17.

ای برادر! برای نیك عالم را ظلمت فرو گرفت، دست دشمن دراز شد، مقام امتحان در میان آمد. انقلاب در مردم افتاد، هر کس براهی رفت و خیالی نمود. جمعی ازد نبال جاهلان که دزدان راهند شتافتند. هر جا حقی بود بقدر امکان دشمن گرفتند. کم کم قلبها سیاه شد. گوشها کر شد. زبان گوینده از کار باز ماند. امکان نه داشت که بجماعت کرها بتوان مطلب گفت که نمی فهمند. اکنون ای برادرزبان گوینده ای هست اگر گوش شنوا داری بیا و الا نمی توانی درک این معنی را بنمائی.

40. Schmidtke, ed., *Correspondance Corbin-Ivanow: Lettres Échangés entre Henry Corbin et Vladimir Ivanow de 1947 à 1966* (Paris, 1999), 21, 23.

41. Ernst, *The Shambhala Guide to Sufism* (Boston, MA, 1997), 18

42. Daftary, *The Ismāʿīlīs: Their History and Doctrines* (Cambridge, 1990), 439. Cf. Ivanow, *Ismaili Literature*, 137–138.

43. Lewisohn, "Nizārī Quhistānī," 242.

44. Daftary, *Ismāʿīlīs*, 468.

45. Ṣadr al-Dīn, "Sab ghaṭ sāmi māro bharapur beṭhā," in *102 Ginānajī: Chopaḍī*, 3rd ed., vol. 4 (Mumbai, 1968 VS/[1912]), 59.

46. Mustanṣir bi'llāh (=Gharīb Mīrzā?), *Pandiyāt*, ed. 42, cf. trans. 26.

47. Cited in introduction to Quhistānī, *Dīwān*, 251; cf. Lewisohn, "Nizārī Quhistānī," 242.

48. See Yeroushalmi, *The Judeo-Persian Poet ʿEmrānī and His Book of Treasure: ʿEmrānī's Ganj-Nāme, a Versified Commentary on the Mishnaic Tractate Abot* (Leiden, 1995), 86–88, cited in Lewisohn, "Nizārī Quhistānī," 251 n102.

49. Daftary, *Ismāʿīlīs*, 469.

50. Cited in Nomoto, "Kitāb al-Islāḥ," 161.

51. Sijistānī, *Kitāb al-Iftikhār*, ed. Poonawala (Beirut, 2000), 29.

52. Daftary, *Ismāʿīlīs*, 467.

53. See Ivanow, Introduction to Mustanṣir bi'llāh (=Gharīb Mīrzā?), *Pandiyāt*, 01, 07.

54. Algar, "The Revolt of Āghā Khān Maḥallātī and the Transference of the Ismāʿīlī Imamate to India," *SI* 29 (1969): 73.

55. Pourjavady, "Ismāʿīlīs and Niʿmatullāhīs," *SI* 41 (1975): 114.

56. Daftary, *Ismāʿīlīs*, 467. See also Boivin, "A Persian Treatise for the Ismāʿīlī Khojas of India: Presentation of the Pandiyāt-i Jawānmardī," in *The Making of Indo-Persian Culture*, et. al. (New Delhi, 2000), 118.

57. Daftary, *Ismāʿīlīs*, 467. See also Maẓharī Kirmānī, "Rābiṭa-yi Ismāʿīliyān bā Ṣūfiyān-i ṭarīqat-i Niʿmat Allāhī," *Ṣūfī* 27 (June 1995): 6–18.

58. Lewisohn, "Nizārī Quhistānī," 244.

59. Ibn Khaldūn, *Muqaddima*, trans. Rosenthal, vol. 2, 187.

60. Lewisohn, "Nizārī Quhistānī," 244.

61. These include *shaykh al-awliyā, kāshif-i asrār-i ḥaqq, shaykh al-shuyūkh*, etc., any of which could refer to an Ismaili luminary or an adept of many other non-Sufi persuasions.

62. Nanji, *The Nizārī Ismāʿīlī Tradition in the Indo-Pakistan Subcontinent* (Delmar, NY, 1978), 167 n165.

63. See Shams, "Vel Chandrabhāṇ nī," in *Chandrabhāṇ ane Surbhāṇ: Banne nī Vel sāthe*, 2nd ed. (Mumbai, 1926), v. 5. The verse is inadvertently cited by Nanji as number 4. The word *sufet* occurs twice. A number of different editions of this composition as well as manuscripts were checked to see if the word *ṣūfī* occurs in any of them, but all concur in the reading *sufet*.

64. See Subhan, *Sufism, Its Saints and Shrines: An Introduction to the Study of Sufism with Special Reference to India and Pakistan*, revised ed. (Lucknow, 1960), 359, in which his name occurs in the traditional list of the order's saints. The *Ta'rīkh-i Burhānpūr* corroborates this testimony. Cited in Ivanow, "The Sect of Imam Shah in Gujrat," *JBBRAS* 12 (1936): 50. See also Dihlawī, *Akhbār al-Akhyār fī Asrār al-Abrār* (Delhi, 1891), 207–208; Ivanow, "Sect of Imam Shah," 34; Konṭrākṭar, *Pīrāṇā-"Satpanth" nī Pol ane Satya no Prakāsh*, 1st ed., vol. 1 (Ahmadābād, India, 1926), 134, Nanji, *Nizārī Ismāʿīlī Tradition*, 77.

65. Not to mention the fact that almost all such Ismaili claims recorded by scholars are extremely recent. See, for example, Daftary, *Ismāʿīlīs*, 705 n38.

66. Chittick, *Faith and Practice of Islam: Three Thirteenth Century Sufi Texts* (Albany, NY, 1992), 177.

67. Nasafī, "Zubdat al-Ḥaqā'iq," in *Panj Risāla dar bayān-i Āfāq wa-Anfus yaʿnī Barābari-yi Ādam wa-ʿĀlam*, ed. Bertel's (Moscow, 1970), 91–207. This volume of five treatises is very interesting, and it is possible that some of the works contained in it date to the period studied in this book. Unfortunately, as this cannot be ascertained, they have not been taken into account here. An extract of another of Nasafī's works, the *Maqṣad-i Aqṣā*, is found in the 968/1560 manuscript containing a number of Ismaili works, including the *Rawḍa-yi Taslīm* and the anonymous *mathnawī* cited in chapter 3. Even more intriguing,

it corresponds very closely to the standard edition in Nasafī, "Maqṣad-i Aqṣā," in *Ganjīna-yi ʿIrfān*, ed. Rabbānī (Tehran, nd), 273–277, except, as Hermann Landolt notes, for "a few omissions of specifically Sufi passages." See his Introduction to Ṭūsī and Ḥasan-i Maḥmūd, *Rawḍa-yi Taslīm*, 4, 245 n11.

68. On Nasafī, see Landolt, "Le Paradoxe de la 'Face de Dieu': ʿAzīz-e Nasafī (VII/XIII siècle) et le 'Monisme Ésoterique de l'Islam,' " *Studia Iranica* 25 (1996), Ridgeon, *Aziz Nasafi* (Richmond, Surrey, 1998); Ridgeon, *Persian Metaphysics and Mysticism* (Richmond, Surrey, 2002).

69. See Landolt, "Nasafi, ʿAzīz b. Moḥammad," in *Encyclopaedia Iranica*, ed. Yarshater, Online edition, http://www.iranica.com/newsite/home/index.isc, accessed April 5, 2006 ed. (London, 1996–), in which the author notes other concepts in which Nasafī displays his responsiveness to Ismaili thought.

70. [Shāh Ṭāhir al-Dakkanī?], "Baʿḍī az Taʾwīlāt-i Gulshan-i Rāz," in *Trilogie Ismaélienne*, ed. Corbin, trans. Corbin (Tehran, 1340 HS/1961); Ivanow, "An Ismaili Interpretation of the Gulshani Raz," *JBBRAS* NS 8 (1932).

71. Quhistānī, *Haft Bāb*, ed. Ivanow, trans. Ivanow, *Haft Bab or "Seven chapters"* (Mumbai, 1959) ed. 4, cf. trans. 4.

72. Ibid, ed. 4–5, cf. trans. 4.

73. Schact, "Aṣḥāb al-Raʾy," in *EI2*, vol. 1 (Leiden, 1960–2004; reprint, CD-ROM v. 1.0).

74. Quhistānī, *Haft Bāb*, ed. 5, cf. trans. 5.

75. In this hemistich, Nizārī has encapsulated numerous layers of meaning, which are impossible to capture in translation. These include, "By the ʿ*ayn* (eye) of ʿ*irf* (patient quest)," "Through blessing (ʿ*urf*) itself," etc.

76. Quhistānī, *Dīwān*, 746. See also Lewisohn, "Nizārī Quhistānī," 237. The meter is the rather uncommon *muḍāriʿ akhrab wa-sālim*.

ما بين حق و باطل ضديتی ست مطلق   تيغی به تار مويی آويخته معلق
ای يار يك نصيحت يارانه بشنو از من   مگرو برای ناقص مشنو حديث احمق
يك بار حای حيرت بر قاف قرب او زن   كز عين عرف گردد ميم محق محقق...
هر ظاهری كه بينی بی باطنی نباشد   بشنو ندای دعوت زين داعی مصدق
با وقت ساز حالی تا وعده بی ستانيم   از كف مدار خالی جام می مروق
من پير خانقاهم يعنی شراب خانه   كرباس و صوف خواهم نه سندس و ستبرق...
مهر كسيست مارا در جان كه وقت معجز   مه را بيك اشاره كردی در آسمان شق
با لحم و دم ما شد مهر ولی مخمر   دانی كدام والی شير مصاف خندق
دانم كنند جهال انكار بر نزاری   غم نيست اگر مقلد گيرد برين سخن دق

77. Ibn Ḥusām Khūsfī, "Birādarān ba-ḥaqq," np; Muʿizzī, "Ismāʿīliyyān-i Īrān," 358–359.

78. Kirmānī, *Rāḥat al-ʿAql*, ed. Ḥusayn and Ḥilmī (Leiden, 1953), 61.

79. ومن مات ولم يعرفْ امام زمانه فقدْ مات ميته جاهليةٍ. Various versions of this tradition from different Islamic schools of thought can be found in Sami Makarem's introduction to Abū al-Fawāris, *al-Risāla fī al-Imāma*, ed. Makarem, trans. Makarem, *The Political Doctrine of the Ismāʿīlīs (The Imamate)* (Delmar, NY, 1977), 60; al-Nuʿmān, *Daʿāʾim al-Islām wa-Dhikr al-Ḥalāl wa-al-Ḥarām wa-al-Qaḍāyā wa-al-Aḥkām*, ed. Fayḍī (Cairo, 1951–1961), vol. 1, 31; Ibn Ḥanbal, *al-Musnad*, ed. Albānī (Cairo, 1986), vol. 4, 96. See also Ṭūsī and Ḥasan-i Maḥmūd, *Rawḍa-yi Taslīm*, ed. 175, trans. 141, 261 n149, which has further citations.

80. A reference to Quran 38:76 and elsewhere.

81. In Ismaili contexts, the expression *mard-i khudā* refers to the Imam, a member of the *daʿwa* being referred to as *mard-i imām*. See Ṭūsī and Ḥasan-i Maḥmūd, *Rawḍa-yi Taslīm*, ed. 219–220, trans. 176–177.

82. Quhistānī, *Dīwān*, 262–263, cf. Lewisohn, "Nizārī Quhistānī," 242–243.

83. Quhistānī, *Haft Bāb*, ed. 5, cf. trans. 5.

84. Ibid, ed. 6–7, trans. 6–7.

85. Ibid, ed. 7–8, cf. trans. 7–8.

86. Haji, "La Doctrine Ismaélienne d'après l'oeuvre d'Abū Isḥāq Qohestānī" (PhD dissertation, Sorbonne, 1975), 63 suggests that this individual held the rank of *dāʿī*. As will be seen from the argument that follows, this is not possible.

87. Quhistānī, *Haft Bāb*, ed. 49–50, trans. 49–50.

88. Ibid.

89. Ibid, ed. 43–44, trans. 43–44.

90. The text is corrupt here, calling blessings upon a plural number of people, while it seems only one is mentioned.

91. Quhistānī, *Haft Bāb*, ed. 9, cf. trans. 8–9.

92. Translated in Morgan, *The Mongols* (Oxford, 1986), 162 from Kāshānī, *Taʾrīkh-i Ūljāytū*, ed. Hambly (Tehran, 1348 HS/1969), 98 with an omitted word from the unique ms, Aya Sofya 3019, f. 178a. Chingiz modified to Genghis.

93. al-Nuʿmān, *Daʿāʾim*, ed. vol. 1, 84–98, trans. vol. 1, 104–122.

94. Ibid, ed. vol. 1, 87, trans. vol. 1, 108.

95. Ibid, ed. vol. 1, 89, trans. vol. 1, 110.

96. Ibid, ed. vol. 1, 88, trans. vol. 1, 109.

97. Ibid, ed. vol. 1, 93, trans. vol. 1, 115, slightly modified. Other texts read "ʿUmar" rather than "ʿAmr."

98. Ibid, ed. vol. 1, 92–95, vol. 1, 114–118.

99. Ibid, ed. vol. 1, 91, cf. trans. vol. 1, 112.

100. See, for example, Mustanṣir bi'llāh (=Gharīb Mīrzā?), *Pandiyāt*, ed. 31, 41, 54, 62, 65, 72 etc., trans. 19, 25, 34, 39, 40, 41, 45, etc.

101. See, for example, Ibid, ed. 23–24, trans. 15.

102. Ivanow, *Ismaili Literature*, 136; Ivanow, *Two Early Ismaili Treatises: Haft-babi Baba Sayyid-na and Matlubu'l-muʾminin by Tusi* (Mumbai, 1933).

103. See, for example, Idrīs ʿImād al-Dīn b. Ḥasan, *ʿUyūn al-akhbār*, vol. 5, 137, cited in Halm, *The Fatimids and Their Traditions of Learning* (London, 1997), 27.

104. These included Ibn al-Ṭuwayr and al-Muṣabbiḥī, see Canard, "Daʿwa," in *EI2*, vol. 2 (Leiden, 1960–2004; reprint, CD-ROM v. 1.0).

105. Mustanṣir bi'llāh (=Gharīb Mīrzā?), *Pandiyāt*, ed. 12–13, cf. trans. 8, reading, as per Ivanow's suggestion, *īmān* in place of *amān*.

106. Ibid, ed. 16–17, cf. trans. 11.

107. Ibid, ed. 15, trans. 10.

108. Ibid, ed. 56–57, cf. trans. 35.

109. Ibid, ed. 52, trans. 32–33.

110. Ibid, ed. 14, cf. trans. 9–10.

111. al-Nuʿmān, *Daʿāʾim*, ed. vol. 1, trans. vol. 1, 101–102.

112. W. Ivanow, Introduction to Mustanṣir bi'llāh (=Gharīb Mīrzā?), *Pandiyāt*, 010–014, cf. Daftary, *Ismāʿīlīs*, 468.

113. Nanji, *Nizārī Ismāʿīlī Tradition*, 85–86.

114. See Khayrkhwāh Harātī, "Qiṭʿāt," in *Taṣnīfāt-i Khayrkhwāh Harātī*, ed. Ivanow, *Taṣnīfāt-i Khayrkhwāh Harātī* (Tehran, 1961), passim; Khayrkhwāh Harātī, "Risāla," in *Taṣnīfāt-i Khayrkhwāh Harātī*, ed. Ivanow, *Taṣnīfāt-i Khayrkhwāh Harātī* (Tehran, 1961), passim.

115. Mustanṣir bi'llāh (=Gharīb Mīrzā?), *Pandiyāt*, ed. 42, cf. trans. 26.

116. See, for example, Ibid, ed. 42, 65, trans. 26, 40.

117. Ibid, ed. 42, trans. 26.

118. Ibid, ed. 43, trans. 26.

119. See, for example, ibid, ed. 32, 55, trans. 20, 34.

120. Ibid, ed. 91, cf. trans. 56.

121. Ibid, ed. 2, cf. trans. 2.

CHAPTER 8

1. Vaglieri, "Fadak," in *EI2*, vol. 2 (Leiden, 1960–2004; reprint, CD-ROM v. 1.0). On the wider implications of allowing Fāṭima to inherit this land, see Jafri, *The Origins and Early Development of Shiʿa Islam* (London, 1979), 63.

2. [pseudo-Nāṣir-i Khusraw: Khayrkhwāh Harātī?], *Kalām-i Pīr*, ed. Ivanow, trans. Ivanow (Mumbai, 1935), ed. 43–44, trans. 36, translation slightly modified.

3. Ibid, 36 n1; Yousofi, "Kāshifī, Kamāl al-Dīn Ḥusayn b. ʿAlī," in *EI2*, vol. 4 (Leiden, 1960–2004; reprint, CD-ROM v. 1.0). These two figures were apparently Sunnis but had clear sympathies for many Shiʿi ideas and concepts.

4. The descendant was none other than Mūsā al-Kāẓim, the son of the Imam Jaʿfar al-Ṣādiq, whom the author of the *Kalām-i Pīr* takes to be a *mustawdaʿ* Imam who acted on the authority of his elder brother, the Imam Ismāʿīl.

5. [pseudo-Nāṣir-i Khusraw: Khayrkhwāh Harātī?], *Kalām-i Pīr*, ed. 44, cf. trans. 36–37.

6. al-Ḥusaynī, *Risāla dar Ḥaqīqat-i Dīn*, ed. Ivanow, facsimile of the autograph copy ed. (Mumbai, 1947), 49; al-Ḥusaynī, *Risāla dar Ḥaqīqat-i Dīn*, trans. Ivanow, *True Meaning of Religion or Risala dar Haqiqati Din*, 2nd ed. (Mumbai, 1933; reprint, Dar es Salam, Tanzania: Shia Imami Ismailia Association for Tanzania, 1970), 49. This very early tradition is treated in great detail in Massignon, "Salmān Pāk et les prémices spirituelles de l'Islam Iranien," in *Opera Minora*, vol. 1 (Beirut, 1963), 455–457.

7. Cf. al-Ḥusaynī, *Ḥaqīqat-i Dīn*, ed. 61, trans. 39.

8. See Lalani, *Early Shīʿī Thought: The Teachings of Imam Muḥammad al-Bāqir* (London, 2000), 52.

9. Khayrkhwāh Harātī, "Risāla," in *Taṣnīfāt-i Khayrkhwāh Harātī*, ed. Ivanow, *Taṣnīfāt-i Khayrkhwāh Harātī* (Tehran, 1961), 2.

10. See, for example, ʿAbd al-Salām, "Alā ay ṭālib-i waḥdat kih mī lāfī kih jūyāyam," in *Kitāb al-Manāqib* ed. Hiz Hāʾīnes Prins Āghā Khān Shīʿa Imāmī Ismāʿīliya Esūsīʾeshan barāʾe Pākistān (Karachi, 1406/1986); ʿAbd al-Salām, "Alā e ṭālib-i waḥdat hamī lāfī kih jūyāyam," in *Qasidas: Great Ismaili Tradition of Central Asia*, ed. The Shia Imami Ismaili Tariqah and Religious Education Board for Pakistan, vol. 1 ([Karachi], nd), Side A, #1; Hūnzāʾī, *Falsafa-yi Duʿā* (Hunza-Gilgit, Pakistan, 1967), 101–109."Risāla-yi Munāẓara," in *Institute of Ismaili Studies Library*, Persian ms, number unknown (London).

11. The text here and further on in this chapter is reconstructed from ʿAbd al-Salām, "Alā ay ṭālib-i waḥdat kih mī lāfī kih jūyāyam," in *Institute of Ismaili Studies Library*, Persian ms 14704 (London); ʿAbd al-Salām, "Alā ay ṭālib-i waḥdat hamī lāfī kih jūyāyam," in *Institute of Ismaili Studies Library*, Persian ms 15033 (London); ʿAbd al-Salām, "Alā e ṭālib," Hiz Hāʾīnes Prins Āghā Khān Shīʿa Imāmī Ismāʿīliya Esūsīʾeshan barāʾe Pākistān, ed., *Kitāb al-Manāqib* (Karachi, 1406/1986), 4–9. The first hemistich of the third verse may also be understood as, "If you wish to achieve command over this world of divinity."

الا ای طالب وحدت همی لافی که جویایم   کلام از من شنو زیرا کتاب الله گویایم
بمکتب خانهء تسلیم شاگرد دل من شو   اگر خواهی که بر رویت در اسرار بگشایم
اگر فرماندهی خواهی درین آفاق لاهوتی   بفرمانم کمر بربند و بشنو هرچه فرمایم

12. Ayoub, "The Speaking Qurʾān and the Silent Qurʾān: A Study of the Principles and Development of Imāmī Shīʿī tafsīr," in *Approaches to the History of the Interpretation of the Qurʾān*, ed. Rippin (Oxford, 1988), 177–197.

13. Ibid, 183. See also n17 on this page in which the author cites al-Kulaynī, *al-Uṣūl min al-Kāfī*, ed. al-Ghifārī, 2 vols. (Tehran, 1388/1968), i, 169, 192, 213. Cf. Poonawala, "Ismāʿīlī taʾwīl of the Qurʾān," in *Approaches to the History of the Interpretation of the Qurʾān*, ed. Rippin (1988), 200 n7.

14. Ayoub, "Speaking Qurʾān," 183, n17.

15. al-Mu'ayyad fī al-Dīn Shīrāzī, *Dīwān*, ed. Ḥusayn (Cairo, 1949), 313. Cf. Qutbuddin, *Al-Mu'ayyad al-Shīrāzī and Fatimid Da'wa Poetry* (Leiden, 2005), 78–80, for further references, translation, and discussion.

يا حُجَّةً مَشْهورةً فِي الوَرَى وطَوْدَ عِلْمٍ اَعْجَزَ المُرْتَقِيْ

A brief outline of al-Mu'ayyad's life can be found in Daftary, *The Ismāʿīlīs: Their History and Doctrines* (Cambridge, 1990), 213–218 and al-Hamdani, "The Fāṭimid Daʿi al-Mu'ayyad: His Life and Work," in *The Great Ismaili Heroes* (Karachi, 1973). More detailed information may be found in Klemm, *Die Mission des fāṭimidischen Agenten al-Mu'ayyad fī d-dīn in Sīrāz* (Frankfurt am Main, 1989), Klemm, *Memoirs of a Mission: The Ismaili Scholar, Statesman and Poet al-Mu'ayyad fi'l-Dīn al-Shīrāzī* (London, 2003). His *sīra* has been studied by al-Hamdani, "The Sira of al Muayyad fid-Din ash-Shirazi" (PhD dissertation, University of London, 1950) and his *dīwān* by Qutbuddin, *Al-Mu'ayyad.*

16. The following discussion is drawn primarily from the thirty-eighth *majlis* in the second tome of the work, see al-Mu'ayyad fī al-Dīn Shīrāzī, *al-Majālis al-Mu'ayyadiyya*, ed. Ḥamīd al-Dīn, vols. 1 and 2 (Mumbai and Oxford, 1975–1986), vol. 2, 215–222; but it also draws from *majlis* forty-five in the first tome, which discusses many of the same topics, pp. 209–214; also al-Mu'ayyad fī al-Dīn Shīrāzī, *al-Majālis al-Mu'ayyadiyya*, trans. Muscati and Moulvi, *Life and Lectures of the Grand Missionary al-Muayyad-fid-Din al-Shirazi* (Karachi, 1950), 137–140.

17. Ṭūsī and Ḥasan-i Maḥmūd, *Rawḍa-yi Taslīm*, ed. Badakhchani, trans. Badakhchani, *Paradise of Submission: A Medieval Treatise on Ismaili Thought* (London, 2005) ed. 128–134, trans. 104–109.

18. See Ṭūsī, *Sayr wa-Sulūk*, ed. Badakhchani, trans. Badakhchani, *Contemplation and Action: The Spiritual Autobiography of a Muslim Scholar* (London, 1998), ed. 14, trans. 46.

19. Ṭūsī, *Āghāz wa-Anjām*, ed. Afshār (Tehran, 1335 HS/1956), chapter 17.

20. Quhistānī, *Dīwān-i Ḥakīm Nizārī Quhistānī*, ed. Muṣaffā (Tehran, 1371 HS/1992), 674–675 and Baiburdi, *Zindagī wa-Āthār-i Nizārī*, trans. Ṣadrī (Tehran, 1370 HS/[1991]), 83. Cf. Hunzai, *Shimmering Light: An Anthology of Ismaili Poetry* (London, 1996), 91–92; Jamal, *Surviving the Mongols: Nizari Quhistani and the Continuity of Ismaili Tradition in Persia* (London, 2002), 96–97; Lewisohn, "Sufism and Ismāʿīlī Doctrine in the Persian Poetry of Nizārī Quhistānī (645–721/1247–1321)," *Iran* 41 (2003): 241.

21. Shams, *Man Samajāṇī [Moṭī]* ([Mumbai?], nd), c. 158, Nūr Muḥammadshāh, *Sat Veṇī Moṭī*, ed. Devarāj, 1st Gujarati ed. (Mumbai, 1975 VS/1919), 154. See also Virani, "Symphony of Gnosis: A Self-Definition of the Ismaili Ginān Literature," in *Reason and Inspiration in Islam: Theology, Philosophy and Mysticism in Muslim Thought*, ed. Lawson (London, 2005), 507–510.

22. Ṭūsī, *Sayr wa-Sulūk*, ed. 17–18, cf. trans. 47–48.

23. A reference to Quran 32:8 and 77:20.

24. Ṭūsī and Ḥasan-i Maḥmūd, *Rawḍa-yi Taslīm*, ed. 134, trans. 109, translation slightly modified.

25. Ḥusayn, "Āmad zamān ānkih maḥabbat ʿīyan kunīm," in *Institute of Ismaili Studies Library*, Persian ms 14698 (London). A few verses from this poem are cited in Muʿizzī, "Ismāʿīliyyān-i Īrān" (MA thesis, Dānishgāh-i Firdawsī, 1371–1372 HS/1992–1993), 171 n100, in which she suggests that this poet may be the same as a certain Mīrzā Ḥusayn. The meter, technically speaking, may be classified as *muḍāriʿ makhbūn akhrab makfūf wa-sālim wa-akhrab wa-maḥdhūf* or even as *ramal makhbūn mushaʿʿas makfūf wa ṣālim*. In reality, it is almost the same as *muḍāriʿ akhrab makfūf maḥdhūf*, wonderfully translated in Thiesen, *A Manual of Classical Persian Prosody: With Chapters on Urdu, Karakhanidic and Ottoman Prosody* (Belgium, 1982), 155 as "the ear-pierced restrained apocopated eightfold similar meter." On the difficulties of classification, see Thiesen, *Classical Persian Prosody*, 153–156, 180.

دل بر کنیم از همه حالات دنیوی	جان را بنور رحمت حق شادمان کنیم
خود را خلاص ساخته از دست دیو نفس	از صدق بندگئ امام زمان کنیم
دلها ز مکر دیو درونی رها کنیم	جان را فدای نام شه انس و جان کنیم
سلطان دین که شاه غریب است نام او	نام بزرگ او همه ورد زبان کنیم
گاه [sic، گاهی] چو طفل و گاه جوانست و گاه پیر	باید که ما حدیث پیمبر نشان کنیم
جانم فدای طبع عزیزی که گفته است	يك بيت از كلام شريفش ادا كنيم
بی شك همان علی است نباید که ذرّه ای	در بندگیش میل بچون و چرا کنیم
گر اهل [شرع ؟] رو سوی کعبه می کنند	ما کعبه حقیقت خود انگوان کنیم
چون در فنا ز زندگی این جهان بقاست	هان تا هوای زندگی جاودان کنیم
گشتیم پیر جمله به تقصیر و معصیت	خود را بنور طاعتش از نو جوان کنیم
چون روح ما ز وسوسه تن خلاص شد	اندر جوار رحمت حق آشیان کنیم
با صدق اگر ز مبداء خود یاد آوریم	رو بر معاد بر صفت عاشقان کنیم...

26. Shams, *Man Samajāṇī [Moṭī]*, c. 7. In this regard, see also Virani, "Symphony of Gnosis," 508–509.

27. Shams, *Shrī Nakaḷaṁk Shāstra : Pīr Shams no Vāek Moṭo*, ed. Chunārā, 1st ed. (Mumbai, 1342/1923), v. 52.

28. Imāmshāh, "Pīr vinā pār na pāmīe," in *100 Ginānanī Chopaḍī*, 5th ed., vol. 3 (Mumbai, 1991 vs/1935), v. 12; cf. Imāmshāh, "Pīyu pīyu kījīe," in *100 Ginānanī Chopaḍī*, 5th ed., vol. 3 (Mumbai, 1991 vs/1935), v. 1 and Ṣadr al-Dīn, "Sīrīe salāmashāhā amane malīyā," in *100 Ginānanī Chopaḍī*, 4th ed., vol. 5 (Mumbai, 1990 vs/1934), v. 3.

29. Satagur Nūr, "Satagur padhāreā tame jāgajo," in *100 Ginānanī Chopaḍī*, 5th ed., vol. 3 (Mumbai, 1991 vs/1935), v. 4.

30. Shams, "Sāmī tamārī vāḍī māṃhe," in *100 Ginānanī Chopaḍī*, 5th ed., vol. 3 (Mumbai, 1991 vs/1935), v. 7; cf. Imāmshāh, "Imāmapurī nagarī ne kuṃvārī kā khetra,"

in *100 Ginānanī Chopaḍī, 60 Ginān: Jugesar tathā Abadhunāṃ (section 2)*, 4th ed., vol. 6 (Mumbai, 1989 vs/1933), v. 6.

31. Shams, "Satagur bheṭeā kem jāṇīe," in *100 Ginān nī Chopaḍī*, 5th ed., vol. 2 (Mumbai, 1993 vs/1936), v. 1.

32. Imāmshāh, "Āj te amar āveā," in *100 Ginān nī Chopaḍī*, 5th ed., vol. 2 (Mumbai, 1993 vs/1936), v. 2.

33. A reference to the famous Quranic phrase, *liman al-mulk*, (40:16). For an Ismaili understanding of this dictum, see Ṭūsī, *Āghāz wa-Anjām*, chapter 2.

34. Dāʿī Anjudānī, "[Qaṣīda-yi dhurriyya]," in *Institute of Ismaili Studies Library*, Persian ms 15030 (London). There are a number of copies of this *qaṣīda* in the manuscripts of the Iranian Ismailis. See Muʿizzī, "Ismāʿīliyyān-i Īrān," 40. Fidā'ī Khurāsānī had quoted it in his "Dānish-i Ahl-i Bīnish," p. 445, cited in Muʿizzī's above mentioned work.

35. Cited in Ṭūsī and Ḥasan-i Maḥmūd, *Rawḍa-yi Taslīm*, ed. 175, trans. 141. In addition to the sources cited in Ṭūsī and Ḥasan-i Maḥmūd, *Rawḍa-yi Taslīm*, 261–262 n151; see also al-Nuʿmān, *Daʿā'im al-Islām fī Dhikr al-Ḥalāl wa-al-Ḥarām*, trans. Fyzee and Poonawala, *The Pillars of Islam*, 2 vols. (New Delhi, 2002–2004), vol. 1, 22; al-Nuʿmān, *Sharḥ al-Akhbār fī faḍā'il al-a'immat al-aṭhār*, ed. al-Jalālī, 3 vols. (Qumm, 1409–1412/1988–1992), vol. 1, 104.

36. Ṭūsī and Ḥasan-i Maḥmūd, *Rawḍa-yi Taslīm*, ed. 175, trans. 141.

37. Ibid, ed. 196–197, trans. 158–159.

38. Darwīsh, "Dilā az manzil-i īn tīrah khākdān bar khīz," in *Institute of Ismaili Studies Library*, Persian ms 14712 (London). Some verses of this poem are quoted in Muʿizzī, "Ismāʿīliyyān-i Īrān," 170–171 n100. The meter is *mujtathth muthamman makhbūn maḥdhūf*.

دلا ز منزل این تیره خاکدان برخیز   چو عاشقان ز سر و مال و ملك و جان بر خیز
بدام دانه دنیا بمانده ای در بند   ببر طمع ز خیالات این و آن بر خیز
مشو فریفتهء این [sic, omit] رنگهای شیطانی   بکار بندگی صاحب الزمان بر خیز
غرور و عشوه دنیا بکافران بگذار   تو مردوار در این دور امتحان بر خیز...
تو ای برادر من گر نجات می خواهی   بدوستاران [بدوستداری آن] شاه انجدان بر خیز..
امام وقت علی زمانه شاه غریب   به بندگیش کمر بسته و ز جان بر خیز...
محل رفتن [و] کوچ است از این جهان درویش   چه مانده ای که برفتند همراهان بر خیز...

39. See note 11 in this chapter.

در این گنجینه نه سقف و چهار ایوان و شش منظر   طلسم گنج معنی دان وجود عالم آرایم
اگر خواهی که روی من به بینی چشم سر بگشا   که چشم سر نه بیند جز ظهور دهر فرسایم
مرا در عالم خاکی کجا بینی بدین دیده   که من در جا و بیجایم بری از جا و ماوایم
اگر خواهی که بشناسی مرا خود را شناس اوّل   بمن هر کو شناسا شد شناسا را شناسایم
ز جام شوق شو سرمست که تا در یابی این معنی   که من گه باده و گه جام و گاهی گشته سقّایم
از آن در اول و آخر نه بینی غیر من چیزی   از این معنی که پنهانست دایم گشته پیدایم

تغیّر نیست در معنی مرا لیك از ره صورت   مبدّل می شوم گاهی بهر شکلی برون آیم
مرا نه جسم دان نه جان مرا نه این شمر نه آن   که من در کون بیچونی ز جسم و جان مبرّایم
نه موجود و نه معدومم نه محسوس و نه معلومم   نه با چون و نه بیچونم نه در جا و نه بیجایم
من آن شمعِ جهان تابم که خورشیدِ جهان آرا   زند پروانه آسا پر ز شوقِ شمع پیرایم
من آن اعجوبهٴ صنعم که چون افشا کنم معنی   دو عالم مشتعل گردد ز نور شعله آرایم
بسیطِ مطلقم در ذات و کلِ جمله کلیات   ولی اجزای موجودات جزوی دان ز اجزایم
مرا گو گردِ احمر دان مرا اکسیرِ اعظم خوان   مرا گوهر مخوان زیرا که من بحر گهر زایم
اگرچه قطره را مانم که از دریا برون افتد   ولی چون قطره بشناسی بدانی همچو دریایم
مثال من بسی بینی ولی از راه کج بینی   اگر توراست بین باشی نه بینی مثل و همتایم
هزاران خانه دارم جا و جایم نیست خود پیدا   هزاران اسم دارم من ولی خود یك مسمّایم
کنون عبد السلامم من ولی از همگنان غمگین   ازین مجلس بخواهم رفت و دیگر بار باز آیم
منم عبد السلام و از من است این بیستون بر پا   بمانندِ ستون در زیر این نه سقفِ مینایم

40. Muʿizzī, "Ismāʿīliyyān-i Īrān," 107 has compared it to the *shaṭḥ*, or ecstatic locutions, of the Sufis.

41. al-Malījī, *al-Majālis al-Mustanṣiriyya*, ed. Ḥusayn (Cairo, [1947]), 27.

42. This is a recognized Shīʿī tradition, reported in slightly different wordings in, for example, al-Kulaynī, *al-Uṣūl min al-Kāfī*, ed. Kamarāʾī (Tehran, 1392/1792) vol. 1, 332–334; Ṭūsī and Ḥasan-i Maḥmūd, *Rawḍa-yi Taslīm*, ed. 148, trans. 120. See also Amir-Moezzi, *The Divine Guide in Early Shiʿism: The Sources of Esotericism in Islam,* trans. Straight (Albany, NY, 1994) 43, 125, 229 n673–n675 for further references.

43. al-Ḥusaynī, *Ḥaqīqat-i Dīn*, 73–74. Cf. translation in al-Ḥusaynī, *Ḥaqīqat-i Dīn*, 48.

44. "al-Salām ay bādashāh-i dīn-o dunyā al-salām," in *Institute of Ismaili Studies Library*, Persian ms 15052 (London). The meter is *ramal muthamman maḥdhūf.*

السلام ای بادشاه دین و دنیا السلام   از خراسان آمدم بهر لقایت یا امام
نیست همره طاعتی کان موجب غفران شود   هست جرم و معصیت بسیار و نفس ناتمام
با چنین کاسد متاعی دارم از لطفت امید   تا بمن بخشی گناه بندگان از خاص و عام
زانکه هستی قادر و حاکم بکل کاینات   معنی این قول روشن گشته از نص کلام
اسم خاصت گشته ظاهر بر جمیع مومنان   شاه غریب و شاه مستنصر وصی شه سلام...

45. The text here was prepared from a collation of the poem in Anṣārī, "Har kih az ʿilm-i ladunī shammaī āgāh shud," in *Institute of Ismaili Studies Library*, Persian ms 15052 (London) and a second, unnumbered ms, also at the Institute of Ismaili Studies. I am grateful to Dr. F. M. Hunzai for indicating to me the existence of the latter, which contains the full name of the poet. The meter is *ramal muthamman maḥdhūf.*

هر که از علم لدنی شمهء آگاه شد   از دل و جان بندهء مستنصر بالله شد
بگذراند پایهء قدر خود از ایوان عرش   هرکه از روی محبت خاك این درگاه شد
بندهء شاهی شدم کز روی عز و منزلت   هر که شد هندوی او بر هر دو عالم شاه شد
بنده ای گشتم چنان مقبل که هر کس دید گفت   بس مبارك بنده ای کش نام عبد الله شد
بود دلخواه من بیدل که بینم روی دوست   لله الحمد آنچه دل بر موجب دلخواه شد
نیست تشبیه تو در آفاق الا ذات تو   لاجرم هر کس ترا بشناخت بی اشباه شد
هر زمان در صورت دیگر بر آمد بو العجب   گاه مستنصر شد و گاهی سلام الله شد
گاه طفل و گاه پیر و گاه برنا می شود   گاه بر معراج رفت و گاه اندر چاه شد
گر بصد صورت بر آید مرد معنی را چه غم   هر کرا بگشود چشم سِر بسویش راه شد
هر که این ره را بتحقیق از پی فرمان نرفت   گر همه مأذون درگهست کو گمراه شد
هر که از امر تو سر پیچید بالله العظیم   گر بصورت پیر درگاهست طفل راه شد
یا خداوندا تو می دانی درین دنیای دون   عمر در غفلت گذشت [و] سال رفت [و] ماه شد
یا خداوندا درین دنیا ز بهر آن جهان   دانهء تخمی نیفکندیم که بیگاه شد
هاتفی در گوش جانم گفت ناگاه [sic، ناگاهان] ز غیب   غم مخور چون این سعادت مر ترا ناگاه شد
گرچه عریانم من از طاعت بدان شادم یقین   هر که شد درویش این درگاه صاحب جاه شد
یا خداوندا اگر گستاخای کردم عظیم   غم نخواهم خورد چون لطف توام همراه شد
هم بنامت ختم کردم زانکه در دنیا و دین   ابتدای کارها بر نام بسم الله شد

46. Amir-Moezzi, *Divine Guide*, 31, 44–45. See also Nāṣir-i Khusraw, *Wajh-i Dīn*, ed. Aavani (Tehran, 1977), 127, and Jaʿfar b. Manṣūr al-Yaman, *Kitāb al-Kashf*, ed. Strothmann (London, 1952), 109.

47. Mustanṣir bi'llāh (=Gharīb Mīrzā?), *Pandiyāt-i Jawānmardī*, ed. Ivanow, trans. Ivanow, *Pandiyat-i Jawanmardi or "Advices of Manliness"* (Leiden, 1953), ed. 17–19, trans. 11–12.

48. Ibid, ed. 85–86, cf. trans. 53. Regarding the weeping of the Prophets, see Quran 17:109, 19:58.

49. al-Mu'ayyad fī al-Dīn Shīrāzī, *Dīwān*, 313. Cf. Qutbuddin, *Al-Mu'ayyad*, 77–80, in which the poem is analyzed and translated. The word *fawd* (hair around the temples) seems to have been misread as *fu'ād* (heart).

أقْسِمُ لَو أنّكَ تَوَّجْتَني   بِتاج كِسرَى مَلِكِ المَشْرِق
و نُلْتَنِي كُلَّ أمُورِ الوَرَى   مَنْ قَدْ مَضَى مِنهم و مَنْ قَدْ بَقِي
وَقُلْتَ أنْ لا نَلْتَقِي سَاعةً   أجَبْتُ يا مولايَ أنْ نَلْتَقِي
لأنَّ اِبعَادَكَ لِي ساعةً   شَيَّبَ فَوْدَيَّ مَعَ المَفْرِق

50. Ṣadr al-Dīn, "Sakhī māhā pad kerī vāt koek jāṇere," in *100 Ginānanī Chopaḍī*, 5th ed., vol. 3 (Mumbai, 1991 vs/1935), vv. 1, 4, 9–13. *Aras paras* in v. 10 may perhaps be *aras kuras*, i.e., *ʿarsh [wa-] kursī*.

51. Mustanṣir bi'llāh (=Gharīb Mīrzā?), *Pandiyāt*, ed. 34–35, trans. 21–22.
52. Ibid, ed. 35, trans. 22.

AFTERWORD

1. Hodgson, "The Ismāʿīlī State," in *The Cambridge History of Iran*, vol. 5 (Cambridge, 1968), 423.
2. Juwaynī, *Taʾrīkh-i Jahāngushāy*, ed. Qazwīnī, 3 vols. (Leiden, 1912–1937), ed. vol. 3, 275, trans. vol. 2, 723.
3. Ibid, ed. vol. 3, 277, trans. vol. 2, 724–725.
4. Ivanow, "My First Meeting with the Ismailis in Persia," *Ilm* 3, no. 3 (December 1977): 16–17, reprinted from Ivanow, "My First Meeting with Ismailis of Persia," *Read and Know* 1 (1966). "I was able to see" corrected to "was I able to see," "expect n life" corrected to "expect in life," and "poor village" corrected to "poor villages."

Bibliography

ʿAbd al-Salām, Imām. "Alā ay ṭālib-i waḥdat hamī lāfī kih jūyāyam," in *Institute of Ismaili Studies Library*, Persian ms 15033. London.

———. "Alā ay ṭālib-i waḥdat kih mī lāfī kih jūyāyam," in *Kitāb al-Manāqib* ed. Hiz Hāʾīnes Prins Āghā Khān Shīʿa Imāmī Ismāʿīliya Esūsīʾeshan barāʾe Pākistān, 4–9. Karachi, 1406/1986.

———. "Alā ay ṭālib-i waḥdat kih mī lāfī kih jūyāyam," in *Institute of Ismaili Studies Library*, Persian ms 14704. London.

———. "Alā e ṭālib-i waḥdat hamī lāfī kih jūyāyam," in *Qasidas: Great Ismaili Tradition of Central Asia*. ed. Audio Visual Department The Shia Imami Ismaili Tariqah and Religious Education Board for Pakistan. Vol. 1, Side A, #1. [Karachi], nd.

[ʿAbd al-Salām, Imām?]. "Panj Sukhan kih Ḥaḍrat-i Shāh Islām Farmūda and," in *Kitāb-i Mustaṭāb-i Haft Bāb-i Dāʿī Abū Isḥāq*. ed. Ḥājī Qudrat Allāh Beg, 125–126. Gilgit, Pakistan, 1962.

Abu-Izzeddin, Nejla Mustafa. *The Druzes: A New Study of Their History, Faith and Society*. Leiden, 1984.

Abū al-Fawāris, Aḥmad b. Yaʿqūb. *al-Risāla fī al-Imāma*. ed. Sami Nasib Makarem. trans. Sami Nasib Makarem. *The Political Doctrine of the Ismāʿīlīs (The Imamate)*. Delmar, NY, 1977.

Abū al-Fidā. "al-Mukhtaṣar [fī] taʾrīkh [or akhbār] al-bashar (extracts with French translation)," in *Recueil des Historiens des Croisades: Historiens Orientaux*. Vol. 1, 1–165. Paris, 1872–1906.

Abū al-Maʿālī, Ḥātim b. ʿImrān (or Maḥmūd) b. Zahrā. "Risālat al-Uṣūl wa-al-Aḥkām," in *Khams Rasāʾil Ismāʿīliyya*. ed. ʿĀrif Tāmir, 99–143. Salamiyya, Syria, 1375/1956.

Abū al-Maʿālī, Muḥammad b. ʿUbayd Allāh al-Ḥusaynī al-ʿAlawī. *Bayān al-Adyān*. ed. ʿAbbās Iqbāl Āshtiyānī and Muḥammad Taqī Dānishpazhūh. Tehran, 1376 HS/1997.

Adae, Guillelmus. *Directorium ad passagium faciendum, in RHC: Documents Arméniens*. Vol. 2. Paris, 1869–1906.

Ādhar, Luṭf ʿAli Beg Begdilī. *Ātishkada*. ed. Ḥasan Sādāt Nāṣirī. Tehran, 1337–1338 HS/1958–1959.

"Afghans' Attack to Alamut Fortress Confirmed." August 28, 2005. Cultural Heritage News Agency, http://www.chn.ir/en/news/?id=5512&section=2 (accessed February 5, 2006).

al-Aflākī, Shams al-Dīn Aḥmad. *Manāqib al-ʿĀrifīn*. ed. Tahsin Yazici. 2 vols. Ankara, 1959.

Akhbār al-dawla al-ʿAbbāsiyya wa-fīhi akhbār al-ʿAbbās wa-waladihi. ed. ʿAbd al-ʿAzīz al-Dūrī and ʿAbd al-Jabbār al-Muṭṭalibī. Beirut, 1971.

Akhtar, Kazi Ahmed Mian. "Shams Tabrizi: Was He an Ismailian." *IC* 10 (January 1936): 131–136.

"al-Salām ay bādashāh-i dīn-o dunyā al-salām," in *Institute of Ismaili Studies Library*, Persian ms 15052. London.

"Alamut Fortress, No Prison." August 29, 2005. Cultural Heritage News Agency, http://www.chn.ir/en/news/?Section=2&id=5522 (accessed February 5, 2006).

Algar, Hamid. "Niʿmat-Allāhiyya," in *EI2*. Vol. 8, 44. Leiden, 1960–2004. Reprint, CD-ROM v. 1.0.

———. "The Revolt of Āghā Khān Maḥallātī and the Transference of the Ismāʿīlī Imamate to India." *SI* 29 (1969): 55–81.

ʿAlī b. Abī Ṭālib. *Nahj al-Balāgha*. ed. Ṣubḥī al-Ṣāliḥ. Beirut, 1387/1967.

Ali, Syed Mujtaba. *The Origin of the Khojāhs and Their Religious Life Today*. Würzburg, 1936.

Amīn-Riyāḥī, Muḥammad. *Taʾrīkh-i Khuy*. Tehran, 1372 HS/1993.

al-Amīnī, ʿAbd al-Ḥusayn Aḥmad al-Najafī. *al-Ghadīr fī al-Kitāb wa-al-Sunna wa-al-Adab*. 2nd ed. 11 vols. Tehran, 1372/1952.

Amir-Moezzi, Mohammad Ali. *The Divine Guide in Early Shiʿism: The Sources of Esotericism in Islam*. trans. David Streight. Albany, NY, 1994.

ʿĀmir b. ʿĀmir al-Baṣrī. Tāʾiyya. ed. Yves Marquet. trans. Yves Marquet. *Poésie ésoterique Ismailiènne: La Tāʾiyya de ʿĀmir b. ʿĀmir al-Baṣrī*. Paris, 1985.

Anṣārī, ʿAbd Allāh. "Har kih az ʿilm-i ladunī shammaī āgāh shud," in *Institute of Ismaili Studies Library*, Persian ms 15052. London.

Asani, Ali Sultaan Ali. *The Harvard Collection of Ismaili Literature in Indic Languages: A Descriptive Catalog and Finding Aid*. Boston, 1992.

———. "The Ismaʿili Gināns: Reflections on Authority and Authorship," in *Mediaeval Ismaʿili History and Thought*. ed. Farhad Daftary, 265–280. Cambridge, 1996.

———. "The Khojki Script: A Legacy of Ismaili Islam in the Indo-Pakistan Subcontinent." *JAOS* 107, no. 3 (1987): 439–449.

Aubin, Jean. *Matériaux pour la biographie de Shāh Niʿmatullāh Walī Kermānī*. Tehran, 1956.

———. "Un Santon Quhistani de l'Époque Timouride." *Revue des Études Islamiques* 35 (1967): 185–216.

Ayalon, David. "The Great Yāsa of Chingiz Khān: A Re-examination." *SI* 33 (1971): 97–140.

Ayoub, Mahmoud. "The Speaking Qur'ān and the Silent Qur'ān: A Study of the Principles and Development of Imāmī Shīʿī tafsīr," in *Approaches to the History of the Interpretation of the Qur'ān*. ed. Andrew Rippin. Oxford, 1988.

Babayan, Kathryn. *Mystics, Monarchs, and Messiahs: Cultural Landscapes of Early Modern Iran*. Cambridge, MA, 2002.

Badakhchani, Sayyed Jalal Hossein. "The Paradise of Submission." PhD dissertation, Oxford University, 1989.

Badakhshānī, Sayyid Suhrāb Walī. *Sī wa-Shish Ṣaḥīfa*. ed. Hushang Ujaqi. Tehran, 1961.

———. *Tuḥfat al-Nāẓirīn*. ed. Ḥājī Qudrat Allāh Beg. Gilgit, Pakistan, 1960.

al-Baghdādī, Abū Manṣūr ʿAbd al-Qāhir b. Ṭāhir. *al-Farq bayna al-Firāq*. trans. Kate Chambers Seelye. *Moslem Schisms and Sects: (al-Farḳ bain al-firāḳ) Being the History of the Various Philosophic Systems Developed in Islam*. New York, 1966.

Baiburdi, Chingiz Gulam-Ali. *Zhizn' i Tvorchestvo Nizari—Persidskogo Poeta XIII–XIV vv*. Moscow, 1966.

———. *Zindagī wa-Āthār-i Nizārī*. trans. Mihnāz Ṣadrī. Tehran, 1370 HS/[1991].

Bashir, Shahzad. "Between Mysticism and Messianism: The Life and Thought of Muhammad Nurbakś (d. 1464)." PhD dissertation, Yale University, 1997.

———. *Fazlallah Astarabadi and the Hurufis*. Oxford, 2005.

al-Bazāʿī, Muḥammad b. al-Faḍl b. ʿAlī. "Kitāb al-Tarātīb al-Sabʿa wa-hiya Sabʿa Tarātīb ʿalā al-Tamām wa-al-Kamāl," in *Akhbār al-Qarāmiṭa*. ed. Suhayl Zakkār. 2nd ed, 287–291. Damascus, 1402/1982.

Bazmee Ansari, A. S. "al-Djūzdjānī," in *EI2*. 2nd ed. Vol. 2, 609. Leiden, 1960–2004. Reprint, CD-ROM v. 1.0.

Bernard, André. "Fear of Book Assasination [sic] Haunts Bibliophile's Musings." *The New York Observer*. December 15, 2003. http://www.nyobserver.com/pages/story.asp?ID=8291. (Accessed January 28, 2004).

Biblia Sacra: iuxta Vulgatam versionem. Ed. Bonifatius Fischer and Robert Weber. Stuttgart: Deutsche Bibelgesellschaft, 1983. http://www.thelatinlibrary.com/bible/prologi.html (accessed February 2, 2006).

Boghā, Māstar Hāsham. *Isamāilī Darpaṇ*. Mumbai, 1323/1906.

Boivin, Michel. "A Persian Treatise for the Ismāʿīlī Khojas of India: Presentation of the Pandiyāt-i Jawānmardī," in *The Making of Indo-Persian Culture*. ed. Muzaffar Alam et al. New Delhi, 2000.

Bosworth, C. E. "Kāwūs, Banū," in *EI2*. Vol. 4, 808. Leiden, 1960–2004. Reprint, CD-ROM v. 1.0.

Bosworth, C. E., and V. Minorsky. "Lāhīdjān," in *EI2*. Vol. 5, 602. Leiden, 1960–2004. Reprint, CD-ROM v. 1.0.

Bosworth, Charles E. "The Ismaʿilis of Quhistān and the Maliks of Nīmrūz or Sīstān," in *Mediaeval Ismaʿili History and Thought*. ed. Farhad Daftary. Cambridge, 1996.

Boyle, John Andrew. "The Death of the Last ʿAbbāsid Caliph: A Contemporary Muslim Account." *Journal of Semitic Studies* 6 (1961).

———. "Dynastic and Political History of the Il-Khans," in *The Cambridge History of Iran*. ed. John Andrew Boyle. Vol. 5. Cambridge, 1968.

Browne, Edward Granville. *A Literary History of Persia*. 4 vols. Cambridge, 1902–1924.

Bruijn, J. T. P. de. *Of Piety and Poetry: The Interaction of Religion and Literature in the Life and Works of Ḥakīm Sanā'ī of Ghazna*. Leiden, 1983.

Bruijn, J. T. P. de. "Sanā'ī," in *EI2*. Vol. 9, 3 Leiden, 1960–2004. Reprint, CD-ROM v. 1.0.

Buhl, F. "Muḥammad b. ʿAbd Allāh b. al-Ḥasan al-Muthannā b. al-Ḥasan b. ʿAlī b. Abī Ṭālib, called al-Nafs al-Zakiyya," in *EI2*. Vol. VII, 388. Leiden, 1960–2004. Reprint, CD-ROM v. 1.0.

Calder, Norman. "Judicial Authority in Imāmī Shīʿī Jurisprudence " *BRISMES* 6, no. 2 (1979): 104–108.

Calmard, J. "Marʿashīs," in *EI2*. Vol. 6, 510. Leiden, 1960–2004. Reprint, CD-ROM v. 1.0.

Canard, M. "Daʿwa," in *EI2*. Vol. 2, 170. Leiden, 1960–2004. Reprint, CD-ROM v. 1.0.

Casanova, M. Paul. "Un nouveau manuscrit de la secte des Assassins." *JA* 11 série, no. 19 (1922): 126–135.

Catafago, Joseph. "Lettre de M. Catafago à M. Mohl." *JA* série 12, no. 12 (1848): 72–78, 485–493.

Chambers, F. M. "The Troubadours and the Assassins." *Modern Language Notes* 64 (1949): 245–251.

Chardin, John. *Voyages de monsieur le chevalier Chardin en Perse et autres lieux de l'orient*. 3 vols. Amsterdam, 1709.

Chittick, William C. *Faith and Practice of Islam: Three Thirteenth Century Sufi Texts*. Albany, NY, 1992.

Chunārā, Alīmāmad Jānmahamad. *Nūram Mobīn: yāne Allāhanī pavitra rasī [English Title: Noorum-Mobin or The Sacred Cord of God*]. ed. Jāfaralī Māhamad Sufī. 4th ed. Mumbai, 1961.

Chunārā, Alīmāmad Jānmāmad. *Nurun Mobīn: athavā Allāhanī pavitra rasī*. 1st ed. Mumbai, 1935.

Clarke, Lynda G. "Early Doctrine of the Shiʿah, According to the Shīʿī Sources." PhD dissertation, McGill University, 1994.

———. "The Rise and Decline of *Taqiyya* in Twelver Shiʿism," in *Reason and Inspiration in Islam: Theology, Philosophy and Mysticism in Muslim Thought*. ed. Todd Lawson. London, 2005.

"Convention on the Prevention and Punishment of the Crime of Genocide." December 9, 1948. Office of the United Nations High Commissioner for Human Rights, http://www.unhchr.ch/html/menu3/b/p_genoci.htm (accessed February 2, 2006).

Corbin, Henry. *Cyclical Time and Ismaili Gnosis*. London, 1983.

———. *En Islam Iranien: Aspects Spirituels et Philosophiques*. 4 vols. Paris, 1971.

———. "The Ismāʿīlī Response to the Polemic of Ghazālī," in *Ismāʿīlī Contributions to Islamic Culture*. ed. S. H. Nasr. trans. James W. Morris, 67–98. Tehran, 1977.

———. *Temple and Contemplation*. trans. Philip Sherrard. London, 1986.

———. *Trilogie Ismaélienne*. Tehran, 1961.

Cortese, Delia. "Eschatology and Power in Mediaeval Persian Ismailism." PhD dissertation, University of London, 1993.

Crone, Patricia. "ʿUthmāniyya," in *EI2*. Vol. 10, 952. Leiden, 1960–2004. Reprint, CD-ROM v. 1.0.

Crowe, Yolande. "Samarḳand," in *EI2*. Vol. 8, 1031. Leiden, 1960–2004. Reprint, CD-ROM v. 1.0.

Daftary, Farhad. *The Assassin Legends: Myths of the Ismailis*. London, 1994.

———. *Ismaili Literature*. London, 2004.

———. *The Ismāʿīlīs: Their History and Doctrines*. Cambridge, 1990.

———. "The Medieval Ismāʿīlīs of the Iranian Lands," in *The Sultan's Turret: Studies in Persian and Turkish Culture*. ed. Carole Hillenbrand. Vol. 2, 43–81. Leiden, 2000.

———. "Persian Historiography of the Early Nizārī Ismāʿīlīs." *Iran* 30 (1992): 91–97.

———. "Shams al-Dīn Muḥammad," in *EI2*. Vol. 9, 295. Leiden, 1960–2004. Reprint, CD-ROM v. 1.0.

———. "Shihāb al-Dīn al-Ḥusaynī, Shāh," in *EI2*. Vol. 9, 435. Leiden, 1960–2004. Reprint, CD-ROM v. 1.0.

———. "W. Ivanow: A Biographical Notice." *Middle Eastern Studies* 8, no. 2 (May 1972): 241–244.

Dāʿī Anjudānī. "[Qaṣīda-yi dhurriyya]," in *Institute of Ismaili Studies Library*, Persian ms 15030. London.

Daragāhavālā, Pīrazādā Sayyad Sadaruddīn. *Tavārīkhe Pīr*. 2 vols. Navasārī, India, 1914–1935.

Darwīsh. "Dilā az manzil-i īn tīrah khākdān bar khīz," in *Institute of Ismaili Studies Library*, Persian ms 14712. London.

Davy, Major William. *Political and Military Institutes of Tamerlane*. Delhi, 1972.

Dawlatshāh, Ibn ʿAlāʾ al-Dawla. *Tadhkirat al-Shuʿarāʾ*. Ed. Edward Granville Browne. London, 1901.

de Bode, Baron C. A. *Travels in Luristan and Arabistan*. Vol. 2. London, 1845.

"Dhoā: sāji: somaṇi: subhuaji," in *The Harvard Collection of Ismaili Literature in Indic Languages, Houghton Library*, Ms Ism K 19. Cambridge, MA.

Dhuā: gaṭ: pāṭ - sāñji: somaṇi: tathā subhuhaji: khās: imāmii: isamāili: khojā: jamātaje: vāsate. Mumbai, 1958 vs/1902.

"Dhuā: vakhatji," in *The Harvard Collection of Ismaili Literature in Indic Languages, Houghton Library*, Ms Ism K 22. Cambridge, MA.

Dihgān, Ibrāhīm. *Kārnāma yā dū bakhsh-i dīgar az taʾrīkh-i Arāk. [Tehran], 1345* HS/1966.

Dihlawī, ʿAbd al-Ḥaqq. *Akhbār al-Akhyār fī Asrār al-Abrār*. Delhi, 1891.

al-Dimashqī, Shams al-Dīn Abū ʿAbd Allāh Muḥāmmad. *Nukhbat al-Dahr fī ʿAjāʾib al-Barr wa-al-Baḥr*. Copenhagen, 1874.

———. *Nukhbat al-Dahr fī ʿAjāʾib al-Barr wa-al-Baḥr*. ed. A. F. Mehren. *Cosmographie de Chems-ed-Din Abou Abdallah Mohammed Ed-Dimichqui*. St. Petersburg, 1866.

———. *Nukhbat al-Dahr fī ʿAjāʾib al-Barr wa-al-Baḥr (Persian translation)*. Shayryūr, 1357 HS/1978.

Dossa, Parin Aziz. "Ritual and Daily Life: Transmission and Interpretation of the Ismaili Tradition in Vancouver." PhD dissertation, University of British Columbia, 1985.

Dughlāt, Mīrzā Ḥaydar. *Taʾrīkh-i Rashīdī*. ed. Wheeler M. Thackston. trans. Wheeler M. Thackston. *Mirza Haydar Dughlat's Tarikh-i Rashidi: A History of the Khans of Moghulistan*. [Cambridge, MA], 1996.

Dumasia, Naoroji M. *The Aga Khan and His Ancestors*. Mumbai, 1939.

Dupree, Louis. "Further Notes on Taqiyya: Afghanistan." *JAOS* 99, no. 4 (October–December 1979): 680–682.

During, Jean. *Musique et mystique dans les traditions de l'Iran*. Tehran, 1989.

Eche, Y. *Les Bibliothèques Arabes Publiques et Semi-Publiques en Mésopotamie, en Syrie et en Egypte au moyen âge*. Damascus, 1967.

Ernst, Carl W. *The Shambhala Guide to Sufism*. Boston, MA, 1997.

Faṣīḥ Khwāfī, Aḥmad b. Jalāl al-Dīn Muḥammad. *Mujmal-i Faṣīḥī*. ed. Maḥmūd Farrukh. 2 vols. Mashhad, 1339–1340 HS/1960–1961.

Fernández-Armesto, Felipe. "Steppes Towards the Future." *The Independent*. March 12, 2004. Independent News and Media, http://www.independent.co.uk/ (accessed March 13, 2004).

Fidāʾī Khurāsānī, Muḥammad b. Zayn al-ʿĀbidīn. *Hidāyat al-Muʾminīn al-Ṭālibīn*. ed. A. A. Semenov. Moscow, 1959.

———. "Hidāyat al-Mu'minīn al-Ṭālibīn," trans. Abhadharasul Salemānānī in *Institute of Ismaili Studies Library*, Khojki ms KH29. London, 1960 vs/[1903] Shrāvaṇ 22.

Firishta, Muḥammad Qāsim Hindūshāh Astarābādī. *Taʾrīkh-i Firishta [a.k.a. Gulshan-i Ibrāhīmī]*. ed. John Briggs. Mumbai, 1832.

Flugel, Gustav. *Die Arabischen, Persischen und Turkischen Handschriften der Kaiserlich-königlichen Hofbibliothek zu Wien*. Wien, 1867.

Gardīzī, ʿAbd al-Ḥayy b. al-Ḍaḥḥāk. *Zayn al-Akhbār*. ed. ʿAbd al-Ḥayy Ḥabībī. Tehran, 1347 HS/1968.

Ghālib, Muṣṭafā. *Aʿlām al-Ismāʿīliyya*. Beirut, 1964.

———. *Sinān Rashīd al-Dīn: Shaykh al-Jabal al-Thālith*. Beirut, 1967.

Gharīb Mīrzā, Imām. "Min Kalām-i Shāh Gharīb Mīrzā," in *Institute of Ismaili Studies Library*, Persian ms 123. London.

al-Ghazālī, Abū Ḥāmid Muḥammad b. Muḥammad al-Ṭūsī. *Faḍāʾiḥ al-Bāṭiniyya wa-Faḍāʾil al-Mustaẓhiriyya*. ed. ʿAbd al-Raḥmān Badawī. Cairo, 1383/1964.

———. *Faḍāʾiḥ al-Bāṭiniyya wa-Faḍāʾil al-Mustaẓhiriyya*. ed. Ignaz Goldziher. *Streitschrift des Gazālī gegen die Bāṭinīya-Sekte*. partial ed. Leiden, 1910.

Gīlānī, Mullā Shaykh ʿAlī. *Taʾrīkh-i Māzandarān*. ed. M. Sutūda. Tehran, 1352 HS/1973.

Goldziher, Ignaz. "Das Prinzip der taḳijja im Islam." *Zeitschrift der Deutschen Morgenländischen Gesellschaft* 60 (1906): 213–226.

Guillaume, J. "Les Ismaéliens dans le Roman de Baybars: Genèse d'un type littéraire." *SI* 84 (1996): 145–179.

Ḥāfiẓ Abrū, ʿAbd Allāh b. Luṭf ʿAlī al-Bihdādīnī. *Dhayl-i Jāmiʿ al-Tawārīkh*. Tehran, 1317 HS/1938.

Haig, T. W., and B. Spuler. "Kart," in *EI2*. Vol. 4, 672. Leiden, 1960–2004. Reprint, CD-ROM v. 1.0.

Haji, Zebunisa A. "La Doctrine Ismaélienne d'après l'oeuvre d'Abū Isḥāq Qohestānī." PhD dissertation, Sorbonne, 1975.

Hajnal, István. "On the History of the Ismāʿīlī 'Hidden Imāms' as Reflected in the Kitāb at-tarātīb as-sabʿa." *The Arabist, Budapest Studies in Arabic (Essays in Honour of Alexander Fodor on his Sixtieth Birthday)* 23 (2001): 101–116.

Halm, Heinz. *Die Kaliefen von Kairo: Die Fatimiden in Ägypten, 973–1074.* Munich, 2003.

———. *The Empire of the Mahdi: The Rise of the Fatimids.* trans. M. Bonner. Leiden, 1996.

———. *The Fatimids and Their Traditions of Learning.* London, 1997.

———. *Shiʿism.* trans. Janet Watson and Marian Hill. 2nd ed. New York, 2004.

———. *Shīʿism.* Edinburgh, 1991.

al-Hamdani, Abbas. "The Fāṭimid Daʿi al-Muʾayyad: His Life and Work," in *The Great Ismaili Heroes.* Karachi, 1973.

———. *The Beginnings of the Ismāʿīlī Daʿwa in Northern India (now Pakistan).* Cairo, 1956.

———. "The Sira of al Muayyad fid-Din ash-Shirazi." PhD dissertation, University of London, 1950.

al-Hamdani, Husain F. "Some Unknown Ismaili Authors and Their Works." *JRAS* (1933): 359–378.

al-Ḥāmidī, Ibrāhīm b. al-Ḥusayn. *Kanz al-Walad.* ed. Muṣṭafā Ghālib. Wiesbaden, 1391/1971.

Hammer-Purgstall, Joseph von. *Die Geschichte der Assassinen aus Morgenländischen Quellen.* Stuttgart and Tübingen, 1818.

———. *The History of the Assassins, Derived from Oriental Sources.* trans. Oswald Charles Wood. London, 1835.

———, ed. *Codices Arabicos, Persicos, Turcicos, Bibliothecae Caesareo-Regio-Palatinae Vindobonensis.* Vindobonae, 1820.

Harvey, L. P. "The Moriscos and the Ḥajj." *BRISMES* 14, no. 1 (1987): 11–24.

Ḥasan Kabīr al-Dīn, Pīr. "Saṃvat chaud so ne bāvan," in *100 Ginān nī Chopaḍī.* 4th ed. Vol. 5, #100. Mumbai, 1990 vs/1934.

———. "Sarave jivuṃnā jāre lekhāṃ lese," in *100 Ginānanī Chopaḍī.* 5th ed. Vol. 2, #18. Mumbai, 1993 vs/1936.

Hidāyat, Riḍā Qulī Khān. *Majmaʿ al-Fuṣaḥāʾ.* ed. Maẓāhir Muṣaffā. Tehran, 1336 HS/1957.

Hillenbrand, Carole. "The Power Struggle Between the Saljuqs and the Ismaʿilis of Alamūt, 487–518/1094–1124: The Saljuq Perspective," in *Mediaeval Ismaʿili History and Thought.* ed. Farhad Daftary. Cambridge, 1996.

Hinds, M. "Miḥna," in *EI2.* Vol. 7, 2. Leiden, 1960–2004. Reprint, CD-ROM v. 1.0.

Hiz Hāʾīnes Prins Āghā Khān Shīʿa Imāmī Ismāʿīliya Esūsīʾeshan barāʾe Pākistān, ed. *Kitāb al-Manāqib.* Karachi, 1406/1986.

Hodgson, M. G. S. "Djaʿfar al-Ṣādiḳ," in *EI2.* Vol. II, 374. Leiden, 1960–2004. Reprint, CD-ROM v. 1.0.

———. "The Ismāʿīlī State," in *The Cambridge History of Iran.* Vol. 5, 422–482. Cambridge, 1968.

———. *The Order of Assassins.* New York, 1980.

Hooda, Vali Mahomed N. "Some Specimens of Satpanth Literature," in *Collectanea*. ed. Wladimir Ivanow. Vol. 1, 55–137. Leiden, 1948.

Hosain, M. Hidayat. "Shāh Ṭāhir of the Deccan." *New Indian Antiquary* 2 (1939): 460–473.

Howard, E. I. *The Shia School of Islam and Its Branches, Especially That of the Imamee-Ismailies: A Speech Delivered by E. I. Howard, Esquire, Barrister-at-Law, in the Bombay High Court, in June, 1866*. Mumbai, 1866.

Howorth, Henry H. *History of the Mongols: From the 9th to the 19th Century*. London, 1876–1927.

Huart, Cl., and H. Masse. "Dawlat-Shāh (Amīr) b. ʿAlāʾ al-Dawla Bakhtīshāh," in *EI2*. Vol. 2, 179. Leiden, 1960–2004. Reprint, CD-ROM v. 1.0.

Ḥudūd al-ʿĀlam. trans. V. Minorsky. *Ḥudūd al-ʿĀlam*, the Regions of the World. 2nd ed. London, 1970.

Hunsberger, Alice C. *Nasir Khusraw: The Ruby of Badakhshan*. London, 2000.

Hunzai, Faquir M. *Shimmering Light: An Anthology of Ismaili Poetry*. London, 1996.

Hunzai, Faquir M., and Rashida Noormohamed Hunzai. *The Holy Ahl-i Bayt in the Prophetic Traditions*. Karachi, 1999.

Hunzāʾī, Naṣīr al-Dīn "Naṣīr." *Falsafa-yi Duʿā*. Hunza-Gilgit, Pakistan, 1967.

———. *Silsila-yi Nūr-i Imāmat*. Karachi, 1957.

Ḥusayn. "Āmad zamān ānkih maḥabbat ʿīyan kunīm," in *Institute of Ismaili Studies Library*, Persian ms 14698. London.

al-Ḥusaynī, Aṣīl al-Dīn ʿAbd Allāh. *Risāla-yi Mazārāt-i Harāt (-Maqṣad al-Iqbāl-i Sulṭāniyya). ed. Fikrī Saljūqī. Vol. 1, Part 1. Kabul, 1967.*

al-Ḥusaynī, Pīr Shihāb al-Dīn Shāh. *Kitāb-i Khiṭābāt-i ʿĀliya*. ed. Hūshang Ujāqī. Mumbai, 1963.

———. *Risāla dar Ḥaqīqat-i Dīn*. trans. Wladimir Ivanow. *True Meaning of Religion or Risala dar Haqiqati Din*. 2nd ed. Mumbai, 1933. Reprint, Dar es Salam, Tanzania: Shia Imami Ismailia Association for Tanzania, 1970.

———. *Risāla dar Ḥaqīqat-i Dīn*. ed. Wladimir Ivanow. Facsimile of the autograph copy ed. Mumbai, 1947.

Ibn al-Athīr, ʿIzz al-Dīn. *Taʾrīkh al-Kāmil [a.k.a. al-Kāmil fī al-Taʾrīkh]*. Cairo, 1303/1885.

Ibn al-Haytham, Abū ʿAbd Allāh Jaʿfar b. Aḥmad al-Aswad. *Kitāb al-Munāẓarāt*. ed. Wilferd Madelung and Paul E. Walker. trans. Wilferd Madelung and Paul E. Walker. *The Advent of the Fatimids: A Contemporary Shiʿi Witness*. London, 2000.

Ibn al-Qalānisī, Abū Yaʿlā Ḥamza b. Asad. *Dhayl Taʾrīkh Dimashq*. ed. H. F. Amedroz. Leiden, 1908.

Ibn al-Walīd, ʿAlī b. Muḥammad. *Dāmigh al-Bāṭil wa-Ḥatf al-Munāḍil*. ed. Muṣṭafā Ghālib. 2 vols. Beirut, 1403/1982.

Ibn Bābawayh, Abū Jaʿfar Muḥammad. *A Shīʿite Creed*. trans. Asaf Ali Asghar Fyzee. Calcutta, 1942.

Ibn Baṭṭuta. *Riḥla*. trans. H. A. R. Gibb. *The Travels of Ibn Battuta*. 4 vols. Cambridge, 1971.

———. *Riḥla*. ed. Ch. Defrémery and B. R. Sanguinetti. trans. Ch. Defrémery and B.R. Sanguinetti. *Voyages d'Ibn Battūta*. Paris, 1853–1859.

Ibn Ḥanbal, Aḥmad b. Muḥammad. *al-Musnad*. ed. M. N. Albānī. Cairo, 1986.

Ibn Ḥusām Khūsfī, Muḥammad. "Birādarān ba-ḥaqq mawsim-i munājāt ast," in *Majmū'a-yi Ash'ār-i Madhhabī*. ed. Anjuman-i ta'līm wa-tarbiyat-i madhhabī-i shī'a-yi imāmiyya ismā'īliyya-i khurāsān, np. Mashhad, Iran, 1995.

Ibn Kathīr, Ismā'īl b. 'Umar. *al-Bidāya wa-al-Nihāya*. Beirut, 1977.

Ibn Khaldūn. *The Muqaddimah: An Introduction to History*. trans. Franz Rosenthal. 3 vols. Princeton, 1967.

Ibn Shaddād, 'Izz al-Dīn. *Ta'rīkh al-Malik al-Ẓāhir*. ed. A. Ḥuṭayṭ. Wiesbaden, 1983.

Ibn Taghrībirdī, Jamāl al-Dīn Abū al-Maḥāsin Yūsuf. *al-Nujūm al-Zāhira fī mulūk Miṣr wa-al-Qāhira*. Cairo, 1348–1391/1929–1972.

Idrīs, 'Imād al-Dīn b. al-Ḥasan b. 'Abd Allāh b. al-Walīd. *'Uyūn al-Akhbār wa-Funūn al-Āthār*. ed. Ayman Fu'ād Sayyid. trans. Paul E. Walker and Maurice A. Pomerantz. *The Fatimids and the Successors in Yaman: The History of an Islamic Community, Arabic Edition and English Summary of Volume 7 of Idrīs 'Imād al-Dīn's 'Uyūn al-Akhbār*. Vol. 7. London, 2002.

———. "Zahr al-Ma'ānī," in *Ismaili Tradition Concerning the Rise of the Fatimids*. ed. Wladimir Ivanow. trans. Wladimir Ivanow, ed. 47–80, trans. 232–274. London, 1942.

Imāmshāh, Sayyid. "Āj te amar āveā," in *100 Ginān nī Chopaḍī*. 5th ed. Vol. 2, #59. Mumbai, 1993 vs/1936.

———. "Imāmapurī nagarī ne kuṃvārī kā khetra," in *100 Ginānanī Chopaḍī, 60 Ginān: Jugesar tathā Abadhunāṃ (section 2)*. 4th ed. Vol. 6, #46 (section 2). Mumbai, 1989 vs/1933.

———. *Janatpurī*. 2nd ed. Mumbai, 1976 vs/1920.

———. *Janatpurī*. [Mumbai?], nd.

———. "Jirebhāīre pīr kabīradīn jomu sīpārīu," in *100 Ginānanī Chopaḍī*. 5th ed. Vol. 1, #27. Mumbai, 1990 vs/1934.

———. "Mumaṇ: Chitāmaṇī," in *12 Girathane: 101 Ginān*. ed. Alādhīn: Gulāmahusen, 413–515. Mumbai, nd [before 1905?].

———. "Pīr vinā pār na pāmīe," in *100 Ginānanī Chopaḍī*. 5th ed, #9. Mumbai, 1991 vs/1935.

———. "Pīyu pīyu kījīe," in *100 Ginānanī Chopaḍī*. 5th ed, #8. Mumbai, 1991 vs/1935.

———. "Shāhā nā khat āyā vīrā jampudīp māṃhe" in *100 Ginānanī Chopaḍī*. 4th ed. Vol. 5, #54. Mumbai, 1990 vs/1934.

———. "Velā pohotī ne ved vīchāro," in *100 Ginānanī Chopaḍī*. 4th ed. Vol. 1, #14. Mumbai, 1990 vs/1934.

Imāmshāh, Sayyid, and Bāī Buḍhāī. *Ekiyāsī: ginānajī: chopaḍī: jeṃmiñj: ginān: 71 pīr: emām: shāhi: ne: bāī: buḍhāījā tathā ginān: 10 gugarījā*. np, 1953 vs/1897.

"Irshād al-Ṭalibīn," in *Institute of Ismaili Studies Library*, Persian ms 15095. London.

Islāmshāh, Imām. "Haft Nukta," in *Institute of Ismaili Studies Library*, Persian ms 43. London.

———. "Haft Nukta," in *Kitāb-i Mustaṭāb-i Haft Bāb-i Dāʿī Abū Isḥāq*. ed. Ḥājī Qudrat Allāh Beg, 115–124. Gilgit, Pakistan, 1962.

Ivanow, Wladimir. *Alamut and Lamasar*. [Tehran], 1960.

———. "A Forgotten Branch of the Ismailis." *JRAS* (1938): 57–79.

———. *A Guide to Ismaili Literature*. London, 1933.

———. *Ibn Al-Qaddah (The Alleged Founder of Ismailism)*. 2nd rev. ed. Mumbai, 1957.

———. "An Ismaili Interpretation of the Gulshani Raz." *JBBRAS* NS 8 (1932): 69–78.

———. *Ismaili Literature: A Bibliographical Survey*. 2nd amplified ed. Tehran, 1963.

———. *Ismaili Tradition Concerning the Rise of the Fatimids*. London, 1942.

———. "An Ismailitic Pedigree." *JASB* NS 18 (1922): 403–406.

———. "Ismailitica 1 and 2." *Memoirs of the Asiatic Society of Bengal* 17 (1922): 1–76.

———. "My First Meeting with Ismailis of Persia." *Read and Know* 1 (1966): 11–14.

———. "My First Meeting with the Ismailis in Persia." *Ilm* 3, no. 3 (December 1977).

———. *Problems in Nasir-i Khusraw's Biography*. Mumbai, 1956.

———. "The Sect of Imam Shah in Gujrat." *JBBRAS* 12 (1936): 19–70.

———. "Shums Tabrez of Multan," in *Professor Muhammad Shafi Presentation Volume*. ed. S. M. Abdullah, 109–118. Lahore, 1955.

———. "Some Muhammadan Shrines in Western India." *Ismaili: Golden Jubilee Number* (1936 January 21): 16–23.

———. "Sufism and Ismailism: Chiragh-Nama." *Revue Iranienne d'Anthropologie* 3 (1959): 13–17.

———. "Tombs of Some Persian Ismaili Imams." *JBBRAS* NS 14 (1938): 49–62.

———. *The Truth-Worshippers of Kurdistan*. 1953.

———. *Two Early Ismaili Treatises: Haft-babi Baba Sayyid-na and Matlubu'l-muʾminin by Tusi*. Mumbai, 1933.

Jaʿfar b. Manṣūr al-Yaman, Abū al-Qāsim. *Kitāb al-Kashf*. ed. Rudolf Strothmann. London, 1952.

Jafri, Syed Husain M. *The Origins and Early Development of Shiʿa Islam*. London, 1979.

Jamal, Nadia Eboo. "The Continuity of the Nizari Ismaili Daʿwa: 1256–1350." PhD dissertation, New York University, 1996.

———. *Surviving the Mongols: Nizari Quhistani and the Continuity of Ismaili Tradition in Persia*. London, 2002.

al-Jurbādhaqānī, Nāṣiḥ b. Ẓafar. *Tarjuma-yi Taʾrīkh-i Yamīnī*. ed. Jaʿfar Shiʿār. Tehran, 1345 HS/1966.

Juwaynī, ʿAlāʾ al-Dīn ʿAṭā-Malik. *Taʾrīkh-i Jahāngushāy*. trans. John Andrew Boyle. *The History of the World-Conqueror*. 2 vols. Cambridge, MA, 1958.

———. *Taʾrīkh-i Jahāngushāy*. ed. Mīrzā Muḥammad Qazwīnī. 3 vols. Leiden, 1912–1937.

Jūzjānī, Minhāj al-Dīn ʿUthmān b. Sirāj. *Ṭabaqāt-i Nāṣirī*. trans. Henry G. Raverty. *The Ṭabaḳāt-i-Nāṣirī: A General History of the Muhammadan Dynasties of Asia*. London, 1881–1899.

———. *Ṭabaqāt-i Nāṣirī*. ed. ʿAbd al-Ḥayy Ḥabībī. 2nd ed. Kabul, 1342–1343 HS/1963–1964.

Kābā, Edaljī Dhanjī. *Khojā Kom nī Tavārīkh [English Title, The History of the Khojas]*. Amarelī, Kāṭhīyāvāḍ, India, 1330/1912.

Kamāl al-Dīn, ʿAlī Muḥammad, and Zarīna Kamāl al-Dīn. *Manāsik Majālis wa-Tasbīḥāt*. Karachi, 2004.

Kāshānī, Jamāl al-Dīn Abū al-Qāsim ʿAbd Allāh b. ʿAlī. *Ta'rīkh-i Ūljāytū*. ed. M. Hambly. Tehran, 1348 HS/1969.

———. *Zubdat al-tawārīkh: bakhsh-i Fāṭimiyān wa-Nizāriyān (partial edition)*. ed. Muḥammad Taqī Dānishpazhūh. 2nd ed. Tehran, 1366 HS/1987.

Kassam, Tazim. *Songs of Wisdom and Circles of Dance: Hymns of the Satpanth Ismaili Muslim Saint, Pir Shams*. Albany, NY, 1995.

Kennedy, Hugh. *The Early ʿAbbāsid Caliphate*. London, 1981.

Khakee, Gulshan. "The Dasa Avatara of the Satpanthi Ismailis and the Imam Shahis of Indo-Pakistan." PhD dissertation, Harvard University, 1972.

Khākī Khurāsānī, Imām Qulī. *Dīwān*. ed. Wladimir Ivanow. *An Abbreviated Version of the Diwan of Khaki Khorasani*. Mumbai, 1933.

Khayrkhwāh Harātī, Muḥammad Riḍā b. Khwāja Sulṭān Ḥusayn Ghūriyānī. "Qiṭʿāt," in *Taṣnīfāt-i Khayrkhwāh Harātī*. ed. Wladimir Ivanow. *Taṣnīfāt-i Khayrkhwāh Harātī*, 77–111. Tehran, 1961.

———. "Risāla," in *Taṣnīfāt-i Khayrkhwāh Harātī*. ed. Wladimir Ivanow. *Taṣnīfāt-i Khayrkhwāh Harātī*, 1–75. Tehran, 1961.

———. *Taṣnīfāt-i Khayrkhwāh-i Harātī*. ed. Wladimir Ivanow. Tehran, 1961.

[Khayrkhwāh Harātī?]. *Faṣl dar Bayān-i Shinākht-i Imām*. ed. Wladimir Ivanow. 3rd rev. ed. Tehran, 1960.

———. *Faṣl dar Bayān-i Shinākht-i Imām*. trans. Wladimir Ivanow. 2nd rev. ed. Mumbai, 1947.

Khūsfī, Muḥammad Ibn Ḥusām. *Dīwān-i Muḥammad b. Ḥusām Khūsfī: Shāmil-i qasīdahā, ghazalhā, tarkībbandhā, tarjīʿbandhā, musammaṭhā, mathnawīhā, qiṭahā, rubāʿīhā*. ed. Aḥmad Aḥmadī Bīrjandī and Sālik Muḥammad Taqī. Mashhad, 1366 HS/1988.

Khwāndamīr, Ghiyāth al-Dīn b. Humām al-Dīn. *Ḥabīb al-Siyar*. ed. J. Humā'ī. Tehran, 1333 HS/1954.

———. *Ḥabīb al-Siyar*. ed. Wheeler M. Thackston. trans. Wheeler M. Thackston. *Habibu's-Siyar, Tome Three. The Reign of the Mongol and the Turk*. Cambridge, MA, 1994.

Kirmānī, Ḥamīd al-Dīn. *Rāḥat al-ʿAql*. ed. Muḥammad Kāmil Ḥusayn and Muḥammad Muṣṭafā Ḥilmī. Leiden, 1953.

Klemm, Verena. *Die Mission des fāṭimidischen Agenten al-Mu'ayyad fī d-dīn in Sīrāz*. Frankfurt am Main, 1989.

———. *Memoirs of a Mission: The Ismaili Scholar, Statesman and Poet al-Mu'ayyad fi'l-Dīn al-Shīrāzī*. London, 2003.

Kohlberg, E. "al-Rāfiḍā or al-Rawāfiḍ," in *EI2*. Vol. VIII, 386. Leiden, 1960–2004. Reprint, CD-ROM v. 1.0.

Kohlberg, Etan. "Imām and Community in the Pre-Ghayba Period," in *Authority and Political Culture in Shiʿism*. ed. S. A. Arjomand, 25–53 Albany, 1988.

———. "Some Imāmī-Shīʿa Views on Taqiyya." *JAOS* 95 (1975): 395–402.

———. "Taqiyya in Shīʿī Theology and Religion," in *Secrecy and Concealment: Studies in the History of Mediterranean and Near Eastern Religions*. ed. H. G. Kippenberg and G. G. Stroumsa, 345–380. Leiden, 1995.

Konṭrākṭar, Paṭel Nārāyaṇjī Rāmjībhāī. *Pīrāṇā-"Satpanth" nī Pol ane Satya no Prakāsh*. 1st ed. Vol. 1. Ahmadābād, India, 1926.

Kramers, J. H. "Ḳūhistān," in *EI2*. Vol. 5, 354. Leiden, 1960–2004. Reprint, CD-ROM v. 1.0.

Kūchak. *Silk-i Gawhar Rīz*. ed. Qudertullah. Dushanbe, Tajikistan, nd.

al-Kulaynī, Abū Jaʿfar Muḥammad b. Yaʿqūb. *al-Uṣūl min al-Kāfī*. ed. ʿAlī Akbar al-Ghifārī. 2 vols. Tehran, 1388/1968.

———. *al-Uṣūl min al-Kāfī*. ed. Muḥammad Bāqir Kamarāʾī. Tehran, 1392 HS/1972.

Laknawī, Ḥāmid Ḥusayn al-Mūsawī. *ʿAbaqāt al-Anwār fī Imāmat al-Aʾimma al-Aṭhār*. 10 vols. [Qumm], 1983–1990.

Lalani, Arzina R. *Early Shīʿī Thought: The Teachings of Imam Muḥammad al-Bāqir*. London, 2000.

Laʿlū (Laʿl Muḥammad) [Khoja Hashim Lalloo], Hāshim. *[Ḥaqq-i Mawjūd?]*. Hyderabad, Sindh, [after 1899: cover damaged].

Lamb, Charles. *The Works of Charles and Mary Lamb: Elia and The Last Essays of Elia*. ed. E. V. Lucas. Project Gutenberg. http://www.gutenberg.org/author/Charles_Lamb (accessed March 15, 2006).

Lammens, H. *Étude sur la règne du calife omaiyade Moʿāwiya 1er*. Paris, 1908.

Landolt, Hermann. "Introduction" in Ṭūsī, Naṣīr al-Dīn Muḥammad b. Muḥammad, and Ḥasan-i Maḥmūd. *Rawḍa-yi Taslīm*. ed. S. J. Badakhchani. trans. S. J. Badakhchani. *Paradise of Submission: A Medieval Treatise on Ismaili Thought*. London, 2005.

———. "Nasafi, ʿAzīz b. Moḥammad," in *Encyclopaedia Iranica*. ed. Ehsan Yarshater. Online edition, http://www.iranica.com/newsite/home/index.isc (accessed April 5, 2006). London, 1996– .

———. "Le Paradoxe de la 'Face de Dieu': ʿAzīz-e Nasafī (VII/XIII siècle) et le 'Monisme Ésoterique de l'Islam.' " *Studia Iranica* 25 (1996): 163–192.

Layish, Aharon. "*Taqiyya* among the Druzes." *Asian and African Studies* 19 (1985): 245–281.

"Le projet de croisade de Philippe VI de Valois." 1997. http://www.geocities.com/Area51/Corridor/7872/croisade.htm (accessed February 2, 2002).

Levi Della Vida, G., and R. G. Khoury. "ʿUthmān b. ʿAffān," in *EI2*. Vol. 10, 946. Leiden, 1960–2004. Reprint, CD-ROM v. 1.0.

Lewis, Bernard. *The Assassins: A Radical Sect in Islam*. London, 1967.

———. "Kamāl al-Dīn's Biography of Rashīd al-Dīn Sinān." *Arabica* 13, no. 3 (1966).

———. *The Origins of Ismailism: A Study of the Historical Background of the Fatimid Caliphate*. New York, 1975.

———. "Some Observations on the Significance of Heresy in the History of Islam." *SI* 6 (1953): 43–63.

Lewis, Franklin D. *Rumi: Past and Present, East and West*. Oxford, 2000.

Lewisohn, Leonard. *Beyond Faith and Infidelity: The Sufi Poetry and Teachings of Mahmud Shabistari*. Surrey, 1995.

———. "Sufism and Ismāʿīlī Doctrine in the Persian Poetry of Nizārī Quhistānī (645–721/1247–1321)." *Iran* 41 (2003): 229–251.

Lockhart, L. "Alamūt," in *EI2*. Vol. 1, 352. Leiden, 1960–2004. Reprint, CD-ROM v. 1.0.

Maclean, Derryl N. *Religion and Society in Arab Sind*. Leiden, 1989.

Madelung, Wilferd. "Ash-Shāfiya—Review." *Zeitschrift der Deutschen Morgenländischen Gesellschaft* 118 (1968): 423–427.

———. "Ash-Shāfiya—Review." *Oriens* 23–24 (1974): 517–518.

———. "Ismāʿīliyya," in *EI2*. Vol. 4, 198. Leiden, 1960–2004. Reprint, CD ROM v. 1.0.

———. "Mulḥid," in *EI2*. Vol. 7, 546. Leiden, 1960–2004. Reprint, CD-ROM v. 1.0.

———. *The Succession to Muhammad*. Cambridge, 1997.

Madelung, Wilferd, and E. Tyan. "ʿIṣmā," in *EI2*. Vol. 4, 182. Leiden, 1960–2004. Reprint, CD-ROM v. 1.0.

Majerczak, R. "Les Ismaéliens de Choughnan." *Revue du Monde Musulman* 24 (1913): 202–218.

al-Majlisī, Muḥammad Bāqir. *Biḥār al-Anwār*. Vol. 16. [Iran], 1305–1315 HS/1926–1936.

Makarem, Sami Nasib. *The Doctrine of the Ismailis*. Beirut, 1972.

Makdisi, George. *Ibn ʿAqīl et la Résurgence de l'Islam traditionaliste au XIe Siècle*. Damascus, 1963.

———. *The Rise of Colleges: Institutions of Learning in Islam and the West*. Edinburgh, 1981.

al-Malījī, Abū al-Qāsim ʿAbd al-Ḥakim b. Wahb. *al-Majālis al-Mustanṣiriyya*. ed. Muḥammad Kāmil Ḥusayn. Cairo, [1947].

Mallison, Françoise. "Les Chants *Garabi* de Pir Shams," in *Littératures Médievales de l'Inde du Nord*. ed. Françoise Mallison, 115–138. Paris, 1991.

Man, John. *Genghis Khan: Life, Death and Resurrection*. London, 2004.

Manz, Beatrice Forbes. "Shāh Rukh," in *EI2*. Vol. 9, 197. Leiden, 1960–2004. Reprint, CD-ROM v. 1.0.

———. "Tīmūr Lang," in *EI2*. Vol. 10, 510. Leiden, 1960–2004. Reprint, CD-ROM v. 1.0.

———. "Ulugh Beg," in *EI2*. Vol. 10, 812. Leiden, 1960–2004. Reprint, CD-ROM v. 1.0.

al-Maqdisī, Muḥammad b. Aḥmad. *Aḥsan al-taqāsīm*. ed. M. J. deGoeje. 2nd ed. Leiden, 1906.

al-Maqrīzī, Taqī al-Dīn Abū al-ʿAbbās Aḥmad b. ʿAlī. *Ittiʿāẓ al-ḥunafāʾ bi-akhbār al-aʾimma al-Fāṭimiyīn al-khulafāʾ*. ed. Jamāl al-Dīn al-Shayyāl and Muḥammad Ḥilmī Muḥammad Aḥmad. 3 vols. Cairo, 1967–1973.

———. *Kitāb al-mawāʿiẓ wa-al-iʿtibār bi-dhikr al-khiṭaṭ wa-al-āthār*. 2 vols. Būlāq, 1270/1854.

Marʿashī, Ẓahīr al-Dīn. *Taʾrīkh-i Gīlān wa-Daylamistān*. ed. Hyacinth Louis Rabino. Rasht, 1330/1912.

———. *Taʾrīkh-i Gīlān wa-Daylamistān*. ed. M. Sutūda. Tehran, 1347 HS/1968.

———. *Taʾrīkh-i Ṭabaristān wa-Rūyān wa-Māzandarān*. ed. Ḥusayn Tasbīḥī. Tehran, 1361 HS/[1983].

Marco Polo. *The Travels of Marco Polo*. trans. Aldo Ricci. New York, 1931.

Marlowe, Christopher. *Tamburlaine the Great: Part I*. ed. Alexander Dyce. Project Gutenberg, November 1997 (accessed February 21, 2006).

Marquet, Yves. "Le Qāḍī Nuʿmān à propos des heptades d'imāms." *Arabica* 25, no. 3 (September 1978): 225–232.

Massignon, Louis. *Hallāj: Mystic and Martyr*. ed. Herbert Mason. trans. Herbert Mason. abridged ed. Princeton, NJ, 1994.

———. "Salmān Pāk et les prémices spirituelles de l'Islam Iranien," in *Opera Minora*. Vol. 1, 450–457. Beirut, 1963.

Maʿṣūm ʿAlīshāh, Muḥammad Maʿṣūm Shīrāzī. *Tarāʾiq al-Ḥaqāʾiq*. ed. Muḥammad Jaʿfar Maḥjūb. Tehran, 1345 HS/1966.

Maẓharī Kirmānī, ʿAlī Aṣghar. "Rābiṭa-yi Ismāʿīliyān bā Ṣūfiyān-i ṭarīqat-i Niʿmat Allāhī." *Ṣūfī* 27 (June 1995): 6–18.

McCarthy, Richard J. *Freedom and Fulfillment*. Boston, 1980.

McEoin, Denis. "Aspects of Militancy and Quietism in Imami Shiʿism." *BRISMES* 11, no. 1 (1984): 18–27.

Melville, Charles. "Ḥamd Allāh Mustawfī's Ẓafarnāmah and the Historiography of the Late Ilkhanid Period," in *Iran and Iranian Studies: Essays in Honor of Iraj Afshar*. ed. Kambiz Eslami, 1–12. Princeton, 1997.

———. "The Īlkhān Öljeitü's Conquest of Gīlān (1307): Rumour and Reality," in *The Mongol Empire and its Legacy*. ed. Reuven Amitai-Preiss and David O. Morgan, 73–125. Leiden, 1999.

Menant, Dominique. "Les Khodjas du Guzarate." *Revue du Monde Musulman* 12 (1910): 214–232, 406–424.

Minorsky, V. "Daylam," in *EI2*. Vol. 2, 189. Leiden, 1960–2004. Reprint, CD-ROM v. 1.0.

———. "Rūyān," in *EI2*. Vol. 8, 650. Leiden, 1960–2004. Reprint, CD-ROM v. 1.0.

Minorsky, V., and C. E. Bosworth. "Māzandarān," in *EI2*. Vol. 6, 935. Leiden, 1960–2004. Reprint, CD-ROM v. 1.0.

Mīrkhwānd, Muḥammad b. Khwāndshāh. *Rawḍat al-Ṣafāʾ*. 10 vols. Tehran, 1338–1339 HS/1959–1960.

———. *Rawḍat al-Ṣafāʾ*. ed. Am. Jourdain. trans. Am. Jourdain. *"Histoire de la dynastie des Ismaéliens de Perse," Notices et Extraits des Manuscrits*. Vol. 9, 1813.

Mirza, Nasseh Ahmad. *Syrian Ismailism: The Ever Living Line of the Imamate*. Richmond, Surrey, 1997.

Mitha, Farouk. *Al-Ghazali and the Ismailis: A Debate on Reason and Authority in Medieval Islam*. London, 2001.

Modarressi, Hossein. *Crisis and Consolidation in the Formative Period of Shīʿite Islam: Abū Jaʿfar ibn Qiba al-Rāzī and His Contribution to Imāmite Shīʿite Thought*. Princeton, NJ, 1993.

Moir, Zawahir. *A Catalogue of the Khojki MSS in the Library of the Ismaili Institute*. London, 1985.

Momen, Moojan. *An Introduction to Shiʿi Islam: The History and Doctrines of Twelver Shiʿism*. New Haven, 1985.

Morgan, David. *Medieval Persia, 1040–1797*. London, 1988.

———. *The Mongols*. Oxford, 1986.

———. "Persian Historians and the Mongols," in *Medieval Historical Writing in the Christian and Islamic Worlds*. ed. David Morgan. London, 1982.

Morris, James Winston. "Taqīyah," in *Encyclopedia of Religion*. ed. Mircea Eliade. Vol. 14, 336–337. New York, 1987.

Moscati, S. "Abū Salama Ḥafs b. Sulaymān al-Khallāl," in *EI2*. Vol. 1, 149. Leiden, 1960–2004. Reprint, CD-ROM v. 1.0.

al-Muʾayyad fī al-Dīn Shīrāzī, Abū Naṣr Hibat Allāh. *al-Majālis al-Muʾayyadiyya*. ed. Muṣṭafā Ghālib. Vols. 1 and 3. Beirut, 1974–1984.

———. *al-Majālis al-Muʾayyadiyya*. ed. Hātim Ḥamīd al-Dīn. Vols. 1 and 2. Mumbai and Oxford, 1975–1986.

———. *al-Majālis al-Muʾayyadiyya*. trans. Jawad Muscati and Khan Bahadur A. M. Moulvi. *Life and Lectures of the Grand Missionary al-Muayyad-fid-Din al-Shirazi*. Karachi, 1950.

———. *Dīwān*. ed. Muḥammad Kāmil Ḥusayn. Cairo, 1949.

Muḥammad Taqī b. ʿAlī Riḍā b. Zayn al-ʿĀbidīn. *Āthār-i Muḥammadī*. Maḥallāt, Iran, 1893.

Muḥammad Zardūz, Khudāwand [Imam Shams al-Dīn Muḥammad?] "Alfāẓ-i Guharbār wa-Durr Nithār," in *Institute of Ismaili Studies Library*, unnumbered Persian ms. London.

Muḥammadshāh, Sayyid. "Sācho tuṃ moro sāṃhīā," in *102 Ginānajī: Chopaḍī*. 3rd ed. Vol. 4, #67. Mumbai, 1968 vs/[1912].

Muʿizzī, Maryam. "Ismāʿīliyyān-i Īrān." MA thesis, Dānishgāh-i Firdawsī, 1371–1372 HS/1992–1993.

Mulukshāh, Shujāʿ al-Mulk b. Sayyid Jamāʿat ʿAlīshāh, and Muḥammad ʿĪsanshāh. *Gulzār-i Shams*. [Multan], 1334/1916.

Mumtaz, Kamil Khan. *Architecture in Pakistan*. Singapore, 1985.

Mustanṣir bi'llāh (=Gharīb Mīrzā?), Imām. *Pandiyāt-i Jawānmardī*. ed. Wladimir Ivanow. trans. Wladimir Ivanow. *Pandiyat-i Jawanmardi or "Advices of Manliness."* Leiden, 1953.

———. "Pandiyāt-i Jawānmardī," in *Institute of Ismaili Studies Library*, Khojki ms KH110. London.

al-Muttaqī, ʿAllāma ʿAlī. *Kanz al-ʿUmmāl*. Beirut, 1399/1979.

Muwaḥḥid, Muḥammad ʿAlī. *Shams-i Tabrīzī*. Tehran, 1996.

Nānajīāṇī, Sachedīnā. *Khojā Vṛttānt*. Ahmadabad, India, 1892.

Nanji, Azim. "The Ginān Tradition among the Nizārī Ismāʿīlīs: Its Value as a Source of their History," in *Actes du XXIXe Congrès international des Orientalistes*. Vol. 3, 143–146. Paris, 1975.

———. "A Khojki Version of the Nizari Ismaili Works: The Pandiyat-i Javanmardi," in *[Proceeding of the] 30th International Congress of Human Sciences in Asia and North Africa: Middle East 1*. ed. Graciel de la Lama, 122–125. Mexico, 1982.

———. *The Nizārī Ismāʿīlī Tradition in the Indo-Pakistan Subcontinent*. Delmar, NY, 1978.

———. "Ritual and Symbolic Aspects of Islam in African Contexts," in *Islam in Local Contexts*. ed. Richard C. Martin. Vol. 17, 102–109. Leiden, 1982.

Nasafī, ʿAzīz-i. "Maqṣad-i Aqṣā," in *Ganjīna-yi ʿIrfān*. ed. Ḥ. Rabbānī. Tehran, nd.

———. "Zubdat al-Ḥaqāʾiq," in *Panj Risāla dar bayān-i Āfāq wa-Anfus yaʿnī Barābari-yi Ādam wa-ʿĀlam*. ed. Andrey Evgen'evich Bertel's, 91–207. Moscow, 1970.

Naṣīr al-Dīn, Pīr. "Huṃ balahārī tame shāhā rājā," in *100 Ginān nī Chopaḍī*. 5th ed. Vol. 2, #57. Mumbai, 1993 VS/1936.

Nāṣir-i Khusraw, Ḥakīm Abū Muʿīn. *Dīwān-i Ashʿār-i Ḥakīm Nāṣir-i Khusraw Qubādiyānī*. ed. Mujtabā Mīnuwī and Mahdī Muḥaqqiq. Tehran, 1357 HS/1978.

———. *Dīwān-i Ashʿār-i Nāṣir-i Khusraw Qubādiyānī: Mushtamil ast bar Rawshanāʾīnāma, Saʿādatnāma, Qasāʾid wa-Muqaṭṭaʿāt*. ed. Naṣr Allāh Taqawī et al. Tehran, 1380 HS/2001.

———. *Gushāyish wa-Rahāyish*. ed. Faquir M. Hunzai. trans. Faquir M. Hunzai. *Knowledge and Liberation: A Treatise on Philosophical Theology*. London, 1998.

———. *Jāmiʿ al-Ḥikmatayn*. ed. Henry Corbin and Muḥammad Muʿīn. *Le Livre Réunissant les Deux Sagesses*. Tehran, 1953.

———. *Khwān al-Ikhwān*. ed. Yaḥyā al-Khashshāb. Cairo, 1940.

———. *Safarnāma*. ed. Muḥammad Dabīr-i Siyāqī. Tehran, 1984.

———. *Wajh-i Dīn*. ed. Gholam-Reza Aavani. Tehran, 1977.

Nawas, J. A. *al-Maʾmūn: Miḥna and Caliphate*. Nijmegen, 1992.

Nazarali, Hasan. *A Brief Outline of Ismaili Rites, Rituals, Ceremonies and Festivals*. [Edmonton, Canada?], nd.

Nikitine, B. "Bādūsbānids," in *EI2*. Vol. 1, 871. Leiden, 1960–2004. Reprint, CD-ROM v. 1.0.

Niʿmat Allāh Walī. *Kulliyāt-i dīwān*. ed. Maḥmūd ʿIlmī. Tehran, 1333 HS/1954.

Niẓām al-Mulk. *Siyar al-Mulūk or Siyāsatnāma*. trans. H. Darke. 2nd ed. London, 1978.

Nomoto, Shin. "Early Ismāʿīlī Thought on Prophecy According to the Kitāb al-Islāḥ by Abū Hātim al-Rāzī (d. ca. 322/934–5)." PhD dissertation, McGill University, 1999.

Nooraly, Zawahir. *Catalogue of Khojki Manuscripts in the Collection of the Ismailia Association for Pakistan (draft copy)*. Karachi, 1971.

al-Nuʿmān, al-Qāḍī Abū Ḥanīfa b. Muḥammad. *Daʿāʾim al-Islām fī Dhikr al-Ḥalāl wa-al-Ḥarām*. trans. Asaf A. A. Fyzee and completely revised and annotated by Ismail Kurban Husein Poonawala. *The Pillars of Islam*. 2 vols. New Delhi, 2002–2004.

———. *Daʿāʾim al-Islām wa-Dhikr al-Ḥalāl wa-al-Ḥarām wa-al-Qaḍāyā wa-al-Aḥkām*. ed. Āṣaf b. ʿAlī Aṣghar Fayḍī. Cairo, 1951–1961.

———. *Kitāb al-Majālis wa-al-Musāyarāt*. ed. al-Ḥabīb al-Faqī, Ibrāhīm Shabbūḥ, and Muḥammad al-Yaʿlāwī. Tunis, 1978.

———. *Kitāb Asās al-Taʾwīl*. ed. ʿĀrif Tāmir. Beirut, [1960].

———. *Kitāb Iftitāḥ al-daʿwa*. ed. Farhat Dachraoui. *Les commencements du califat Fatimid au Maghreb: Kitāb Iftitāḥ al-daʿwa du Cadi Nuʿman*. Tunis, 1975.

———. *Risālat Iftitāḥ al-Daʿwa*. ed. Wadād al-Qāḍī. Beirut, 1971.

———. *Sharḥ al-Akhbār fī faḍāʾil al-aʾimmat al-aṭhār*. ed. al-Sayyid Muḥammad al-Ḥusaynī al-Jalālī. 3 vols. Qumm, 1409–1412/1988–1992.

———. *Taʾwīl al-Daʿāʾim*. ed. Muḥammad Ḥasan al-Aʿẓamī. 3 vols. Cairo, 1967–1972.

———. *Ikhtilāf Uṣūl al-Madhāhib*. ed. Muṣṭafā Ghālib. Beirut, 1393/1973.

Nūr Muḥammadshāh, Sayyid. *Sat Varaṇī Moṭī*. [Mumbai ?], nd.

———. "Sat Varaṇi Moṭi ni Vel," in *Personal Library of Mr Abdulrasool Mawji*. Calgary, Canada.

Sat Varaṇī Moṭi nī Vel [a.k.a. Sat Veṇī nī Vel]. Mumbai, 1962 vs/1905.

———. *Sat Veṇī Moṭī*. ed. Lālajī: bhāī: Devarāj. 1st Gujarati ed. Mumbai, 1975 vs/1919.

Nūrbakhsh, Muḥammad. *Risāla al-Hudā*. ed. Shahzad Bashir. *Between Mysticism and Messianism: The Life and Thought of Muhammad Nūrbakś (d. 1464)*. New Haven, 1997.

Orwell, George. *Nineteen Eighty-four*. New York, 1992.

Petrushevsky, I. P. "The Socio-Economic Conditions of Iran under the Il-Khāns," in *The Cambridge History of Iran*. Vol. 5, 484–488. Cambridge, 1968.

Picklay, Abdus Salam. *History of the Ismailis*. Mumbai, 1940.

Poonawala, Ismail K. *Biobibliography of Ismāʿīlī Literature*. Malibu, CA, 1977.

———. "An Ismāʿīlī Refutation of al-Ghazālī," in *Middle East 1 30th International Congress of Human Sciences in Asia and North Africa 1976*. ed. Graciela de la Lama, 131–134. Mexico City, 1982.

———. "Ismāʿīlī ta'wīl of the Qur'ān," in *Approaches to the History of the Interpretation of the Qur'ān*. ed. Andrew Rippin. Oxford, 1988. 199–222.

Pourjavady, Nasrollah Peter Lamborn Wilson. "Ismāʿīlīs and Niʿmatullāhīs." *SI* 41 (1975): 113–135.

[pseudo-Aḥmad b. Muḥammad Ardabīlī]. *Ḥadīqat al-Shīʿa*. Tehran, 1964.

[pseudo-Ḥasan-i Ṣabbaḥ]. "Haft Bāb-i Bābā Sayyidnā," in *Two Early Ismaili Treatises*. ed. Wladimir Ivanow, 4–42. Mumbai, 1933.

[pseudo-Nāṣir-i Khusraw: Khayrkhwāh Harātī?]. *Kalām-i Pīr*. ed. Wladimir Ivanow. trans. Wladimir Ivanow. Mumbai, 1935.

[pseudo-Shihāb al-Dīn Abū Firās]. *al-Qaṣīda al-Shāfiya*. ed. Sami Nassib Makarem. trans. Sami Nassib Makarem. *Ash-Shāfiya (The Healer): An Ismāʿīlī Poem Attributed to Shihāb ad-Dīn Abū Firās*. Beirut, 1966.

———. *al-Qaṣīda al-Shāfiya*. ed. ʿĀrif Tāmir. Beirut, 1967.

Qā'inī, Jalāl-i. "Naṣā'iḥ-i Shāhrukhī," in *Österreichische Nationalbibliothek*, Monastic Microfilm Project Number 22 249, University Microfilms, Codex Vindobonensis Palatinus. A.f. 112 (Flügel 1858). Vienna, 1970.

Qāsim Tushtarī (Turshīzī?). "[Risāla dar Maʿrifat-i Khāliq]," in *Institute of Ismaili Studies Library*, Persian ms 814. London.

———. "[Risāla dar Maʿrifat-i Khāliq]," in *Institute of Ismaili Studies Library*, Persian ms 15048. London.

Qazwīnī, Ḥamd Allāh Mustawfī. *Nuzhat al-Qulūb*. ed. Guy Le Strange. trans. Guy Le Strange. *The Geographical Part of the Nuzhat al-Qulūb*. Leiden, 1915–1919.

———. *Ta'rīkh-i Guzīda*. ed. Edward Granville Browne. trans. Edward Granville Browne. *The Ta'rīkh-i Guzīda: or, "Select History."* Leiden, 1910–1913.

———. *Ẓafarnāma*. ed. Naṣr Allāh Pūrjawādī and N. Rastigār. facsimile ed. 2 vols. Tehran, 1377 HS/1999.

Qazwīnī, Muḥammad. *Yāddāshthā-yi Qazwīnī*. ed. Īraj Afshār. Vol. 8. Tehran, 1332–1354 HS/1953–1975.

Quhistānī, Bū Isḥāq. *Haft Bāb*. ed. Wladimir Ivanow. trans. Wladimir Ivanow. *Haft Bab or "Seven Chapters."* Mumbai, 1959.

Quhistānī, Nizārī. *Dīwān-i Ḥakīm Nizārī Quhistānī*. ed. Maẓāhir Muṣaffā. Tehran, 1371 HS/1992.

———. "Safarnāma," in *The Continuity of the Nizari Ismaili Daʿwa*. ed. Nadia Eboo Jamal 257–298. PhD dissertation, New York University, 1996.

al-Qummī, Abū Jaʿfar Muḥammad b. al-Ḥasan al-Ṣaffār. *Baṣāʾir al-Darajāt fī Faḍāʾil Āl Muḥammad*. ed. Muḥsin Kūcha Bāghī. [Tabrīz?], [1960].

al-Qummī, Saʿd b. ʿAbd Allāh. *Kitāb al-maqālāt wa-al-firaq*. ed. M. J. Mashkūr. Tehran, 1963.

Qutbuddin, Bazat-Tahera. "al-Muʾayyad fī al-Dīn al-Shīrāzī: Founder of a New Tradition of Fāṭimid Daʿwa Poetry." PhD dissertation, Harvard University, 1999.

Qutbuddin, Tahera. *Al-Muʾayyad al-Shīrāzī and Fatimid Daʿwa Poetry*. Leiden, 2005.

Rabino, Hyacinth Louis. "Les Dynasties du Māzandarān." *JA* 228 (1936): 397–474.

———. "Les Dynasties locales du Gīlān et du Daylam." *JA* 237 (1949): 301–350.

———. *Mazandaran and Astarabad*. London, 1928.

———. *Les Provinces Caspiennes de la Perse: Le Guīlān*. Paris, 1917.

———. "Rulers of Gīlān." *JRAS* (1920): 277–296.

———. "Rulers of Lahijan and Fuman, in Gilan, Persia." *JRAS* (1918): 88–89, 94.

Rajabalī, Ramajānali, ed. *Khojā Isamāilī Kelenḍar ane Dīrekaṭarī: 1910*. Mumbai, 1910.

Rājgīrī, Mīr Sayyid Manjhan Shaṭṭārī. *Madhumālatī*. trans. Aditya Behl and Simon Weightman. *Madhumālatī: An Indian Sufi Romance*. Oxford, 2000.

Rashīd al-Dīn, Faḍl Allāh Ṭabīb. *Jāmiʿ al-Tawārīkh*. trans. Wheeler M. Thackston. *Jamiʿu't-tawarikh: Compendium of Chronicles*. 3 vols. Cambridge, MA, 1998.

———. *Jāmiʿ al-Tawārīkh*. ed. B. Karīmī. Tehran, 1338 HS/1959.

Rāzī, Amīn Aḥmad. *Haft Iqlīm*. ed. Jawād Fāḍil. Tehran, nd.

Reckendorf, H. "ʿAmmār b. Yāsir," in *EI2*. Vol. 1, 448. Leiden, 1960–2004. Reprint, CD-ROM v. 1.0.

Rematulā, Jāfarbhāī. *Khojā Kom no Itihās*. Mumbai, 1905.

Ridgeon, Lloyd. *Aziz Nasafi*. Richmond, Surrey, 1998.

———. *Persian Metaphysics and Mysticism*. Richmond, Surrey, 2002.

"Risāla-yi Munāẓara," in *Institute of Ismaili Studies Library*, Persian ms, accession number unknown. London.

"Risāla-yi Ṣirāṭ al-Mustaqīm," in *Institute of Ismaili Studies Library*, Persian ms 15034. London.

"Risāla-yi Ṣirāṭ al-Mustaqīm," in *Seekers of Union: The Ismailis from the Mongol Debacle to the Eve of the Safavid Revolution*. ed. Shafique N. Virani. trans. Shafique N. Virani. *The Epistle of the Right Path*, ed. 220–231, trans. 209–219. PhD dissertation, Harvard University, 2001.

Robinson, B. W. "Miʿrādj," in *EI2*. Vol. 7, 97. Leiden, 1960–2004. Reprint, CD-ROM v. 1.0.

Rypka, J. "Poets and Prose Writers of the Late Saljuq and Mongol Periods," in *The Cambridge History of Iran*. Cambridge, 1968.

Sachedina, Abdulaziz Abdulhussein. *Islamic Messianism: The Idea of Mahdi in Twelver Shiʿism*. Albany, NY, 1981.

Sacy, A. I. Silvestre de. "Mémoire sur la dynastie des Assassins." *Mémoirs de l'Institut Royal de France* 4 (1818): 1–84.

Sacy, Antoine I. Silvestre de. *Exposé de la religion des Druzes*. 2 vols. Paris, 1838.

Sadik Ali, Mumtaz Ali Tajdin. *101 Ismaili Heroes: (Late 19th Century to Present Age)*. Vol. 1. Karachi, 2003.

Sadik Ali, Mumtaz Ali Tajjdin. "Pir Shahabu'd Din Shah al-Husayni," in *The Great Ismaili Heroes*. Karachi, 1973.

Ṣadr al-Dīn, Pīr. "Aj sahi māhādin bujo bhev," in *100 Ginānanī Chopaḍī*. 5th ed. Vol. 1, #57. Mumbai, 1990 vs/1934.

———. "Ālamot gaḍh pāṭaṇ delam des bhāire," in *100 Ginānanī Chopaḍī*. 5th ed. Vol. 2, #39. Mumbai, 1993 vs/1936.

———. "Āshā: trī: trī: lokā :l: dhara-alī: hek: vado: sāmī," in *102 Ginānajī: Chopaḍī:* ed. Lālajī: bhāī: Devarāj. 2nd ed. Vol. 4, 10–12. Mumbai, 1961 vs/[1905].

———. "Āshājī sacho tuṃ alakh nirījan agam agochar," in *102 Ginānajī: Chopaḍī*. 3rd ed. Vol. 4, #4. Mumbai, 1968 vs/[1912].

———. "Āvo mārā munivar bhāiḍā hojī," in *100 Ginānanī Chopaḍī*. 5th ed. Vol. 2, #11. Mumbai, 1993 vs/1936.

———. "Bhāīr bhāṅā ma ṭaḍo," in *100 Ginānanī Chopaḍī*. 5th ed. Vol. 3, #81. Mumbai, 1991 vs/1935.

———. "Des delamame shāhā harī avatareo," in *100 Ginānanī Chopaḍī*. 4th ed. Vol. 6, #29. Mumbai, 1989 vs/1933.

———. "Dhan dhan ājano dāḍalore ame harīvar pāyājī," in *100 Ginānanī Chopaḍī*. 4th ed. Vol. 5, #42. Mumbai, 1990 vs/1934.

———. "Ejio: āeo: āeo: haṃsejo: var: rājā:," in *102 Ginānajī: Chopaḍī:* ed. Lālajī: bhāī: Devarāj. 2nd ed. Vol. 4, 33–34. Mumbai, 1961 vs/[1905].

———. "Hame umāyā ne kāyam pāyā," in *100 Ginānanī Chopaḍī*. 4th ed. Vol. 5, #93. Mumbai, 1990 vs/1934.

———. "Jampu meṃ jampu meṃ var shāhā ache," in *100 Ginānanī Chopaḍī*. 5th ed. Vol. 2, #87. Mumbai, 1993 vs/1936.

———. "Jem jem jugatasuṃ pirīt karevā," in *100 Ginānanī Chopaḍī*. 5th ed. Vol. 2, #35. Mumbai, 1993 vs/1936.

———. "Jituṃ: lāl: sirie: e: sāraṅg: dhar-āshā: tribhovar: vado: sāmī:," in *102 Ginānajī: Chopaḍī:* ed. Lālajī: bhāī: Devarāj. 2nd ed. Vol. 4, 8–10. Mumbai, 1961 vs/[1905].

———. "Jugā jug shāhā avatāraj dhareā [a.k.a. Sen Akhāḍo]," in *100 Ginānanī Chopaḍī*. 5th ed. Vol. 2, #26. Mumbai, 1993 vs/1936.

———. "Jugame phīre shāhājī munerī," in *102 Ginānajī: Chopaḍī*. 3rd ed. Vol. 4, #3. Mumbai, 1968 vs/[1912].

———. "Kāṃ bāndho māyā puravase ho kāyā pur," in *100 Ginānanī Chopaḍī*. 4th ed. Vol. 6, #8. Mumbai, 1989 vs/1933.

———. "Kiratā: jugeṃ: dhuār: utar: dise: huaḍā," in *102 Ginānajī: Chopaḍī:* ed. Lālajī: bhāī: Devarāj. 2nd ed. Vol. 4, 46–47. Mumbai, 1961 vs/[1905].

———. "More āshājī harovar sarovar," in *102 Ginānajī: Chopaḍī*. 3rd ed. Vol. 4, #41. Mumbai, 1968 vs/[1912].

———. "Namo: te: shāhā: nur ke" in *102 Ginānajī: Chopaḍī:* ed. Lālajī: bhāī: Devarāj. 2nd ed. Vol. 4, 4–6. Mumbai, 1961 vs/[1905].

———. "Pañchame [sic] āyā shāhā paratak pāyā," in *100 Ginānanī Chopaḍī*. 5th ed. Vol. 3, #46. Mumbai, 1991 vs/1935.

———. "Pāchham: dese: parabhu: paratak: beṭhā," in *102 Ginānajī: Chopaḍī:* ed. Lālajī: bhāī: Devarāj. 2nd ed. Vol. 4, 54–58. Mumbai, 1961 vs/[1905].

———. "Pāchham: dese thi: parabhu: padhāreā," in *102 Ginānajī: Chopaḍī:* ed. Lālajī: bhāī: Devarāj. 2nd ed. Vol. 4, 52–54. Mumbai, 1961 vs/[1905].

———. "Payalore nām sāhebajo vado līje," in *102 Ginānajī: Chopaḍī*. 3rd ed. Vol. 4, #82. Mumbai, 1968 vs/[1912].

———. "Sab ghaṭ sāmi māro bharapur beṭhā," in *102 Ginānajī: Chopaḍī*. 3rd ed. Vol. 4, #59. Mumbai, 1968 vs/[1912].

———. "Sakhī māhā pad kerī vāt koek jāṇere," in *100 Ginānanī Chopaḍī*. 5th ed. Vol. 3, #30. Mumbai, 1991 vs/1935.

———. "Sāmi rājā jampuadipe umāeoji," in *100 Ginānanī Chopaḍī*. 5th ed. Vol. 1, #66. Mumbai, 1990 vs/1934.

———. "Sāmi rājo āve jaṅgī ḍhol vajāve," in *100 Ginānanī Chopaḍī*. 5th ed. Vol. 2, #32. Mumbai, 1993 vs/1936.

———. "Sansār sāgar madhe vān āpaṇā satagure noriyāṃre," in *100 Ginānanī Chopaḍī*. 5th ed. Vol. 1, #68. Mumbai, 1990 vs/1934.

———. "Shāhāke hek man āṃhī sirevo," in *102 Ginānajī: Chopaḍī*. 3rd ed. Vol. 4, #48. Mumbai, 1968 vs/[1912].

———. "Shāhāke: hekamaṃn: āaṃhi: sirevo: jire: yārā: mumanājio," in *102 Ginānajī: Chopaḍī:* ed. Lālajī: bhāī: Devarāj. 2nd ed. Vol. 4, 65–67. Mumbai, 1961 vs/[1905].

———. "Sīrīe salāmashāhā amane malīyā," in *100 Ginānanī Chopaḍī*. 4th ed. Vol. 5, #10. Mumbai, 1990 vs/1934.

———. "Thar thar moman bhāī koī koī raheseji," in *100 Ginānanī Chopaḍī*. 4th ed. Vol. 5, #50. Mumbai, 1990 vs/1934.

———. "Yārā anat kiroḍie vadhāīuṃ," in *102 Ginānajī: Chopaḍī*. 3rd ed. Vol. 4, #29. Mumbai, 1968 vs/[1912].

Ṣafā, Dhabīḥ Allāh. *Taʾrīkh-i Adabiyāt-i Īrān*. Tehran, 1352 HS/1973.

Ṣāhib al-Dīn, Pīr. "Āo gatīure bhandhe," in *100 Ginānanī Chopaḍī*. 5th ed. Vol. 3, #74. Mumbai, 1991 vs/1935.

Saleh, Shakib. "The Use of Bāṭinī, Fidāʾī and Ḥashīshī Sources in the Writings of the Arab Sunni Historians." *SI* 82 (1995): 35–43.

Sām Mīrzā. *Tuḥfa-yi Sāmī*. ed. R. Humāyūn-Farrukh. Tehran, nd.

Satagur Nūr, Pīr. "Satagur padhāreā tame jāgajo," in *100 Ginānanī Chopaḍī*. 5th ed., Vol. 2, #83. Mumbai, 1991 vs/1935.

Savory, R. M. "Ḳāsim-i Anwār," in *EI2*. Vol. 4, 721. Leiden, 1960–2004. Reprint, CD-ROM v. 1.0.

Sayf b. Muḥammad b. Yaʿqūb. *Taʾrīkh Nāma-yi Harāt*. ed. M. Z. Ṣiddīqī. Calcutta, 1944.

Schact, J. "Aṣḥāb al-Ra'y," in *EI2*. Vol. 1, 691. Leiden, 1960–2004. Reprint, CD-ROM v. 1.0.

Schimmel, Annemarie. *Islam in the Indian Subcontinent*. Leiden, 1980

———. *Make a Shield from Wisdom: Selected Verses from Nāṣir-i Khusraw's Dīvān*. London, 1993.

———. "Shams-i Tabrīz(ī)," in *EI2*. Vol. 9, 298. Leiden, 1960–2004. Reprint, CD-ROM v. 1.0.

Schmidtke, Sabine, ed. *Correspondance Corbin-Ivanow: Lettres Échangés entre Henry Corbin et Vladimir Ivanow de 1947 à 1966*. Paris, 1999.

Sells, Michael A., ed. *Early Islamic Mysticism: Sufi, Quran, Miraj, Poetic and Theological Writings*. New York, 1996.

Semenov, Aleksandr Aleksandrovich. "Iz oblasti religioznikh verovaniy gornikh tadzhikov [On the Religious Beliefs of the Mountain Tajiks]." *ȁtnograficheskoe obozrenie (Moscow)* 47, no. 4 (1900): 81–88.

———. "Iz oblasti religioznikh verovaniy shughnanskikh ismailitov [On the Religious Beliefs of the Ismailis of Shughnān]." *Mir Islam (St Petersburg)* 1, no. 44 (1912): 523–561.

———. "Opisanie ismailitskikh rukopisey, sobranikh A. A. Semyonovim [Description of Ismāʿīlī manuscripts, A. A. Semenov's collection]." *Izvestiya Rossiyskoy Akademii Nauk/Bulletin de l'Académie des Sciences de Russie (Petrograd)* 6 série, no. 12 (1918): 2171–2202.

Shackle, Christopher, and Zawahir Moir. *Ismaili Hymns from South Asia: An Introduction to the Ginans*. London, 1992.

[Shāh Ṭāhir al-Dakkanī?]. "Baʿḍī az Ta'wīlāt-i Gulshan-i Rāz," in *Trilogie Ismaélienne*. ed. Henry Corbin. trans. Henry Corbin, ed. 131–161, trans. 1–174. Tehran, 1340 HS/ 1961.

Shāmī, Niẓām al-Dīn. *Ẓafarnāma*. ed. Felix Tauer. trans. Felix Tauer. *Histoire des Conquêtes de Tamerlan, Intitulée Ẓafarnāma*. Prague, 1937–1956.

Shams, Pīr. "Bhulā: ma: bhule: bhamajore: hinduo," in *28 Garabī: pīr: samas nī*. ed. Lālajī: bhāī: Devarāj. 2nd ed. 22–23. Mumbai, 1913.

———. "Bhulo: bhulotebhulo: bhamaraḍore: lol," in *28 Garabī: pīr: samas nī*. ed. Lālajī: bhāī: Devarāj. 2nd ed., 11–12. Mumbai, 1913.

———. "Cheto: cheto: te: chañchal: chetiyāre: lol," in *28 Garabī: pīr: samas nī*. ed. Lālajī: bhāī: Devarāj. 2nd ed. 14–15. Mumbai, 1913.

———. "E sabhāgā har puchh nind [sic] niravāṇ pañjetan," in *100 Ginānanī Chopaḍī*. 5th ed. Vol. 2, #71. Mumbai, 1993 vs/1936.

———. "Evi: garabi: sampuraṇ: sār," in *28 Garabī: pīr: samas nī*. ed. Lālaji: bhāi: Devarāj. 2nd ed., 35–36. Mumbai, 1913.

———. "Gur: āvatā: sarave: rāt," in *28 Garabī: pīr: samas nī*. ed. Lālajī: bhāī: Devarāj. 2nd ed. 4–5. Mumbai, 1913.

———. "*Gur vachane chālea*," in *100 Ginānanī Chopaḍī*. 4th ed. Vol. 4. Mumbai, 1989 vs/1933.

———. "Gure: kāḍhichhe: pāvaḷ: hāthe," in *28 Garabī: pīr: samas nī*. ed. Lālajī: bhāī: Devarāj. 2nd ed. 33–34. Mumbai, 1913.

———. "Jīv tuṃ jāvā de," in *100 Ginānanī Chopaḍī*. 5th ed. Vol. 2, #49. Mumbai, 1993 vs/1936.

———. "Ke: tame: amiras: pijo: din: ne: rāt," in *28 Garabī: pīr: samas nī*. ed. Lālajī: bhāī: Devarāj. 2nd ed., 5–6. Mumbai, 1913.

———. *Man Samajāṇī [Moṭī]*. [Mumbai?], nd.

———. "*Nar: kāsamanā: pharamānathī: gur: shamas: pīr: ||: ramavā nīsareāremā*," in *12 Girathane: 101 Ginān*. ed. Alādhīn: Gulāmahusen. Mumbai, nd [before 1905?].

———. "Nar: kāsham nā: pharamān thī:," in *28 Garabī: pīr: samas nī*. ed. Lālajī: bhāī: Devarāj. 2nd ed., 20–21. Mumbai, 1913.

———. "Sāmī tamārī vāḍī māṃhe," in *100 Ginānanī Chopaḍī*. 5th ed. Vol. 3, #24. Mumbai, 1991 vs/1935.

———. "Satagur bheṭeā kem jāṇīe," in *100 Ginān nī Chopaḍī*. 5th ed. Vol. 2, #66. Mumbai, 1993 vs/1936.

———. "Satagur: samash: em: kahere: gāphalo: kem: utaraso: pār," in *28 Garabī: pīr: samas nī*. ed. Lālajī: bhāī: Devarāj. 2nd ed., 17–18. Mumbai, 1913.

———. "Shāhānī sarevāe tame jāgajo," in *100 Ginānanī Chopaḍī*. 5th ed. Vol. 1, #85. Mumbai, 1990 vs/1934.

———. *Shrī Nakaḷaṁk Shāstra : Pīr Shams no Vāek Moṭo*. ed. Alīmāmad Jānmāmad Chunārā. 1st ed. Mumbai, 1342/1923.

———. "Tiyāṃ thī ame āveā uñchamāṃ," in *100 Ginānanī Chopaḍī*. 4th ed. Vol. 6, #37. Mumbai, 1989 vs/1933.

———. "Vel Chandrabhāṇ nī," in *Chandrabhāṇ ane Surbhāṇ: Banne nī Vel sāthe*. 2nd ed., 14–17. Mumbai, 1926.

Shams al-Dīn Muḥammad?, Imām. "Alfāẓ-i Guharbār," in *Institute of Ismaili Studies Library*, Persian ms 15071. London.

———. "Alfāẓ-i Guharbār," in *Institute of Ismaili Studies Library*, Persian ms 15077. London.

———. "Alfāẓ-i Guharbār," in *Institute of Ismaili Studies Library*, Persian ms 15092. London.

———. "[No Title]," in *Institute of Ismaili Studies Library*, Persian ms 814, 105. London, 1313/1895.

Shams al-Dīn Tabrīzī. *Maqālāt-i Shams-i Tabrīzī*. ed. Muḥammad ʿAlī Muwaḥḥid. 2 vols. Tehran, 1990.

Shams-i Tabrīz. "*Sāqī-yi bā wafā manam dam hama dam ʿAlī ʿAlī*," in *Kitāb al-Manāqib*. ed. Hiz Hāʾīnes Prins Āghā Khān Shīʿa Imāmī Ismāʿīliya Esūsīʾeshan barāʾe Pākistān, 66–67. Karachi, 1406/1986.

———. "*Sāqiy-i bā wafā manam dam hama dam ʿAlī ʿAlī*," in *Manāqib: Surūda shuda dar huḍūr-i Mawlānā Ḥāḍir Imām dar dawrān-i bāzdīd-i Pākistān, Aktūbar 2000, bā tarjamāy-i Inglīsī*. ed. The Shia Imami Ismaili Tariqah and Religious Education Board for Pakistan, Side A, #1. [Karachi], [Soon after October 2000].

———. "Sāqīy-i bā wafā manam dam hama dam ʿAlī ʿAlī," in *Medā Lāl Qalandar*. ed. ʿĀbida Parwīn.

———. "*Sāqi-yi bā wafā manam dam hama dam ʿAlī ʿAlī*," in *Qasidas: Great Ismaili Tradition of Central Asia*. ed. Audio Visual Department The Shia Imami

Ismaili Tariqah and Religious Education Board for Pakistan. Vol. 1, Side A, #4. [Karachi], nd.

———. "Tā Ṣūrat-i Paywand-i Jahān būd ʿAlī būd," in *Gulzār-i Shams*. ed. Shujāʿ al-Mulk b. Sayyid Jamāʿat ʿAlīshāh Mulukshāh and Muḥammad ʿĪsanshāh, 350–351. [Multan], 1334/1916.

———. "Tā Ṣūrat-i Paywand-i Jahān būd ʿAlī būd," in *Kitāb al-Manāqib*. ed. Hiz Hāʾines Prins Āghā Khān Shīʿa Imāmī Ismāʿīliya Esūsīʾeshan barāʾe Pākistān, 56–64. Karachi, 1406/1986.

———. "Tā Ṣūrat-o Paywand-i Jahān būd ʿAlī būd," in *Majmūʿa-yi Ashʿār-i Madhhabī*. ed. Anjuman-i taʿlīm wa-tarbiyat-i madhhabī-i shīʿa-yi imāmiyya ismāʿīliyya-i khurāsān, np. Mashhad, Iran, 1995.

"Sharḥ al-Marātib," in *Institute of Ismaili Studies Library*, Persian ms 15077. London.

"Sharḥ al-Marātib," in *Institute of Ismaili Studies Library*, Persian ms 15092. London.

"Sharḥ al-Marātib," in *Institute of Ismaili Studies Library*, Persian ms 15093. London.

"Sharḥ-i Marātib," in *Tuḥfat al-Nāẓirīn*. ed. Ḥājī Qudrat Allāh Beg, 88–95. Gilgit, Pakistan, 1960.

Sharpe, Eric J. *Comparative Religion: A History*. 2nd ed. La Salle, IL, 1986.

Shushtarī, Qāḍī Sayyid Nūr Allāh b. ʿAbd Allāh. *Majālis al-Muʾminīn*. Tehran, 1299/1882.

———. *Majālis al-Muʾminīn*. Tehran, 1375–1376/1955–1956.

Sijistānī, Abū Yaʿqūb. *Kitāb al-Iftikhār*. ed. Ismail K. Poonawala. Beirut, 2000.

Smith, J. M., Jr. "Djalāyir, Djalāyirid," in *EI2*. Vol. 2, 401. Leiden, 1960–2004. Reprint, CD-ROM v. 1.0.

Soudavar, A. "Ẓafarnāma wa-Shāhnāma-yi Mustawfī" *Īrānshināsī* 7, no. 4 (1996): 752–761.

Spuler, B. "Gīlān," in *EI2*. Vol. 2, 1111. Leiden, 1960–2004. Reprint, CD-ROM v. 1.0.

———. "Ḥasanak," in *EI2*. Vol. 3, 255. Leiden, 1960–2004. Reprint, CD-ROM v. 1.0.

Stavridès, Yves. "Ils ont massacré les livres au lance-roquette." *Express*. January 10, 2002. Groupe Express-Expansion, http://www.lexpress.fr/info/monde/dossier/afghanistan/dossier.asp?ida=418403 (accessed February 28, 2006).

Steigerwald, Diane. "La dissimulation (*taqiyya*) de la foi dans le Shiʿisme Ismaelien." *Studies in Religion/Sciences Religieuses* 27 (1988): 39–59.

Stern, Samuel Miklos. "The Early Ismāʿīlī Missionaries in North-West Persia and in Khurāsān and Transoxiana." *BSO(A)S* 23 (1960): 56–90.

———. "Heterodox Ismāʿīlism at the Time of al-Muʿizz." *BSO(A)S* 17 (1955): 10–33.

———. "Ismāʿīlī Propaganda and Fatimid Rule in Sind," in *Studies in Early Ismāʿīlism*, 177–188. Leiden, 1983.

Strothmann, R., and M. Djebli. "Taḳiyya," in *EI2*. Vol. 10, 135. Leiden, 1960–2004. Reprint, CD-ROM v. 1.0.

Subhan, John A. *Sufism, Its Saints and Shrines: An Introduction to the Study of Sufism with Special Reference to India and Pakistan*. Revised ed. Lucknow, 1960.

Subtelny, Maria Eva. "The Sunni Revival under Shāh-Rukh and Its Promoters: A Study of the Connection between Ideology and Higher Learning in Timurid Iran," in *Proceedings of the 27th Meeting of Haneda Memorial Hall Symposium on Central Asia and Iran: August 30, 1993*, 16–21. Kyoto, 1994.

Subtelny, Maria Eva, and Anas B. Khalidov. "The Curriculum of Islamic Higher Learning in Timurid Iran in the Light of the Sunni Revival under Shāh-Rukh." *JAOS* 115, no. 2 (1995): 217–222.

Sutūda, Manūchihr Ibrāhīm. *Az Āstarā tā Astarābād*. 10 vols. Tehran, 1366 HS/1987.

Sykes, Percy Molesworth. *A History of Persia*. 2 vols. London, 1915.

al-Ṭabarsī, al-Faḍl b. al-Ḥasan. *Majmaʿ al-bayān fī tafsīr al-Qurʾān*. Vol. 3. Beirut, 1954–1957.

al-Tabrīzī, Abū ʿAbd Allāh Muḥammad b. ʿAbd Allāh al-Khaṭīb. *Mishkāt al-Maṣābīḥ*. ed. Muḥammad Nāṣir al-Dīn al-Albānī. Beirut, 1961.

Tāmir, ʿĀrif. *al-Imāma fī al-Islām*. Beirut, [1964].

———. "Furūʿ al-shajarat al-Ismāʿīliyya." *al-Mashriq* 51 (1957): 581–612.

———. "Ḥaqīqat Ikhwān al-Ṣafāʾ wa-Khullān al-Wafāʾ." *al-Mashriq* 51 (1957): 129–172.

———, ed. *Arbaʿ Rasāʾil Ismāʿīliyya*. Salamiyya, Syria, 1952.

———, ed. *Khams Rasāʾil Ismāʿīliyya*. Salamiyya, Syria, 1375/1956.

Thackston, Wheeler M. *A Millennium of Classical Persian Poetry: A Guide to the Reading and Understanding of Persian Poetry from the Tenth to the Twentieth Century*. Bethesda, MD, 1994.

Thiesen, Finn. *A Manual of Classical Persian Prosody: With Chapters on Urdu, Karakhanidic and Ottoman Prosody*. Belgium, 1982.

Turkumān, Iskandar Beg Munshī. *Taʾrīkh-i ʿĀlamārā-yi ʿAbbāsī*. 2 vols. Tehran, 1971.

———. *Taʾrīkh-i ʿĀlamārā-yi ʿAbbāsī*. Tehran, 1314/1897.

al-Ṭūsī, Abū Jaʿfar Muḥammad b. Ḥasan. *Ikhtiyār maʿrifat al-rijāl, al-maʿrūf bi-rijāl al-Kashshī*. ed. Ḥasan al-Muṣṭafawī. Mashhad, Iran, 1348 HS/1969.

Ṭūsī, Naṣīr al-Dīn Muḥammad b. Muḥammad. *Āghāz wa-Anjām*. ed. I. Afshār. Tehran, 1335 HS/1956.

———. *Sayr wa-Sulūk*. ed. S. J. Badakhchani. trans. S. J. Badakhchani. *Contemplation and Action: The Spiritual Autobiography of a Muslim Scholar*. London, 1998.

Ṭūsī, Naṣīr al-Dīn Muḥammad b. Muḥammad, and Ḥasan-i Maḥmūd. *Rawḍa-yi Taslīm*. ed. S. J. Badakhchani. trans. S. J. Badakhchani. *Paradise of Submission: A Medieval Treatise on Ismaili Thought*. London, 2005.

Vaglieri, L. Veccia. "Fadak," in *EI2*. Vol. 2, 725. Leiden, 1960–2004. Reprint, CD-ROM v. 1.0.

———. "Ghadīr Khumm," in *EI2*. Vol. 2, 993. Leiden, 1960–2004. Reprint, CD-ROM v. 1.0.

———. "Ibrahīm b. ʿAbd Allāh," in *EI2*. Vol. 3, 983. Leiden, 1960–2004. Reprint, CD-ROM v. 1.0.

van den Berg, Gabrielle Rachel. "Minstrel Poetry from the Pamir Mountains: A Study on the Songs and Poems of the Ismāʿīlīs of Tajik Badakshan." PhD dissertation, State University of Leiden, 1997.

Vatikiotis, Panayiotis J. *The Fatimid Theory of State*. Lahore, [1957].

Virani, Shafique N. "Ahl al-Bayt," in *Encyclopedia of Religion*. ed. Lindsay Jones. Vol. 1, 198–199. New York, 2005.

———. "The Days of Creation in the Thought of Nāṣir Khusraw," in *Nāṣir Khusraw: Yesterday, Today, Tomorrow*. ed. Sarfaroz Niyozov and Ramazon Nazariev. Khujand, Tajikistan, 2004, 74–83.

———. "The Eagle Returns: Evidence of Continued Ismāʿīlī Activity at Alamūt and in the South Caspian Region following the Mongol Conquests." *JAOS* 123 (2003): 351–370.

———. "Seekers of Union: The Ismailis from the Mongol Debacle to the Eve of the Safavid Revolution." PhD dissertation, Harvard University, 2001.

———. "Symphony of Gnosis: A Self-Definition of the Ismaili Ginān Literature," in *Reason and Inspiration in Islam: Theology, Philosophy and Mysticism in Muslim Thought*. ed. Todd Lawson, 503–521. London, 2005.

———. "The Voice of Truth: Life and Works of Sayyid Nūr Muḥammad Shāh, a 15th/16th Century Ismāʿīlī Mystic." MA thesis, McGill University, 1995.

Walad, Sulṭān. *Mathnawī-yi Waladī*. ed. Jalāl al-Dīn Humāʾī. Tehran, 1316/1937.

Walker, Paul E. *Exploring an Islamic Empire: Fatimid History and Its Sources*. London, 2002.

Ward, L. J. "The Ẓafarnāma of Ḥamd Allāh Mustaufī and the Il-khan Dynasty of Iran." PhD dissertation, University of Manchester?, 1983.

Wilkinson, J. C. "The Ibāḍī Imāma." *BSO(A)S* 39, no. 3 (1976): 535–551.

Willey, Peter. *Eagle's Nest: Ismaili Castles in Iran and Syria*. London, 2005.

Yazdī, Sharaf al-Dīn ʿAlī. *Ẓafarnāma*. Delhi, 1972.

———. *Ẓafarnāma*. ed. Muḥammad ʿAbbāsī. Tehran, 1336 HS/1957.

Yeroushalmi, David. *The Judeo-Persian Poet ʿEmrānī and His Book of Treasure: ʿEmrānī's Ganj-Nāme, a versified Commentary on the Mishnaic Tractate Abot*. Leiden, 1995.

Yousofi, Gholam Hosein. "Kāshifī, Kamāl al-Dīn Ḥusayn b. ʿAlī," in *EI2*. Vol. 4, 703. Leiden, 1960–2004. Reprint, CD-ROM v. 1.0.

Ẓahīr al-Dīn, ed. *Muhammedanische Quellen zur geschichte der Südlichen Küstenländer des Kaspischen Meeres*. ed. B. Dorn. Vol. 1. St. Petersburg, 1850.

Zaman, Muhammad Qasim. *Religion and Politics Under the Early ʿAbbāsids: The Emergence of the Proto-Sunnī Elite*. Leiden, 1997.

Zamānī. "Ay dar miyān-i jān," in *Institute of Ismaili Studies Library*, Persian ms 14718. London.

Zettersteen, K. V. "ʿAbd Allāh b. al-Ḥasan b. al-Ḥasan," in *EI2*. Vol. 1, 45. Leiden, 1960–2004. Reprint, CD-ROM v. 1.0.

Index

In the index, entries may be transcribed in either their Arabic or Persian form, reflecting usage in the sources. The Arabic definite article "al-" is ignored in alphabetization. Books and other treatises are referenced under the names of their authors, if these are known with some degree of certainty.